World Yearbook of Education 2025

The World Yearbook of Education 2025 analyzes teacher policies and the governance of the teaching profession in the contemporary context of major societal changes and globalizing processes.

The first volume dedicated to an overview of globalized teacher policies and their implications for the status of the teaching profession across the world, this book reflects the ambition to advance the debate on the challenges and opportunities associated with the teaching profession. It recognizes that teacher policy is situated at the crossroads of three logics that have changed and become more complex due to globalization processes since the 1970s: the logic of teacher policy regulation has shifted from state-centric government toward pluriscalar global governance; the logic of employment relations has shifted to a flexibility paradigm; the logic of teacher education has shifted from the transmission of knowledge in teacher education to teachers' lifelong learning. In line with the objective to analyze the governance of the teaching profession in the contemporary context of major societal changes and globalizing processes, this book is organized into three parts, focusing on:

- teacher policies as global governance and public policy;
- teacher labor markets, employment relations, and careers and the institutional transformations in the world of work and employment; and
- the reconfiguration of teachers' work and the learning of teachers.

Its contributors use different methodological approaches to draw on a range of case studies and analyses of national, regional, and global patterns. A timely and important contribution to discussions of the future of the teaching profession across the world, the *World Yearbook of Education 2025* is ideal reading for policymakers, the professional teaching community, researchers, graduate students, and anyone interested in education policy-related areas such as public policy, comparative education, and sociology of education.

Xavier Dumay is Professor of Education at UCLouvain, Belgium.

Tore Bernt Sorensen is Lecturer of Education at the School of Education, University of Glasgow, UK.

Lynn Paine is Professor of Teacher Education at Michigan State University, USA.

World Yearbook of Education

Series editors:

Julie Allan
University of Birmingham, UK

Antoni Verger
Universitat Autònoma de Barcelona, Spain

Examining a different topical subject each year, these fascinating books put forward a wide range of perspectives and dialogue from all over the world. With the best and most pivotal work of leading educational thinkers and writers from 1965 to the present day, these essential reference titles provide a complete history of the development of education around the globe. Available individually or in library-ready sets, this is the indispensable atlas of education, mapping ever changing aspects of theory, policy, teaching and learning.

Titles in the series:

World Yearbook of Education 2020
Schooling, Governance and Inequalities
Edited by Julie Allan, Valerie Harwood and Clara Rübner Jørgensen

World Yearbook of Education 2022
Education, Schooling and the Global Universalization of Nationalism
Edited by Daniel Tröhler, Nelli Piattoeva and William F. Pinar

World Yearbook of Education 2023
Racialization and Educational Inequality in Global Perspective
Edited By Janelle Scott and Monisha Bajaj

World Yearbook of Education 2024
Digitalisation of Education in the Era of Algorithms, Automation and Artificial Intelligence
Edited By Ben Williamson, Janja Komljenovic and Kalervo Gulson

World Yearbook of Education 2025
The Teaching Profession in a Globalizing World: Governance, Career, Learning
Edited by Xavier Dumay, Tore Bernt Sorensen, and Lynn Paine

For more information about this series, please visit: www.routledge.com/World-Yearbook-of-Education/book-series/WYBE

World Yearbook of Education 2025

The Teaching Profession in a Globalizing World: Governance, Career, Learning

Edited by Xavier Dumay,
Tore Bernt Sorensen, and Lynn Paine

LONDON AND NEW YORK

Designed cover image: Getty Images

First published 2025
by Routledge
4 Park Square, Milton Park, Abingdon, Oxon OX14 4RN

and by Routledge
605 Third Avenue, New York, NY 10158

Routledge is an imprint of the Taylor & Francis Group, an informa business

© 2025 selection and editorial matter, Xavier Dumay, Tore Bernt Sorensen, and Lynn Paine; individual chapters, the contributors

The right of Xavier Dumay, Tore Bernt Sorensen and Lynn Paine to be identified as the authors of the editorial material, and of the authors for their individual chapters, has been asserted in accordance with sections 77 and 78 of the Copyright, Designs and Patents Act 1988.

All rights reserved. No part of this book may be reprinted or reproduced or utilised in any form or by any electronic, mechanical, or other means, now known or hereafter invented, including photocopying and recording, or in any information storage or retrieval system, without permission in writing from the publishers.

Trademark notice: Product or corporate names may be trademarks or registered trademarks, and are used only for identification and explanation without intent to infringe.

British Library Cataloguing-in-Publication Data
A catalogue record for this book is available from the British Library

ISBN: 978-1-032-57945-0 (hbk)
ISBN: 978-1-032-57944-3 (pbk)
ISBN: 978-1-003-44173-1 (ebk)

DOI: 10.4324/9781003441731

Typeset in ITC Galliard Pro
by KnowledgeWorks Global Ltd.

Contents

About the Editors — vii
List of Contributors — viii

Introduction – The Teaching Profession in a Globalizing World: Governance, Career, Learning — 1
XAVIER DUMAY, TORE BERNT SORENSEN, AND LYNN PAINE

PART I
The Global Governance of Teachers and the Teaching Profession — 23

1 Between Teachers' Governance and Development: Shifting Emphases, Methods, and Global Policy Trends in Teacher Appraisal — 25
GERARD FERRER-ESTEBAN, CLARA FONTDEVILA, AND ANTONI VERGER

2 "Agency Work": Teachers, the OECD, and the "Happiness Turn" — 56
SUSAN L. ROBERTSON AND CARLOS NAVIA CANALES

3 Educational Hierarchies and "The Voice of the Teaching Profession": Organized Teachers' Participation in Global Governance — 74
NINA BASCIA

4 Representations of Teachers and Teaching in the Public Space: Exploring the Interplay between Policy and Media Constructions of Teacher Supply in Australia and England — 88
KATHRYN SPICKSLEY AND NICOLE MOCKLER

PART II
Labor Market Policies and Teachers' Careers: Shifting Toward Flexibility and Fragmentation — 109

5 Teacher Shortages and Contract Teachers in the Global South — 111
AMITA CHUDGAR AND MARTIAL DEMBÉLÉ

6 The Expanded Presence of Second-Career Teachers: Redefining the Teaching Profession and Career — 129
THIBAULT COPPE

7 The Teaching Profession in India: Growth, Diversification, and Feminization — 143
PADMA M. SARANGAPANI, MYTHILI RAMCHAND, AND JYOTI BAWANE

8 The Future of Teacher Education and Teacher Professionalism in the Face of Global Policy Trends — 160
MARIA TERESA TATTO

PART III
New Configurations of Teachers' Work and Learning — 177

9 Platformed Professionalities: What Digital Platforms Do to Teacher Professionality — 179
MATHIAS DECUYPERE AND STEVEN LEWIS

10 Working from Professional and Political Scripts: Teach for All and the Globalization of a (Domestic) Teacher Education Model — 196
MATTHEW A. M. THOMAS AND ELISABETH E. LEFEBVRE

11 Teacher Leadership and Professional Status in World Culture — 212
GERALD K. LETENDRE

12 The Socio-Politics of Teachers' Learning: Global Insights — 229
IAN HARDY

Index — 245

About the Editors

Xavier Dumay is Professor of Education at UCLouvain, Belgium. His research interests include the globalization of education and educational policy, new institutional theory, global politics, and changing forms of education. His recent books include the *Oxford Handbook of Education and Globalization* (together with Paola Mattei, Eric Mangez, and Jacqueline Behrend), and the *Liberalization of Teacher Employment Regimes in Europe*, both published by Oxford University Press.

Tore Bernt Sorensen is Lecturer in Education at the School of Education, University of Glasgow. Tore's scholarship concerns global education governance, public policy analysis, and the teaching profession. His recent research was published in *European Educational Research Journal, Journal of Education and Work, Comparative Education Review*, and *Globalisation, Societies and Education*. Tore also edited the handbook section "Globalization and Teacher Education" in *The Palgrave Handbook of Teacher Education Research* (Editor-in-Chief, Ian Menter).

Lynn Paine is Professor of Teacher Education at Michigan State University, USA. Her research focuses on comparative and international education and the sociology of education, with an emphasis on the comparative study of teachers, teaching and teacher education, and the relationship between educational policy and practice. She has co-authored books on the university and teachers (with Harry Judge, Michel Lemosse, and Michael Sedlak) and systems of comprehensive teacher induction (with Edward Britton, David Pimm, and Senta Raizen). Her recent work examines global reform discourses of teaching and teacher development.

Contributors

Nina Bascia is Professor Emerita at the Ontario Institute for Studies in Education of the University of Toronto. Her expertise covers the intersection of educational policy and teachers' work. She has studied teacher organizations internationally for over thirty-five years at school, local, and jurisdictional levels around the world. She is co-editor of a Routledge series, *Critical Perspectives on Teaching and Teachers' Work* and is currently working on an international handbook on that topic for the series.

Jyoti Bawane is Professor at the National Council for Educational Research and Training. She has engaged in research areas relating to understanding the teaching profession, initiatives improving school education, and online education. She served on the national team for reviewing the teacher education in selected Indian states and represented the National Council for Teacher Education (NCTE) as a member for the drafting of the curriculum framework for teacher education. She was member of the research and authoring team of the State of teachers, teaching, and teacher education report for India, 2023: The right teacher for every child. Her recent publication is the co-edited volume *The Imbecile's Guide to Public Philosophy*, Routledge, 2021.

Carlos Navia Canales is a PhD student at the University of Cambridge. Given his work in citizenship education, he was selected as one of the 100 young leaders in Chile. He is a co-host of the podcast *Aula Divergente*, a FreshEd production, which discusses educational policies in Latin America. Carlos is interested in both education as a human right and the impact of neoliberalism in discourses about the educability of emotions, working as an advisor on these fields for public institutions.

Amita Chudgar is Professor of education policy and interim associate dean of international studies at Michigan State University's College of Education. Amita's work has engaged with teacher labor markets in diverse global context. She has published on challenges of teacher distribution, teacher shortages, teacher preparation, and teachers in low-cost private education sector. She has worked extensively on contract teacher policies and their implications in various national contexts. Her work has been recognized by prestigious grants and awards from the academy. She also engages with the policy arena primarily through her work with the International Task Force on Teachers'. Recently she was part of a team that provided background support to the UN High-Level Panel on the Teaching Profession.

Thibault Coppe is currently Assistant Professor of Educational Sciences at the University of Groningen in the Netherlands, affiliated with the GION Education/Research group. He is a former FNRS/FRESH grant recipient (Belgium). His research interests focus on the comparative analysis of policies affecting second-career teachers and how these teachers experience their daily professional life locally. Through his research, he has developed a strong interest in reflecting on the use of various methods in the social sciences (quantitative, qualitative, and mixed) and in exploring the nexus between research and practice.

Mathias Decuypere is Professor of School Development and Governance at the Zurich University of Teacher Education (Switzerland), as well as affiliated to KU Leuven (Belgium). His research adopts an international, macro-level perspective on educational policymaking and governance. It is interested in how distinct global developments in governance (e.g., behavioral governance; platform governance; synthetic governance) affect local school practices.

Martial Dembélé is a Full Professor of education at the Université de Montréal and holds the UNESCO Chair in Education Policy and the Teaching Profession. His teaching, research, and consulting activities have been in the areas of school improvement, teacher issues, international development in education, and accountability in education. Professor Dembélé has written extensively on these topics, always with a comparative lens, e.g., *Global Perspectives on Teacher Learning: Improving Policy and Practice*, Quality Education in Africa: Challenges and Prospects, *More and Better Teachers for Quality Education for All, A Review of the Use of Contract Teachers in Sub-Saharan Africa*, and *Private Provision of Teacher Preparation*.

Gerard Ferrer-Esteban is Lecturer at the Faculty of Psychology and Education Sciences at the Universitat Oberta de Catalunya (UOC). He holds a PhD in Sociology from the Universitat Autònoma de Barcelona (UAB), with a focus on school autonomy and inequalities. His research areas include educational policy, school segregation, and educational inequalities. Ferrer-Esteban has extensive experience in research and academia in both Spain and Italy. He has worked at the Agnelli Foundation in Italy and on R&D projects funded by the European Research Council and the Spanish Ministries of Education and of Economy, and Competitiveness.

Clara Fontdevila is British Academy Postdoctoral Fellow at the School of Education of the University of Glasgow. Her research focuses on the comparative analysis of education policy and politics, with a particular interest in the origins and contemporary restructuring of education markets, and the expansion and institutionalization of learning assessments. In the past, she has participated in different competitive research projects, including REFORMED, focusing on the dissemination of school autonomy and accountability reforms; and Dual Apprenticeship, focusing on the recontextualization of dual training programs. She has also held research and consultancy contracts with different organizations, including the Open Societies Foundation, Education International, and UNESCO.

Ian Hardy is Associate Professor in the School of Education at The University of Queensland, Brisbane, Australia. Dr Hardy's research focuses on the nature and impact of education policy, particularly in relation to institutionalized educational settings such as schools and universities. Dr Hardy also has a sustained interest and focus upon education in varying national and international settings and his work explores how educational policy and practice reflect the influence of a range of scalar relations – local, state/provincial, regional, national, international, and global. He is lead author of the recently published volume *Shaping School Success: Empowering Educational Leaders* (Routledge; 2025), and author of *School Reform in an Era of Standardization: Authentic Accountabilities* (Routledge; 2021).

Elisabeth E. Lefebvre is Associate Professor of Education at Bethel University in Minnesota. Her interdisciplinary research explores the mutually constitutive and historical relationships between schooling and childhood, as well as the ways in which discourses surrounding schools and schooling impact student and teacher experiences. Elisabeth's work has appeared in *Comparative Education Review, Discourse, International Journal of Educational Development, Journal of Education Policy, Teachers College Record, Teaching and Teacher Education*, among other journals, as well as in books including *Children and Youth as Subjects, Objects Agents* (Palgrave Macmillan, 2021), and *Progressive Neoliberalism in Education* (Routledge, 2022).

Gerald K. LeTendre, holds the Batschelet Chair in the College of Education at Penn State where he also served as Chair of the Education Policy Studies Department. His books include *Improving Teacher Quality* (co-authored with Motoko Akiba), *Promoting and Sustaining a Quality Teacher Workforce* (co-edited with Alex Wiseman), and *The International Handbook of Teacher Quality and Policy* (co-edited with Motoko Akiba). He is a former editor of *The American Journal of Education*, and his current research focuses on globalization, the state, and the teaching profession.

Steven Lewis is Associate Professor of Comparative Education at Australian Catholic University. His research is located across policy sociology, comparative and international education, and critical geography. Steven is interested in how education policy making and governance, and teacher professional learning and expertise, are being reshaped by new forms of digital data, algorithms and infrastructures, as well as emerging policy temporalities and spaces. His most recent books include *Assembling Comparison: Understanding Education Policy through Mobility and Assemblage* (Bristol University Press, 2024) and *PISA, Policy and the OECD: Respatialising Global Educational Governance Through PISA for Schools* (Springer, 2020).

Nicole Mockler is Professor of Education at the University of Sydney, Australia, and Honorary Research Fellow in the Department of Education at the University of Oxford, UK. She was awarded her PhD in Education at the University of Sydney in 2008 and also holds a Master of Arts in History/Gender Studies and a Master of Science in Applied Statistics. Nicole's research interests are in the areas of teachers' work and professional learning; education policy and politics; and curriculum and pedagogy. In 2022 Nicole was awarded the Australian Council for Educational Leadership Dr Paul Brock Memorial Medal.

Mythili Ramchand is Professor at the Centre of Excellence in Teacher Education, Tata Institute of Social Sciences, Mumbai, INDIA. She has anchored design of several teacher education programs across the country including the Post Graduate Certificate in Contemporary Education Perspectives for teacher Educators and the BEd-MEd Innovative programme. She is currently engaged in comparative research on initial teacher education in BRICS countries and the United Kingdom. She was member of the research and authoring team of the State of teachers, teaching, and teacher education report for India, 2023: The right teacher for every child. Her most recent publication is the coedited volume *Learning without Burden: Where are We a Quarter Century after the Yash Pal Committee Report*, Routledge, 2023.

Susan Lee Robertson is Professor of Sociology of Education at the University of Cambridge, and Distinguished Visiting Professor, Aarhus University, Denmark. She has held academic posts in Australia and New Zealand prior to the UK. Susan writes extensively on globalization, governance, transformations of the state and education. Her recent book is on the *Post Pandemic University*. Susan is founding editor of *Globalization, Societies and Education*, and currently co-editor.

Padma M. Sarangapani is Professor and Chair of the Centre of Excellence in Teacher Education, Tata Institute of Social Sciences, Mumbai, INDIA. Her research and publications are in the area of curriculum, pedagogy and culture, teacher education, and education policy. She has designed and led several large scale initiatives in collaboration with States to strengthen systems of teacher education and school curriculum, and the development of innovative teaching programs. She has served on national and UNESCO committees as an expert. She led the research and authoring team of the State of teachers, teaching and teacher education report for India, 2023: The right teacher for every child. Her most recent publication is the coedited volume *Education, Teaching, and Learning: Discourses, Cultures, and Conversations*, Orient Blackswan, 2023.

Kathryn Spicksley is British Academy Postdoctoral Fellow at the University of Birmingham, UK. Her research explores the relationship between cultural discourse on education and teachers' working lives and professional identities. Her doctoral dissertation, which won the 2022 BERA Doctoral Thesis Award, explored the professional identities of early career teachers working in multi-academy trust primary schools in England. Prior to studying for her PhD, Kathryn worked as an early years teacher.

Maria Teresa Tatto holds the prestigious position of Southwest Borderlands Professor of Comparative Education at Arizona State University. Her research delves into the intricacies of education system reform and its impact on creating more equitable and accessible educational opportunities for disadvantaged populations. Notably, she has developed a unique theoretical framework that analyzes the relationships between teacher preparation research, policy, and practice. Her contributions to the field have been recognized through her former presidency of the Comparative and International Education Society, her Honorary Research Fellowship at the University of Oxford, her Fellowship at Kellogg College England, and her Fellowship in the American Educational Research Association.

Matthew A.M. Thomas is Senior Lecturer in International and Comparative Education at the University of Glasgow, where he also leads the Education Leadership and Policy group. His research examines education policies, pedagogical practices, and teacher and higher education. Matthew has worked as a public school teacher in the United States and researcher, teacher educator, and international development practitioner in Australia, Indonesia, Mali, Nigeria, Tanzania, and Zambia. Most recently, Matthew is the co-editor of *Examining Teach For All* (Routledge, 2021), *The Bloomsbury Handbook of Theory in Comparative and International Education* (Bloomsbury, 2021), and *Australian Universities* (Sydney University Press, 2022).

Antoni Verger is a Professor of Sociology at the Universitat Autònoma de Barcelona and a Research Fellow at the Catalan Institution for Research and Advanced Studies (ICREA). His research focuses on educational reform processes, viewed through the lenses of comparative and global policy studies. In recent years, he has specialized in the study of privatization, school autonomy, and accountability reforms. He has led multiple research projects in these fields through competitive grants awarded by the European Research Council, the Marie S. Curie program, Erasmus Plus, Fulbright, and the Spanish Research Agency.

Introduction – The Teaching Profession in a Globalizing World

Governance, Career, Learning

Xavier Dumay, Tore Bernt Sorensen, and Lynn Paine

Introduction: Objectives of the Volume

Teachers and the teaching profession have been a recurring focus of the World Yearbooks of Education (WYBE) since the inception of the series in 1965. Even before being named WYBE, the Yearbook of Education 1963, edited by George F. Bereday, was devoted to "the education and training of teachers," accompanied by an observation that has been invoked so often since, "the strength of an educational system must depend largely on the quality of its teachers." Several approaches have subsequently been adopted for the study of teachers in the series, reflecting the problems and research interests of different periods: the attractiveness of the profession and teacher shortages in the face of profound demographic changes during the period of educational expansion in the 1960s (International WYBE 1963), the training and professional development of teachers in the context of rapid technological innovations (WYBE 1980), and teacher education from a governing and cultural perspective (WYBE 2002). More recently, WYBE 2013 was concerned with the politics of (de)professionalization and the renegotiation of the boundaries of teachers' work within local, national, and global spaces, reflecting the growing interest in the dynamics of globalization.

Focusing on the teaching profession, this volume continues the journey begun back in 1963. Like WYBE 2013, the volume considers how globalization is reshaping the work of educators. However, rather than drawing on the sociology of professions and work as this previous volume did, WYBE 2025 adopts a public policy perspective. This means that the volume seeks to situate teacher policy as implicated in "the set of activities that governments engage in for the purpose of changing their economy and society" (Peters, 2015, p. 1), and in particular, contemporary developments in the governance of teachers and the teaching profession globally, labor markets for teachers, and teacher education and learning.

Global Governance and a Global Field of Teacher Policy

It is almost surprising that it has taken so long for a volume of the WYBE to adopt this lens on teacher policy, given the significant institutional and policy developments related to the teaching profession over the past 40 years.

DOI: 10.4324/9781003441731-1

Since the ground-breaking 1966 ILO/UNESCO Report of Recommendations on the Status of the Teaching Profession (ILO/UNESCO, 2016), teachers and the teaching profession have increasingly been the subject of global discourses and various governance mechanisms, to the point of becoming a major policy avenue and a policy field in its own right, imbricated with education policy yet not reducible to it.

Some definitions are necessary, as "governance" has come to be one of the most widely applied concepts in education policy and research, with many different meanings both analytically and normatively (Wilkins & Mifsud, 2024). The definition by Capano et al. (2015, p. 316) incorporates several of the important key features:

> Governance refers to the possible ways in which policy actors, including governments, combine to solve collective problems and thus affect the ways in which policy processes are steered. Governance modes can be based on different mixes of coordination principles (hierarchy, market and network), but even in the more extreme horizontal arrangement they need to be steered – that is, they need to be led towards constructive, positive coordination.

Given the scope of this volume, we are particularly interested in global governance which concerns "the exercise of authority across national borders as well as consented norms and rules beyond the nation state, both of them justified with reference to common goods or transnational problems" (Zürn, 2018, pp. 3–4).

This broad definition calls for a few qualifications. First, while global governance does not need to apply to the entire globe, it suggests a pluralization of governance actors and typically involves international (intergovernmental) or transnational (cross-border) institutions (Zürn, 2018; for an indicative inventory of teacher policy actors, see Paine et al., 2016, p. 720). This is also evident for teacher policy. Corresponding with the strengthened attention directed toward teachers and teaching in policy and research globally from the 1990s onward, a widening range of actors have become increasingly involved in the governance of teachers and teacher education, including intergovernmental (IGOs) and supranational organizations, aid agencies, private corporations, and consultancies such as Pearson, McKinsey, and Google, and foundations and venture philanthropies like the Ford Foundation and the Bill and Melinda Gates Foundation (Paine et al., 2017; Robertson, 2016). In particular, the main IGOs in global education governance include the Organization for Economic Cooperation and Development (OECD), the United Nations Educational, Scientific and Cultural Organization (UNESCO), and the World Bank. Moreover, in the European region, the European Union (EU) has also become increasingly active since the 2000s (Sorensen & Dumay, 2024). These are all prominent actors in teacher policy too, and they tend to define their teacher policy interests differently and with different emphases, reflecting their historical legacy, evolving roles, and adaptation in global governance (Hossain, 2022; Paine et al., 2016; Robertson, 2016).

Second, hierarchy and different power capacities are integral parts of global governance (Zürn, 2018). The literature has demonstrated the influence, modus operandi, and value orientations of the main IGOs engaging with education and teacher policy, since they were created as part of the post-WWII architecture, UNESCO having been succinctly labeled "the idealist," the World Bank "the master of coercion," and the OECD "the master of persuasion" (Elfert & Ydesen, 2023, pp. 29–38). Yet, questions of authority, hierarchy, and legitimacy in the global governance of teachers tend to remain blurry due to the limited political mandates of these IGOs, reflected in the emphasis on consensus, networks, and mobilization in global teacher policy discourses. In this respect, the analysis of the OECD's "pluri-dimensionality," being simultaneously actor, multilateral arena, and instrument for governments and other actors in global governance (Centeno, 2021), also applies to the other main IGOs, further complicating the identification of power capacities and hierarchies between governance actors. In global governance, state governments often remain the central type of players, whether they choose to play a central role or not (Capano et al., 2015). This is also evident in the governing of education sectors (Tröhler et al., 2021), with the important qualification that the power capacities of states to resist, adapt to, influence, and set out directions in global governance vary enormously (Hossain, 2022; Tröhler, 2021).

Third, global governance involves an element of "publicness," whether carried out by non-state or state actors, as it seeks to legitimize itself by invoking a sense of "public interest," regardless other underlying motivations (Zürn, 2018). This feature is also evident for education and teacher policy. Not least the "quality" of teachers (cf. George Bereday in 1963) has often been represented as a sort of panacea in addressing a range of policy problems with major import for economies and societies, such as educational inequalities, student inclusion, and system "performance" and effectiveness more broadly. In other words, teacher policy has been harnessed for solving problems represented to be in the public interest (Depaepe & Smeyers, 2008).

In the discourses of IGOs, policy issues related to teachers have been grouped under the umbrella of "teacher policy." Teacher policies cover a wide range of teacher-related issues that can be grouped into three main areas: i) teacher education, certification, continuous professional development, and learning; ii) labor market policies, including teacher recruitment, the allocation and distribution of teachers across workplaces, teacher mobility, career design, and the scope of teachers' work; and iii) the governance of teachers, including accountability systems and teacher evaluation. Hence, the teaching profession is affected by transformations of work and employment (teachers as workers), public policy (teaching as public service profession), and education (teachers as educators and learners). Whilst the strong influence of economics in the social sciences and public policy overall is well-recognized (Fourcade et al., 2015), we suggest that it is not simply a matter of education and employment policy becoming embedded, subordinated, or nested within an economic regime. The ubiquitous emphasis on learning and development across societies is a powerful reminder of the complex dynamics between regimes.

WYBE 2025 seeks to bring together the three policy areas of teacher education and learning, employment, and governance, while considering their mutual implications in the global governance of teachers. The structure of the volume reflects our objective to address these areas in an integrated fashion, thereby advancing the research literature on teacher policy which has tended to concentrate on each of these areas without much consideration of scholarship concerned with the other areas, or the implications between teachers' learning, employment, and governance.

The Shifting Logics of Teacher Policy: Governance, Flexible Employment, and Learning

The existing literature on the governance of the teaching profession in the context of globalization has concentrated on the re-scaling of governance and the emergence and consolidation of a global policy field concerned with teacher policy since the 1990s (Akiba, 2017; Paine et al., 2016; Robertson, 2013; Sorensen & Robertson, 2020). This wide-ranging literature has often been concerned with the unfolding tensions between new forms of accountability, the trust-based "embedded accountability" (Dubnick, 2006) of the teaching profession, professional autonomy, and the varied implications for the notion of teacher professionalism in different settings (Verger et al., 2023). Meanwhile, the literature on teacher labor markets and labor market policies is certainly the one that has focused most clearly on issues of educational quality, examining the factors that influence career decisions among the teacher workforce, the distribution of teachers across schools, and the educational opportunities of students (Lankford et al., 2002; Loeb & Béteille, 2009; Luschei & Chudgar, 2016). Finally, the literature on teacher education has primarily been concerned with the contribution of initial teacher education and training and continuing professional development (CDP) to the formation of teaching professionalism and the knowledge base of the profession (e.g., Darling-Hammond et al., 2017; Menter, 2023; Schmidt et al., 2011; Tatto et al., 2013), including also the risks of deprofessionalization posed by the introduction of alternative entries and routes into the profession (Darling-Hammond et al., 2002; Tatto & Pippin, 2017). To varying degrees, these literatures have considered the dynamics of globalization (Sorensen & Dumay, 2021). While it is clear that parts of the literature on the governance of the profession have largely embraced this dimension, this is less the case in the twin literatures on teacher labor market policy and teacher education and professional development, although seminal contributions have paved the way (Labaree, 2017; Paine et al., 2016). This means that we know little about the interfaces between globalization dynamics and teacher labor markets, including working conditions, career paths, collective mobilization, and industrial relations. Meanwhile, the numerous comparative studies of national variations in teacher education curriculum, structure, and policies have tended to treat globalization as a context justifying the comparison of different models (often conceived as "best practice") rather than an analytical entry in its own right (Sorensen & Dumay, 2021).

As mentioned above, the entry point for this volume is that developments in the three policy areas of teacher learning, employment, and governance are mutually implicated, suggesting the need to develop a dialogue between these different fields of research and to make globalization a central part of the analysis of teacher policy. We start from the observation that teacher policy is situated at the crossroads of three logics that have changed and become more complex due to globalization processes since the 1970s: the logic of teacher policy regulation has shifted from state-centric government toward pluriscalar global governance (Sorensen & Robertson, 2020); the logic of employment relations has shifted to a flexibility paradigm (Dumay, 2025); the logic of teacher education has shifted from the transmission of knowledge in teacher education to teachers' lifelong learning and "learning as a norm" (Vanden Broeck & Mangez, 2016). In line with our objective to integrate different analytical perspectives on teacher policy, the volume aims to theorize how the teaching profession and teacher policies have been shaped by these three shifts. WYBE 2025 argues that because of the scale and complexity of the challenges facing societies and their education systems, a global perspective is essential to making sense of the developments outlined above.

One of the central arguments in this volume is that as globalization evolves, the historical forms of the teaching profession (initial teacher education, bureaucratic careers, and bureaucratic and embedded notions of accountability) are changing. Historically, teacher education and the processes that regulate teachers' education, work and employment have been primarily national affairs. In the 19th and 20th centuries, teaching emerged as a public profession in the context of the development of modern states (Dumay & Burn, 2023). The development of the teaching profession in most countries was progressively structured around three dimensions: initial education, the curriculum of which was determined in a dialogue between public authorities and the profession; an employment framework that ensured long-term bureaucratic careers; and public accountability mechanisms.

In most countries of the "global North,"[1] and beyond due to the legacies of colonialism, initial teacher education has emerged as the cornerstone of teacher education and professional development, with the implicit idea that it is possible and desirable to prepare teachers for a long professional career. In the context of the comprehensive school reform movement that developed in most education systems after World War II, most countries significantly expanded and harmonized models of initial teacher education, often in conjunction with university support. CDP was then gradually seen as a complement to this initial training (Hoyle & Megarry, 1980), with the aim of adapting teachers to the increasing complexity of the work and to rapid technological change, in the perspective of a long career in teaching. More generally, this vision of initial teacher education corresponded to the modern conception of time and the future as (relatively) predictable and controllable (see Dumay & Mangez, 2024).

Similarly, teachers' careers and employment frameworks have expanded over the course of the twentieth century with the development of public administration, labor law, and industrial relations in the context of developing modern states, with the bureaucratic long-term career as its central and symbolic figure (Dumay, 2025; Dumay & Burn, 2023). The development of protective employment frameworks and long careers faced a dual challenge: the need to respond to workers' demands for higher employment and social standards, most often articulated through teachers' unions, but also to the interest of states, whose public forces were expanding, in being able to count on a captive workforce to match the stakes invested in school systems at the time. Once again, the long-term perspective of careers, and the bureaucratic framework that structures them, matched to a certain conception of time, which is that of a predictable and plannable time, and a relationship to space, through the constitution of a domestic workforce meeting criteria that largely limit the mobility of teachers outside national borders.

Finally, systems of accountability, as they developed over the 20th century, mainly corresponded to a logic of bureaucratic accountability which verifies compliance with rules (curricula, assessment of learning, timetables, etc.), and not directly student results or the value added by teachers or schools to student learning involved in the post-bureaucratic governance of educational systems (Maroy, 2009). The logic of bureaucratic accountability, centered on the control of inputs (certification, years of training), was to some extent aligned with professional forms of accountability based on mutual accountability and trust in professional norms and values (Hopmann, 2008), which have shifted to a reliance on more explicit and specific standards and contracts (Holloway et al., 2017).

This book thus examines how these central forms of teacher education and professional development, careers, and governance have changed with the development of globalization and the globalization of teacher policy. We aim to analyze how these shifts have informed global teacher policy and how they have reshaped the teaching profession in a globalizing context. WYBE 2025 therefore analyzes teacher policy and the governance of the teaching profession in the contemporary context of major societal shifts and globalizing processes, such as the development of global governance (Zürn, 2018), the flexibilization of employment regimes and the liberalization of labor relations (Baccaro & Howell, 2017; Kalleberg, 2018; Thelen, 2014), and the expansion of lifelong learning (Milana, 2017), to name a few of the major changes that cut across public policy and administration, work and employment, and education.

Although this volume analyzes global transformations in the teaching profession, our starting point is emphatically not that the regulation of the teaching profession is becoming more homogeneous or converging toward a world model. Rather, we understand the processes and outcomes of governance as complex, contingent, and vernacular (Dumay, forthcoming). The volume includes a large number of case studies covering many regions of the world. More than geographical diversity, however, we have sought to include cases and processes of globalization that are theoretically divergent and hence underpins our argument concerning the complex outcomes of governance, observation that contextual constraints influence policy options, as well as actors' perception/definition of the "problem." The chapters across sections reflect the ambition to capture some of the variation and simultaneously recognize the symbolic power of certain emerging/circulating ideas and/or of certain transnational entities shaping the conversation. Recent comparative analyses of the teaching profession (Dumay & Burn, 2023; Voisin & Dumay, 2020) have demonstrated that although the teaching profession worldwide shares common traits, sometimes summarized as semi-professions (Etzioni, 1969), the cultural roots and modes of regulation pertaining to the teaching profession differ from one system to another, implying varied outcomes of globalization processes (Dumay, 2025). For instance, Voisin and Dumay (2020) suggested that dominant patterns and key rationales underpin the regulation of the teaching profession in different contexts, shaping the institutional landscape of the teaching profession and the ways in which education systems organize and regulate teacher education, teaching labor markets, and professional accountability.

Finally, the volume pays special attention to the representation and role of teachers and the teaching profession in governance, employment models, and learning. The literature on education and teacher policy tends to consider teachers and the teaching profession as targets of reform. In particular, the field of educational policy implementation (see Spillane et al., 2002) considers teachers and the profession as mediators of the relationship between policy and students and their learning. Although contemporary studies have emphasized the importance of individual and collective teacher agency (Hallett, 2010), they remain largely indexed to an understanding of the role of teachers and the teaching profession as targets of reform, including analyses of the ways teachers individually and collectively, resist to reforms (Connell, 2009; Paine & Zeichner, 2012; Seddon et al., 2013). In recent years, however, the sociology of globalization and the professions has emphasized the need to understand how professionals themselves, through but not limited to professional associations or unions, actively participate in the global transformations of their profession. Scott (2013) theorized that the professions in modern society have taken a leading role in the creation and maintenance of institutions, based on the concept of "institutional agents," which underpins the role of professionals in the development of the institutional framework in which they work. We are therefore particularly interested in showing how, and to which extent, the teaching profession and teachers as institutional agents contribute to the development and diffusion of global ideas and practices. This includes how they actively participate in the governance of their profession through professional associations and trade unions, which have been increasingly active at the transnational levels over recent decades reflected, for example, in the re-scaling of arrangements for social dialogue, consultation, and industrial relations. The recent UN High-Level Panel on the Teaching Profession and the annual series of International Summits on the Teaching Profession highlight this re-orientation in global governance. For the former, the United Nations, together with the International Labour Organization and UNESCO, launched in 2024 a high-level panel on the teaching profession to "allow teachers to become drivers of change in education" (International Labour Organization, UN, & UNESCO, 2024). For the latter, the OECD and Education International, the major global federation of teacher unions, have since 2011 brought together education ministers and union leaders from selected countries, demonstrating a degree of inclusion of representatives of teaching profession in debates and regulations beyond the national level (Paine et al., 2017).

Corresponding with our conception of teacher policy, the book has three Parts, concentrating on the emphatic global shifts in governance, labor markets, and careers, and teachers' learning, respectively. The sections below briefly review these shifts, with reference to the chapters included in the volume as well as existing key literature.

The Global Governance of Teachers and the Teaching Profession

Among the volume's three sections, Part I speaks most directly, in analytical terms, to public policy, global governance, and the global field of teacher policy. From different perspectives and with different foci, the four chapters in this section thus analyze the governance of teachers, considering the ways contemporary policies related to teachers are developed, diffused, and enacted globally, as well as their ideational underpinnings.

In particular, the chapters in Part I engage with i) shifting emphases in teacher evaluation and appraisal (Ferrer-Esteban, Fontdevila & Verger, Chapter 1); ii) the OECD's recent focus on teacher well-being and students' social and emotional skills (Robertson & Navia Canales, Chapter 2); iii) the capacity of teacher organizations to represent the interests of teachers in global governance (Bascia, Chapter 3); and iv) the interplay between policy and media constructions of teacher supply (Spicksley & Mockler, Chapter 4).

The chapters relate to several of the key debates on teacher policy and global governance. First, in highlighting the processes and outcomes of pluri-scalar governance as complex, contingent, and vernacular, the chapters corroborate the argument that the regulation of the teaching profession is not converging toward a world model (Dumay, 2025; Paine et al., 2016). In particular, Ferrer-Esteban and colleagues' comparative analysis of teacher evaluation and appraisal policies since the early 2000s thus suggests that national institutions, and especially teacher regulatory regimes (Voisin & Dumay, 2020), continue to mediate the enactment of these types of policies. Meanwhile, Spicksley and

Mockler identify a complex relationship between policy and media texts in Australia and England, where these national contexts play a significant mediating role in how teachers are constructed within the media.

Importantly, the vernacular globalization argument does not imply that there are not any powerful agencies pursuing their agendas, a point that leads to the issues of hierarchy, authority, and pluralization of actors in global governance. Robertson and Navia Canales demonstrate the capacity of the OECD, arguably the most influential organization in global debates on teacher policy since the 1990s, to pick up and frame emerging policy issues, such as wellbeing and socio-emotional skills, and put them on the global policy and research agenda, in ways that are consistent with the organization's preference for neoliberal ideas. While the OECD has become a fixture in contemporary global education governance, their chapter is also an account of the organization's continuous adaptation to changing circumstances to stay relevant in a fluid and volatile political field (see Carroll & Kellow, 2011). Bascia's chapter discusses the hierarchies and the pluralization of actors in global governance, focusing on the role of teacher unions, which have become more visible at the global level since the 2000s. In contrast to Robertson and Navia Canales' actor perspective on the OECD, Bascia's interest in the organization is mainly due to its function as a multilateral arena (Centeno, 2021), where teacher unions, among numerous other types of organisations, take part in debates on teacher policy and programs. Bascia's chapter highlights the complexity and hierarchies of global governance, both in terms of inter-organizational relations, where the inclusion of teacher unions in national and global policymaking often remains symbolic, as well as intra-organizational relations and procedures shaping the representation of the teaching profession. In the literature on global education governance, intra-organizational relations often remain neglected, which is unfortunate given the number of meta-organizations – characterized by having organizations rather than individuals as members – engaging in global governance (Ahrne & Brunsson, 2008).

While the roles and activities of state authorities might be changing as the political field has become globalized (Dale, 2005), the findings by Ferrer-Esteban and colleagues align with the observation that state authorities remain central players in governance – whether they choose to play a central role or not – thus highlighting a sense of continuity in an otherwise dynamic and complex environment. In this way, their chapter illustrates that rather than the simplistic distinction between state-centric "old governance" and society-centric "new governance" (the latter assuming the ability of society to govern itself via market, networks, and other decentralized forms of interactions), it is constructive in theoretical and empirical terms to understand governance as a broader concept than government (Capano et al., 2015). This implies that transformations in the patterns of governance do not necessarily reflect a zero-sum game, where the "global" gains what the national "loses" (Dale, 2005).

The chapters thus suggest that although there is by now a substantial literature on teacher governance, the particular dynamics associated with authority, hierarchy and legitimacy in global governance remain pertinent empirical questions. Studies might here draw inspiration from the longstanding debate in the public policy literatures about the "shadow of hierarchy" as necessary scope condition to activate the voluntary mechanisms leading toward constructive and effective coordination (Börzel, 2010; Héritier & Lehmkuhl, 2008). Does the very large critical literature about the roles of IGOs in education, combined with research findings about the continued centrality of state authorities and the strengthened presence of commercial interests in global governance, indicate the lack of hierarchy in the global governance of education and teachers that may potentially lead to constructive coordination, tangible results, and even a notion of *progress*? In considering this question, it appears critical that state authorities have a crucial role in defining the distribution of the labor of governance, including the scope of action for themselves and other policy actors.

The chapters also provide important insights about the "publicness" and invocation of "public interest" in global governance (Zürn, 2018). Depending on agenda-setting and the framing of policy issues, this feature is closely related to the notion of "educationalization," whereby education sectors are mobilized to address social and economic problems in society (Depaepe & Smeyers, 2008; Tröhler, 2016). In their chapter about the interplay between policy and media constructions of teacher supply, Spicksley and Mockler address the mobilization of public interest most directly. An underexplored issue in research, they are concerned with how teachers and teaching are created as an object of public and political interest, shaping public expectations to teachers, and involving media corporations as important commercial actors in a globalized field. Their chapter is a powerful example of the epistemic gains of analyzing teacher governance with a wider lens, considering the dynamics between different types of texts and actors. The two chapters by Bascia, and Robertson and Navia Canales, are also concerned with the mobilization of public interest and educationalization. With its focus on the OECD, the latter chapter concentrates on the single most adept policy actor in global education governance in terms of generating public interest for its activities (consider PISA, the OECD Programme for International Student Assessment), and the organization's recent activities about teacher well-being and students' socio-emotional skills continue to be framed by the contribution of education sectors to the economy and society. Meanwhile, Bascia's chapter about the complexities and complications of teacher unions' objective, and especially those of Education International at the global level, to represent the teaching profession, suggests that unions, like other major players in global governance, have an interest in mobilizing public interest about education and teacher policies in order raise their status and attract resources (Bridges, 2008).

In combination, the chapters in Part I indicate an important reorientation in the global governance of teachers from the 2010s onwards. When the attention directed toward teachers and teaching gained momentum in the 1990s and the first decade of the 2000s, global policy discourses tended to embrace human capital theory, market-based and high-stakes accountability, flexibilization, and performance pay for teachers (Sorensen & Robertson, 2020). Especially emblematic and influential outputs of this era include the "Teachers Matter" report (OECD, 2005) and the "first McKinsey report" (Barber & Mourshed, 2007). Since the 2010s, there has been a shift in the understanding and framing of policy issues away from market-based and high-stakes accountability, toward an acknowledgment of the importance of teachers' professional autonomy. This observation is especially supported by the chapter in this volume by Ferrer-Esteban and colleagues, which demonstrates the expanding scope of teacher evaluations and more diverse array of methods since the 2000s, thereby reducing the emphasis on student performance and standardized assessment data, which was previously predominant in global governance discourses. The shift is also related to another trend mentioned above, concerning the increasing recognition in global policy discourses of teachers as institutional agents (Scott, 2013) and the need to include the profession in policy making, as discussed in Bascia's chapter. When situating these trends in the wider landscape of education sector reform, characterized by a declining emphasis in global policy discourses on major structural system reform (Bromley et al., 2021), as well as more sensitivity toward system-specific features and contextual factors in reform processes, the increasing level of complexity and, perhaps, contingency, in the global field of teacher policy becomes clear. While it would be premature to declare that these recent trends in combination amount to a paradigm shift in global teacher policy, they do suggest a pertinent research agenda. In this respect, the chapters in Part I, as well as the volume overall, highlight the variation in policy outcomes of global governance processes in different settings, as well as the need for critical inquiry (see especially chapters by Robertson & Navia Canales, and Bascia) to unpack ideational underpinnings and potential discrepancies between discourses of inclusion, well-being, equality, and the actual workings and outcomes of teacher policy making.

Labor Market Policies and Teachers' Careers: Shifting toward Flexibility and Fragmentation

Part II concentrates on the global transformations of the worlds of work, employment, and careers, an underexplored area in scholarship concerned with the teaching profession and globalization (Sorensen & Dumay, 2021). Two sets of significant lines of reform – in public management and in education expansion – have together led to shifts in teaching that have moved toward a vision of the teacher labor market oriented toward flexibility and the creation of a teaching labor force that is increasingly fragmented. As argued in the discussion above, there is no singular global policy in play, yet – as the chapters in Part II suggest – teaching has experienced a widespread remaking of temporal, spatial, and relational boundaries. The heightened attention to the importance of teaching (for education as a project, for national development, for the economy) has paradoxically resulted in the combination of greater calls for professionalism and growing challenges to a vision of a coherent, self-regulated profession. The chapters in this section explore the complex and shifting relationship of employment, work, careers, and the profession.

In the 20th century, teaching careers in most countries took the form of long bureaucratic careers. Teachers were prepared in specific programs, usually provided by universities or other higher education institutions in partnership with schools which serve as practicum sites. In addition, teachers' labor markets in most high-income countries historically have been regulated as an internal and professional labor market. But the introduction of New Public Management-oriented approaches changed the framework for managing teaching. This was certainly the case as many national systems addressed problems resulting from the expansion of schooling after the press for Education for All. In the Global South, teacher shortage has led to widespread borrowing of the model of contract teachers as a contingent labor group (Chudgar & Dembélé, Chapter 5). Whether in the Global North or Global South, the teaching profession has been shaped in recent decades by a vision of a profession characterized by a flexibility paradigm (Dumay, 2025).

The teaching profession has, over the last decades, gone through important global changes in terms of the status and attractiveness of the profession, mobility, and labor markets. Existing research indicates a crisis in teacher supply in many countries, reflecting a decline in the relative social and economic status of the teaching profession in some contexts, as well as the push for expansion of first primary and then secondary schooling in many countries and the severe impact of the COVID-19 pandemic in most. The teacher workforce has in many systems become more diversified in terms of possible pathways for entering the profession (e.g., second-career teachers), contractual conditions and required levels of qualification. The growing variation in teacher characteristics is associated with the increasing fragmentation of educational provision and the teaching profession. High rates of teacher attrition are widespread, particularly among novice teachers who are more likely to be confronted with less favorable employment conditions.

Part II examines these relationships between global evolutions of employment, careers, and work, and the evolutions visible in labor markets for teachers and teachers' careers across the world. In particular, it looks at how the narratives of policy reform are circulating, how policy issues are represented, framed, and dealt with in different sites globally, and the consequences of these for the profession. The section explores four major themes: (1) the diminished attractiveness of the teaching profession and the challenge in recruitment of "high-quality" teachers; (2) teacher shortages and teacher attrition; (3) new modes of entrance into the profession and the diversification of the teaching workforce; and (4) tensions between policy solutions to the shortages problem and policy solutions to concerns about "quality." This section sought out chapters that drew on phenomena in different regions of the world and that could explore how historical, cultural, political, and economic contexts shape teacher policy.

In prior decades, central concerns have been about whether teaching is a profession and how to professionalize teaching (Burbules & Densmore, 1991; Etzioni 1969; Ingersoll & Perda, 2008; Labaree, 1992; Lortie, 1975; Shulman, 1987). Today we need to ask fresh questions about the teaching profession. Shifts globally and within countries, as well as challenges to the status of teaching, have produced "traveling policies" of solutions to problems that in global reform rhetoric identify strengthening the teaching profession as the key to improving education quality. From the OECD (2005) "Teachers Matter" to the McKinsey report's regularly cited claim that "the quality of an education system cannot exceed the quality of its teachers" (Barber & Mourshed, 2007, p. 16), to UNESCO's recent "Global Report on Teachers" (UNESCO & International Task Force on Teachers for Education 2030, 2024), the argument about the significance of teachers, as well as the need to transform the profession, has become a narrative that echoes across global, national, and local contexts. While there has not been a universal approach to these issues, nonetheless what have become widely shared policy solutions – the use of contract teachers and second-career teachers, opening up alternative entries to teaching, new forms of teacher assessment, and more – now raise questions about how one can talk about teachers as sharing a profession.

Diversification currently characterizes the teaching force in many countries. While the cases drawn on in this part make clear that there is diversity within and across national and regional contexts, in recent years a pattern of increasing fragmentation of the profession has emerged. The rise of more varied routes into teaching, as well as greater diversity in teacher preparation within a national system, produces new answers to the question of who teachers are, how they are recruited and enter the field, and what their work and careers entail.

Much of the impetus for the heightened fragmentation of the profession derives from teacher shortages. The marketization of teaching has become a "magical" solution (Ball, 1998) to this problem in many contexts. As Chudgar and Dembélé (Chapter 5) argue, for example, contract teacher policy approaches to teacher shortages in low- and middle-income countries have profound implications for educational systems, their learners, and the teaching profession itself. Indeed, shortages have been leading much of the global reform narrative in the Global South: see for example UNESCO's Global Teacher Report's subtitle: "Addressing teacher shortages and transforming the profession." Yet shortages are part of the explanation for reforms in recruitment, entry, and preparation of teachers in the Global North as well, as Coppe (Chapter 6) explains. These policy approaches have reshaped the contours of the profession – who enters, how long they stay, how much there is a shared identity among teachers. The chapter by Sarangapani and colleagues (Chapter 7), along with Chudgar and Dembélé's, reminds us that uneven distribution, with resultant surplus and shortage of teachers, within a country adds to the complex set of motivations for new teacher policy. Across the chapters, we see the evidence of traveling reforms and global vernacularization.

The complex roles of actors in and mechanisms for such shifts – whether international financial institutions' pressing structural adjustment policies on national governments (requiring them to reduce the percentage of national funds spent on educator salaries) or the spread through summits and reports about "best practices" for managing the educator workforce – are important to understand as boundary remaking (Seddon et al., 2013). Teacher labor market policy no longer reflects (or is influenced by) only the nation-state; additionally, it constructs new boundaries of (and within) the teaching force.

The transformation of the teaching profession globally is equally important a story about shifting ideas about quality – what teacher quality is, how it can be produced, assessed, and maintained, as well as who determines these. Research suggests there is no single pattern of teacher policy (Voisin & Dumay, 2020), and the chapters document this as well, while still noting some broad patterns. Tatto (Chapter 8) explores patterns of solutions that have been taken up, in part from concern about quality. At the same time that quality has become a watchword for reform (Sayed et al., 2018), an increasingly diverse set of actors have arrived on the scene to reshape the profession – from non-state and transnational actors creating models of short-term teacher preparation (Lefebvre et al., 2022) to international organizations providing metrics and guidelines for defining, producing, hiring, and supporting "quality teaching" (see, for example, the World Bank's Global Platform for Successful Teachers) (Béteille & Evans, 2019).

The chapters in this section explore these issues of shortage and quality, fragmentation and redefinition of teachers' work and teacher quality. Together they offer national case studies (Sarangapani et al.), examinations of patterns within regions (Tatto), considerations of what appear as emerging global trends (Chudgar and Dembele; Coppe; Tatto), powered by global governance and involvement or steering of government, IGO and INGO, and non-state actors. The diversification (and heightened precarity) of the teaching workforce, relocation of recruitment and preparation, and redefinition of careers and teacher work all, as these chapter suggest, arrive as widely shared solutions. Such "solutions" also engender new problems. The chapters point to the need for more research to understand the policies, their impact, implications, and possibilities for the profession.

New Configurations of Teachers' Work and Learning

Part III delves into contemporary transformations of (teacher) education and the temporal, social and topical expansion of learning. It looks at how the shift from education to learning, the development of lifelong learning and continuous professional development, and the digitization of education, work, and CPD are reorganizing the status of the teaching profession and teachers' work, transcending profession boundaries and reconfiguring contexts and modalities of teachers' learning. It deals with four trends, each of which is the subject of a chapter: the digitization of teacher professional learning (Decuypere & Lewis,

Chapter 9), teacher learning in transnational spaces and projects (Thomas & Lefebvre, Chapter 10), the greater division of labor, specialization of work, and teacher leadership (LeTendre, Chapter 11); and the coexistence of multiple conceptions of teacher learning in work contexts (Hardy, Chapter 12). These trends all revolve around the idea of "learning as a norm" (Mangez & Vanden Broeck, 2020) and the adaptation of the teaching profession to more uncertain, unstable, and changing contexts and crises.

The contributions show in different ways that the form of learning implies a different conception of time, space, and profession. In contrast to the form of (teacher) training, the form of learning implies a shorter, more flexible relationship with time, reflecting a view of the future that is more uncertain and open-ended. Learning often takes place through projects that have a temporary organizational form and non-permanent structures. For example, Decuypere and Lewis analyze the European Commission's European School Education Platform as an example of how such platforms promote a projectified version of teacher professionalism and learning that implies time-bounded, teacher-centered learning. In the same vein, Thomas and Lefebvre examine how learning and socialization into the profession can be imagined in short modules that prepare teachers for a short teaching assignment, as is the case for teachers entering the profession through the Teach For All (TFAll) program. They show how such a redesign of initial training is made possible by scripts such as "recruiting the best and the brightest," and the candidates' ability to "learn quickly" and "work restlessly."

The relationship to space is also changing profoundly. Learning and training space is both virtual and rooted in organizations. The proliferation of learning and professional development platforms plunges teachers (at different stages of their careers) into virtualized learning devices and communities, disconnecting them from the workplace, highlighted by Decuypere and Lewis who point out that teachers' learning is not only projectified but also platformed. But learning is also increasingly tied to the work context, in local communities of colleagues in various leadership and advisory roles. In this regard, LeTendre's chapter shows that workplace learning and organizational professionalism have become global trends, supported in particular by the changing discourse of IOs emphasizing teacher professionalism (OECD, 2016; Hardy, Chapter 12).

Finally, the form of learning implies new conceptions of professionalism and professionals: professionalism is conceived in terms that are much more focused on the individuals themselves and their work contexts; and professionals are expected to be entrepreneurs of themselves and responsible for their own development. This argument is well developed by Lewis and Decuypere, who show that platformed learning implies new conceptions of teacher professionalism that emphasize new kinds of knowledge (i.e., soft skills) and accountability models (i.e., accountability for project outcomes). Hardy, for his part, suggests that rival conceptions of professionalism are in tension in most school systems, i.e., neoliberal conceptions emphasizing work prescriptions and output-based control, and more professionally oriented conceptions underpinned by trust in professional judgment. The two conceptions carry different visions of teacher learning: the former sees learning as instrumental to accountability goals, the latter approaches learning in a more open way.

In practice, different forms of teacher education and learning coexist. As LeTendre analyzes in his chapter on teacher leadership, old cultural forms (of teacher leadership, as in the case of Japan) are hybridized by new political and institutional influences (which may give new or different meanings to practices or concepts). Depending on their histories and trajectories, not all education systems are equally sensitive to the development of more open and flexible forms of learning. Voisin and Dumay (2020) suggest that the teaching profession is embedded in regulatory configurations (which may be bureaucratic, market-based, or professional) that make it more or less receptive to alternative conceptions of the profession and professional learning. It's no coincidence, for example, that the TFAll program originated in the United States and has seen its strongest development in education systems such as England and Australia (Thomas & Lefebvre); or that the deployment of neoliberal conceptions of teacher learning, while widespread around the world, is more visible in some places than others (Hardy).

However, contributions in Part III also highlight that it is precisely one of the characteristics of alternative learning systems that they are highly flexible while retaining the core of what makes them what they are. Teacher work and learning is, paradoxically, highly scripted, and adaptable. As noted by Thomas and Lefebvre about TFAll, scripts as flexible narratives that allow for embodied improvisation, reinterpretation, and even revision. Despite differences in implementation and philosophies, TFAll affiliates adapt the "unifying principles" to their specific contexts while maintaining a remarkably similar language. In the same way, Decuypere and Lewis point out that "project-based" "self-centered" professionalization, although it can take very different forms (digital or not; international or local, etc.), has become a central, and even necessary, aspect of teacher professionality in relation to which teachers are required to position themselves.

Teacher professionalism (and teacher learning) is also increasingly seen in relation to workplaces and contexts, and job-embedded learning. Not only in education, the exercise of professionalism is now defined in organizational terms, encompassing the logics of organization and market, managerialism and commercialism (Evetts, 2003). The logic of organizational professionalism, as noted by LeTendre in this volume, has been widely promoted by some leading international organizations, such as the OECD, under the concept of the learning organization. In some systems, however, this is a strong logic rooted in a country's history and culture. In a country like Japan, for example, teaching careers have historically been structured around multiple roles and professional positions in the workplace that allow teachers to advance professionally. However, these long-standing cultural logics have recently been undermined by new concepts such as teacher leadership. Both historical and contemporary forms of organizational professionalism, often combined according to the stronger or weaker influences of neoliberal conceptions of the teaching profession and teacher learning (Hardy), involve a complex redefinition of professional labor relations and teacher agency. Labor relations are both hierarchical and heterarchical, and teacher agency is both enhanced and constrained.

These blurred boundaries and relationships should also invite us to question the real power of teachers to reshape their profession. The sociology of work has amply demonstrated that for many occupations, job specialization is associated with higher status. But the trend toward greater specialization in teaching seems less clear-cut. Mathou et al. (2023) and Thomas and Lefebvre in this volume also argue that the increasing complexity of work environments is reflected in the greater precariousness of work, particularly in contexts where neoliberal influences are strong (see Hardy). But more than that, it raises the question of who controls teachers' work, to paraphrase Richard Ingersoll. Decuypere and Lewis suggest that the expertise/knowledge base of teachers and the teaching profession has been externalized in platforms and in new kinds of experts, those who master organizational logics (project, platforms) more than professional logics (linked to teaching content or pedagogy). Complementarily, these new forms of learning and work organization can also be seen as political forms and processes in themselves. Thomas and Lefebvre, for example, rightly point out that TFAll is both a professional and a political script. Decuypere and Lewis, in the same vein, see the project form increasingly used as a governance technique to stimulate and instill specific forms of learning. These alternative forms are above all a political form or script, as they bring existing practices and ideas into tension and friction. Even if they remain largely peripheral, they carry within them the seeds of a theory of change that implies, more than a direction or directions to take, the need for constant change, which obviously fit much more with the form of (teacher) learning than with that of (teacher) education.

Concluding Remarks

WYBE 2025 – the teaching profession in a globalizing world: governance, career and learning – develops an original framework for considering, from a globalization and public policy perspective, the ways in which the logics of governance, employment, and education, all three of which constitute this emerging public policy field, are evolving and transforming. It therefore calls for a decompartmentalization of research on the governance of the teaching profession, teacher labor markets, and teacher education and learning to better capture how the shifting logics that organize them are intertwined and reorganize the status of the teaching profession in a globalizing world. Concepts such as (teacher) careers or intriguing, relatively new tropes in global conversations such as teacher well-being, resilience, and self-care (see Robertson and Navia, this volume) offer relevant ways to further understand and disentangle the intersections of the three logics of governance, labor market, and learning.

WYBE 2025 also invites further reflection on the ways and conditions under which teachers, through unions, professional associations, and (professional) social movements in general, are agents of change in the globalized field of education and teacher policy. Indeed, the question that remains largely unanswered – in the field of educational research, but not only – is that of the mechanisms of globalization of professions, and the ways in which these mechanisms (of representation, contestation, and legitimation, to name a few) impact on central processes for profession such as professional development models, modes of recruitment, and labor markets and careers.

Finally, WYBE 2025 questions the singularity of the field of teacher policy – at the intersection of the public sector, employment, finance, and educational reform – but at the same time invites our research community to understand teacher policy as a reflection of new developments in educational policy that may point to more contextualized, contingent, and less structural patterns of reform which in fact implies renewed reflection on new forms of teacher professionalism, which can be organizational as invoked by IGOs, but not only.

Note

1 Here and throughout this chapter and volume, we recognize the difficulty of naming groups of countries. Like many scholars, we struggle with finding ways to speak about more than a single country without overgeneralizing or ignoring historical complexities, cultural meanings, and political dynamics and inequities. All classifications seem problematic. At times in this introduction, we use commonly used terms (such as low- and middle-income countries) of international financial organizations when the economic distinctions are most salient; at other times we refer to what – at the time of this writing – are often referred to as countries in the Global South or Global North. This issue is a reminder of the challenge of thinking "globally"; the inadequacy of terms to capture complexity, history, and variation; and impermanence (and temporality) of frameworks constructed by research and policy. Readers will note that chapter authors chose their own approach to classifying countries, reflecting their diverse theoretical and disciplinary perspectives.

References

Ahrne, G., & Brunsson, N. (2008). *Meta-organizations*. Edward Elgar.
Akiba, M. (2017). Editor's introduction: Understanding cross-national differences in globalized teacher reforms. *Educational Researcher, 46*(4), 153–68.
Baccaro, L., & Howell, C. (2017). *Trajectories of neoliberal transformation. European industrial relations since the 1970s*. Cambridge University Press.
Ball, S. J. (1998). Big policies/small world: An introduction to international perspectives in education policy. *Comparative Education, 34*(2), 119–130.
Barber, M., & Mourshed, M. (2007). *How the world's best-performing school systems come out on top*. McKinsey & Company.
Béteille, T., & Evans, D. K. (2019). *Successful teachers, successful students: Recruiting and supporting society's most crucial profession*. World Bank Group.
Börzel, T. A. (2010). European Governance: Negotiation and competition in the shadow of hierarchy. *JCMS: Journal of Common Market Studies, 48*(2), 191–219.

Bridges, D. (2008). Educationalization: On the appropriateness of asking educational institutions to solve social and economic problems. *Educational Theory*, 58(4), 461–474.
Bromley, P., Overbey, L., Furuta, J., & Kijima, R. (2021). Education reform in the twenty-first century: Declining emphases in international organisation reports, 1998–2018. *Globalisation, Societies and Education*, 19(1), 23–40.
Burbules, N. C., & Densmore, K. (1991). The limits of making teaching a profession. *Educational Policy*, 5(1), 44–63.
Capano, G., Howlett, M., & Ramesh, M. (2015). Bringing governments back in: Governance and governing in comparative policy analysis. *Journal of Comparative Policy Analysis: Research and Practice*, 17(4), 311–321.
Carroll, P., & Kellow, A. (2011). *The OECD: A study of organisational adaptation*. Edward Elgar.
Centeno, V. G. (2021). The OECD: Actor, arena, instrument. *Globalisation, Societies and Education*, 19(2), 108–121.
Connell, R. (2009). Good teachers on dangerous ground: Towards a new view of teacher quality and professionalism. *Critical Studies in Education*, 50(3), 213–229.
Dale, R. (2005). Globalisation, knowledge economy and comparative education. *Comparative Education*, 41(2), 117–149.
Darling-Hammond, L., Chung, R., & Frelow, F. (2002). Variation in teacher preparation: How well do different pathways prepare teachers to teach? *Journal of Teacher Education*, 53(4), 286–302.
Darling-Hammond, L., Burns, D., Campbell, C., Goodwin, A. L., Hammerness, K., Low, E. L., ... & Zeichner, K. (2017). *Empowered educators: How high-performing systems shape teaching quality around the world*. John Wiley & Sons.
Depaepe, M., & Smeyers, P. (2008). Educationalization as an ongoing modernization process. *Educational Theory*, 58(4), 379–389.
Dubnick, M. J. (2006). "Orders of Accountability." *Paper presented at the World Ethics Forum*, Oxford, UK. Retrieved from http://pubpages.unh.edu/dubnick/papers/2006/oxford2006.pdf
Dumay, X. (Ed.) (2025). *The liberalization of teacher employment regimes in Europe*. Oxford University Press.
Dumay, X., & Burn, K. (2023). *The status of the teaching profession: Interactions between historical and new forms of segmentation*. Routledge.
Dumay, X., & Mangez, E. (2024). Social theory, globalization, and education. In P. Mattei, X. Dumay, E. Mangez, & J. Behrend (Eds.), *The Oxford handbook of education and globalization* (pp. 3–26). Oxford University Press.
Elfert, M., & Ydesen, C. (2023). *Global governance of education: The historical and contemporary entanglements of UNESCO, the OECD and the World Bank*. Springer.
Etzioni, A. (1969). *The semi-professions and their organization: Teachers, nurses, social workers*. The Free Press.
Evetts, J. (2003). The Sociological Analysis of Professionalism: Occupational Change in the Modern World. *International Sociology*, 18(2), 395–415.
Fourcade, M., Ollion, E., & Algan, Y. (2015). The superiority of economists. *Journal of Economic Perspectives*, 29(1), 89–114.
Hallett, T. (2010). The myth incarnate: Recoupling processes, turmoil, and inhabited Institutions in an urban elementary school. *American Sociological Review*, 75(1), 52–74.
Héritier, A., & Lehmkuhl, D. (2008). The shadow of hierarchy and new modes of governance. *Journal of Public Policy*, 28(1), 1–17.
Holloway, J., Sorensen, T. B., & Verger, A. (2017). Global perspectives on high-stakes teacher accountability policies: An introduction. *Education Policy Analysis Archives*, 25, 1–18.
Hopmann, S. T. (2008). No child, no school, no state left behind: Schooling in the age of accountability. *Journal of Curriculum Studies*, 40(4), 417–456.

Hossain, M. (2022). Diffusing "Destandardization" reforms across educational systems in low- and middle-income countries: The case of the world bank, 1965 to 2020. *Sociology of Education*, 95(4), 320–339.

Hoyle, E., & Megarry, J. (Eds.). (1980). *World yearbook of education 1980. The professional development of teachers*. Routledge.

Ingersoll, R. M., & Perda, D. (2008). The status of teaching as a profession. In J. Ballantine & J. Spade (Eds.), *Schools and society: A sociological approach to education*, (pp. 106–118). Pine Forge Press

International Labour Organization and UNESCO (2016). *ILO/UNESCO recommendation concerning the status of teachers (1966) and UNESCO recommendation concerning the status of higher-education teaching personnel (1997)*. International Labour Office.

International Labour Organization, UN and UNESCO (2024). *Transforming the teaching profession: Recommendations and summary of deliberations of the United Nations secretary-General's high-level panel on the teaching profession*. International Labour Office.

Kalleberg, A. L. (2018). *Precarious lives. Job insecurity and well-being in rich democracies*. Polity Press.

Labaree, D. (1992). Power, knowledge, and the rationalization of teaching: A genealogy of the movement to professionalize teaching. *Harvard Educational Review*, 62(2), 123–155.

Labaree, D. F. (2017). Futures of the field of education. In G. Whitty, & J. Furlong (Eds.), *Knowledge and the study of education: An international exploration* (pp. 277–283). Symposium Books.

Lankford, H., Loeb, S., & Wyckoff, J. (2002). Teacher sorting and the plight of urban schools: A descriptive analysis. *Educational Evaluation and Policy Analysis*, 24(1), 37–62.

Lefebvre, E. E., Pradhan, S., & Thomas, M. A. M. (2022). The discursive utility of the global, local, and national: Teach for all in Africa. *Comparative Education Review*, 66(4), 620–642.

Loeb, S., & Béteille, T. (2009). Teacher quality and teacher labor markets. In G. Sykes, B. Schneider, & D. N. Plank (Eds.), *Handbook of education policy research* (pp. 596–612). Routledge.

Lortie, D. C. (1975). *Schoolteacher: A sociological study*. University of Chicago Press.

Luschei, T. F., & Chudgar, A. (2016). *Teacher distribution in developing countries: Teachers of marginalized students in India, Mexico, and Tanzania*. Springer.

Mangez, E., & Vanden Broeck, P. (2020). The history of the future and the shifting forms of education. *Educational Philosophy and Theory*, 20(6), 676–687.

Maroy, C. (2009). Convergences and hybridization of educational policies around 'post-bureaucratic' models of regulation. *Compare: A Journal of Comparative and International Education*, 39(1), 71–84.

Mathou, C., Sarazin, M., & Dumay, X. (2023). Reshaped teachers' careers? New patterns and the fragmentation of the teaching profession in England. *British Journal of Sociology of Education*, 44(3), 397–417.

Menter, I. (2023). Teacher education research in the twenty-first century. In I. Menter (Ed.), *The Palgrave handbook of teacher education research* (pp. 3–31). Palgrave Macmillan.

Milana, M. (2017). *Global networks, local actions: Rethinking adult education policy in the 21st century*. Routledge.

OECD (2005). *Teachers matter: Attracting, developing and retaining effective teachers, education and training policy*. OECD Publishing. Accessed on 13 May 2024.

OECD (2016). *Teaching in Focus: Teacher Professionalism*. OECD publishing. Accessed on 26 August 2024.

Paine, L., Aydarova, E., & Syahril, I. (2017). Globalization and teacher education. In D. J. Clandinin, & J. Husu (Eds.), *The Sage handbook of research on teacher education* (pp. 1133–1148). Sage.
Paine, L., Blömeke, S., & Aydarova, O. (2016). Teachers and teaching in the context of globalization. In D. H. Gitomer & C. A. Bell (Eds.), *Handbook of research on teaching* (fifth ed.) (pp. 717–786). American Educational Research Association.
Paine, L., & Zeichner, K. (2012). The local and the global in reforming teaching and teacher education. *Comparative Education Review*, 56(4), 569–83.
Peters, B. G. (2015). *Advanced introduction to public policy*. Edward Elgar.
Robertson, S. L. (2013). Teachers' work, denationalization, and transformations in the field of symbolic control: A comparative account. In T. Seddon, & J. S. Levin (Eds.), *World yearbook of education 2013. Educators, professionalism and politics: Global transitions, national spaces and professional projects* (pp. 77–96). Routledge.
Robertson, S. L. (2016). The global governance of teachers' work. In K. Mundy, A. Green, B. Lingard, & A. Verger (Eds.), *The handbook of global education policy* (pp. 275–290). Wiley-Blackwell.
Sayed, Y., Ahmed, R., & Mogliacci, R. (2018). *The 2030 global education agenda and teachers, teaching and teacher education* (Version 1). University of Sussex.
Schmidt, W. H., Blömeke, S., Tatto, M. T., Hsieh, F. J., Cogan, L., Houang, R. T., & Schwille, J. (2011). *Teacher education matters: A study of middle school mathematics teacher preparation in six countries*. Teachers College Press, Columbia University.
Scott, R. W. (2013). Lords of the dance: Professionals as institutional agents". *Organization Studies*, 29(2), 219–238.
Seddon, T., & Levin, J. S. (Eds.). (2013). *World yearbook of education 2013. Educators, professionalism and politics: Global transitions, national spaces and professional projects*. Routledge.
Seddon, T., Ozga, J., & Levin, J. S. (2013). Global transitions and teacher professionalism. In T. Seddon, & S.J. Levin (Eds.), *World yearbook of education 2013. Educators, professionalism and politics: Global transitions, national spaces and professional projects*. Routledge.
Shulman, L. (1987). Knowledge and teaching: Foundations of the new reform. *Harvard Educational Review*, 57(1), 1–23.
Sorensen, T. B., & Dumay, X. (2021). The teaching professions and globalization: A scoping review of the anglophone research literature. *Comparative Education Review*, 65(4), 725–749.
Sorensen, T. B., & Dumay, X. (2024). The European Union's governance of teachers and the evolution of a bridging issue field since the mid-2000s. *European Educational Research Journal*, 23(2), 237–260.
Sorensen, T. B., & Robertson, S. L. (2020). Ordinalization and the OECD's governance of teachers. *Comparative Education Review*, 64(1), 21–45.
Spillane, J. P., Reiser, B. J., & Reimer, T. (2002). Policy implementation and cognition: Reframing and refocusing implementation research. *Review of Educational Research*, 72(3), 387–431.
Tatto, M. T., & Pippin, J. (2017). The quest for quality and the rise of accountability systems in teacher education. In D.J. Clandinin, & J. Husu (Eds.). *The Sage Handbook of Research on Teacher Education* (pp. 68–89). Sage.
Thelen, K. (2014). *Varieties of liberalization and the new politics of social solidarity*. Cambridge University Press.
Tröhler, D. (2016). educationalization of social problems and the educationalization of the modern world. In M. Peters (Ed.), *Encyclopedia of educational philosophy and theory*. Springer.
Tröhler, D. (2021). Magical enchantments and the nation's silencing: Educational research agendas under the spell of globalization. In D. Tröhler, N. Piattoeva, &

W. F. Pinar (Eds.), *World yearbook of education 2022: Education, schooling and the global universalization of nationalism* (pp. 7–25). Routledge.

Tröhler, D., Piattoeva, N., & Pinar, W. F. (Eds.). (2021). *World yearbook of education 2022: education, schooling and the global universalization of nationalism.* Routledge.

UNESCO & International Task Force on Teachers for Education 2030 (2024). *Global report on teachers: Addressing teacher shortages and transforming the profession.* UNESCO.

Vanden Broeck P. & Mangez E. (2016) Learning as a Norm, paper presented at the European Conference on Educational Research, Network 28: sociologies of education, Dublin, August 24, 2016.

Verger, A., Parcerisa, L., & Quilabert, E. (2023). *The trajectory, instrumentation and enactment of global education reform: Analyses of 'school autonomy with accountability' reforms in different settings.* Comparative International and Education Society Annual Conference 2023 Formal Panel Session, Washington D.C. 18–22 February 2023.

Voisin, A., & Dumay, X. (2020). How do educational systems regulate the teaching profession and teachers' work? A typological approach to institutional foundations and models of regulation. *Teaching and Teacher Education, 96*, 103–144.

Wilkins, A. W., & Mifsud, D. (2024). What is governance? Projects, objects and analytics in education. *Journal of Education Policy, 39*(3), 349–365.

Zürn, M. (2018). *A theory of global governance: Authority, legitimacy, and contestation.* Oxford University Press.

Part I

The Global Governance of Teachers and the Teaching Profession

1 Between Teachers' Governance and Development

Shifting Emphases, Methods, and Global Policy Trends in Teacher Appraisal

Gerard Ferrer-Esteban, Clara Fontdevila, and Antoni Verger

Introduction

In 2007, the McKinsey report *How the World's Best-Performing School Systems Come Out on Top* famously asserted that "the quality of an educational system cannot exceed the quality of its teachers" (Barber & Moursed, 2017, p. 16). Despite attracting considerable criticism, the statement spread rapidly, exemplifying the centrality of the notions of teacher effectiveness and teacher quality. These notions gained currency in an era marked by a growing focus on quality assurance in education, a burgeoning interest in cross-national assessments, and the ascendance of outcomes based management approaches in the public sector. A clear manifestation of the teacher-effectiveness agenda has been the intensification of teacher appraisal arrangements. Since the mid-2000s, the increasing emphasis on teacher effectiveness has led to numerous policies aimed at monitoring and evaluating teacher work, both collectively and individually (Williams & Engel, 2012). Countries have developed evaluation frameworks combining different instruments such as external assessments, standards, and performance-based incentives to regulate teachers' work and career progression.

Such policies have precipitated a shift in the governance of the teaching profession, reshaping aspects of teachers' work including work conditions, career trajectories, and external support. Nonetheless, and perhaps more critically, these reforms have also affected teachers' professional identities and societal valuation. Policies entailing the routine observation and assessment of teachers' work have made some educators feel less trusted by educational authorities, undermining their sense of autonomy and control. Accordingly, teacher appraisal reforms have been the object of a vibrant academic and policy debate concerned with their merits and drawbacks (Lavigne et al., 2014; Smith & Holloway, 2020).

As this chapter shows, teacher appraisal policies have been evolving and diversifying. The early emphasis on accountability and control has given way to a greater focus on appraisal as a tool for professional growth and instructional improvement. This discursive shift is evident in international organizations (IOs) and transnational fora, as early proponents now advocate for more

DOI: 10.4324/9781003441731-3

comprehensive and sophisticated systems. However, domestic implications remain unclear. The contested nature of teacher-appraisal schemes, along with their uneasy fit with certain administrative and educational cultures, has led several countries to experiment new policies. It is increasingly clear that global discourses vary widely in their translation into concrete evaluation policies – both across and within nations.

Teacher appraisal epitomizes the fluid and mutating nature of policy instruments in education governance. It serves as a magnifying lens for examining policy convergence and divergence dynamics – given the varied meanings, uses, and implementation of apparently similar instruments. This heterogeneity begs for a critical interrogation of the factors driving policy adoption and adaptation. Building on such premises, this chapter is organized as follows. The first section reviews the global debate on teacher appraisal by mapping the evolution of methods and their key proponents. The second section introduces the study's analytical and methodological approach. The third section presents our main results, exploring the worldwide evolution of teacher appraisal methods, focusing on the influence of partisan politics and teachers' regulations. We conclude by reflecting on the contingent relationship between global policy trends and their adoption and enactment across contexts.

The Twists and Turns of Teacher Appraisal: An Overview of the Global Debate

Teachers' evaluation policies have been long established in many educational systems. Historically, external actors like inspectors or school boards predominantly conducted teacher evaluations, following a range of administrative procedures. This approach significantly shifted in the 1980s and 1990s with emerging educational improvement and innovation trends to include practices like teachers' self-evaluation, peer evaluation, and even more disruptive methodologies like action research (Huber & Skedsmo, 2016). This marked a shift from top-down models to a collaborative and formative approach valuing teachers' autonomy and reflective practice for professional development (O'Leary, 2022; Ridge & Lavigne, 2020).

At the millennium's turn, reforms placed teachers at the center of efforts to enhance educational outcomes, aligning teacher evaluation with broader quality assurance and performance-based accountability agendas. Consequently, teacher appraisal became more visible and experienced a transformation both in form and purpose. Teacher appraisal began to rely on a few new sources of information – most notably, externally administered assessments measuring student achievement. Reforms across different countries coincided in using narrow outcome metrics, focusing more on the individual teacher (Holloway et al., 2017; Smith & Kubacka, 2017). The rise of value-added models (VAMs), aimed at estimating teacher contribution to learning growth via standardized tests (Hallinger et al., 2014), represents one of the most visible manifestations of this procedural shift. Though mainly used in the United States and the

United Kingdom, VAMs' disruptive nature significantly impacted the international educational debate (AERA, 2015).

In the early 2000s, teacher evaluation tools were thus put at the service of a broader accountability agenda and attached to different material or administrative rewards and sanctions, including changes in compensation and opportunities for career progression (Isoré, 2009). Teacher appraisal reforms emphasized efficiency and were portrayed to encourage teachers' efforts in promoting students learning (Mathwasa & Duku, 2015). The *Teachers Matter* publication of the Organisation for Economic Co-operation and Development (OECD, 2005) exemplified this iteration and helped consolidate teacher appraisal policies among key IOs. The report underscored the necessity of incentivizing good teaching through transparent and systematic evaluations, even when altering work arrangements. Besides the OECD, entities such as the World Bank, Bill and Melinda Gates Foundation, and McKinsey adopted this policy approach in the 2000s (Robertson, 2012). Although these organizations favored different approaches, consistent with their roles and preferences, the focus on teacher quality was central and enhanced the legitimacy of teacher reforms internationally.

However, recent developments suggest another shift. The IOs that championed a managerial approach to teachers' work, evaluation, and management have begun to acknowledge the limits of this perspective. There is growing consensus on prioritizing teacher well-being and re-professionalizing teaching – a move toward restoring the dignity and recognizing the complexity of educators' work. The OECD now advocates a more balanced approach to teacher policy, clearly exemplifying this discursive change. Remarkably, these shifts have been years in the making and cannot be disconnected from the engagement with other education stakeholders and social partners – most notably, teachers. In the early 2010s, the OECD, in collaboration with Education International (the global federation of teacher unions), initiated dialogues via summits that underscored the importance of teacher appraisal frameworks focusing on professional development and feedback (Sorensen, 2021).

This reimagined approach to teacher appraisal was supported by OECD's research initiatives, such as *Synergies for Better Learning* (OECD, 2013). The explicit acknowledgment that "there are risks that the developmental function of teacher appraisal is undermined when it is too closely associated with high-stakes appraisal for accountability purposes" (p. 332) is particularly emblematic of this shift. The 2020s marked a turn toward an even more cautious approach to teacher appraisal, as captured by one of the OECDs current flagship projects, *New Professionalism and the Future of Teaching*, which refrains from referring to teacher evaluation as a primary professionalization tool (OECD, 2022).

This shift has often been linked to high-stakes teacher evaluation not improving student learning (Bleiberg et al., 2021; Di Carlo, 2023). It is also a response to the general realization that the overemphasis on accountability and performance metrics can inadvertently erode teachers' professional standing. Teacher appraisal pressures have often led to widespread issues of declining morale, as well as mounting stress for educators and school leaders (Jerrim & Sims, 2022; Larsen, 2005; Sutcher et al., 2019). Accordingly, many educational systems are shifting from narrow teacher-appraisal systems to more comprehensive approaches that enhance teacher professionalism (Ávalos, 2022).

Overall, there is evidence of a discursive shift on the question of teacher appraisal – at least within transnational and academic circles. However, it remains unclear how and to what extent such changes have impacted domestic policy agendas and what are their consequences. Indeed, teacher appraisal policies are unlikely to have followed a linear trajectory. As discussed above, teacher appraisal reforms are often disruptive and likely to spark political contestation and opposition. In addition, while certain administrative cultures may easily accommodate teacher appraisal schemes, their institutional fit and feasibility in other contexts are doubtful. Similar policies such as performance-based school accountability schemes have indeed shown notoriously erratic trajectories across countries (Högberg & Lindgren, 2021; Teltemann & Jude, 2019). Yet, evidence of teacher appraisal reform trajectories is limited.

Understanding the Enactment of Teacher Appraisal Reforms: Analytical Pointers and Empirical Strategy

Scholars concerned with the global circulation of policy ideas have drawn attention to the need for interrogating the policy convergence thesis; the idea that, because of globalizing policy trends, countries are becoming more alike. Such realization has given rise to different literatures concerned with the identification of sources of variation or points of mediation (cf. Hay, 2004). Thus, the global discourse emphasizing the need to reinforce teacher appraisal does not guarantee uniform policy arrangements across countries or linear trajectories. To test this premise, our study examines these policies' enactment and evolution, addressing how institutional features and contingencies affect policy change. This section focuses on two key national institutions identified by comparative social policy as mediators in recontextualizing global policy trends: partisan politics and regulatory regimes.

This section introduces these two determinants, adjusting them to the education sector's specificities, and hypothesizes their effects on teacher-appraisal policy. Next, we outline the empirical strategy, with particular attention to the data sources used to operationalize the variables of interest.

Explaining Policy Divergence: The Role of Institutional Mediations

First, *partisan ideologies* and the balance of power among different political forces (and politically active organizations) are amply recognized as key factors shaping the configuration of public policies, including the content and nature of educational reforms (Busemeyer, 2014; Taylor & Henry, 2000). Such factors would not only impact the probability of adoption of certain policies but also their implementation and stability over time. Hence, it can be assumed that partisan politics are likely to intervene decisively in all dimensions of governmental action – but especially in relation to politically charged policy issues. Given its disruptive and divisive impact, this is often the case with teacher-appraisal policies. Indeed, high-stakes accountability reforms are rarely received with indifference among the teacher profession (Verger et al., 2019) – given that they often entail important changes in the working conditions and social status of the profession, but also because they are often adopted as part of broader reform packages concerned with the governance of the education system.

The political salience of teacher-appraisal reforms can be safely assumed, yet partisan preferences and alliances on such questions defy simple generalizations. The relationship between political orientation and education policy preferences has thus acquired an element of unpredictability as a result of broader trends, including increasingly complex patterns of party competition and the transformation of major political parties (cf. Gingrich, 2011; Häusermann et al., 2013). The lack of straightforward connections between political ideology and policy preferences is particularly evident in the case of accountability-related education reforms (Verger et al., 2019). Quality assurance discourses in education, embraced across the political spectrum, can serve different and even competing objectives. School and teacher evaluation policies, often associated with right-wing forces, can serve a school effectiveness agenda, but they may also be motivated by a pro-equity agenda aimed at reducing so-called learning gaps, which is associated with left-leaning forces. Additionally, although teacher appraisal reforms were initially informed by a managerial ethos, they have also proved capable of accommodating a professionalization agenda that puts a premium on the autonomy of the teaching workforce.

The complex alignment between political parties and key stakeholders (Giudici et al., 2023) adds another layer of complexity. Formal or organic ties between the government, tasked with the implementation of reforms, and organizations representing the teaching profession are likely to condition the reception of attempted policy changes. Teacher-career reforms negotiated with major teachers' unions might fare better than those unilaterally championed by a government. Once again, political alliances increasingly have become unpredictable when it comes to teacher reform. While social-democratic governments are often assumed to be more receptive to the input of teachers' unions and grassroots, there is evidence that the alliance between trade unions and social-democratic parties has eroded since the 1990s (Allern et al., 2017; Howell, 2001). Hence, while the cooperation between teacher unions and left-leaning governments is likely to favor the durability of teacher appraisal reforms, such connections cannot be taken for granted but need to be empirically examined.

Existing regulatory regimes also play a key role in the enactment of educational reforms; they can either facilitate or hinder change, depending on their ability to mediate between external pressures and internal structures and capabilities. Regulatory regimes thus exemplify the mediating role played by institutional architectures. Research on the impact of institutional architectures has tended to focus on administrative regimes, which have repeatedly been found to mediate in the reception of global trends and external pressures, conditioning which paradigms are retained and how they are adapted to local contexts (Peters & Pierre, 2012; Pollitt & Bouckaert, 2017). In the context of educational reforms, national education administrations operate as a key mediating variable, as they present a series of regulatory and organizational particularities that need to be considered to understand enactment processes. In the case of teacher reforms, the regulation of the teaching profession, which has been found to vary markedly across different world regions, can be expected to play a crucial role in mediating the enactment of the quality assurance paradigm. Here, the work of Voisin and Dumay (2020) is particularly relevant. Building on the premise that the institutional foundations regulating the teaching profession differ sharply across countries, they propose four models that shape the quality and distribution of teachers and structure the professional environment within which teachers operate. These models or regimes differ on a range of variables such as the nature of teacher preparation programs, labor market regulations, and the prevailing divisions of labor, including the relative levels of teacher autonomy and the prevailing forms of accountability. The four regimes can be summarized as follows:[1]

- A *market regime*, guided by the principles of flexibility and competition, relying on a combination of performance, managerial and market-based accountability, and limited levels of teacher autonomy.
- A *rules regime*, characterized by highly centralized and bureaucratic regulations governing the teaching profession, privileging external and hierarchical forms of control, based on bureaucratic rules.
- A *training regime*, centered around the notions of expertise and professional autonomy and equipping teachers with high levels of autonomy and trust on the part of educational authorities. This regime privileges professional rather than hierarchical forms of control.
- A *professional skills regime*, which puts a premium on practical skills and highly selective training schemes and combines the reliance on bureaucratic rules and professional standards.

These different regimes vary greatly in their compatibility with various forms of teacher appraisal. At one end of the spectrum, the market regime can be expected to adopt performance-based approaches (Paufler & Sloat, 2020). Appraisal schemes relying on student achievement metrics are similarly aligned with the professional skills regime, as these countries rely heavily on the strict monitoring of teachers' work as well as on centrally defined curricular guidelines and learning outcomes. Conversely, performance-based teacher-appraisal policies might be a less natural fit within the professional training regime, as educators in these countries tend to have the necessary skills to collect and interpret feedback from students and colleagues informally. To them, increasing teacher inspection and surveillance might undermine teachers' passion for their work and make the profession less attractive (cf. Asia Society, 2013). Policies that strengthen external accountability are also likely to generate significant resistance in systems where the rules regime prevails. In such contexts, characterized by a de facto high degree of teacher autonomy and soft accountability, teacher evaluation arises from bureaucratic requirements applied with considerable discretion, usually by inspection services, sometimes in a ritual manner (Isoré, 2009). Thus, attempts to introduce more rigorous teacher appraisal practices have been especially contentious and faced significant resistance (Checchi & Mattei, 2021).

Data Sources and Methodological Approach

Our chapter examines the multiple and changing manifestations of teacher appraisal reforms to make sense of the diverse trajectories regarding teacher appraisal policies. Specifically, we aim to (a) map the evolution of teacher appraisal schemes; (b) determine the relative levels of similarity exhibited by such policies within and across different groups of countries, and (c) examine the explanatory force of different national institutions mediating in the enactment of teacher appraisal agendas.

To this end, we conducted a series of analyses using the OECD's Program for International Student Assessment (PISA) dataset, which covered data from 15 to 39 countries and included up to five or six assessment cycles, depending on the specific analysis. These cycles included the years 2003, 2009, 2012, 2015, 2018, and 2022. We specifically analyzed responses to PISA's questionnaires administered to school principals focusing on school practices. Despite its limitations, this remains one of the few comparable data sources to gain insight into the enactment of teacher appraisal reforms and their penetration into school routines and practices.

We have treated our country-level dataset as panel data and conducted random effects models, including wave-fixed effects to account for global trends and policy shifts that might impact educational practices across countries.[2] This approach allows us to control for time-specific influences, such as international educational movements, economic cycles, and widespread policy reforms, which could confound the relationship between teachers' regulatory regimes or partisan politics and the methods of teacher assessment. We assume that unobserved country-specific effects (such as cultural, institutional, and historical factors) are random and uncorrelated with other regressors within our model.[3] This enables us to estimate time-invariant explanatory variables that remain constant over time yet vary across countries. The random-effects framework offers greater efficiency compared to a fixed-effects model, provided that the assumption of uncorrelated effects holds.

We focus on two explanatory variables in different specifications: teacher regulatory regimes and partisan politics. To examine the explanatory power of *teacher regulatory regimes*, we rely on the classification developed by

32 World Yearbook of Education 2025

Voisin and Dumay (2020) synthesized above. Building on this typology, our study classifies countries according to the following groups (n=15):[4]

- *Market regime:* Australia, Chile, New Zealand, United Kingdom, United States
- *Rules regime:* France, Italy, Portugal, Spain
- *Training regime:* Denmark, Finland, Norway
- *Professional skills regime:* Japan, Singapore, South Korea

To examine the impact of *partisan politics*, we rely on an *ad-hoc* classification of countries according to the ideological orientation of the prevailing political force for the 1995–2020 period (n=39). For the operationalization of this variable, we drew on data extracted from the *Database of Political Institutions 2020*, compiled by the Inter-American Development Bank, and classified countries according to the following categories:

- *Left-leaning countries:* countries in which the chief executive identifies with the Left for more than 60% of the years over the 1995–2020 period.
- *Right-leaning countries:* countries in which the chief executive identifies with the Right for more than 60% of the years over the 1995–2020 period.
- *Other:* countries in which the chief executive identifies with the Centre for more than 60% of the years over the 1995–2020 period, or in which neither Right nor Left parties have dominated for more than 60% of the years over the 1995–2020 period.

Change and Continuity in Teacher-Evaluation Methods

In this section, we first map the evolution of different teacher appraisal methods globally, to subsequently test the explanatory power of partisan politics and teacher regulatory regimes in shaping policy-related trends.

Table 1.1 shows that the use of all methods has experienced an uptake since the early 2000s – albeit to a different extent. The use of these methods peaked in 2015 but has undergone a slight decline according to PISA 2022,

Table 1.1 Percentage of students in schools where, during the previous academic year, the following methods were used to monitor teachers' practice.

	Tests/assessments of student achievement	Teacher peer review	Principal or senior staff observations of lessons	Observation of classes by inspectors or other external persons
2003	0.647	0.595	0.669	0.303
2009	0.689	0.661	0.785	0.425
2012	0.816	0.680	0.777	0.383
2015	0.851	0.739	0.865	0.522
2018	n.d.	n.d.	n.d.	n.d.
2022	0.787	0.665	0.845	0.441

Source: OECD-PISA 2003–2022.

presumably connected with the impact of COVID-19 on education policy. Moreover, the order of the most widely used methods has remained relatively stable over time: both in 2003 and 2022, *observations by senior personnel* and *assessments of student achievement* were the most common methods to evaluate teachers' practices. These were followed by *teacher peer review*, and, at a considerable distance, *observations of classes by inspectors or other stakeholders external to schools*. This pattern confirms that assessment data remains a crucial source of information for teacher evaluation purposes and one that has tended to gain importance over time. Likewise, the reliance on internal forms of evaluation by school leadership is a widespread method, though with a minor decline between 2015 and 2022.

Such general trends, resulting from cross-country averages, conceal however a much more complex reality. An overview of country-level averages indicates that education systems exhibit different and even diverging trajectories. For instance, regarding the *use of student achievement data from tests to monitor teacher practice*, Figure 1.1 shows different country patterns in implementing this appraisal method. Some countries show a clear incremental trend (i.e., a consistent or substantial increase between 2003 and 2015), including Norway, Denmark, or Sweden. Few countries feature a declining tendency, including Finland, Canada, or the United Kingdom, whereas a third group exhibits relatively stable trajectories (e.g., Chile or Israel). Finally, some countries feature more inconsistent or even erratic behavior, with noticeable variations over the years, such as Iceland, Portugal, or Spain. A similar pattern can be observed for other monitoring methods (see Figures A1.1–A1.3 in Appendix). The only constant is thus the very *lack* of a consistent trend across countries.

Considering the dissimilar nature of policy trends observed at a country level, the following step in our research is to analyze the trends in relation to specific groups of countries, to test whether and to what extent partisan politics and teacher regulatory regimes might play a determining role in shaping policies tendencies.

Teacher Regulatory Regimes and Teacher Appraisal

To better understand how our statistical models explain the variance in how teachers are monitored in different countries, we first resort to the *rho* statistic, which measures the inherent between-country variability, a key feature in panel studies that deal with data across multiple periods and entities. Next, we examine the between R-squared values, which tell us how effectively our models explain the observed differences between countries, considering the rho statistic. Lastly, we explore the relationship between regulatory regimes and the methods of teacher monitoring, with an emphasis on specifying the contribution of these regimes to explaining between-country differences.

Our findings show that the rho statistic varies considerably across models. This indicates that country-specific factors impact quite differently on how teachers are monitored. For instance, *using performance data for judgments* and

34 *World Yearbook of Education 2025*

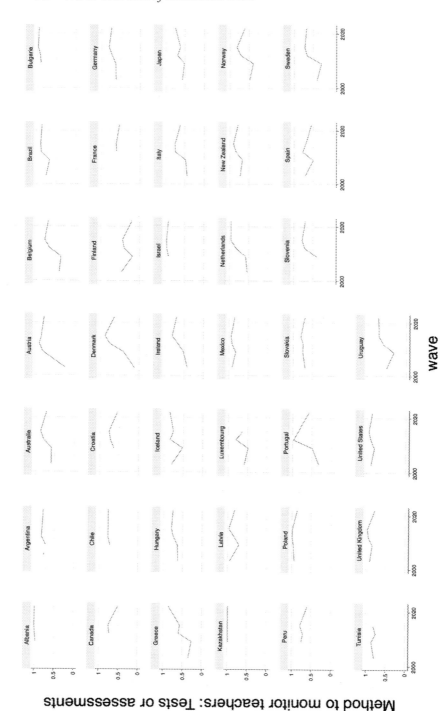

Figure 1.1 Percentage of students in schools where tests or assessments were used to monitor teachers' practice, by country.
Source: Authors' elaboration, based on OECD-PISA 2003–2022.

principal/staff observations both have a rho value of 0.60 (Tables A1.1 and A1.2, see Model 3, in Appendix), meaning that a significant amount of the variation can be attributed to differences between countries. This suggests that national characteristics, policies, or contexts play a big role in shaping teacher evaluation methods. The highest rho values are observed in the models for *external inspector observations* and *teacher peer review* at 0.82 and 0.78, respectively. These high values imply that even more of the variation in these methods is due to country-level differences, suggesting that their enactment is heavily shaped by specific country characteristics.

The models to explore the teaching profession regulatory regimes have considerable yet varying explanatory power. As indicated by the overall R-squared reported in Tables A1.1 and A1.2, there are noticeable differences in how much each model explains the variation between countries regarding the teacher monitoring methods implemented. These variations highlight the influence of country-specific factors on teacher monitoring practices. Models focusing on *judging teachers' effectiveness based on performance data*, and *principal or senior staff observations*, show high between-country explanatory power, with between R-squared values of 92% and 95%, respectively. These high values indicate that the models effectively account for differences in these practices across nations. Conversely, the model focusing on *external inspections* shows a low between R-squared value (17%), which suggests that numerous factors influencing this method's adoption remain unaccounted for. Lastly, the models focusing on *teacher peer review* and *tests to monitor teachers* exhibit moderate to high R-squared values (51% and 84%, respectively), indicating that these models are reasonably good at explaining the differences in these methods' penetration across countries.

The statistical models also demonstrate that teachers' regulatory regimes significantly affect which methods countries use to monitor teachers' work. The professional skills regime and, to a lesser extent, the market regime appear to have a broad and substantial influence on the adoption of several evaluation methods. These regimes are positively associated with certain monitoring methods, a pattern that remains robust even after introducing additional controls. Specifically, the professional skills regime shows a strong positive relationship with the *use of performance data for teacher appraisals*, a relationship that holds after accounting for wave effects and other covariates (Figure 1.2 and Models 1–3 in Table A1.1). When considering only the regulatory model as a covariate, the model for performance data use in teacher appraisals reveals an overall R-squared of 0.59 and a between R-squared of 0.77, indicating a substantial explanatory power both within and between countries. The second regime most strongly associated with the use of performance data for teacher appraisal is the market regime, followed by the rules regime. Countries with the training regime generally show less inclination to employ data-driven approaches in evaluating teachers.

This pattern holds across different methods of teacher monitoring, including *tests or assessments* and *teacher peer reviews*, concerning which the

36 World Yearbook of Education 2025

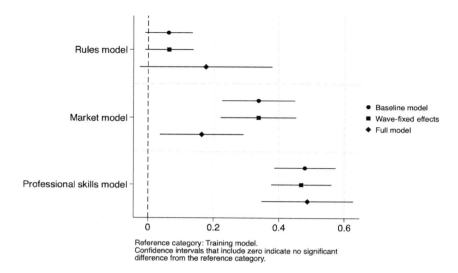

Figure 1.2 Teacher regulatory regimes and performance data use to judge teachers' work.
Source: OECD-PISA 2003–2022.
Note: The coefficients displayed in the graph are derived from random-effects models applied to our panel data at the country level. Please refer to Appendix for additional details.

professional skills and market regimes exhibit a significant positive association (see Figures 1.3a and 1.3c). Regarding *tests or assessments* as a monitoring method, the overall R-squared is 0.37 with a between R-squared of 0.63 when only the regulatory regime is included, reflecting a notable explanatory capacity of the regimes, particularly between countries (Model 1 in Table A1.2). For teacher peer reviews, the overall and between R-squared values are 0.40 and 0.47, respectively, indicating a moderate explanatory power of regulatory regimes alone (Model 7 in Table A1.2). Although countries with a rules regime also show a significant association with these two monitoring methods, the relationship is less strong than that of the professional skills and market regimes.

When it comes to *observations by principals or senior staff*, the professional skills regime consistently shows a strong and positive relationship. This trend is evident with an overall R-squared of 0.78 and a between R-squared of 0.88 when only the regulatory regime is considered (Model 10 in Table A1.2). This high explanatory power suggests that the regulatory regime significantly influences the prevalence of this practice both within and across countries. The professional skills regime significantly outperforms the rules regime, which serves as the reference category in the model. The market regime also shows greater engagement with principal or senior staff observations compared to the rules regime, yet the strength of this association decreases, reaching marginal significance in the fully specified model (Figure 1.3d). This decline suggests

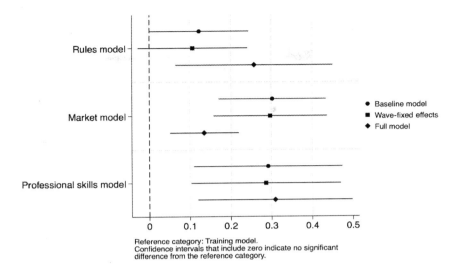

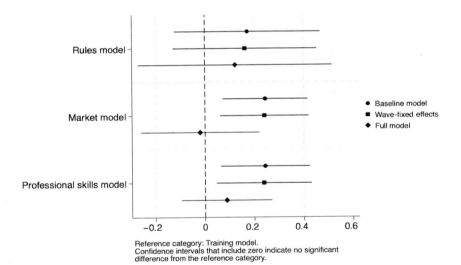

Figure 1.3 Teacher regulatory regimes and methods to monitor teachers' practice. (a) Monitoring method: Tests or assessments. (b) Monitoring method: Observation of classes by inspectors or other external personnel. (c) Monitoring method: Teacher peer review. (d) Monitoring method: Principal or senior staff observations of lessons.

Source: OECD-PISA 2003–2022.

Note: The coefficients displayed in the graph are derived from random-effects models applied to our panel data at the country level. Please refer to the appendix for additional details.

(*Continued*)

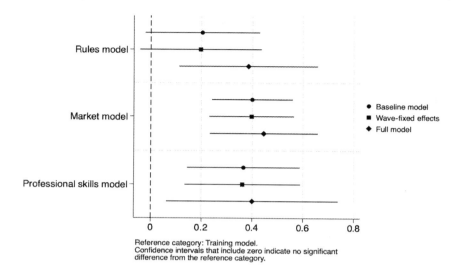

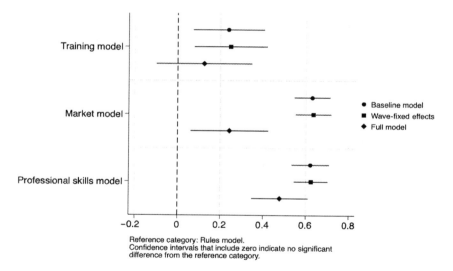

Figure 1.3 (Continued)

that time-variant factors might play a crucial role in shaping this practice. The lower coefficient for the rules regime could indicate a cultural or policy-driven aversion toward adopting principal-led monitoring methods.

In the model that examines how teachers are monitored by *inspectors or external personnel observations*, none of the regulatory approaches significantly affect this method once we adjust for other factors (refer to Figure 1.3b and Model 6 in Table A1.2). When using only regulatory regimes, both the overall and between

R-squared values are quite low at 0.16 (see Model 4 in Table A1.2). These identical values suggest that regulatory regimes alone cannot fully explain how frequently teachers are monitored by external observers. The consistency of these values, whether looking at within-country or between-country differences, points to more complex factors influencing the adoption of external observation practices, which are not solely tied to regulatory regimes.

The Impact of Partisan Politics

When incorporating countries' political orientation into the analysis, we find a broad range of rho values, which indicate the complex ways in which various elements, including political dynamics, interact to influence teacher appraisal practices. Qualitative monitoring methods and subjective judgments, like *peer reviews and observations by inspectors or senior staff* (with rho values of 0.73, 0.78, and 0.85, respectively, as shown in Models 9, 6, and 12 in Table A1.4), are particularly sensitive to the social, political, and educational environments of countries, reflecting significant between-country variations. In contrast, the rho value for the model that examines the *use of performance data to judge teachers' effectiveness* (see Model 3 in Table A1.3) stands at 0.69, which is higher than the rho value of 0.60 found in models focused on regulatory regimes. This indicates that, in combination, the variables included in the model significantly contribute to explaining the differences between countries. On the other hand, the application of *tests or assessments as monitoring methods* shows a lower rho value of 0.48 (see Model 3 in Table A1.4), which suggests a more uniform usage across countries compared to the rho of 0.72 seen in models with regulatory regimes as primary predictors.

The models we used show differing levels of explanatory power. According to the between R-squared values, which are derived from the overall R-squared values from Tables A1.3 and A1.4, the models that include political orientation as a factor have a wide range of effectiveness. For example, these models only explain 7% of the variations in *external inspections* but go up to 55% in evaluating the *use of performance data for appraising teachers*. This significant disparity indicates the presence of numerous unobserved factors that could be influencing the enactment of these methods, potentially more so than those observable in the regulatory regimes.

This variability reveals that while the models do explain some differences between countries in methods like *using performance data to assess teachers' effectiveness* (55%) and *using principal observations for teacher appraisal* (43%), their impact is not consistently strong. Especially, the very low between R-squared value of 7% for external inspections suggests that there are many important aspects that our models are not capturing, which affects our understanding of how widely this method is used in schools. Therefore, models incorporating countries' political orientation might not be as effective in capturing the complex factors influencing the adoption of certain monitoring methods compared to those focusing on regulatory regimes.

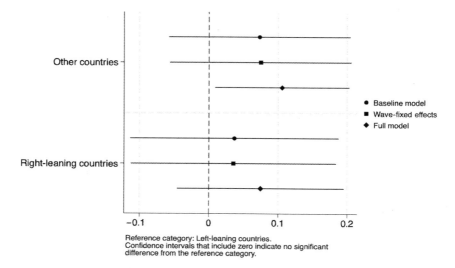

Figure 1.4 Partisan politics and performance data used to judge teachers' work.
Source: OECD-PISA 2003–2022.
Note: The coefficients displayed in the graph are derived from random-effects models applied to our panel data at the country level. Please refer to Appendix for additional details.

Regarding the association between political orientation and specific teacher monitoring methods, our models reveal varying results depending on the method in question. For *assessing teachers through performance data*, countries where neither the right nor the left is prevalent show a positive and marginally significant association (10%), with a coefficient of 0.11 in the fully specified model, suggesting that these countries tend to favor such learning data-driven approaches (see Figure 1.4 and Model 3 in Table A1.3). Right-leaning countries also show a positive association with this method, but the relationship is not statistically significant.

Compared to left-leaning countries, right-wing countries show distinct associations with the adoption of specific monitoring methods in education. These countries are positively associated with the *use of tests or assessments as monitoring tools* (as shown in Figure 1.5a and Model 3 in Table A1.4) and negatively associated with the *use of teacher peer reviews* (Figure 1.5c and Model 9 in Table A1.4). This finding indicates that right-leaning countries are more inclined to implement learning data-driven monitoring methods and less likely to adopt process-oriented qualitative appraisal methods such as peer reviews. However, it is worth noting that, when considering only political orientation, these associations have very low between R-squared values, indicating almost negligible explanatory power.

Monitoring methods based on *observations by inspectors or other external personnel*, or on *principal or senior staff observations*, show no statistically significant relationships across political orientations (see Figures 1.5b and 1.5d).

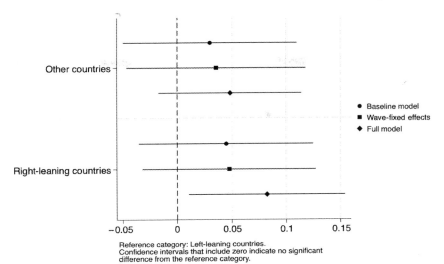

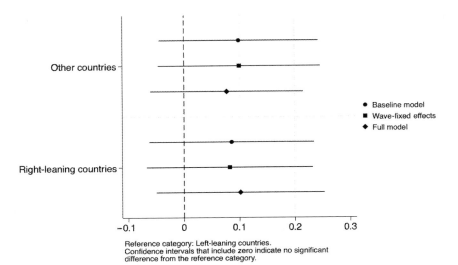

Figure 1.5 Partisan politics and methods to monitor teachers' practice. (a) Monitoring method: Tests or assessments. (b) Monitoring method: Observation of classes by inspectors or other external personnel. (c) Monitoring method: Teacher peer review. (d) Monitoring method: Principal or senior staff observations of lessons.

Source: OECD-PISA 2003–2022.

Note: The coefficients displayed in the graph are derived from random-effects models applied to our panel data at the country level. Please refer to Appendix for additional details.

(Continued)

42 World Yearbook of Education 2025

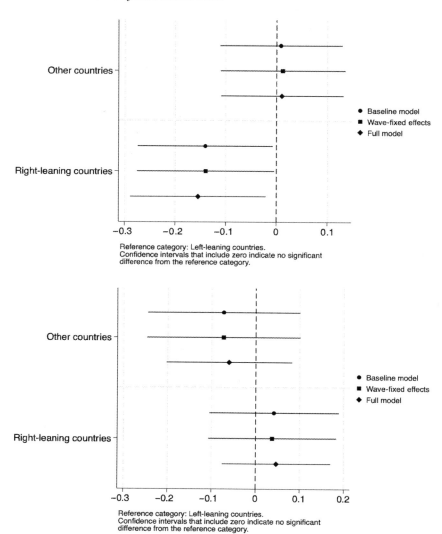

Figure 1.5 (Continued)

This outcome is consistent with the low between R-squared values of 0.04 for inspector-led observations and 0.06 for principal-led observations (see Models 4 and 10 in Table A1.4). These results suggest that political orientation alone has only a marginal influence on the use of these monitoring methods.

Discussion and Conclusions

In this chapter, we have explored the evolving nature of teacher appraisal reforms, charting their development across different countries and examining their dynamic nature. Our findings confirm that teacher evaluation has expanded in the last two decades, incorporating an increasingly wider variety of methods. Globally circulating discourses around teacher appraisal no longer privilege students' academic achievements in standardized tests, as seemed to be the case in the mid-2000s, at least for some pioneering countries. Even if standardized tests continue to play a significant role (in fact, their importance as a source of teacher appraisal has increased over time), their centrality has somewhat diminished as they represent just one component of an increasingly comprehensive appraisal toolkit. This toolkit includes various methods and sources of information, both internal and external, enabling a more nuanced assessment of teacher work. Thus, while still intersecting with performance-based accountability and the regulatory control of teachers' work, teacher appraisal policies have the potential to promote more holistic approaches to teacher effectiveness, encouraging the formative use of most evaluation methods.

Our results also indicate that although teacher appraisal policies do not follow a uniform path, it is possible to discern patterns based on the influence of domestic factors. Specifically, teacher regulatory regimes demonstrate considerable explanatory power, albeit this varies across teacher monitoring methods. Countries with regulatory regimes aligned with performance- and market-based forms of accountability are more likely to adopt external teacher appraisal methods. Specifically, the professional skills and market regimes are more inclined to use performance data in evaluating teachers compared to the other regimes, emphasizing the reliance of the former on assessment data. In general, even if regulatory regimes appear to enjoy considerable explanatory power for most teacher appraisal methods, the use of observations by inspectors and external staff is less influenced by such regimes, suggesting that a more complex interplay of factors is involved in the enactment of this method.

Our analyses also suggest that the impact of partisan politics is comparably more limited and uneven. Political orientation has little influence on external inspections or principal-led observations, which indicates that it is not a driver of these methods. Hence, certain teacher appraisal methods are adopted and persist regardless of the prevailing political climate. However, partisan politics seems to have a greater influence on other appraisal methods. Specifically, in countries with predominantly right-wing governments, there is a greater propensity to use student achievement data in teacher appraisals, along with lesser reliance on peer-review methods. This pattern may reflect a reduced trust in the teaching profession's self-regulatory capacity under right-leaning administrations. This can also be indicative of alignment with an outcomes-based evaluation culture and managerial rhetoric, which are more often mobilized by right-wing forces.

Finally, our results also point to the disruptive impact of COVID-19 on education policy priorities. The pandemic appears to have put a halt to the trajectory of teacher-appraisal methods, with a relative backlash in their use. This shift aligns with changes observed in the discourse of IOs, where there is now an intensified focus on post-pandemic policies that prioritize teacher well-being, encourage collaboration, and promote autonomy. These policies aim to support teachers' needs, as a necessary condition for the development of resilient and adaptive educational systems (Zancajo et al., 2022). However, while the pandemic has clearly motivated a reevaluation of teacher policies, the nature, scope, and permanence of these policy changes remain uncertain.

Future Research Directions

While exploratory, our findings contribute to a better understanding of the limitations of existing literature and suggest areas for further research. First, our study highlights the risks of excessive attention on Anglo-American countries in teacher appraisal research. The debate around the potential and dangers of teacher appraisal is largely shaped by dynamics observed in a subset of countries that have pioneered particularly disruptive reforms. This debate has often centered around reforms driven by a managerial *ethos* and evaluation arrangements that privilege accountability over developmental and formative roles. Yet, our results reveal a more complex teacher reform landscape. Numerous countries favor approaches that diverge from the model of teacher governance that predominates in Anglo-American settings, indicating that internationally, polymorphic patterns of teacher appraisal prevail over a uniform global testing culture. Future research should delve deeper into the complexities of implementing teacher appraisal systems across diverse contexts. It should also inquire into the normative underpinnings of these policies and their implications for teachers' working conditions and professional identities.

Second, while our focus was on partisan politics and teacher regulatory regimes as main mediation points, our results suggest that making sense of the contingent nature of teacher reforms requires a deeper look at additional factors and institutions not covered in this chapter. Specifically, the impact of party politics extends beyond mere power dynamics among different party families. The changing alliances between major political forces and key education stakeholders, including teacher unions and other interest groups like families, warrant further research. Likewise, further work is needed to make sense of the dynamic nature of teacher regulatory regimes. These regimes do not only exhibit path dependency but have also been reshaped by theories such as new public management and public choice. Understanding the mediating impact of regulatory regimes requires a closer examination of the ongoing processes of hybridization and transformation that these regimes have undergone.

Notes

1 For this chapter, our synthesis of the four regimes focuses on the prevailing forms of accountability and autonomy associated with each regime.
2 An extended explanation of the empirical models has been included in Appendix.
3 This assumption is also based on the Hausman test, which was conducted to determine the suitability of using a random-effects model for our analysis. The test did not reveal any systematic differences between the coefficients estimated by both

fixed-effects and random-effects models, suggesting that the unique errors (entity-specific random component in the RE model) are not correlated with the regressors. Consequently, we failed to reject the null hypothesis, indicating the suitability of the random-effects model for efficiency gains in our estimation.
4 For the specific analysis of teacher regulatory regimes, our study focuses uniquely on the subset of 15 countries included in Voisin and Dumay's (2020) classification. For the analysis of the influence of partisan politics, we extended our analysis to a larger sample (n=39).
5 This assumption is also based on the Hausman test, which was conducted to determine the suitability of using a random-effects model for our analysis. The test did not reveal any systematic differences between the coefficients estimated by both fixed-effects and random-effects models, suggesting that the unique errors (entity-specific random component in the RE model) are not correlated with the regressors. Consequently, we failed to reject the null hypothesis, indicating the suitability of the random-effects model for efficiency gains in our estimation.

References

AERA. (2015). AERA statement on use of value-added Models (VAM) for the evaluation of educators and educator preparation programs. *Educational Researcher, 44*(8), 448–452. https://doi.org/10.3102/0013189X15618385

Allern, E. H., Bale, T., & Otjes, S. (2017). The relationship between left-of-centre parties and trade unions in contemporary democracies. In E. H. Allern, & T. Bale (Eds.), *Left of-centre parties and trade unions in the twenty-first century* (pp. 280–309). Oxford University Press.

Asia Society. (2013). Teacher Quality: The 2013 International Summit on the Teaching Profession. https://asiasociety.org/files/teachingsummit2013.pdf

Ávalos, B. (2022). Teacher professionalism and performance appraisal: A critical discussion. In J. Manzi, Y. Sun, & R. M. García (Eds.), *Teacher evaluation around the world: Experiences, dilemmas and future challenges* (pp. 93–109). Springer.

Barber, M., & Mourshed, M. (2017). *How the world's best-performing school systems come out on top*. McKinsey and Company.

Bleiberg, J., Brunner, E., Harbatkin, E., Kraft, M. A., & Springer, M. G. (2021). The effect of teacher evaluation on achievement and attainment: Evidence from statewide reforms (Working Paper No. 21-496).

Busemeyer, M. R. (2014). *Skills and inequality. Partisan politics and the political economy of education reforms in Western welfare states*. Cambridge University Press.

Checchi, D., & Mattei, P. (2021). Merit pay for schoolteachers in Italy, 2015–2016: A new regime of education accountability? *Comparative Education Review, 65*(3), 445–466.

Di Carlo, M. (2023). *The rise and fall of the teacher evaluation reform empire*. Available in: https://www.shankerinstitute.org/blog/rise-and-fall-teacher-evaluation-reform-empire

Gingrich, J. (2011). *Making markets in the welfare state: The politics of varying market reforms*. Cambridge University Press.

Giudici, A., Gingrich, J., Chevalier, T., & Haslberger, M. (2023). Center-right parties and post-war secondary education. *Comparative Politics, 55*(2), 193–218.

Hallinger, P., Heck, R. H., & Murphy, J. (2014). Teacher evaluation and school improvement: An analysis of the evidence. *Educational Assessment, Evaluation and Accountability, 26*, 5–28.

Häusermann, S., Picot, G., & Geering, D. (2013). Review article: Rethinking party politics and the welfare state – Recent advances in the literature. *British Journal of Political Science, 43*(1), 221–240.

Hay, C. (2004). Common trajectories, variable paces, divergent outcomes? Models of European capitalism under conditions of complex economic interdependence. *Review of International Political Economy, 11*(2), 231–262.

Högberg, B., & Lindgren, J. (2021). Outcome-based accountability regimes in OECD countries: A global policy model? *Comparative Education, 57*(3), 301–321.

Holloway, J., Sorensen, T., & Verger, A. (2017). Global perspectives on high-stakes teacher accountability policies: An introduction. *Education Policy Analysis Archives, 25,* 85, https://doi.org/10.14507/epaa.25.3325

Howell, C. (2001). The end of the relationship between social democratic parties and trade unions? *Studies in Political Economy, 65*(1), 7–37.

Huber, S. G., & Skedsmo, G. (2016). Teacher evaluation–accountability and improving teaching practices. *Educational Assessment, Evaluation and Accountability, 28,* 105–109.

Isoré, M. (2009). *Teacher evaluation: Current practices in OECD countries and a literature review* (OECD Education Working Paper No. 23). OECD.

Jerrim, J., & Sims, S. (2022). School accountability and teacher stress: International evidence from the OECD TALIS study. *Educational Assessment, Evaluation and Accountability, 34*(1), 5–32.

Larsen, M. A. (2005). A critical analysis of teacher evaluation policy trends. *Australian Journal of Education, 49*(3), 292–305.

Lavigne, A. L., Good, T. L., & Marx, R. W. (2014). Introduction to high-stakes teacher evaluation: High cost–big losses. *Teachers College Record, 116*(1), 1–5.

Mathwasa, J., & Duku, N. (2015). Teachers at crossroads: Teacher professional development through the performance appraisal system at primary school level in the Bulawayo metropolitan province: An assessment. *Journal of Social Sciences, 45*(3), 221–235.

OECD. (2005). *Teachers matter: Attracting, developing and retaining effective teachers.* OECD.

OECD. (2013). *Synergies for better learning: An international perspective on evaluation and assessment.* OECD.

OECD. (2022). *Introduction to ambition loops: An introduction to the multi-national stakeholder study on new professionalism and the future of teaching.* Centre for Educational Research and Innovation (CERI). OECD.

O'Leary, M. (2022). Rethinking teachers professional learning through unseen observation. *Professional Development in Education.* https://doi.org/10.1080/19415257.2022.2125551.

Paufler, N. A., & Sloat, E. F. (2020). Using standards to evaluate accountability policy in context: School administrator and teacher perceptions of a teacher evaluation system. *Studies in Educational Evaluation, 64,* 100806.

Peters, B. G., & Pierre, J. (2012). *The SAGE handbook of public administration.* SAGE.

Pollitt, C., & Bouckaert, G. (2017). *Public management reform: A comparative analysis–into the age of austerity.* Oxford University Press.

Ridge, B. L., & Lavigne, A. L. (2020). Improving instructional practice through peer observation and feedback: A review of the literature. *Education Policy Analysis Archives, 28,* 61.

Robertson, S. L. (2012). Placing teachers in global governance agendas. *Comparative Education Review, 56*(4), 584–607.

Smith, W. C., & Holloway, J. (2020). School testing culture and teacher satisfaction. *Educational Assessment, Evaluation and Accountability, 32,* 461–479.

Smith, W. C., & Kubacka, K. (2017). The emphasis of student test scores in teacher appraisal systems. *Education Policy Analysis Archives, 25*(86). https://doi.org/10.14507/epaa.25.2889

Sorensen, T. B. (2021). The space for challenge in transnational education governance: The case of education international and the OECD TALIS programme. *Discourse: Studies in the Cultural Politics of Education, 42*(4), 572–589. https://doi.org/10.1080/01596306.2020.1718611.

Sutcher, L., Darling-Hammond, L., & Carver-Thomas, D., 2019. Understanding teacher shortages: An analysis of teacher supply and demand in the United States. *Education Policy Analysis Archives*, 27(35). http://dx.doi.org/10.14507/epaa.27.3696

Taylor, S., & Henry, M. (2000). Globalisation and educational policymaking: A case study. *Educational Theory*, 50(4), 487–503.

Teltemann, J., & Jude, N. (2019). Assessments and accountability in secondary education: International trends. *Research in Comparative and International Education*, 14(2), 249–271.

Verger, A., Fontdevila, C., & Parcerisa, L. (2019). Reforming governance through policy instruments: How and to what extent standards, tests and accountability in education spread worldwide. *Discourse: Studies in the Cultural Politics of Education*, 40(2), 248–270.

Voisin, A., & Dumay, X. (2020). How do educational systems regulate the teaching profession and teachers work? A typological approach to institutional foundations and models of regulation. *Teaching and Teacher Education*, 96, 103144.

Williams, J. H., & Engel, L. C. (2012). How do other countries evaluate teachers? *Phi Delta Kappan*, 94(4), 53–57.

Zancajo, A., Verger, A., & Bolea, P. (2022). Digitalization and beyond: The effects of covid-19 on post-pandemic educational policy and delivery in Europe. *Policy and Society*, 41(1), 111–128.

Appendix

Methodological Notes

We have treated our country-level dataset as panel data and conducted random-effects models, including wave-fixed effects to account for global trends and policy shifts that might impact educational practices across countries. This allows us to control for time-specific influences, such as international educational movements, economic cycles, and widespread policy reforms, that could confound the relationship between the teachers' regulatory regime or the partisan politics and the teacher assessment methods. We assume that unobserved country-specific effects – such as cultural, institutional, and historical factors – are random and uncorrelated with the other regressors within our model.[5] This allows us to estimate time-invariant explanatory variables, which remain constant over time yet vary across countries. The random-effects framework offers greater efficiency compared to a fixed-effects model, provided the assumption of uncorrelated effects holds true.

To address the potential for correlated errors within countries – errors that could arise from national circumstances or country-level shocks – we have clustered standard errors at the country level. This is particularly pertinent to panel data, where repeated observations across time within the same countries can introduce serial correlations. By clustering standard errors by country, we recognize that shared economic trends or policy shifts might simultaneously impact all data points within a country. This strategy is a more conservative approach that ensures our standard errors remain robust to these intra-country correlations, enhancing the reliability and accuracy of our findings.

This approach, which combines random effects, wave-fixed effects, and clustered standard errors, is well-suited for our dataset. It includes a limited temporal span but a broad group of countries, thereby enabling an analysis that makes use of the variation inherent both within countries over time and across countries.

$$Y_{it} = \alpha + \sum_{j=1}^{J} \gamma_j D_{ji}^t + \sum_{t=1}^{T} \delta_j W_i^t + \beta_1 GDP_i^t + \beta_2 SES\_sch_i^t + \beta_3 Private_i^t + \beta_4 Aut\_staff_i^t + \beta_5 Aut\_curr_i^t + \beta_6 Size_i^t + u_i + \varepsilon_i^t$$

where

Y_{it} is the dependent variable for country i at time t, which reflects the teachers' appraisal methods employed in schools: teacher peer reviews, principal, or senior staff observations of lessons, classroom observations conducted by inspectors or external personnel, and tests or assessments to monitor teachers. To show the prevalence of the appraisal methods across schools in different countries, the variables are measured as the percentage of students attending schools where principals report the use of each specific method. In this way, we provide a student-weighted measure, rather than a simple count of schools, reflecting the impact of such methods on the student population.

α is the constant term.

γ_j are the coefficients for the dummy variables D_{ji}^t, which represents the different categories of our explanatory variables for country i at time t.

δ_t are the coefficients for the wave (time points) fixed effects W_i^t, which captures time-specific influences that are common to all countries.

We included control factors in our models, such as the countries' GDP (GDP_i^t), the proportion of private schools ($Private_i^t$), the schools' average index of the Economic, Social and Cultural Index as measured in PISA ($SES\_sch_i^t$), measures of school autonomy in staffing and curriculum ($Aut\_staff_i^t$ and $Aut\_curr_i^t$), and the average school size ($Size_i^t$). These variables were chosen for their theoretical and empirical relevance to our outcomes and, along with wave-fixed effects, provide an appropriate framework for examining the variations in teachers' assessment methods and align with our study's aim to offer a contextually informed analysis.

Finally, u_i is the unobserved country-specific random effect, while ε_i^t is the error term.

Between Teachers' Governance and Development 49

Figure A1.1 Percentage of students in schools where teacher peer reviews (of lesson plans, assessment instruments, lessons) were used to monitor teachers' practice, by country.

Source: Authors' elaboration, based on OECD-PISA 2003–2022.

50 *World Yearbook of Education 2025*

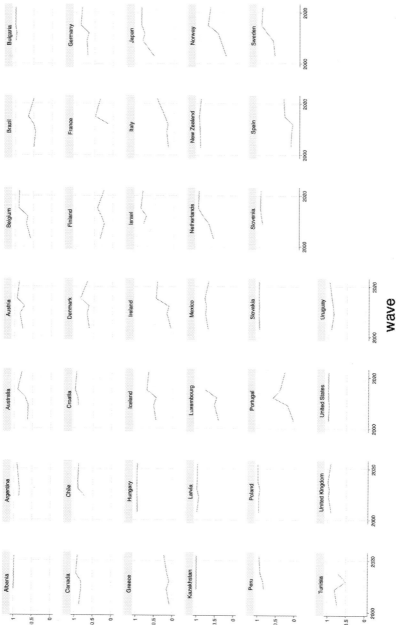

Figure A1.2 Percentage of students in schools where principal or senior staff observations of lessons were used to monitor teachers' practice, by country.

Source: Authors' elaboration, based on OECD-PISA 2003–2022.

Between Teachers' Governance and Development 51

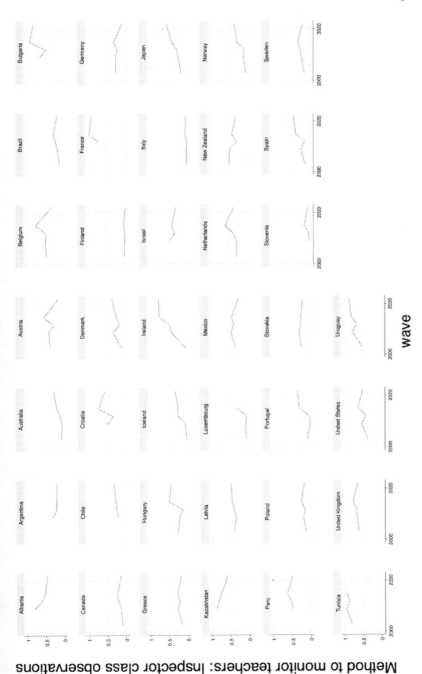

Figure A1.3 Percentage of students in schools where observations of classes by inspectors or other persons external to the school were used to monitor teachers' practice, by country.

Source: Authors' elaboration, based on OECD-PISA 2003–2022.

Full Regression Tables

Table A1.1 Teacher regulatory regimes and performance data use to judge teacher's work.

		Performance data is used to: Make judgments about teachers' effectiveness		
		(1)	(2)	(3)
Ref. category:	Rules regime	0.063	0.064	0.177
Training	Market regime	0.338***	0.338***	0.164**
regime	Professional skills regime	0.480***	0.469***	0.488***
Wave-fixed effects		No	Yes	Yes
Controls		No	No	Yes
Country observations		15	15	15
Country-by-wave observations		84	84	84
R-squared	Within	0.00	0.46	0.50
	Between	0.77	0.78	0.92
	Overall	0.59	0.70	0.82
Rho		0.45	0.65	0.60

Source: OECD-PISA 2003–2022. Countries that have participated in at least 4 PISA waves were selected.
Note: Standard errors in parentheses. $*p < 0.10$, $**p < 0.05$, $***p < 0.01$.

Table A1.2 Teacher regulatory regimes and methods to monitor teachers' practice.

		Method to monitor teachers' practice: Tests or assessments of student achievement		
		(1)	(2)	(3)
Ref. category:	Rules regime	0.123*	0.107	0.257**
Training	Market regime	0.302***	0.297***	0.135**
regime	Professional skills regime	0.292***	0.286**	0.309**
Wave-fixed effects		No	Yes	Yes
Controls		No	No	Yes
Country observations		15	15	15
Country-by-wave observations		71	71	71
R-squared	Within	0.00	0.49	0.56
	Between	0.63	0.62	0.84
	Overall	0.37	0.57	0.72
Rho		0.26	0.48	0.24

(*Continued*)

Table A1.2 (Continued)

		Method to monitor teachers' practice: Observation of classes by inspectors or other external personnel		
		(4)	(5)	(6)
Ref. category:	Rules regime	0.172	0.162	0.122
Training	Market regime	0.244**	0.240**	−0.020
regime	Professional skills regime	0.244**	0.239**	0.088
Controls		No	No	Yes
Wave-fixed effects		No	Yes	Yes
Country observations		15	15	15
Country-by-wave observations		71	71	71
R-squared	Within	0.00	0.35	0.45
	Between	0.16	0.19	0.17
	Overall	0.16	0.24	0.27
Rho		0.81	0.73	0.82

		Method to monitor teachers' practice: Teacher peer review		
		(7)	(8)	(9)
Ref. category:	Rules regime	0.203	0.196	0.385**
Training	Market regime	0.340***	0.397***	0.445***
regime	Professional skills regime	0.366**	0.362**	0.400**
Controls		No	No	Yes
Wave-fixed effects		No	Yes	Yes
Country observations		15	15	15
Country-by-wave observations		71	71	71
R-squared	Within	0.00	0.1845	0.28
	Between	0.47	0.45	0.51
	Overall	0.40	0.42	0.49
Rho		0.75	0.78	0.78

		Method to monitor teachers' practice: Principal or senior staff observations of lessons		
		(10)	(11)	(12)
Ref. category:	Training regime	0.238**	0.248**	0.020
Rules	Market regime	0.630***	0.635***	0.172*
regime	Professional skills regime	0.621***	0.624***	0.475***
Controls		No	No	Yes
Wave-fixed effects		No	Yes	Yes
Country observations		15	15	15
Country-by-wave observations		71	71	71
R-squared	Within	0.00	0.34	0.52
	Between	0.88	0.89	0.95
	Overall	0.78	0.82	0.90
Rho		0.42	0.58	0.60

Source: OECD-PISA 2003–2022. Countries that have participated in at least 4 PISA waves were selected.

Note: Standard errors in parentheses. *$p < 0.10$, **$p < 0.05$, ***$p < 0.01$.

Table A1.3 Partisan politics and performance data use to judge teachers' work.

		Performance data is used to make judgments about teachers' effectiveness		
		(1)	(2)	(3)
Ref. category: Left-leaning countries	Other political orientation	0.073	0.075	0.106*
	Right-leaning countries	0.037	0.035	0.075
Wave-fixed effects		No	Yes	Yes
Controls		No	No	Yes
Country observations		39	39	39
Country-by-wave observations		216	216	216
R-squared	Within	0.00	0.46	0.45
	Between	0.02	0.04	0.55
	Overall	0.02	0.13	0.52
Rho		0.76	0.83	0.69

Source: OECD-PISA 2003–2022. Countries that have participated in at least 4 PISA waves were selected.
Note: Standard errors in parentheses. $*p < 0.10$, $**p < 0.05$, $***p < 0.01$.

Table A1.4 Partisan politics and methods to monitor teachers' practice.

		Method to monitor teachers' practice: Tests or assessments of student achievement		
		(1)	(2)	(3)
Ref. category: Left-leaning countries	Other political orientation	0.030	0.036	0.048
	Right-leaning countries	0.045	0.048	0.082**
Wave-fixed effects		No	Yes	Yes
Controls		No	No	Yes
Country observations		39	39	39
Country-by-wave observations		178	178	178
R-squared	Within	0.00	0.43	0.44
	Between	0.01	0.01	0.53
	Overall	0.01	0.19	0.48
Rho		0.46	0.60	0.48

		Method to monitor teachers' practice: Observation of classes by inspectors or other external personnel		
		(4)	(5)	(6)
Ref. category: Left-leaning countries	Other political orientation	0.098	0.099	0.077
	Right-leaning countries	0.086	0.083	0.102
Wave-fixed effects		No	Yes	Yes
Controls		No	No	Yes
Country observations		39	39	39
Country-by-wave observations		178	178	178
R-squared	Within	0.00	0.32	0.38
	Between	0.04	0.06	0.07
	Overall	0.03	0.10	0.12
Rho		0.78	0.81	0.78

(Continued)

Table A1.4 (Continued)

		Method to monitor teachers' practice: Teacher peer review		
		(7)	*(8)*	*(9)*
Ref. category: Left-leaning countries	Other political orientation	0.011	0.013	0.011
	Right-leaning countries	−0.141*	−0.140*	−0.155**
Wave-fixed effects		No	Yes	Yes
Controls		No	No	Yes
Country observations		39	39	39
Country-by-wave observations		178	178	178
R-squared	Within	0.00	0.17	0.19
	Between	0.09	0.08	0.19
	Overall	0.07	0.10	0.19
Rho		0.74	0.77	0.73

		Method to monitor teachers' practice: Principal or senior staff observations of lessons		
		(10)	*(11)*	*(12)*
Ref. category: Left-leaning countries	Other political orientation	−0.073	−0.073	−0.060
	Right-leaning countries	0.042	0.038	0.047
Wave-fixed effects		No	Yes	Yes
Controls		No	No	Yes
Country observations		39	39	39
Country-by-wave observations		178	178	178
R-squared	Within	0.00	0.40	0.43
	Between	0.06	0.04	0.43
	Overall	0.03	0.08	0.41
Rho		0.86	0.90	0.85

Source: OECD-PISA 2003–2022. Countries that have participated in at least 4 PISA waves were selected.

Note: Standard errors in parentheses. *$p < 0.10$, **$p < 0.05$, ***$p < 0.01$.

2 "Agency Work"
Teachers, the OECD, and the "Happiness Turn"

Susan L. Robertson and Carlos Navia Canales

Introduction

In 2021, the Organisation for Economic Co-operation and Development (OECD) launched the results of its newest assessment program for 10- and 15-year-old students, the 2019 *International Survey on Social and Emotional Skills* (SSES). The OECD insisted on the importance of measuring social and emotional skills stating: "… they are indispensable for a peaceful and prosperous future, and for the cohesion of societies" and they "predict important life outcomes in various domains such as academic achievement, employment and health" (OECD, 2023, p. 1). This would require new efforts from teachers to redress what the survey results suggested was a shortfall in teachers' awareness of the state of student's social and emotional learning.

Yet teachers, too, were in the OECD's sights regarding social and emotional well-being. New items on teacher well-being were added to the teacher questionnaire component of the OECD's Program of International Student Assessment (PISA) 2021. The results showed a low level of teacher well-being, high levels of absenteeism, and teacher attrition (Viac & Fraser, 2020, p. 7). In short, teachers were distinctly "unhappy" professionals teaching "unhappy" students in their classrooms. In the OECD's view, this demands a shift in teachers' efforts to shape a new kind of socio-emotionally skilled student, whilst attending to their own well-being.

At first glance, this recent shift in policy focus for the OECD is a welcome change. Critics pointed to the OECD's preoccupation with cognitive skills, an impoverished understanding of students as "human capital," and teachers as mid-wives for student learning for capitalism (Sorensen & Robertson, 2020). In 2014, an Open Letter (coordinated by Meyer & Zahedi, 2014, p. 872), signed by many from the international education community, was sent to OECD Director, Andreas Schleicher, outlining the "… negative consequences of the PISA rankings" (p. 872), including competitive individualism. They concluded: "… PISA has further increased the already high stress-level in our schools, which endangers the well-being of our students and teachers" (p. 873).

Was the OECD listening and responding to these concerns, and did their new concern for their happiness, well-being, and social and emotional

DOI: 10.4324/9781003441731-4

development suggest a reorientation? Other policies of the OECD also suggested a new set of strategic priorities were being pursued. For example, the launch of its *Future of Education and Skills 2030* (OECD, 2018) placed student well-being, student agency, and reflexivity at the center of its new education strategy (Robertson & Beech, 2023). Did recognition of the social suggest matters of class politics and its effects were higher up the OECD's agenda? And, if so, would teachers be given new space for a different kind of accountability to emerge?

In this chapter, we explore what this shift means for teachers, arguing it is important to look beyond the "commonsense" appeal of happiness and well-being (Pawson & Tilly, 1997). Understood in theoretical terms, we argue this requires a rather different kind of "agency work" on the part of teachers and their students; effort directed to the body and emotions, rather than cognition. To this end, we draw on Archer's (1988, 1995) morphogenetic approach to understanding transformations *over time* (Archer refers to time as T) in structure, culture, and agency to make visible projects aimed at the restructuring of social categories (or T1) (a reconceptualized ideal student and teacher), setting in motion new structurally selective interactions (of teacher and student agency) (or T2), leading to social transformation (or social statis) (and T3).

Two forms of critique guide our work; first, a societal and capitalist critique of the pathologies of neoliberalism increasingly apparent in education systems; and second, an empirical analysis of OECD well-being measures, and how they reflect a particular ontology and epistemology. We'll argue that the OECD's understanding of happiness, well-being and social and emotional skills, draws upon a Benthamite utilitarian understanding of happiness, and on personality psychology as a means of understanding the self. Both have origins in the 18th and 19th century and share a concern with measuring and utility maximizing.

The chapter unfolds via four lines of argument, from a diagnosis of the current condition to a close examination of happiness policies, their politics, outcomes, and contradictions. We'll argue that despite the underlying causes of the current malaise around student productivity and teacher commitment, to which happiness is the antidote, its focus on student personality and assumptions about malleability, as well as claims regarding personality as transcultural and transhistorial, continues to align OECD happiness policies with neoliberal tenets focused on self-regulation, control for the economy and cultural domination. And the contradictions abound, including the fact that one of the key *causes* of the decline in mental health and well-being, the implementation of neoliberal informed policies continues to be offered as the solution.

Inconvenient Truths

The OECD has been confronted with a set of inconvenient truths arising from more than three decades of neoliberal policies: (i) its promise "of all boats rising" as a result of competition leading to economic growth has not materialized (cf. OECD, 2008, 2021; Piketty, 2014; Streeck, 2014); (ii) a downturn in student PISA scores globally (OECD, 2023); (iii) problematic teacher recruitment and retention in many education systems; and (iv) low measures of teacher and student happiness and well-being. We elaborate on these four inconvenient truths below, though draw different conclusions as to causes and consequences.

Growing Inequalities, Populist Politics and Reduced Social Cohesion

The first decade of the 21st century came to a spectacular end in 2008, with the big economies teetering on the edge of a global financial crisis, whilst the banks themselves were bailed out by their respective states as too big to fail. State spending on public sectors, including education, were pared back, justified by austerity measures. It was increasingly clear that the OECD's promise "of all boats rising" as a result of competition leading to economic growth had not materialized. Indeed, the story was quite the reverse (cf. OECD, 2008, 2011b, 2015; Piketty, 2014; Streeck, 2014). The incomes of the middle and working classes had eroded, whilst incredible levels of wealth were now concentrated in a small fraction of elite managers and owners of capital (Davies, 2018; Piketty, 2014). More than this, the very wealthy, the 1% of the top 10%, can be shown to have pulled even further away following the 2008 crisis (Streeck, 2014). Davies (2015) also points to rising levels of precarity linked to poorly paid workers who depend on access to credit to augment low pay, foodbanks, and charity. We also note the growing entanglement of the finance sector in education giving rise to unprecedented levels of indebtedness to pay for fees and private tutoring (cf. Brown, 2022; Robertson & Nestore, 2022).

The OECD was aware of these growing disparities and social inequalities (cf. OECD, 2008, 2011a). Acknowledging that income inequality in its member states was at its highest level in the last 50 years, the OECD Secretary General stated: "We have reached a tipping point. Inequality can no longer be treated as an afterthought. We need to focus the debate on how the benefits of growth are distributed" (OECD, 2015, p. 7). As early as 2008, an OECD report *Growing Unequal? Income Distribution and Poverty in OECD Countries* flagged rising income inequalities and poverty across a range of OECD countries. However, the OECD was insistent what was needed was more adequate statistical infrastructures to monitor changes in income inequality over time (OECD, 2008, p. 3).

In 2011, the OECD returned to the issue of growing global inequalities in *Divided We Stand* (OECD, 2011a), whilst its 2015 Report, *In it Together*, stated: "The gap between rich and poor keeps widening... ...in many OECD countries inequality is today at its highest since data collection started" (OECD, 2015, p. 3).

Today, in OECD countries, the richest 10% of the population earn 9.6 times the income of the poorest 10%. In the 1980s, this ratio stood at 7:1 rising to 8:1 in the 1990s and 9:1 in the 2000s... ...at the lower end of the income distribution, real household incomes fell substantially in countries hit hardest by the crisis.

(OECD, 2015, p. 15)

These were startling figures and an admission by the OECD its policy priorities had failed (Robertson & Beech, 2023). The United States, once a more equal society with scope for social mobility, had become one of the more unequal societies in the world. Davies notes:

...research shows that whilst the income of the American people rose by 58% between 1978 and 2015, the income of the bottom half actually fell by 15% over the same period. The gains were clustered heavily among those at the top end of the income distribution: the top 10% of earners experienced a 115% increase over this period, while the top 0.001% saw their incomes rise by an astonishing 685%. The richer one is the faster one's wealth and income has grown. The practical implication of this data is that half of the American population experienced no form of economic progress in nearly 40 years.

(2018, pp. 76–77)

Such levels of inequality are not only linked to poverty, health, and poor education outcomes (see Marmot, 2011; Marmot et al., 2020; OECD, 2020b), they raise important social and political concerns over how to motivate individuals to stay in poorly paid work, how to legitimate such unequal outcomes, and how to manage antagonisms around immigration and "others." Davies asks: "What if the greatest threat to capitalism, at least in the liberal West is simply lack of enthusiasm and activity? Without a certain level of commitment on the part of employees, businesses run into some very tangible problems, which soon show up in their profits" (p. 105). This appears to be happening for teachers and their students.

Declines in Students' PISA Results

In 2023, the OECD reported a decline in student performance across the OECD on its flagship assessment program – PISA (see Figure 2.1). Compared to 2018, OECD data indicates that mean performance fell by 10 score points in reading and by almost 15 score points in mathematics, equivalent to three-quarters of a year's worth of learning. The decline in mathematics performance is three times greater than any previous consecutive change (OECD, 2023, p. 5). This trend, they argued, is more pronounced in 18 countries and economies, where more than 60% of 15-year-olds are falling behind.

Was this the result of COVID-19, or were other factors at play? Was it an outcome of testing fatigue amongst students and their teachers, or had the appetite to stay in the race to the top been increasingly blunted? Or perhaps

60 World Yearbook of Education 2025

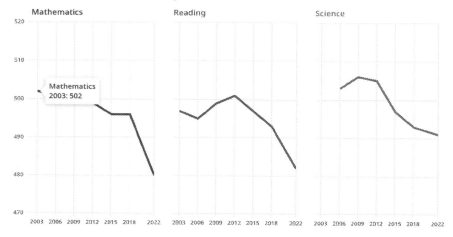

Figure 2.1 Trends in mathematics, reading and science performance, PISA test scores, and OECD average.

the effects of increased levels of poverty on learners, and austerity policies for schools? Or did these scores justify a shift in policy and strategy for the OECD in line with its extension of assessment instruments into new spheres (Sorensen et al., 2021)? Either way, this decline in scores over time is used to legitimate a new policy strategy from the OECD.

Teacher Recruitment and Attrition

The OECD has sought to bring teachers and their work to center stage, arguing that "teachers matter" (Robertson, 2012). Their launch of the *Teaching and Learning International Survey* (TALIS) in 2014, followed by a further set of rounds, was supported by teacher unions concerned to bring to light differences across OECD countries regarding hours of work and issues of teacher work stress (Sorensen, 2017).

The OECD also included a number of new items on their 2019 PISA survey aimed at teachers and well-being. The data shows teacher well-being at an all-time low: the reasons cited by teachers included declining budgets, growing managerialism, over-assessment of them and their students, little professional autonomy, weak public support, and a shared view that teaching is not a valued profession. On average, and across countries participating in TALIS 2018, only one in four teachers believed teaching is a profession valued in society (Viac & Fraser, 2020).

In many countries, this has led to high levels of turnover, as well as issues of retention and recruitment. In 2020, the OECD (see Viac & Fraser, 2020, p. 9) presented a depressing picture on teacher retention. In the United States, about

30% of teachers leave the profession in the first five years after graduation, rising to 50% in high-poverty areas (McCallum et al., 2017). Levels of attrition rates are similar in Australia and the United Kingdom. By way of contrast, Finland and Singapore record rates of around 3 or 4%.

Declines in Student Well-being

Yet the well-being of school students in the world's rich countries, and especially those countries who have adopted neoliberal policies with zeal, also tell a depressing story. In a UNICEF Report published in 2020 on 41 OECD and European Union countries, some figures stand out: in 12 of 41 countries, less than 75% of children aged 15 have high life satisfaction (p. 12); in almost half of the rich countries, more than one in five children live in poverty, in overcrowded housing, and with little play space. And many of the wealthiest countries do not convert good economic and social conditions into consistently high child well-being outcomes.

UNICEF's measures are different from the OECD's (which we elaborate below) (UNICEF, 2020, p. 9). The United States is in the bottom third for all outcomes, whilst the United Kingdom is in the bottom third for two of the three sets of outcomes. Only the Scandinavian countries are in the top third for all outcomes; the latter notable for their welfare policies giving rise to greater levels of equality. These poor results align with those from leading researchers, such as Pickett and Wilkinson (2009), Milanovic (2011), Marmot (2011), Streeck (2014), and Mijs (2021).

What are we to make of this state of affairs? To the OECD, this malaise implies a failure of individual courage, compassion, character fortitude, and creativity (OECD, 2023) warranting an intervention. Our view is that competitive individualism and ordinal instruments of governing, such as PISA and the TALIS, generate pathologies in teachers and their students (Fourcade, 2016; Sorensen & Robertson, 2020). Espeland and Sauder (2016) described these ranking instruments as "engines of anxiety."

What is triggered in OECD policies is a redefinition of the ideal student and teacher, and the rolling out of governing strategies (policies, assessment instruments, results) intended at setting in motion transformations in the agency work of teachers and students.

The Happiness Turn

We now introduce the empirical focus of this chapter; the OECD's happiness turn evidenced in a series of indicative flagship initiatives; the *Better Life Initiative* (2011b); the 2018 *PISA Global Competence Framework* (OECD, 2020a); *the Future of Education and Skills 2030* strategy; and the 2019 *International SSES* program and results (OECD, 2023). We focus specifically on the underpinning constructs in these policy documents, and the claims the OECD uses to justify their development as assessment tools.

We begin with the OECD's *Better Life Initiative* launched in 2008 by French President, Nicolas Sarkozy, at the height of the global financial crisis.

> Everyone aspires to a good life. But what does a "good" (or better) life mean? In recent years, concerns have emerged that standard macroeconomic statistics, such as GDP, which for a long time had been used as proxies to measure well-being, failed to give a true account of people's current and future living conditions.
>
> (OECD, 2011b, p. 1)

The *Better Life Initiative* proposed a broad relationship between education and well-being and sought to present the best set of comparable well-being indicators for advanced and emerging economies, whilst "...better policies need to be based on sound evidence and a broad focus: not only on people's income and financial conditions, but also on their health, their competencies, on the quality of the environment, where they live and work, their overall life satisfaction" (OECD, 2011b, p. 3). These included their material living conditions, education and skills, and subjective well-being. The subjective well-being dimension aimed to provide information on whether people felt satisfied with their lives, understood as states of happiness and usefulness (OECD, 2011b, 2020b). Subjective well-being is made up of three indicators: life satisfaction, positive affect, and negative affect, which act in a complementary manner to provide information on individuals' perception of their own lives (seen as a whole) or on specific events. Indicators, of course, also lead on to assessment tools, and in this case, tolls aimed at advancing the means to reinscribe agency.

We note important conceptual limitations in this work by the OECD. There is no clear definition of social-emotional skills, only that the latter would be differentiated from cognitive skills, such as literacy, numeracy, and IT skills (OECD, 2011b). This is confirmed when social and emotional skills are compared with *personality traits*, which are also treated as non-cognitive abilities. The notion of personality traits will gain relevance and appear in the 2019 SSES which we detail below, understood in both cases as "...relatively enduring patterns of thoughts, feelings and behaviors that reflect the tendency to respond in certain ways under certain circumstances" (OECD, 2011b, p. 30, 2023, p. 15). Yet we encounter a contradictory assumption; that personality traits *can* be modified, despite noting their enduring qualities.

Nor is "affect" defined. It is presented as having important components that measure subjective well-being, classified along a continuum from positive to negative without clear differentiating criterion. Only examples are used to differentiate the former from the latter. While positive effects capture experiences of feelings, such as happiness, joy, excitement, or love, negative effects describe people's experience of feelings such as anger, pain, or sadness. Emotions, socio-emotional skills, and effects are thus treated as non-cognitive entities. Therefore, a negative affect/emotion, such as anger or sadness, is to be understood as a response to a limited experience that does not involve any cognitive component.

This, we argue, suggests not only a simplification of the complex nature of emotions but most importantly it reduces their malleability through education to an exercise of control over them. This perspective thus ignores multiple relevant aspects, leading us to ask: are control and management the proper mechanisms to educate emotions? Are affects/emotions related to cognition? Could a feeling of anger or sadness experienced by a group of students be productively explored, rather than trying to escape from it? Can sadness, anger, or pain be justified (for various reasons, including political and social factors) and understood as an opportunity for dialogue between teachers and students? We return to these questions in our conclusion.

A second initiative by the OECD is the PISA global competences framework (Martini & Robertson, 2022; OECD, 2020; Robertson, 2021) developed as a response to the pathologies raised in the section titled Inconvenient Truths. The hope was to measure students' "global competences"; as a set of values, beliefs, and skills that indicate an orientation of the learner to "others" and their different experiences of, and views on, the world. Yet this initiative ran into trouble. The OECD sought to generate a universal measure of global competencies, and a one-size-fits-all test; a formula that had proven highly successful since its launch in 2000. But many of the indicators were viewed as problematic, and the underpinning episteme (Western middle-class culture) was called into question (Auld & Morris, 2019; Rappleye et al., 2020). The shift to working with culture were, in the end, watered down and realigned with the OECD's economic mandate (Martini & Robertson, 2022). This pattern is repeated regarding their work on social and emotional learning.

A third policy initiative is the OECD's *Future of Education and Skills 2030* (OECD, 2018) which launched a new agenda for the OECD around well-being again appearing to depart from the one the OECD had promoted for three decades (Sorensen et al., 2021). Individual and societal well-being, student agency, and the centrality of stakeholders in education were now highlighted as central concepts. Yet scrutinized closely, it is evident that its conception of agency is a liberal understanding of the human, as making "free choices"; a set of assumptions Archer (1995. p. 7) describes as the "upward conflation" of the actor's agency. Causal efficacy is granted to the agent, whilst structures are given no autonomy.

The final initiative is the *SSES* conducted in 2019. In 2023, the OECD presented the results, providing information about the social and emotional skills of students at the age of 10 and 15, considering factors such as students' socioeconomic background and gender. The notion of social and emotional skills used by the survey contrasts them with cognitive skills and compares them to personality traits or, simply, character. Thus, the report indicates that education should not only promote cognitive skills but also character fortitude (OECD, 2023). Similar to the *Better Lives Initiative* (detailed above), social and emotional skills represent; "…individual capacities that can be manifested in consistent patterns of thoughts, feelings and behaviors" (OECD, 2023, p. 15).

The socio-emotional skills measured by the 2019 survey are based on the *Big Five Personality Model* from personality psychology. According to this model, it is possible to identify a five-factor structure of personality characteristics, reflected in the following domains: "openness," "conscientiousness," "extraversion," "agreeableness," and "neuroticism." Here we make four observations regarding these personality traits (Kankaraš & Suarez-Alvarez, 2019).

First, though the OECD framework acknowledges personality is broadly fixed, they insist it is also malleable, can be modified, is teachable, and is transcultural and transhistoral (OECD, 2023). In short, this framework is appropriate for all OECD participating countries. It is the job of policymakers and educators around the world to promote and balance these socio-emotional skills, along with those that are cognitive, as they are viewed as indispensable in an increasingly demanding, changing, and unpredictable world (OECD, 2023).

Second, in the Big Five Personality Model, neuroticism is linked in the 2019 survey to individuals' abilities to deal with negative emotions. Specifically, the domain is presented as "emotional regulation," again using a similar approach to the *Better Life Initiative* (OECD, 2011). For example, the skill of emotional control is described in terms of regulating anger and irritation in the face of frustration. A behavior that reflects this skill is controlling emotions in situations of conflict, or ways of managing getting upset easily, or being moody. Again, we ask: is there an oversimplification of the nature of the emotion "anger"? What does it mean to control anger? Can the anger of students (perhaps justified even by social and political factors) and its causes be productively explored in a dialogue between themselves as students and their teachers (Zembylas, 2007)?

Third, stress resistance is described as; "…effectiveness in modulating anxiety and being able to calmly solve problems (is relaxed, handles stress well)" (Chernyshenko et al., 2018, p. 110). Yet, how easy is it for a student to control anxiety? What happens when anxiety finds its roots in complex causes, including the social and political model of coexistence, in precarity, or in the face of social violence? Should teachers consider this? Is the nature of an emotion being simplified again under the pretext of educating/controlling it? The OECD conceptual framework (Chernyshenko et al., 2018) developed for the SSES does not offer answers to these questions.

Finally, skill optimism is described as: "…positive and optimistic expectations for self and life in general" (Chernyshenko et al., 2018, p. 110). A behavior that would account for this is generally being in a "good mood." In contrast, those who often feel sad or tend to feel insecure would not have this ability (Chernyshenko et al., 2018). In addition to being confusing and vague, it seems to us these descriptions of appropriate and inappropriate behaviors put great pressure on students, making them responsible for emotional control (as if it were easy) and placing on them the burden of anesthetizing their experience of negative "affects" (anger, sad), potentially leaving their deeper situated causes (societal/structural) unaddressed.

In sum, what is clear is the objective of obtaining good academic performance involves oversimplifying the educability of emotions and reducing their purpose to that of control or management. The understanding of emotions and effects as non-cognitive and momentary entities opens the possibility for neglecting the complex causes behind them and, with that, losing opportunities to pursue a deeper reflective process within schools about the nature of the society that they live in, the causes of social injustices and other inequalities, and how they might be managed. The managing work is to be done by the student, as work on their personality, whilst the teacher's classroom activities are to guide the students' new agency work (Archer, 1995). Happy students are assumed to produce happy teachers, and vice versa. Finally, the OECD's understandings of personality, happiness, and emotions continue to be ideationally framed in a western-centric ontology; that of utility, individualism, competition, and the management of oneself. This opens the OECD to the critique of colonialism, in turn generating problems of legitimation, an issue we return to in the conclusion.

Teachers' "Agency Work" – Laboring on Producing Student Happiness

Teacher' and student' well-being are thus understood as two sides of the same coin in supporting quality teaching (Viac & Fraser, 2020. p. 44). Its PISA results suggest that "...students in happy schools (schools where life satisfaction is above the average in the country) reported a higher level of support from their teachers than students in 'unhappy' schools (where life satisfaction is below the average)" (p. 44). And whilst the OECD's reports note the importance of socio-demographic and socio-economic contextual factors, teacher and student well-being is reduced to cognitive, personality and psychological factors which can be "treated" by encouraging "grit," "mindfulness," "resilience," "compassion," and so on.

We suggest these treatments of a student's personality deficiencies are aimed at securing self-regulation are intended: (i) to ensure a productive worker; (ii) as an incentive for workers following their investment in developing well-being, grit, and compassion via greater rewards (promotion, bonuses); and (iii) to contribute to the expansion of a new economy of consumption of meditation and other "products" which completes the circuit of capital.

Regarding the first, the productive worker, Davies (2015) notes that there is a clear economic incentive for managers to consider the positive attitude of employees. Studies show that workers are more productive when they feel happy, possibly by as much as an additional 12% of output (cf., Oswald et al., 2015). And in workplaces where workers feel respected, listened to, consulted, and involved, they're more likely to work harder and less likely to take sick leave. This does not describe most teachers currently in the education system. Indeed, quite the opposite.

The second dimension, acquiring a state of well-being by developing grit, resilience, and self-efficacy, is incentivized through training, and the promise of workplace rewards (promotion, bonuses). This is clearly on the mind of the OECD when it promotes professional development programs aimed at teachers, or when it encourages teachers to invest in "grit" activities with students, viewing this as an investment that will generate rewards in terms of learning, securing employment, and better remuneration. Now happiness, as an input, is viewed something like a form of capital; happier people achieve more in their careers.

The third concerns the commercializing of well-being solutions aimed at promoting social and emotional skills, well-being, and happiness. We can chart the rise of happiness as simultaneously a zeitgeist (whose gurus and high priests were celebrated at the World Economic Forum in 2014), business (the management consulting group McKinsey has been key broker of happiness products), and instrument of governing (Davies, 2015). Both the happiness industry itself and happiness as a program and product are deeply imbricated with politics. Whose concept of happiness and well-being is at the heart of this movement? And why grit and resilience, and not some other set of concepts?

And whose interests are being served? One answer is that the rise of happiness as a major policy priority and trajectory is tied to the sale of various meditation products and a major industry with a distinct political economy and set of politics, which includes education. The US meditation industry in 2023, for example, was assessed by industry experts to be around US$ 1 billion annually, including mindfulness activities (Vennare, 2023). Similarly, "resilience" is now big business benefitting from government priorities; it is an attribute that characterizes communities and countries, a product to be sold by financial and professional services businesses and allied consultancy firms, and a way of framing conferences and specific tasks that make up the work of government (UK Cabinet Office, 2023).

Governing Happiness: Utilitarianism Meets Psychology Again

In this section, we step back to place the OECD's happiness turn in the governance of teachers into a longer-standing philosophical approach which we suggest is informed by Benthamite utilitarianism, on the one hand, and behavioral psychology, on the other.

Tribe (2008) argues by the early 2000s, happiness emerged as a possible alternative index for governing societies. A number of books captured the zeitgeist of the time; for instance, Bruni and Porta's (2005) *Economics and Happiness*, and Layard's (2006) *Happiness: Lessons from a New Science*. Layard was taken by the idea happiness could be measured and "...there could be more to human welfare than economic growth, rising incomes and the price mechanism" (Tribe, 2008, p. 462). These techniques of governing could be combined to improve the efficiency and rationality of the state and for the owners of capital the productivity of the worker.

Davies (2015) shows that political philosopher, Jeremy Bentham, was particularly taken with Priestley's (1768) *Essay on First Principles of Government* and his reflections of how best to govern a society efficiently; where "...the good and the happiness of the members, that is the majority of the members of any state, is the great standard by which everything relating to that state must finally be determined" (Davies, 2015, p. 13). This was described as a "eureka" moment for Bentham because it meant if you could develop instruments, techniques, and methods for measuring the greatest happiness for the greatest number, then one could turn this into a founding principle of efficient government.

Bentham would go on to devise all kinds of schemes and technologies which he believed could improve the efficiency and rationality of the state, including ways of thinking about our propensity to pursue pleasure, on the one hand, and avoid pain, on the other. Bentham's preoccupations at the time with measuring happiness can be regarded as the beginning of a science of happiness, and a critical component in achieving a rational form of politics and law (Davies, 2015). Others were to follow, including William Stanley Jevons, whose calculations around markets, utility, and pleasure (rational consumer) were subsequently to produce the idea of homo-economicus. Still others, like Gustav Fechner (1850) in Germany, sought to use mathematical ratios to calculate pain and pleasure (Davies, 2015). The link to current tropes and treatments, of grit, resilience, and mindfulness, are examples of interventions aimed at managing our bodies and their experiences. However, this emerging science of happiness is not concerned with happiness in any ethereal or ethical sense; rather, if happiness was a physical occurrence in the body (as in physical pleasure or pain), if it could be understood and measured, it could also be manipulated.

The 19th century was also a time of great inventiveness, with the creation of measuring tools, including devices for assessing blood pressure, pulse rates, and eye movements, all aimed at seeking to understand what it was that humans were thinking and feeling, including pleasure and pain. Up until this point, the classical political economists had no discernible concern with psychological questions of feelings. Yet these experiments and measures came to form the foundation of behavioral psychology (Davies, 2015). When intertwined with economics and mathematics, they could be translated into measuring tools that in turn would enable governors, like the OECD, to manage populations.

Conclusions

In this conclusion, we reflect on what the OECD's turn to happiness reveals as a mode of governing. For teachers, despite acknowledging the wider conditions of their work contributing to poor teacher recruitment, attrition, and health outcomes, the solution for the OECD is not to be found in restructuring their work but in amelioration activities, such as teachers' professional development focused on well-being. For students, their happiness is to be operationalized using personality psychology as a framework: of "openness," "conscientiousness," "extraversion," "agreeableness," and "neuroticism," along with self-efficacy' and "achievement motivation" (OECD, 2021, p. 18). These traits are to be worked on by the teacher and the student via "treatments" like "grit" to produce a happy student.

Probing deeper, we ask: looked at from the vantage point of now, will this "happiness turn" result in the social transformations the OECD hopes for? To answer this question, we return to Archer's (1995, pp. 140–141) morphogenetic approach which focuses on structures, agency and culture; of structural conditioning (T1), socio-cultural interactions (T2), and structural elaboration or structural reproduction (T3). For us, this means attending to processes, relations and emergences – from a "pre-existing" social form, to a "during," and then "an after."

In relation to T1 and T2, we identified a series of ongoing policies being promoted by the OECD to develop well-being and social and emotional skills in students, which appear to challenge the dominance of a narrow range of cognitive skills in students (mathematics, literacy, science) reinforced by the OECD's PISA league tables. We noted the recent downturn in PISA scores, as well as concerns over teacher' well-being. Presumably, by the OECD linking the social and emotional well-being to assumptions about student achievement, on the one hand, and teacher happiness, on the other, concerns over student productivity are resolved. This will require new practices on the part of teachers in schools in relation to students (T2). We note, however, that the OECD's commitment to PISA's cognitive skills does not disappear; rather it sits alongside the happiness turn.

We make the following observations. First, whilst teachers are being asked to labor differently in schools in relation to students to stimulate a new kind of "self" work, the outcomes are not over-determined, and it is not evident what kind of social transformations might occur. For sure, new programs are likely to be promoted in schools aimed at students' social and emotional well-being. But we might also conclude that what is being added by the OECD are socio-emotional skills to be developed by teachers in students aimed at managing the pathologies of neoliberalism. Rather than a deviation from neoliberalism, we posit that the "happiness turn" is an extension of neoliberalism, or in Peck's (2010) terms, "neoliberalization." By this, he means neoliberalization is a process of managing the contradictions and crises from previous rounds of policymaking.

Rather than a transformation in the neoliberal social order to something else, we see transformations taking place in neoliberalism as an organizing ideology to direct the agency work of teachers and their students (T3) more concertedly. The disciplinary and biopolitical technologies of Hayek's market order; of pain, frustration and stigmatization by the governor is to be more determinedly matched by the grit and resilience of the governed. Ibled (2023, p. 81) describes this as the "optimistic cruelty" of Hayek's market order: "… the willingness to see or orchestrate the suffering of others," not as a side-effect of neoliberal theories, but the putting into practice a key tenet of the neoliberal project.

Second, the OECD's understanding of social and emotional skills is also full of elisions, narrowings, and contradictions, which in the long run will set up new tensions and contradictions to be managed. For example, the OECD: (i) equates social and emotional skills to a specific rendering of personality (the Big Five Personality Model); (ii) personality is viewed as composed of relatively *enduring* traits in a person yet paradoxically these traits are *malleable*; (iii) social and emotional skills are assumed to explain the gap in academic performance between low and high socio-economic status student yet evidence suggests that it explains very little; and (iv) its model of personality is viewed as transhistorical, transversal and transcultural, to enable it to be used across its member and non-member states. As we detail below, these assumptions are deeply problematic, and it is possible the OECD's new assessment regime will have either limited impact on students, or if so, in ways unintended though not wholly unexpected.

On the latter issue, we have already seen that those participating in the OECD's program of assessment have called into question the OECD's assumptions about the universal nature of culture (Martini & Robertson, 2022). Yet looked at more closely, we can see that the idea of well-being and happiness continues to align with the ideational regime that the OECD operates in; utility, individualism, competition, and the management of oneself. This is because it is ontologically grounded in the rational, liberal, individualism of Bentham's utilitarian governing project, and a narrow Eurocentric understanding of personality.

This, in turn, exposes the OECD to further critique; of propagating colonialism, and one that the OECD will need to manage to ensure country buy-in to their program. On this issue, Rappleye et al. (2020) show how the OECD's well-being and happiness measures are deeply problematic. Packaged as a universal, they suffer from being telescoped from a large multi-dimensional approach to one which, when operationalized, carries multiple biases toward individualism, life satisfaction, and achievement motivation. As Rappleye et al. (2020, p. 269) note, standing out from the crowd in a Japanese classroom "… might not be deemed the best situation," yet this is precisely what is being valued here in the OECD's concept of achievement, and an atomized individual. They observe; there is "…a startling lack of cultural attunement (linguistic, theoretical, etc.) that operates behind the façade of OECD technical precision" (Rappleye et al., 2023, p. 2).

Gruijters et al. (2023) also dispute the OECD's account of the causal effects of social and emotional skills on achievement which we suggest will destabilize efforts to suture into place a new commonsense. Using OECD PISA indicators and data, Gruijters et al., show that though several socio-emotional skills measured in PISA, such as a growth mindset, "...have a strong association with learning outcomes. In combination, however, these skills explain no more than 8.8% of the socio-economic gap in learning outcomes" (p. 16). Rather, they argue that sociology offers us a far better account of why teachers feel as they do, or why student engagement with education competition is stalling. In this regard, a social class-informed analysis provides a far better explanation of the economic, social, and economic resources that shape the dispositions and accomplishments of students, and the settings (school and community) in which teachers work, than psychology.

Third, the OECD – like Bentham – is more concerned with simple levers for governing, such as their PISA rankings. Following the same Benthamite utility logic, they have prioritized governing using a pared-back understanding of social and emotional well-being as a utility index. And using an ordinal instrument (PISA) that compares one territory (city, country) with another, it is teachers and their students who are encouraged to respond by turning in on themselves to seek a state of "happiness." In doing so they inoculate themselves against "seeing" the ills of the world. This is an instrumental view of happiness, and not one that is captured by notions of the good life.

Looked at from the opposite direction, one should also ask: why shouldn't we feel sad, if not outrage, at the growing levels of inequality that characterize our education settings, communities, and societies (Freytag et al., 2022)? Surely *always* being in a state of happiness means ignoring the pain we experience, or the pain of others (from an excess of competition, precarity, inequality, or stigmatization. In this rendering, happiness is both an anesthetic against anxiety and pain, and a product for sale in the education marketplace. A perfect formula for predatory capitalism. We buy products to inoculate ourselves with happiness via selling "grit" and "resilience." And new forms of treachery also emerge as possibilities; of the state, technology companies, or schools, promoting wearable technology or face recognition technologies to register the emotions of students taking us into the realm of hyper-surveillance.

In conclusion, we argue that we need to deploy socio-political and philosophical resources to make sense of the happiness turn and the new kind of agency work asked of teachers. Sociology of the kind we have outlined above enables us to make visible the absence of a concern for the social, and how social worlds are produced (in the form of structural inequalitie, and subjectivities), at the level of the self, community and society. Politics provides us with the resources to see how projects of governing can and are anchored in particular understandings of order, such as Benthamite utilitarianism. And finally, philosophy can generate the resources to think more reflectively and critically about the good life and what this means for workers like teachers in the institutions, sectors, and communities in which they work and what this means for a democratic and just society.

References

Archer, M. (1988). *Culture and agency: The place of culture in social theory*. Cambridge University Press.
Archer, M. (1995). *Realist social theory: The morphogenetic approach*. Cambridge University Press.
Auld, E., & Morris, P. (2019). Science by streetlight and the OECD's measure of global competence: A new yardstick for internationalisation? *Policy Futures in Education*, 17(6), 67–698.
Brown, P. (2022). Higher education, credentialism, and social mobility. In J. E. Côté, & S. Pickard (Eds.), *Routledge handbook of the sociology of higher education* (pp. 351–362). Routledge.
Bruni, L., & Porta, P. L. (2005). *Economics and happiness: Framing the analysis*. Oxford University Press.
Chernyshenko, O. S., Kankaraš, M., & Drasgow, F. (2018). Social and emotional skills for student success and wellbeing: Conceptual framework for the OECD study on social and emotional skill. *OECD Education Working Papers* (173). OECD.
Dardot, P., Guéguen, H., Laval, C., & Sauvetre, P. (2021). *Le choix, de la guerre civile: Une autre historie neoliberalism*. Lux.
Davies, W. (2015). *The happiness industry: How the government and big eletedusiness sold us well-being*. Verso.
Davies, W. (2018). *Nervous states: Democracy and the decline of reason*. Verso.
Espeland, W. N., & Sauder, M. (2016). *Engines of anxiety: Academic rankings, reputation, and accountability*. Russel Sage Foundation.
Fourcade, M. (2016). Ordinalization: Lewis A. Coser memorial award for theoretical agenda setting. *Sociological Theory*, 34(3), 175–195.
Freytag, T., Lauen, D. L., & Robertson, S. L. (2021). *Space, place and education settings: An introduction*. Springer.
Gruijters, R., Raabe, I. J., & Hübner, N. (2023). Socio-emotional skills and the socioeconomic achievement gap. *Sociology of Education*, 1–28. https://doi.org/10.1177/00380407231216424
Ibled, C. (2023). The 'optimistic cruelty' of Hayek's market order: Neoliberalism, pain and social selection. *Theory, Culture and Society*, 40(3), 81–101.
Kankaraš, M., & Suarez-Alvarez, J. (2019). Assessment framework of the OECD study on social and emotional skills. *OECD education working paper (207)*. OECD.
Layard, R. (2006). *Happiness: Lessons from a new science*. Penguin.
Marmot, M. (2011). *Fair society, healthy lives. Strategic review of health inequalities in England post-2010*. https://www.parliament.uk/globalassets/documents/fair-society-healthy-lives-full-report.pdf
Marmot, M., Allen, J. B. T., Goldblatt, P., & Morrison, J. (2020). *Health equity in England: The Marmot review 10 years on*. www.instituteofhealthequity.org/resources-reports/marmot-review-10-years-on/the-marmot-review-10-years-on-full-report.pdf
Martini, M., & Robertson, S. L. (2022). Erasures and equivalences: Negotiating the politics of culture in the OECD's global competence project. *Compare: A Journal of Comparative and International Education*, 1–18. https://doi.org/10.1080/03057925.2022.2084035
McCallum, F., Price, D., Graham, A., & Morrison, A. (2017). Teacher wellbeing: A review of the literature. *Association of Independent Schools of NSW*, Sydney, Australia.
Meyer, H.-D., & Zahedi, K. (2014). Open letter to Andreas Schleicher, OECD, Paris. *Policy Futures in Education*, 12(7), 872–878.
Mijs, J. (2021). The paradox of inequality: Income inequality and belief in meritocracy go hand in hand. *Socio-Economic Review*, 19(1), 7–35. https://doi.org/10.1093/ser/mwy051

Milanovic, B. (2011). *The haves and the have-nots: A brief and idiosyncratic history of global inequality*. Basic Books.
OECD. (2008). *Growing unequal? Income distribution and poverty in OECD countries*. https://doi.org/10.1787/9789264044197-en
OECD. (2011a). *How's life? Measuring well-being*. https://doi.org/10.1787/23089679
OECD. (2011b). *Divided we stand: Why inequality keeps rising*. https://doi.org/10.1787/9789264119536-en
OECD. (2015). *In it together: Why less inequality benefits all*. https://doi.org/10.1787/9789264235120-en
OECD (2016). *Global competency for an inclusive world*. Paris: OECD.
OECD. (2018). *The future of education and skills: Learning compass 2030*. oecd.org: https://www.oecd.org/education/2030-project/teaching-and-learning/learning/
OECD. (2020a). *PISA 2018 results (volume VI) are students ready to thrive in an interconnected world*. OECD Publishing. https://doi.org/10.1787/d5f68679-en
OECD. (2020b). *How's life? 2020: Measuring well-being*. https://doi.org/10.1787/9870c393-en
OECD. (2021). *Beyond academic learning: First results from survey on social and emotional skills*. https://doi.org/10.1787/92a11084-en
OECD. (2023). *PISA 2022 results: The state of learning and equity in education* (Vol. 1). https://doi.org/10.1787/19963777
Office UK Cabinet. (2023). *The UK government resilience framework (HTML)*. GOV.UK: https://www.gov.uk/government/publications/the-uk-government-resilience-framework/the-uk-government-resilience-framework-html
Oswald, A., Proto, E., & Sgroi, D. (2015). Happiness and productivity. *Jouranl of Labour Economics, 33*(4), 789–822.
Pawson, R., & Tilly, N. (1997). *Realistic evaluation*. Sage.
Peck, J. (2010). *Constructions of neoliberal reason*. Oxford University Press.
Pickett, K., & Wilkinson, R. (2009). *The spirit level*. Penguin.
Piketty, T. (2014). *Capital in the twenty-first century*. Harvard University Press.
Priestley, J. B. (1768). *An essay on the first principles of government*. J. Johnson.
Rappleye, J., Komatsu, H., U., Y., Krys, K., & Markus, H. (2020). Better policies for better lives'? Constructive critique of the OECD's (mis) measure of student well-being. *Journal of Education Policy, 35*(2), 258–282.
Rappleye, J., Komatsu, H., Uchida, Y., Tsai, J., & Markus, H. (2023). The OECD's 'Well-being 2030' agenda: How PISA's affective turn gets lost in translation. *Comparative Education*. https://doi.org/10.1080/03050068.2023.2273640.
Robertson, S. L. (2012). Placing teachers in global governance agendas. *Comparative Education Review, 56*(3), 377–406.
Robertson, S. L. (2021). Provincializing the OECD-PISA global competences project. *Globalisation, Societies and Education, 19*(2), 167–182.
Robertson, S. L., & Beech, J. (2023). 'Promises promises': International organisations. *Comparative Education*. https://doi.org/10.1080/03050068.2023.2287938.
Robertson, S. L., & Nestore, M. (2022). Education cleavages and the rise of authoritarian populism. *Globalisation, Societies and Education, 20*(2), 110–123.
Sorensen, T. (2017). *Work in progress: The political construction of the OECD programme teaching and learning international survey*. PhD Thesis. University of Bristol, Graduate School of Education.
Sorensen, T., & Robertson, S. (2020). Ordinalisation and the global governance of teachers. *Comparative Education Review, 61*(1), 21–45.
Sorensen, T., Ydesen, C., & Robertson, S. L. (2021). Re-reading the OECD and education: The emergence of a global governing complex–an introduction. *Globalisation, Societies and Education, 19*(2), 99–107.
Streeck, W. (2014). *Buying time*. Verso.

Tribe, K. (2008). Happiness: What's the use? *Economy and Society, 37*(3), 460–468.
UNICEF (2020). *Worlds of influence understanding what shapes child well-being in rich countries.* https://www.unicef.org/media/77571/file/Worlds-of-Influence-understanding-what-shapes-child-well-being-in-rich-countries-2020.pdf
Vennare, J. (2023). *Fitt Insider.* https://insider.fitt.co/meditation-mindfulness-startups/
Viac, C., & Fraser, P. (2020). *Teachers' wellbeing: A framework for data collection and analysis. OECD working paper (213).* OECD.
Zembylas, M. (2007). Mobilizing anger for social justice: The politicization of the emotions in education. *Teaching Education, 18*(1), 15–28.

3 Educational Hierarchies and "The Voice of the Teaching Profession"

Organized Teachers' Participation in Global Governance

Nina Bascia

Introduction: The Research Base on Teachers and Their Unions

The title of this chapter is more than a bit of a mouthful. That is, both individually and in combination, "the teaching profession," "global governance," "teacher voice," and "organized teachers" are ambiguous and oxymoronic terms. First, the concept of a "teaching profession" is fraught with contradictory meanings, not least of which is the distinction between what teachers and others understand to be the characteristics of a professional body and whether the locus of authority sits within or outside of that body. Next, there are no organizations (teachers or otherwise) that possess jurisdictional power to mandate educational practice at the global level; their clout lies in influencing others in one way or another. Third, as a massive and heterogeneous body of educators working in a variety of diverse circumstances, teachers cannot be said to speak with a unified voice. Finally, teacher organizations (unions), usually understood as their lawful representatives vis-à-vis employers and other formal educational authorities, are structured hierarchically in a manner reflecting that of the educational systems within which they work, such that the diversity of teachers' occupational interests and concerns are filtered and synthesized through multiple organizational layers.

Nonetheless, the chapter's title has some merit. In the post-World War II era, a period when global organizations such as the Organisation of Economic Cooperation and Development (OECD) and the World Bank emerged and proliferated, several international teacher organizations emerged (Sorensen & Robertson, 2017), the most comprehensive being Education International (EI), the umbrella organization for teacher unions around the world. In addition to providing a range of supports to its nearly 4000 affiliate organizations, EI interacts with a number of other global players in order to advocate for teachers' interests at that level. And while neither EI nor the global organizations with which it interacts can be said to participate in governance in a binding way, they employ various dialogic and material strategies to persuade governmental jurisdictions to adopt their preferred versions of educational futures.

DOI: 10.4324/9781003441731-5

Teacher unions have existed for decades – some for over a century – in many jurisdictions around the world (Bascia & Osmond, 2013; Smaller, 2015; Spaull, 1984). They are only provisionally linked to formal governance structures, if at all; it is when they "upset the applecart" of system-directed business-as-usual that they become recognized as forces to contend with (Bascia & Osmond, 2012). Many teacher members tend to ignore the need for their presence except if and when they are in need of union advocacy, whether individually or collectively (Bascia, 1994).

In parallel fashion, teacher organizations have appeared less frequently in educational research than is merited, absent from studies of educational policy and teachers' work alike. When they are present, it is usually in the form of a passing comment rather than as central players. For example, the placement of teacher union matters in educational handbooks is as segregated chapters rather than as part of the fabric of educational policy and practice. In recent years, their treatment by researchers has improved somewhat, extending beyond generally antipathetic or ambivalent portrayals (e.g., Boyd et al., 2000; Eberts & Stone, 1986; Moe, 2001, 2011) to more nuanced and balanced treatments: beyond the research intended for mainstream policy analysts is emergent scholarship on the relationship between teacher unions and teachers' work (e.g., Bascia, 2023; Bocking, 2020; Carter et al., 2010; Lawn, 1985), as well as on educators' efforts in many countries to establish "social justice" organizations, grounded in issues of schooling and yet linked to broader social movements (e.g., Jones, 2005; Stark et al., 2022; Tarlau & Lira, 2025). As the inclusion of this chapter in the Yearbook demonstrates, teacher organizations recently have become objects of some interest in treatments of "teacher quality" at the global level (e.g., Akiba & LeTendre, 2017; Bascia, 2004, 2017; Robertson, 2012; Sinyolo, 2017; Sorensen & Robertson, 2017).

To what extent can teacher unions claim to represent teachers' interests? Several claims have been made about the challenges they face in bridging the schism that exists between teachers and their organizations: the relative isolation of teaching work (see Cochran-Smith & Lytle, 1992), school structures and cultures that privilege individualism over collectivity (Connell, 1995, 2009; Hargreaves & Fullan, 2000; Little, 1990; Lortie, 2020), and a lack of personal awareness among many teachers to situations where union intervention might seem beneficial (Pogodzinski, 2015). These hypotheses, upon reflection, appear to be time- and location-bound: teachers' work patterns, relationships with other educators, their political orientations, and experience with educational politics vary markedly, not only across jurisdictions around the globe but even within the same school settings (Bascia, 1994). Meanwhile, very little attention has been paid to the *structural factors* that inhibit the capacity of teacher organizations to make claims that they speak for all or even most teachers. This chapter raises fundamental questions about the capacity of teachers' organizations, particularly at the global level, to serve as conduits for teachers' concerns so that they can be considered in relation to educational governance. While the focus is ultimately at the global level, these concerns are salient throughout education systems.

My research trajectory over the past several decades has centered on a range of teacher union-related topics, often grounded empirically in several contrasting cases in order to develop robust hypotheses about the social, political, and organizational dynamics underlying teaching and teacher organizations. This scholarship has privileged teachers' perspectives over those of the union officials, policymakers, and educational administrators that dominate mainstream policy research. Much of my work has focused on teacher organizations in Canada and the United States, but I have also conducted research in South American, European, African, and Asian-Pacific jurisdictions. While independently conducted interviews have been the primary source of data, survey and collaborative research have broadened the breadth of my studies, which have focused on how teachers' union involvement must be understood in the context of their work roles at the school level (Bascia, 1994, 1997, 1998); the constraints on teacher unions' involvement in local governance (Bascia et al., 1997; Lieberman & Bascia, 1990), jurisdictional (state, province or national) (Bascia, 2005, 2009, 2023; Bascia et al., 2023); organizational analyses (Bascia, 2023); and the contextual factors that shape teacher organization participation in international comparison (Bascia, 2004, 2017; Bascia & Osmond, 2013, 2015; Bascia & Stevenson, 2017). The breadth of this work affords me a nuanced understanding of the relationships between teachers and their organizations.

The research base for the section of this chapter on teacher organizational participation in governance at the global level is rooted in my and others' knowledge of the work of EI, through research initiatives I conducted for the organization (Bascia & Osmond, 2013; Bascia & Stevenson, 2017), roughly a dozen conversations with EI staff between 2011 and 2022, in-person observations of International Summits on the Teaching Profession in 2011 and 2015, co-sponsored by EI and the OECD, and familiarity with the research on international organizations' efforts to influence educational practice more broadly. There is a burgeoning literature base on the educational goals and activities of international organizations such as the OECD and the World Bank, as well as corporate entities with an interest in education, such as Pearson, including reviews of the ways they characterize teachers and teaching as of paramount importance to student learning and yet seem always intent on finding ways to control them (see, e.g., Mundy et al., 2016; Robertson, 2012; Sorensen, 2021; Verger & Altinyelken, 2013; Verger et al., 2016). Still, there is scant peer-reviewed published research on teacher organizations' own strategic goals and their relations to other organizational entities at the global level. Research published by Sorensen (2021), both independently and in collaboration with Susan L. Robertson (Sorensen & Robertson, 2017) focusing on the purposes and activities of EI in its collaboration with the OECD on the Teaching and Learning International Survey (TALIS), has been particularly helpful in this regard.

The next section of the chapter focuses on issues surrounding teaching and teacher union engagement at school, district, and state/provincial levels, particularly with respect to the hierarchical nature of educational systems, especially "labor issues" and the diversity of teachers' personal and occupational concerns. The third section reveals how similar dynamics challenge teacher organizations advocacy for teachers at the global level, including a "democratic deficit" that characterizes relations between the umbrella organization representing teacher unions worldwide and its affiliate members, and the challenges facing EI with respect to reframing the dominant discourse about teachers and teaching. The final section of the chapter considers the critical role teacher organizations play vis-à-vis educational governance at every level of the educational system.

The Challenges Facing Teachers and Their Unions

There is a hierarchical relationship between teachers and their educational system superiors to some extent in educational systems around the world. One of the earliest cases of social organization considered by institutional theorists such as Meyer and Rowan (1977) was the modern educational system, a powerful and persuasive structure based on a "scientific management" paradigm, where business firms (such as the Ford Motors factory) and the Prussian military provided the basic hierarchical, bureaucratic organizational model, in this case with teacher-workers at the bottom, charged with implementing the plans and policies promulgated by successive layers of authoritative decision makers. This system architecture persists into the present, making it extremely difficult for teachers to engage in shaping the policies that shape their work, and the authority of teachers' representative organizations is seriously constrained. Indeed, in some countries, such as South Korea, as well as many southern states in the United States, teacher organizations lack formal legal standing – and actually may be illegal, as has become the case in Turkey. In other jurisdictions, even where their presence is enshrined in law, their standing and their involvement in educational decision-making may be precarious, ebbing and flowing at the will of the particular government or administration of the day (Maharaj & Bascia, 2021). In yet other contexts, even longstanding beliefs and traditions of involving labor unions in policy settings may be circumvented by governments choosing to act without meaningful consultation, resulting in policies that run counterproductive to good teaching practice (Bascia & Osmond, 2012).

From the perspective of Canadian and US educational system leaders, there were compelling reasons for their establishment of mass school systems over a century ago at local and provincial/state levels: in an era of massive immigration to North America, these systems were intended to ensure cultural and political assimilation and to develop loyalty and compliance in future workers for growing industrial economies (Harper, 1997; Prentice & Houston, 1975). The new structures were part of a larger transformation of public institutions into more accountable and credible bodies (Fine-Meyer, 2012). Championed by new, so-called "progressive" school superintendents, these new systems designed and manifested:

> centralized, highly structured procedures ... compatible with an assembly-line view of the educational process. The image of a moving conveyer belt on which students were placed while teachers performed a predetermined series of operations on them was a powerful metaphor for order and efficiency.
> (Darling-Hammond, 1996, p. 38)

The management principles upon which these systems were constructed "made a firm distinction between managers, who were to do all the thinking, and workers, who were to conduct routine tasks following procedures developed by the managers" (p. 40). From the late 1800s onward, in both countries, teachers, especially women, organized to improve their working conditions and to pursue material improvements in their salaries and pensions, tenure, and other benefits, in order to raise teaching to the status of a career (Gitlin & Margonis, 1995; Larson, 1977; Smaller, 2015; Urban, 1982). School system leaders countered that teachers' concerns with their own material improvement demonstrated a lack of professionalism (Bascia & Osmond, 2012).

It was thus that in the mid-20th century, when the right to and procedures relating to teachers' collective bargaining were legislated, Canadian province by province and state by state in the United States, they developed within an already hierarchically structured environment that from the outset limited the scope of teachers' engagement in educational decision-making. Collective bargaining rights initially represented a "great bargain" (Carlson, 1992), in the sense that they gave unionized teachers the right to negotiate salary, benefits, and working conditions, while substantive policy domains, governing such issues as curriculum and educational funding, remained under the exclusive jurisdiction of system decision makers. Over time, this compromise has both reflected and reinforced teachers' subordinate position in the educational systems of the two countries.

Within the education sector, school administrators governed teachers' work; up a level, school district leaders directed the activities of both school administrators and teachers; state/provincial officials governed district-level as well as school-level matters; and, in many cases, national-level jurisdictions governed all of the above. The greater the distance between teaching and policy-setting, the greater the prospect that administrative directives cannot take the realities of classroom-level teaching and learning into.

The Persistence of "Labor" Issues

Tautologically, because teachers' working conditions are considered labor issues rather than so-called "professional" matters, they often are seen by policy actors as irrelevant when it comes to setting educational policy (Shields & Knapp, 1997), and as having little to do with the quality of students' learning conditions (Bascia & Rottmann, 2011). Some educational researchers characterize them as "feel good" issues that might increase teacher satisfaction, useful to encourage teacher compliance with administrative directives (Leithwood, 2006; Louis & Smith, 1991); educational decision makers may view teaching conditions as actually as bargaining trade-offs *in competition* with student learning in a zero-sum resource environment, (McDonnell & Pascal, 1979). School and local educational agency administrators increasingly are required to respond to system edicts issued down the hierarchy and are often unable to reconcile them with ensuring the quality of teachers' working conditions. Teacher unions are the only entities that pay substantive attention to the actual conditions of teachers' work, which inevitably shape the conditions of students' learning (Bascia, 2023).

Even while teachers have been recognized as the most critical factor to the quality of student learning (see Sorensen & Robertson, 2017; Verger & Altinyelken, 2013), as teachers' representatives who interact with educational decision makers, teacher unions thus have only a peripheral role in formal educational governance. Instead, without formal authority to participate in policy-setting, their power vis-à-vis educational decision-making tends to rely on their persuasive skills. In sum, educational governance suffers from an absence of attention to the issues and perspectives of educators whose work is closest to educational practice and that matters the most to the achievement of educational system goals. This pattern persists at all system levels, exacerbated to the extent that decision-making occurs at greater distances from teaching practice.

Teachers' issues, ranging from low pay and job insecurity to inadequate educational funding to overtly stated disrespect reported in the media, have persisted since the early days of the advent of mass systems of education. Howard Stevenson and I (Bascia & Stevenson, 2017) argue that these issues are one and the same: that is, it is not possible for teachers to meaningfully engage in so-called professional activities without attending to so-called labor issues – or perhaps it would be better to challenge the prevailing discourse and reframe teaching conditions as professional conditions.

The Diversity of Teachers' Concerns

A second factor complicating the match between policy making and practice is the tendency of standardized policy strategies to view teachers as faceless, interchangeable workers ("the teacher work force"). The variability of teachers' professional concerns and the variety of teaching realities fly in the face of educational system directives. Further, there are profound implications for the effectiveness of unions' organizational advocacy on their behalf (Bascia, 2008). What teachers want and need from their unions depends on who they are, where they are, and the kinds of students and programs with which they work. Descriptions of teachers in educational policy research view them as a homogeneous mass or, perhaps, in micropolitical terms, as belonging to distinct factions (see, e.g., Oakes et al., 1997). A common perspective of union scholars is that teachers are selfish dupes operating out of self-interest, solely concerned with material issues, responding with suspicion when union leaders express an interest in reform (see McDonnell & Pascal, 1979; Olsen, 1965), and readily manipulated by ambitious union officials. Closer glimpses of what teachers value, however, demonstrate strong concerns about their working conditions as firmly connected to student learning and well-being – and tremendous variation in what they want from their unions and why. The structural conditions of teaching engender certain different needs and wants. Teachers' social class, race, gender, and other demographic variations play out in significant ways in schools, as does teachers' subordinate status relative to administrators and policymakers. These are the very factors that often drive teachers to turn to unions for resolution and restitution and yet, somewhat paradoxically, to cause some to possess ambivalent feelings toward their organizations (Bascia, 2008b, 2023).

An earlier union study (Bascia, 1994) suggests that teachers, even in the same workplaces, run the gamut, from articulating strong anti-union sentiments, through apathy, to persistent and passionate union affiliation, their "common sense" perspectives arising from complex sets of personal and work-related factors. Some teachers, both individually and collectively, find themselves faced with situations where they believe they have not been treated fairly and seek out union advocacy in response. Other teachers will not necessarily recognize the value of union representation ("Why would you need association protection for your job unless you have hassles? And there are so few things that you can be hassled about in teaching" – p. 39). The extent to which teachers' understanding of the value of union advocacy is an individual or a larger, shared phenomenon also depends on whether, in a given educational context, teachers work primarily independently or, conversely, have opportunities to develop personal and professional relationships that allow them to see the value of union advocacy for their colleagues – for example, a teacher in a socially tightly knit school recognizes that "teachers get desperate.... To be raising a family, ... to want to educate those children ... and realize that another [employer] will pay more, you become angry" (Bascia, 1994, p. 32). There are important variations in how teachers' relationships with colleagues play out in different school contexts (see also Little, 1990; McLaughlin & Talbert, 2001). In some schools, union affiliation is generally seen as a positive component of staff identity; in other schools, it's up to the individual teacher to choose whether or not union identity "suits me."

Teachers work in different environments – in urban, suburban, or rural schools; in inner city or more privileged neighborhoods; with transient or stable student populations. These settings create different conditions for teaching and learning. Teachers who work with immigrant children, children with special needs, or any other population of students for whom academic success is not easily achieved have greater need for the access to support, information, and influence made available through close union affiliation (Bascia, 1998b). Conversely, those in higher-status teaching roles (e.g., science instructors) may also become union-active out of a sense of entitlement, an expectation that resources should and must be made available for their programs, and outrage when they discover teachers' exclusion from decision-making (Bascia, 1997, 1998).

Another factor complicating the answer to the question "What do teachers want from their unions?" is that teachers change over the course of their careers. Their skills as teachers grow, and their need for on-the-job support shifts. What piques their interest in terms of learning and taking on new challenges changes over time. As they age, their energy levels may change. Their personal lives may alter over time as personal responsibilities ebb and flow. Why and when teachers become interested in union involvement changes as a result: younger teachers are more likely to be attracted by high-quality teaching-related professional learning, more seasoned teachers by the availability of new professional opportunities and the opportunity to develop leadership skills. Teachers of different generational cohorts will have experienced different occupational histories: eras of particular reform ideas, professional opportunities and constraints, and union prominence or invisibility (Bascia, 1994, 1997, 1998, 2008a).

All of these differences make it challenging for teacher organizations to identify priorities that will be meaningful to all or even many teachers. Failing to recognize the roots and complexity of teacher diversity, many union leaders search for organizational initiatives that offend no one but end up satisfying few. In such situations, union leadership may become autocratic and authoritarian. Participatory decision-making structures become mere window dressing, their agendas and procedures manipulated, while real decision-making rests in the hands of a small number of people or even an individual (Bascia, 2008a). Perhaps ironically, ignoring or hiding conflict sends a signal to teachers that their organization is not accessible to everyone, and in the process reduces the information and ideas available to staff members as they attempt to work on teachers' behalf. Facing hostility from educational system superiors and a growing number of demands from their members for support, many unions adopt a "triage" approach, choosing to mount few or even a single agenda item in order to ration scarce organizational resources (Bascia, 2005). But focusing on a narrowed agenda usually backfires: both teachers and others instinctively recognize the inadequacy of the vision driving the agenda, and many teachers are left, again, with the contention that their organization does not support them. Sorensen and Robertson's (2017) concept of "democratic deficit," referring to the dynamics among affiliate members of global teacher organizations, is equally useful in describing the challenges inherent to teacher union organizations of any size and diversity of membership.

This section has presented two related arguments: first, that the origins and hierarchical structure of education systems make it difficult for teacher unions to influence decision making, and second, that unions are challenged in their attempts to respond effectively the diversity of teachers' interest. The rules of hierarchy dictate that the greater the distance between teaching practice and union organization, the greater the likelihood that union organizations will be unable to read the variety of teachers' particular concerns. The effectiveness of union advocacy has a poorer chance of appropriate response at the district level than at the school level, poorer again at the state/provincial level, even worse at the national level and, as the next section attests, particularly troublesome at the global level, where sheer numbers of teachers and organizations may render organizational representation particularly challenging (see Bascia, 1994; also McDonnell & Pascal, 1979; Olson, 1965).

Teachers' Organizational Involvement in Governance at the International Level

Educational International, created in 1993, is the umbrella organization for teacher unions around the world, it has as its affiliates nearly four hundred member organizations in over 170 countries and territories and represents over 30 million education personnel (Education International, 2024). Conversations with EI staff and perusal of its website reveal, despite its small staff and modest budget, its ambitious agenda: to catalyze improvements to teaching through social dialogue. It employs a variety of organizational strategies. Educational news from around the world is made available through EI's website. It has considered setting up offices to conduct educational research in regions of the world that lack the funding to establish their own, and it supports the development of regional networks of teacher unions in less wealthy jurisdictions – for example, sponsoring meeting opportunities for the staff of Sub-Saharan African country-level organizations so that they may share information and build greater organizational capacity. It commissions and publishes the results of both literature reviews and original empirical studies on issues of topical interest (recent examples available on the EI website include artificial intelligence in education, teaching materials, copyright access issues, pedagogical strategies, educational reforms, privatization, and teacher unions themselves) – critically covering relevant topics vis a vis current policy discourses and providing cutting-edge research for teachers, educational researchers, and policymakers that would otherwise be nonexistent. Some of the empirical research sponsored by EI focus on specific countries or regions; also commissioned are multi-case comparative studies in order to derive robust recommendations that can be considered in a wide range of social and geographic contexts.

EI also engages with other international organizations with the intention of injecting "teachers' voice" into global discourses on education, using its partnership activities with the OECD to engage in the "politics of knowledge as a lever for teacher voice in transnational governance" (Sorensen, 2021, p. 572).

For instance, EI co-sponsors annual International Summits on the Teaching Profession with the OECD and a host government. These Summits bring together teacher union and educational officials from a number of countries around the world to learn about and discuss topical ideas of common interest (Paine et al., 2017). It has also influenced, albeit in a limited way, the substance of OECD's Teaching and Learning International Survey (TALIS). One of the recurrent issues associated with TALIS concerns the extent to which the various dimensions of teaching and other school-level factors surveyed in TALIS might be linked to students' academic performance in mathematics, science and reading internationally, as captured through the repeated administration of the Program for International Student Assessment (PISA) (Sorensen, 2021).

Challenges to the Incorporation of "The Voice of the Teaching Profession" in Global Discourses

EI's efforts to incorporate teachers' perspectives and concerns in global-level discourses that undergird the policy recommendations of international organizations are subject several obstacles that broadly echo the major impediments encountered by teacher organizations at other levels. As delineated in this section, these include structural inequities within the organization between wealthier and less wealthy member countries, as well as power imbalances between EI and the OECD. Reinforcing these are the status of the different research methods and data sources underlying TALIS and PISA.

"Democratic Deficits." Similar to the challenges to democratic participation among teachers in their union settings identified previously in this chapter is what Sorensen and Robertson (2017, p. 127) term "democratic deficits" within EI at the global level. In national contexts where more than one union represents teachers, not all unions are necessarily EI affiliates, such that many teachers' perspectives systematically are left out. Furthermore, while EI attempts to ensure greater equity of access through such structural mechanisms as vice presidents for each of the world continents on its leadership team and an executive board with regional committees, it is my observation that wealthier countries (and so-called Western countries) provide the lion's share of the funding that enables EI to function, such that a handful of organizations have a disproportionate influence over EI's goals and strategies.

The Dynamic Nature of Authority Relations. As stated earlier, organizational organizations' involvement in "global governance" is somewhat indirect, since these organizations do not wield the rule of law over national governments; instead, their authority vis a vis educational policy and practice is based on what Sellar and Lingard (2013) call "epistemological governance" (in Sorensen, 2021, p. 575). The OECD's influence is especially linked to its administration of PISA, which has engendered a competitive dynamic among countries, which can be employed to persuade lower-ranking jurisdictions to adopt OECD-recommended reforms. Another powerful strategy for international organizations assertions of influence is monetary: the World Bank provides funding to lower-income countries, and thus rewards or punishes jurisdictions financially on the basis of their compliance with Bank-recommended practices. In this arena, where authority lies outside the realm of formal, legislatively designated governance, there are parallels to the formal educational hierarchy: organizations representing teachers are subordinate to those that dictate policy recommendations: such that EI possesses junior partner status in its relationships with the OECD and the World Bank.

Sorensen and Robertson (2017) characterize EI's achievements as "ambiguous." EI gained access to the TALIS Board in the late 2000s, critically engaged with TALIS themes and survey items, and has been able to refer to TALIS findings to advance teachers' interests (Sorensen, 2021). On the one hand, via the International Summits and their work on the TALIS Board, EI has introduced and to some extent has influenced the prevailing discourse about teachers and teaching, as evidenced by changes to the major foci of subsequent administrations of the survey, but there are powerful discourses that go the other way. On the one hand, teacher well-being is becoming more widely and persistently considered as (somehow) linked to student learning; but on the other hand, OECD's interest in teacher pay-for-performance schemes persists, as does its contention, contrary to teachers' claims, that class size mostly does not matter to the success of teaching and learning. Reinforcing the prevailing status dynamics are contentions about the kinds of evidence employed by TALIS (the self-reports of school-based educators vs. "objective" quantitative data associated with PISA) and whose evidence "counts."

Conclusion

This chapter has discussed how unequal relations challenge teacher organizations' capacity to advocate for teachers at all levels of educational systems, and how those challenges occur through a variety of mechanisms.

First, the chapter indicated a kind of crisis in governance and a critical disconnect between teachers' work and contemporary policy-making. At school, local educational authority, and formal jurisdictional levels, the prevailing model of schooling makes sharp distinctions between policy decision makers and implementers. This is compounded by limits on what teacher organizations can legally negotiate, the persistence of inadequate teaching conditions that mitigate against teachers' abilities to work optimally, and a multilayered system structure. The heterogeneity of teachers' work contexts and concerns also make it difficult for teacher unions to successfully advocate for teachers' occupational issues.

At a global level, EI, the umbrella organization for teacher unions worldwide, is challenged in its efforts to represent "teachers' voice" for similar reasons, most notably by EI's internal structure, particularly with respect to relationships among affiliate member organizations, and by its power relative to other organizations intent to influencing educational policy.

This chapter's review of the literature, as well as my career's research trajectory, thus lead to the contention of the necessity of teacher unions' efforts to minimize the harm caused by unequal power relations. While their success tends to be limited and their challenges persist, as Stevenson and Mercer (2015) have suggested, where they do not exist, they must be (re)invented. For teachers, individually and collectively, the organization of teachers ought to be a critical dimension of educational governance.

References

Akiba, M., & LeTendre, G. K. (Eds.). (2017). *International handbook of teacher quality and policy*. Routledge.

Bascia, N. (1994). *Unions in teachers' professional lives*. Teachers College Press.

Bascia, N. (1997). Invisible leadership: Teachers' union activity in schools. *Alberta Journal of Educational Research, 43*(2), 151–165.

Bascia, N. (1998). Women teachers, union affiliation, and the future of North American teacher unionism. *Teaching and Teacher Education, 14*(5), 551–563.

Bascia, N. (2000). The other side of the equation: Teachers' professional development and the organizational capacity of teacher unions. *Educational Policy, 14*(3), 385–404.

Bascia, N. (2004). Teacher unions and the teaching workforce: Mismatch or vital contribution? In M. Smylie, & D. Miretzky (Eds.), *Addressing teacher workforce issues effectively: institutional, political and philosophical barriers* (pp. 326–347). University of Chicago Press.

Bascia, N. (2005). Triage or tapestry: Teacher unions' contributions to systemic educational reform. In N. Bascia, A. Cumming, A. Datnow, K. Leithwood, & D. Livingstone (Eds.), *International handbook of educational policy* (pp. 593–609). Kluwer Academic Press.

Bascia, N. (2008a). Learning through struggle: How the Alberta Teachers' association maintains an even keel. In K. Church, N. Bascia, & E. Shragge (Eds.), *Learning through community* (pp. 169–186). Springer.

Bascia, N. (2008b). What teachers want from their unions: What the literature tells us. In L. Weiner (Ed.), *The global assault on teaching, teachers and their unions* (pp. 95–108). Palgrave Macmillan.

Bascia, N. (2017). Teacher unions and teacher quality. In M. Akiba, & G. K. LeTendre (Eds.), *Routledge international handbook of teacher quality and policy*. Routledge.

Bascia, N. (2023). *Teachers' work during the pandemic*. Routledge.

Bascia, N., & Osmond, P. (2012). *Teacher unions and educational reform*. National Education Association.

Bascia, N., & Osmond, P. (2013). *Teacher union governmental relations in the context of educational reform*. Education International.

Bascia, N., & Rottmann, C. (2011). What's so important about teachers' working conditions? The fatal flaw in North American educational reform. *Journal of Education Policy, 26*(6), 787–802.

Bascia, N., & Stevenson, H. (2017). *Organizing teaching: Developing the power of the profession*. Education International.

Bascia, N., Stiegelbauer, S., Jacka, N., Watson, N., & Fullan, M. (1997). *Teacher associations and school reform: Building stronger connections*. National Education Association.

Bocking, P. (2020). *Public education, neoliberalism, and teachers: New York, Mexico City, Toronto*. University of Toronto Press.

Boyd, W. L., Plank, D. N., & Sykes, G. (2000). *Teachers unions in hard times. Conflicting missions? Teachers unions and educational reforms*. Brookings Institution Press.

Carlson, D. (1992). *Teachers and crisis: Urban school reform and teachers' work culture* (Vol. 1). Routledge.

Carter, B., Stevenson, H., & Passy, R. (2010). *Industrial relations in education: Transforming the school workforce*. Routledge.

Cochran-Smith, M., & Lytle, S. L. (1992). Communities for teacher research: Fringe or forefront? *American Journal of Education, 100*(3), 298–324.

Connell, R. W. (1995). Transformative labour: Theorizing the politics of teachers' work. In M. K. Ginsburg (Ed.), *The politics of Educators' work and lives* (pp. 91–114). Garland.

Connell, R. (2009). Good teachers on dangerous ground: Towards a new view of teacher quality and professionalism. *Critical Studies in Education, 50*(3), 213–229.

Darling-Hammond, L. (1996). *The right to learn*. Jossey-Bass.

Eberts, R. W., & Stone, J. A. (1986). Teacher unions and the cost of public education. *Economic Inquiry, 24*(4), 631–643.

Education International (2024). Education International. Retrieved March 12, 2024, from ei-ie.org/en

Fine-Meyer, R. (2012). *Including women: The establishment and integration of Canadian women's history into Toronto Ontario classrooms 1968–1993*. University of Toronto.

Gitlin, A., & Margonis, F. (1995). The political aspect of reform: Teacher resistance as good sense. *American Journal of Education, 103*(4), 377–405.

Hargreaves, A., & Fullan, M. (2000). Mentoring in the new millennium. *Theory into Practice, 39*(1), 50–56.

Harper, H. (1997). Difference and diversity in Ontario schooling. *Canadian Journal of Education/Revue Canadienne De l'éducation, 22*(2), 192–206. https://doi.org/10.2307/1585907

Jones, K. (2005). Remaking education in Western Europe. *European Educational Research Journal, 4*(3), 228–242. https://doi.org/10.2304/eerj.2005.4.3.7

Larson, M. S. (1977). *The rise of professionalism: A sociological analysis*. University of California Press.

Lawn, M. (Ed.). (1985). *The politics of teacher unionism: International perspectives*. Croom Helm.

Leithwood, K. (2006). *Teacher working conditions that matter: Evidence for change*. Elementary Teachers' Federation of Ontario.

Lieberman, A., & Bascia, N. (1990). *Assessment of the California policy trust agreement project*. Prepared for PACE (Policy Analysis for California Education) and the Stuart Foundation, Spring.

Little, J. W. (1990). The persistence of privacy: Autonomy and initiative in teachers' professional relations. *Teachers College Record, 91*(4), 509–536.

Lortie, D. C. (2020). *Schoolteacher: A sociological study*. University of Chicago Press.

Louis, K. S., & Smith, B. (1991). Restructuring, teacher engagement and school culture: Perspectives on school reform and the improvement of teacher's work. *School Effectiveness and School Improvement, 2*(1), 34–52.

Maharaj, S., & Bascia, N. (2021). Teachers' organizations and educational reform: Resistance and beyond. *Canadian Journal of Educational Administration and Policy*, (196), 34–48.

McDonnell, L., & Pascal, A. H. (1979). *Organized teachers in American schools*. The RAND Corporation.

McLaughlin, M. W., & Talbert, J. E. (2001). *Professional communities and the work of high school teaching*. University of Chicago Press.

Meyer, J. W., & Rowan, B. (1977). Institutionalized organizations: Formal structure as myth and ceremony. *American Journal of Sociology, 83*(2), 340–363.

Moe, T. M. (2001). Teachers unions and the public schools. In T. M. Moe (Ed.), *A primer on America's schools* (pp. 151–184). Hoover Institution Press.

Moe, T. M. (2011). *Special interest: Teachers unions and America's public schools.* Brookings Institution Press.
Mundy, K., Green, A., Lingard, B., & Verger, A. (Eds.). (2016). *Handbook of global education policy.* John Wiley & Sons.
Oakes, J., Wells, A. S., Jones, M., & Datnow, A. (1997). Detracking: The social construction of ability, cultural politics, and resistance to reform. *Teachers College Record, 98*(3), 482–510.
Olson, M. (1965). *The logic of collective action.* Cambridge Harvard University Press.
Paine, L., Aydarova, E., & Syahril, I. (2017). Globalization and teacher education. In D. J. Clandinin, & J. Husu (Eds.), *The SAGE handbook of research on teacher education* (Vol. 2, pp. 1133–1148). SAGE.
Pogodzinski, B. (2015). The formal and information contexts of union socialization. In N. Bascia (Ed.), *Teacher unions in public education.* Palgrave Macmillan.
Prentice, A. L., & Houston, S. E. (Eds.). (1975). *Family, school & society in nineteenth-century Canada.* Oxford University Press.
Robertson, S. L. (2012). Placing teachers in global governance agendas. *Comparative Education Review, 56*(4), 584–607.
Sellar, S., & Lingard, B. (2013). The OECD and global governance in education. *Journal of Education Policy, 28*(5), 710–725.
Shields, P., & Knapp, M. (1997). The promise and limits of school-based reform: A national snapshot. *Phi Delta Kappan, 79*(4), 288–294.
Sinyolo, D. (2017). Improving teacher quality, status and conditions: The role of teacher organisations. In M. Akiba, & G. K. LeTendre (Eds.), *Routledge international handbook of teacher quality and policy.* Routledge.
Smaller, H. (2015). Gender and status: Ontario teachers' associations in the nineteenth century. In N. Bascia (Ed.), *Teacher unions in public education: Politics, history, and the future* (pp. 11–31). Palgrave Macmillan.
Sorensen, T. B. (2021). The space for challenge in transnational education governance: The case of education international and The OECD TALIS programme. *Discourse: Studies in the Cultural Politics of Education, 42*(4), 572–589.
Sorensen, T. B., & Robertson, S. L. (2017). The OECD program TALIS and framing, measuring, and selling quality teacher™. In M. Akiba, & G. K. LeTendre (Eds.), *International handbook of teacher quality and policy* (pp. 117–131). Routledge.
Spaull, A. (1984). The origins and formation of teachers' unions in nineteenth century Australia. *Critical Studies in Education, 26*(1), 134–168.
Stark, L. W., Dyke, E., & Maton, R. (2022). Afterword: Reflections on contemporary educator movements. *Critical Education, 13*(4), 50–57.
Stevenson, H., & Mercer, J. (2015). Education reform in England and the emergence of social movement unionism: The national union of teachers in England. In N. Bascia (Ed.), *Teacher unions in public education: Politics, history, and the future* (pp. 169–187). Palgrave Macmillan.
Tarlau, R., & Lira, A. (2025). Teacher activism: Global perspectives on the role of teachers in social movements. In N. Bascia, & R. Maton (Eds.), *Handbook on teachers' work.* Routledge.
Urban, W. J. (1982). *Why teachers organized.* Wayne State University Press.
Verger, A., & Altinyelken, H. K. (2013). *Global managerial education reforms and teachers.* Education International.
Verger, A., Fontdevila, C., & Zancajo, A. (2016). *The privatization of education: A political economy of global education reform.* Teachers College Press.

4 Representations of Teachers and Teaching in the Public Space

Exploring the Interplay between Policy and Media Constructions of Teacher Supply in Australia and England

Kathryn Spicksley and Nicole Mockler

Introduction

The relationship between education policy and media discourses of education is complex. While it has long been claimed that beyond citizens' own schooling experience, the mainstream print media makes the most significant contribution to their understanding of schooling and teachers' work (Mills & Keddie, 2010), less focus has been placed on the discursive interaction of education policy and media texts in shaping public discourses of education. This interaction is significant because teachers are subject to complex and ongoing demands from policymakers which are worked up and reworked through media coverage.

The interdiscursive relationship between policy and media has been theorized via the concept of "mediatization," first coined by Norman Fairclough (2000) in the introduction to his major work on the language of New Labour in the United Kingdom (UK). Fairclough argued that "mediatization" constituted a fundamental shift in the relationship between mass media, politics, and government, brought about by the growth of information and communication technologies. Specifically in relation to education, Rawolle has argued for an understanding of the complexity of mediatization processes:

> ...the mediatisation of education policy [is] not easily reduced to the complete dominance of media logic over policy logic or the steering of the media by policy makers. Media coverage can be influential in introducing emerging themes that are subsequently adopted as policy themes in policy texts.
>
> (2010, p. 35)

Previous studies exploring mediatization and education policy include Hattam et al.'s (2009) analysis of the recursive flow of ideas between a key policymaker and media commentator, and Tamir and Davidson's (2011) historical analysis of media coverage of New Jersey education policy debates.

DOI: 10.4324/9781003441731-6

Issues of newsworthiness – the "criteria employed by journalists to measure and therefore "judge" the newsworthiness of events" (Richardson, 2007, p. 91) – also play an important role in the interplay between policy and media discourses. News values, such as consonance, eliteness, impact, negativity/positivity, personalization, proximity, superlativeness, timeliness, and unexpectedness (Bednarek & Caple, 2017), are put to work by different news outlets in different ways, depending on the "imagined" preferences' (Richardson, 2007) of their audiences. In the case of media discourses of education, these preferences are shaped by the near-universal experience of schooling, which provides a baseline understanding of education-related phenomena (Mockler, 2022), but also by local contexts and particularities, among them enactments of globalized policies inflected by "local vernaculars" (Rizvi & Lingard, 2010).

This chapter charts recent research on representations of teachers in the public space, extending current research through a focus on policy and media constructions of teacher supply, a common touchstone for contemporary discussions of teachers and their work. We argue that despite the pervasiveness of globalizing discourses in education – and the tendency for these to be reflected and amplified through the work of the print media – that these globalizing discourses are sometimes disrupted by local conditions and circumstances. Drawing on a range of transnational and national policy texts and a custom-built corpus of over 6,000 media texts published in Australia and England between 2018 and 2022, we use discourse analysis to provide a worked example of the complexity of the discursive interaction between policy and media discourses. Our analysis highlights the impact of the COVID-19 pandemic on discursive practices around teacher supply, most notably in English media texts; as such, this chapter argues that national events, as mediated through news outlets, have the potential to disrupt globalizing discourses about education – regardless of how hegemonic or normative such discourses may at first appear.

Media Representations of Education

As highlighted in Baroutsis and Lingard's (2023) systematic research synthesis, the field of research focused on news, new media, and education policy is a small but rapidly expanding one. Much of the published research focuses on representations of different aspects of education or teachers' work (e.g., Barnes, 2022; Gautreaux & Delgado, 2016; Punakallio & Dervin, 2015), or media reporting of particular policy reforms (e.g., Baroutsis & Lingard, 2017; Edling & Liljestrand, 2020; Gautreaux & Delgado, 2016; Hansen, 2009).

Over the past two decades, the growing significance of international and national standardized testing, including the Organisation for Economic Cooperation and Development's (OECD) Programme for International Student Assessment (PISA), has generated a global body of research focused on national media coverage of these programs. Studies include Takayama's (2008, 2010) examination of the politics of international PISA-related league tables in Japan; Waldow's (2009) review of Germany's response to the 2001 "PISA-shock experienced in Germany"; 'Yemini and Gordon's (2017) examination of the effects of reporting of national and international standardized tests in Israel; and Baroutsis and Lingard's (2017) longitudinal account of portrayals of PISA performance in Australia. A growing body of work also exists that is focused on comparing media responses to PISA across different countries (Hopfenbeck & Görgen, 2017; Waldow et al., 2014). Much of this work focuses not only on representations of the testing programs themselves but also on the implied quality of the local school system, often pointing to manifestations of "PISA panic" (Alexander, 2012) in the media. As Stack (2007) argues:

> there is a consistent discourse in which test results come to stand for the state of American education and global strength. This discourse affects what is taught, how it is taught and how the success and failure of students, teachers and school leaders is judged.
>
> (p. 106)

Indeed, research suggests that crisis and panic narratives are common in media representations of education, with two particular crises used as regular touchstones. The crisis of "teacher quality" has been observed in research conducted in Australia (Barnes, 2022; Keogh & Garrick, 2011; Mockler, 2014; Shine, 2015) but also in the United States (Cohen, 2010; Ulmer, 2016) and on a comparative basis across Saudi Arabia, South Africa, Oman, Bangladesh, and Australia (Alhamdan et al., 2014). Second, the associated crisis of declining educational standards, observed in Australia (Baroutsis, 2016; Blackmore & Thorpe, 2003; McLeod, 1989; Thomas, 2003), the United Kingdom (Pettigrew & MacLure, 1997; Warmington & Murphy, 2004), Chile (Cabalin, 2015), and the United States (Stack, 2007), has also been shown to feature heavily in news coverage of education. Within this research, crises in education are understood to play a critical role in shaping media representations across time and place.

Scholars of education policy are paying increasing attention to the ways in which teacher accountability is framed in media narratives, and the possible impact that this may have on public perceptions of teachers and teaching (e.g., Baroutsis, 2016; Cohen, 2010; Mockler, 2023). However, much of this published research into media representations of teaching focuses on texts published from the 1980s onwards, as legislation governing increased accountability measures began to be introduced in high-income countries. Such studies provide a diachronic perspective on media representations of teachers during this key period of heightening teacher accountability but are unable – unfortunately – to provide clear insights around the evolution between education policy and media discourses over a longer period of time,

Representations of Teachers and Teaching in the Public Space 91

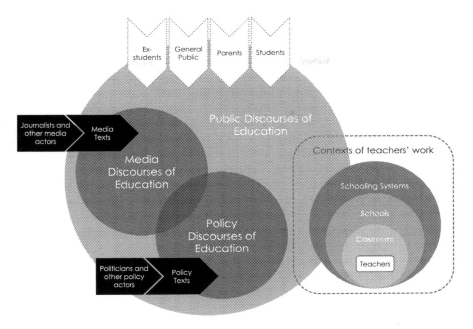

Figure 4.1 Public discourses of education and contexts of teachers work (from Mockler, 2023).

before such policy mandates became commonplace. Furthermore, as Shine (2017, p. 1696) argues, the "impact of such coverage [on teachers] has rarely been directly examined."

The interplay and mutual relationship between education policy discourses and media discourses of education in the production of public understandings and expectations of teachers is an emerging area of research interest (Wallace, 1993; Blackmore & Thorpe, 2003). One of us (Mockler, 2023) has previously theorized this relationship as represented in Figure 4.1. Within this theorization, media and policy discourses of education – each products of the respective work of journalists and other media actors, and politicians and other policy actors – are understood as overlapping "layers" within broader public discourses of education. Members of the public taking up a variety of different subject-positions (including as ex-students, parents, and so on) both consume and contribute to the expansion and re-shaping of these public discourses, while teachers (also members of the "general public") experience the consequences of these discourses in the course of their work, nested within classrooms, within schools, within schooling systems, and as members of "the public" themselves. In this way, media discourses of education contribute to the cultural-discursive arrangements (Kemmis et al., 2014) that frame and shape teachers' work, normalizing some conversations and assessments and rendering different things "sayable" and "unsayable."

Teacher Supply as a Global Issue

Problems with attracting, retaining, and deploying teachers are common in education systems across the globe (Craig, 2017; UNESCO, 2023). However, the way in which these problematisations are framed appears to differ according to the relative wealth of the nations under scrutiny. In the Global South, discourse around teacher supply often constructs short-term "absenteeism" as the key policy problem. Reports, such as *The Oxfam Education Report* (Watkins, 2000), and more recently UNICEF's *Time to Teach* (Karamperidou et al., 2020), exemplify this discursive trend:

> Adequate teaching time is a vital ingredient for good-quality education. Effective instruction demands that 800–1000 hours of teaching are provided each year. Unfortunately, most school systems fall short of this mark [...] Teacher absenteeism, often linked to economic pressures, is a major contributory factor.
>
> (Watkins, 2000, p. 112)

> Teachers attending lessons and spending quality time on task is a prerequisite to learning. However, in sub-Saharan Africa, teacher absenteeism ranges from 15 to 45 per cent. Teacher absenteeism and reduced time on task wastes valuable financial resources, short-changes students and is one of the most cumbersome obstacles on the path toward the education Sustainable Development Goal.
>
> (Karamperidou et al., 2020, p. 6)

In such texts, teacher absenteeism is constructed primarily as a quantitative issue, with policy solutions targeted at increasing time on task. Teachers in low-income countries are reportedly absent from the classroom for a range of reasons, but these short-term absences are often associated with wider structural problems (such as transport infrastructure, or localized conflict) rather than being located within the teachers themselves.

In contrast, within high-income countries located in the Global North, more attention has been focused on psychological issues such as dissatisfaction, demotivation, and burnout amongst teaching staff, leading to high attrition rates (Kinman et al., 2011; Madigan & Kim, 2021; Richards et al., 2018; Whitehead et al., 2000). Teacher attrition is increasingly being positioned as a public health issue in high-income countries (Agyapong et al., 2022; Arvidsson et al., 2019). A concern with teacher supply as a long-term issue, informed primarily by psychological factors, is apparent in a number of recent policy documents published by the OECD and in high-income nation-states:

> Modern education systems evolve in a context of growing teacher shortages, frequent turnover and a low attractiveness of the profession. In such

a context where these challenges interrelate, there is an urgent need to better understand the well-being of teachers and its implications on the teaching and learning nexus.

(Viac & Fraser, 2020, p. 4)

[W]e continue to find that teachers who reported poor well-being were more likely to say that they were considering leaving their jobs than their counterparts.

(Doan et al., 2023, p. 8)

According to the UK's Health and Safety Executive, teaching staff and education professionals report the highest rates of work-related stress, depression and anxiety in Britain […] this report is a detailed investigation of well-being in the education profession.

(Office for Standards in Education UK, 2019, p. 4)

Critical education researchers exploring teacher supply in the Global North have argued that in high-income countries, policymakers' positioning of education as the primary route to increased national competitiveness and economic security has resulted in widened responsibilities for classroom teachers, leading to both heightened workload and a process of work intensification (Apple, 2004; Creagh et al., 2023; Easthope & Easthope, 2000). In high-income countries, therefore, discussions around teacher supply tend to foreground qualitative analyses of teachers working lives, offering policy solutions that seek to increase psychological well-being among teachers.

However, discursive similarities can nevertheless be detected in the strategies deployed to frame teacher supply problems across the Global North and Global South. One example of such assonance can be identified in problematizations which foreground the previously discussed "crisis" in teacher quality as a factor impacting on teacher supply. Such concerns around the quality of teachers are a common feature of discussions around teacher supply conducted at a global level, often focusing on attracting teachers with appropriate qualifications or training in low-income countries (e.g., Schleicher, 2011; UNESCO, 2015; Watkins, 2000). However, these concerns are also taken up and deployed in national policy contexts in countries fiscally located within the Global North. For example, policymakers in both Australia and England have constructed the improvement of teacher quality as a core policy priority within education (Allen & Sims, 2018; Mockler, 2014; Vickers, 2015; Wilkins, 2015), despite teaching being a graduate-entry profession, and requiring an additional teacher training qualification (Australian Institute for Teaching and School Leadership, 2024; Department for Education UK, 2024).

Comparing Two Cases: Focusing on the Relationship between Policy and media Discourse in Australia and England

In this section, our intention is to provide a specific example charting the discursive interplay between policy texts and media texts, focusing on Australia and England. In both nations, policymakers increasingly position teacher supply as a policy problem in need of a solution (Commonwealth of Australia Education Ministers Meeting, 2022; Department for Education UK, 2019). Difficulties with teacher supply are also a regular focus of education reportage across both countries (e.g., Henry, 2023; Precel, 2023). Australia and England acted as comparative contexts, allowing an investigation into the mediatization of globalizing policy discourses across two high-income countries. We took a recursive approach (Baker, 2012), working between six policy texts (Table 4.1) and two large media corpora, composed of media texts from Australia and England (Table 4.2).

We chose to analyze two texts published by the OECD as exemplifying policy texts which had a global reach (Table 4.1). The global influence of the OECD in driving neoliberal education policy worldwide is an established focus of educational research (Lewis, 2017; Lingard & Sellar, 2016; Meyer & Benavot, 2013; Sørensen et al., 2021), as the OECD effectively leverages mechanisms of "soft power" in order to effect changes in education policy at a national level (Knodel et al., 2013). Following Berkovich and Benoliel (2019), we recognize a distinction between OECD reports on the Teaching and Learning International Survey (TALIS), and background reports issued by the organisers of the OECD's annual International Summit on the Teaching Profession (ISTP), in terms of both purpose and audience. These two types of texts are therefore informed by differing discursive practices informing their production, distribution, and consumption (Fairclough, 1992). However, regardless of the circumstances in which these documents arose, OECD

Table 4.1 Policy texts.

Title	Organization	Year	Author(s)	Policy focus
Preparing Teachers and Developing School Leaders for the 21st Century	OECD	2012	Andreas Schleicher (Ed)	Global
TALIS 2018 Results: Teachers and School Leaders as Valued Professionals, Volume II	OECD	2020	n/a	Global
Review of the National School Reform Agreement: Study Report	Australian Government Productivity Commission	2022	n/a	National [Australia]
The National Teacher Workforce Action Plan	Education Ministers Meeting	2022	n/a	National [Australia]
Recruitment and Retention Strategy	Department for Education	2019	n/a	National [England]
Recruitment and Retention Briefing	House of Commons Library	2022	Robert Long Shadi Danechi	National [England]

Table 4.2 Media corpora.

Name	Number of texts	Tokens (words)	Date range	Subcorpora
Australia Media Corpus (AMC)	2,238	1,939,811	2018–2022	**The Age** (left leaning) – 1,182 texts, 974,945 tokens **The Australian** (right leaning) – 1,056 texts, 964,866 tokens
England Media Corpus (EMC)	4,817	14,824,812	2018–2022	**The Guardian** (left leaning) – 3387 texts, 13690234 tokens **The Telegraph** (right leaning) – 1,430 texts, 1,134,578 tokens

publications on education policy are conferred with a high status by national policymakers, and therefore arguably contribute to an increasing standardization of teaching practices worldwide, or in the very least a standardization in the discursive framing of teacher policy and practice. The OECD plays "a key role in encoding what it means to be an effective [education] system, a competent learner, and an excellent teacher" (Sørensen et al., 2021, p. 101), and it does so through To provide diversity in our sample, we chose to analyze one publication reporting on TALIS and one written for the ISTP.

Alongside the "global" OECD texts, we also analyzed two national texts concerned with teacher supply – two produced in Australia and two produced in England (Table 4.1). Again, we selected texts that were produced with different audiences and purposes in mind to capture a range of discursive strategies deployed by policymakers. However, it is important to recognize that policy texts have a life beyond their immediate intentions and are received and interpreted in diverse and unintended ways by a range of policy actors (Ball et al., 2012; Singh et al., 2013).

The database LexisNexis was used to collate two corpora of media documents from the target nations of Australia and England between 2018 and 2022. The media corpora were composed of all texts from the selected newspapers which included the word teacher(s) at least three times, providing consistency in corpus construction across the Australia Media Corpus (AMC) and England Media Corpus (EMC). In order to provide balance and to explore potential discursive patterns across different media outlets with different political leanings, articles from both right-leaning and left-leaning newspapers were incorporated into both corpora (Table 4.2).

We combined close readings of the selected policy and media texts, utilizing Bacchi's "*What's the Problem Represented to be?*" (WPR) approach to policy analysis. The WPR approach is a six-stage, poststructural analysis process that focuses on identifying how problems are represented in texts, what interpretations are silenced by these representations, and the material effects that such representations are likely to have (Bacchi, 2012; Bacchi & Goodwin, 2016). Additionally, given the size of the media corpora, when undertaking media analysis we borrowed analysis and visualization strategies from computer-aided

96 *World Yearbook of Education 2025*

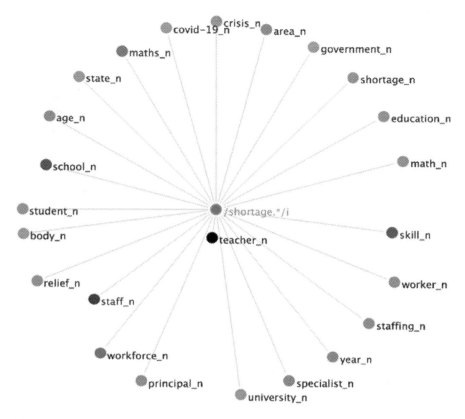

Figure 4.2 Collocation analysis of shortage* in the AMC.

methods of corpus-assisted discourse analysis (Baker, 2012; Mautner, 2009). These strategies involved the generation of GraphColls (e.g., Figure 4.2) which indicate statistical relationships between words (or "collocations"), and the generation of concordance lines, which identify each occurrence of a target word within its immediate context. Both analyses were undertaken through the corpus linguistics software LancsBox (Brezina et al., 2021).

The media corpora covered a period of significant instability as the COVID-19 pandemic caused global disruptions to schooling; this unprecedented global event had a significant impact on news reporting focused on the field of education, and beyond. Between January 2020 and March 2022, UNESCO records schools in England as being fully closed for 16 weeks, and partially open for 11 weeks. The same dataset shows schools in Australia as being partially open for 46 weeks during the same period (UNESCO Institute of Statistics, 2022). As such, the national educational context 2020 and 2022 looked very different across Australia and England, and consequently our analysis revealed significant differences in the corpora with regard to occurrences of the term *COVID-19*. Whereas in the AMC, *COVID-19* occurs 779 times in 375 texts (with a relative frequency of 4.06 occurrences per 10,000 words), in the EMC, *COVID-19* occurs 27,032 times in 888 texts (with a relative frequency of 18.23 occurrences per 10,000 words). These frequencies indicate a significant difference in the way that journalistic reporting around education was conducted across Australia and England during 2020–2022.

Teacher "Shortages" in Policy and Media Texts

In this penultimate section, we focus our discussion on one key difference between the AMC and the EMC, concerned with the deployment of the word *shortage(s)* in relation to teacher supply across policy and media texts. Our discussion of this specific issue is intended to provide an illustration of the complex and contingent relationship between education policy at both global and national levels, and how these policies are received, interpreted and further deployed in the media space.

Our WPR analysis of policy texts indicated areas of alignment and dissonance across global and national policy texts, as well as illustrating the range and complexity of discourses associated with the policy issue of teacher supply. One specific complexity noticed on analyzing the six policy texts in detail was the deployment of the word "shortage" with regard to teacher supply issues. In the OECD texts, teacher shortages are constructed as a global educational problem, transcending national supply issues:

> All in all, teacher shortage is a significant problem in many of the summit countries, although its levels vary significantly across educational levels, subjects and schools.
> (Schleicher, 2012, p. 58)

However, within national policy texts, the problem of teacher shortages is often presented as one of recruitment or retention difficulties. This is particularly obvious in policy texts from England:

> Alongside the recruitment of new teachers, the retention of existing teachers is a key component in maintaining teacher numbers.
> (Long and Danechi, 2022, p. 15)

> Early career retention is now the biggest challenge that we face. And it is where government can help to make the biggest difference by investing significantly.
> (DfE, 2019, p. 20)

Such discursive strategies are of interest because they present solutions offered by policymakers (namely, to recruit more teachers, and to keep more teachers in the classroom for longer) as the policy problem to be solved, therefore, obfuscating the core issue of teacher supply and, in doing so, tacitly closing off particular solutions. This observed divergence between global and national policy texts around the issue of teacher shortages provided a "way in" to exploring the media corpora in detail, comparing the ways in which teacher shortages were constructed across the AMC and the EMC.

The AMC evinces a strong association between *teacher* and *shortage**,[1] with a collocation frequency of 226. Furthermore, a high number of collocates associated with the word *shortage** in the AMC are also linked to education, including *school, maths, education, student,* and *principal* (Figure 4.2).

The word *shortage** in the AMC therefore appears to be deployed primarily in the context of teacher supply, as supported by the following concordance lines:

[16][2] There is already a chronic **shortage** of **teachers** of mathematics
[29] leading to a **shortage** of qualified and experienced **teachers**
[22] Meredith Peace dismissed concerns of a **teacher shortage**
[50] Concerns higher standards will lead to a **shortage** of **teachers** seem premature
[42] Collins said the pandemic had exacerbated **teacher shortages**
[95] There is no greater risk than a looming **teacher shortage**. **Teachers** are seriously overworked

Concordance lines indicate a number of discursive positions taken up and deployed within the Australian media. These include arguments both for [16] and against [22] the existence of a teacher shortage and debates around why teacher shortages might be developing, including the COVID-19 pandemic [42] and teachers' working conditions [95]. Discussion around teacher shortages in the AMC therefore appears to be complex, both supporting and contesting the discourses offered in global and national policy texts. However, both collocation analysis and concordances support a claim that the AMC evidences a concern with teacher *shortages* specifically. Such concern evidences a coherence between the Australian media texts, and both global and Australian policy texts, wherein a concern with teacher shortages is understood as a policy issue discretely located within education.

The focus on teacher shortages evidenced in the AMC offers a contrast to the EMC, where the nouns most frequently associated with *shortage** are also connected with a wide range of supply issues, beyond education (Figure 4.3).

High-frequency noun collocates of *shortage** including *food* (collocation frequency of 75) and *vaccine* (collocation frequency of 55), alongside less frequent collocates such as *petrol, oxygen, bed, medicine, equipment, ivermectin,* and *doctor* (Figure 4.3) indicate a discursive concern in the EMC with shortages of key resources, particularly in the area of medicine and healthcare.

Representations of Teachers and Teaching in the Public Space 99

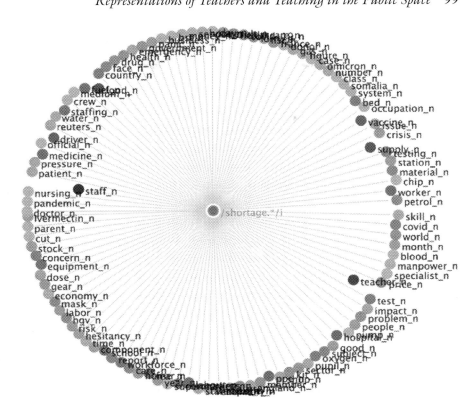

Figure 4.3 Collocation analysis of shortage* in the EMC.

Indeed, the most frequent collocate of *shortage** in the EMC is *staff*, with a collocation frequency of 236:

[521] Meanwhile, a **staffing shortage** is so severe that the hospital
[567] Laboratory owners failed to deal with **staff shortages** and increase pay
[723] Crisis as care homes suffering unprecedented **staff shortages** are forced to stop taking patients
[1217] Pharmacies have been slammed by **staffing shortages,** either because employees are out sick
[1229] Headteachers in England warn **staff shortages** due to **teachers** isolating will be "challenging"
[1285] surging Omicron infections leading to **staff shortages** that have disrupted supply chains

The EMC is therefore concerned with shortages across a range of employment sectors, in contrast to the AMC which is more clearly focused on education.

The differenceS in lexical patternings associated with *shortage** across the AMC and the EMC are significant, because they indicate a different media orientation toward teachers across the two nations. In Australia, the teacher shortage is constructed within media texts as an issue specific to education. However, in England, a shortage of teachers is constructed also as part of a wider shortage of necessary resources and workers in key professions.

After *staff*, *teacher* is the highest frequency collocate of *shortage** in the EMC (136); however, many concordances evidence a discursive entanglement between teacher shortages and COVID-19, rather than a more general teacher shortage:

[838] Schools are also experiencing **teacher shortages** because staff are contracting the virus
[855] Air purifiers would help stop virus spreading in schools as fears grow of **teacher shortages**
[1105] A spiralling **teacher shortage** due to sickness and Covid-related absence

Indeed, such discursive entanglements are not unique to the EMC; there are also examples of teacher shortages being linked to COVID-19 in the AMC:

[368] **Teacher shortages** from Covid-19 absenteeism
[128] Hampered by ongoing **teacher shortages** caused by COVID-19 and influenza
[230] Schools bracing for a potential **teacher shortage** if Omicron cases spike again

Positioning COVID-19 as a cause of teacher shortages is therefore evident across both Australian and English media discussions around education post-2020. As such, there are similarities in the way that media outlets across both nations reiterate globalizing discourses that construct and maintain fears around the impact of teacher supply problems. In both countries, extant discourses that draw on fears around teacher supply are incorporated into discussions that are primarily shaped by emergent national conversations around the impact of the COVID-19 pandemic.

Media narratives of teacher supply are therefore shaped not only by the hegemonic, globalizing discourses of policymakers, but also by national and local events which are considered newsworthy by journalists and media outlets. Such negotiations of globalizing policy discourses within this wider national context are particularly evident in one illustrative text from the EMC, published in the right-leaning *The Daily Telegraph*, in which the recruitment of teachers is discussed as part of a national public sector recruitment drive:

Small businesses have been particularly impacted by the pandemic, with 23 percent cutting jobs in the last quarter [...] the Prime Minister has urged more people to take advantage of the career opportunities available in schools, hospitals, prisons and police stations. [...] The Government has promised to recruit 20,000 more police officers, 50,000 nurses and 6,000 doctors, while also boosting teachers' starting salaries to £30,000 by 2022 to improve the calibre of candidates and retention.

(Yorke, 2020)

Whereas plans to recruit police offices, nurses, and doctors are expressed in purely quantitative terms, the recruitment of teachers is constructed in Yorke's reportage as a qualitative problem, with an intention to "improve the calibre of candidates." An alignment can therefore be identified with both global and national policy documents which discursively entangle issues of teacher supply with those of teacher quality. However, in Yorke's text, such globalizing discourses on education are embedded within a wider discussion of employment difficulties, which is primarily intended to address perceived interest amongst the general public in the economic consequences of the COVID-19 pandemic.

Our exploration of *shortage** across the AMC and the EMC therefore revealed the complex relationship between policy constructions of teacher supply, and their interdiscursive reiteration in media texts. Although globalizing discourses which foreground fears around teacher supply and teacher quality were evident in media texts, these themes were subject to a process of mediatization in order to account for national context, and concomitant considerations around newsworthiness. Such findings suggest that media outlets offer a space in which globalizing discourses on education can be negotiated and adapted, if perhaps not completely resisted.

Conclusion

This chapter has served to highlight the complicated relationship between education policy and media texts in the shaping of understandings of education within the public space. While across both Australia and England, we see issues that dominate policy discussions and debates reflected and refracted in media discussions of education, the ways in which they are treated vary. In the case of the Australian policy and media texts, there is largely an assonance in the discussion of teacher shortages, where the problematizations developed in the policy texts are amplified and extended in media reporting. We also, interestingly, see media articles in this context that are focused on teachers substantively *about* issues to do with schooling and education: it is unusual in the AMC to find an article that includes significant discussion around teachers, but that is not either predominantly focused on education. This is very different to the EMC, where many articles are substantively about wider societal issues – most obviously the COVID-19 pandemic – wherein teacher shortages are effectively one variant of a range of other, sometimes more pressing problems. This may, of course, be at least partly a reflection of the particularities of the timeframe addressed by the study, with 2018–2022 including the key pandemic years of 2020 and 2021. However, it is important to note that the

COVID-19 pandemic did not shape media discourses around education in the same way across both Australia and England. Given the different approaches to and effects of pandemic management in the two national contexts, the "airplay" taken up by the pandemic and the associated topics of interest appear very different in the two countries.

Our analysis of the AMC and the EMC illustrates the dominance of media coverage of the COVID-19 pandemic in England between 2020 and 2021, indicating that during this period stories considered newsworthy were, on the whole, directly related to the pandemic. During this period, challenges in particular policy areas that may previously have been reported on as discrete issues – such as educational problems with teacher supply – could be subsumed within the reporting of wider supply and staffing issues associated with the COVID-19 pandemic. From an educational standpoint, such reporting strategies had the effect of compressing educational reflection on the specific, long-term difficulties governments face in addressing teacher shortages within current globalized, neoliberal education climates. Such reporting strategies indicate that media outlets do not simply regurgitate global policy agendas, even when reconfigured by and through national policymakers. Instead, journalists reinscribe policy discourse in accordance with what they perceive to be local agendas and considerations of news values, sometimes in defiance of wider globalizing discourses. Media outlets are therefore actively involved in discursive practices that work to either support or contest politicians' claims. Our findings suggest that the media can hold a space in which globalizing discourses can be challenged or transformed. This is important to note, as it is claimed that the news media exerts a "powerful influence on mass political behaviour" (Ladd & Lenz, 2009, p. 394).

Stepping back from the specific contexts of Australia and England, our study has theoretical implications for future studies concerning the relationship between education policy and its presentation in the media. Our findings support the argument of Rawolle (2010), that there is not a clear and predictable pathway in the mediatization of education policy discourses, but that mediatization can progress across different, uncertain routes. It is not the case that education policy is unproblematically adopted and disseminated by media actors; further research is therefore needed on the relationships between media outlets and policymakers and on their combined, or individual, impact on public perceptions of teachers and teaching. Furthermore, differences between the AMC and EMC in the foregrounding of COVID-19 suggest that the issue of newsworthiness – which has hitherto been somewhat neglected in scholarly studies around the relationship between education policy and media reportage – plays a significant role in journalistic decision-making around educational issues. This finding should have implications for future, comparative studies of media texts across different localities, with greater attention paid to the way in which national events impact on considerations of what is judged to be a "newsworthy" educational issue. As we found with the EMC, national events have the potential to shape educational narratives, shifting the focus of readers from concerns about discrete educational issues to wider societal problems. Our study suggests there is fruitful research to be undertaken to better understand the relationship between media narratives of educational crisis, and narratives of wider social decline.

Undoubtedly, the specific timescale of the two media corpora – covering the period of the COVID-19 pandemic from early 2020 onwards – had a significant influence on our data and, consequently, our analysis and findings. This was not a "normal" period in education history, but a period of rapid upheaval, in which both policymakers and journalists worked to make sense of a complex and unpredictable global catastrophe. Research has indicated that the role played by teachers was often downplayed or neglected in media coverage (Beames et al., 2021), as news outlets focused primarily on the heroism of healthcare workers (Spicksley & Franklin, 2023). Studies by Nerlino (2023) and Kim et al. (2024) have shown that teachers perceived a shift in media constructions of the teaching profession as the COVID-19 pandemic progressed, from initial admiration and construction of teachers as heroic frontline workers, to more negative constructions later. It is possible that both public perceptions and media constructions of teachers during the COVID-19 pandemic could have varied not only with regard to diachronic factors but also according to locality, with media outlets in some countries portraying teachers in a more positive light than others. Indeed, given the findings presented in this chapter, it is perhaps expected that media presentations of teachers during COVID-19 would be – to a certain extent – contingent on national circumstances and wider policies around epidemiological management. However, comparative research exploring the ways in which teachers were presented in the media across different nations is currently limited, indicating a gap in the research that requires addressing.

What is most evident through our analysis is that the relationship between policy and media discourses of education is more fluid than linear. Even around issues such as teacher supply (where there is strong attention across different national contexts on the part of both policymakers and media outlets) a range of different local social and political factors influence, and in some cases interrupt, the transference of ideas from policy to media reportage and back again. Far from providing simple accounts of the "mediatization" (Lingard & Rawolle, 2004) of education policy, our analysis suggests that nuanced and detailed tracking of ideas central to education policy through the varying contexts of media production is required, in order to gain a coherent picture of the role of the media in both shaping and reflecting public discourses of education.

Notes

1 We employed the wildcard symbol (*) to search simultaneously for *shortage* and *shortages*.
2 These numbers are generated by LancsBox and provide an ID number for each concordance line.

References

Agyapong, B., Obuobi-Donkor, G., Burback, L., & Wei, Y. (2022). Stress, burnout, anxiety and depression among teachers: A scoping review. *International Journal of Environmental Research and Public Health*, *19*(17), 10706.

Alexander, R. J. (2012). Moral panic, miracle cures and educational policy: What can we really learn from international comparison? *Scottish Educational Review*, *44*(1), 4–21.

Alhamdan, B., Al-Saadi, K., Baroutsis, A., Du Plessis, A., Hamid, O. M., & Honan, E. (2014). Media representation of teachers across five countries. *Comparative Education*, *50*(4), 490–505.

Allen, R., & Sims, S. (2018). Do pupils from low-income families get low-quality teachers? Indirect evidence from English schools. *Oxford Review of Education*, *44*(4), 441–458.

Apple, M. W. (2004). Creating difference: Neo-liberalism, neo-conservatism and the politics of educational reform. *Educational Policy*, *18*(1), 12–44.

Arvidsson, I., Leo, U., Larsson, A., Håkansson, C., Persson, R., & Björk, J. (2019). Burnout among school teachers: Quantitative and qualitative results from a follow-up study in Southern Sweden. *BMC Public Health*, *19*(1), 1–13.

Australian Institute for Teaching and School Leadership. (2024). *Become a registered teacher*. AITSL. Retrieved January 28, 2024, from https://www.aitsl.edu.au/prepare-to-be-a-teacher/become-a-registered-teacher

Bacchi, C. (2012). Introducing the 'What's the problem represented to be?' approach. In A. Bletsas, & C. Beasley (Eds.), *Engaging with carol bacchi: Strategic interventions and exchanges* (pp. 21–24). University of Adelaide Press.

Bacchi, C., & Goodwin, S. (2016). *Poststructural policy analysis: A guide to practice*. Springer Nature.

Baker, P. (2012). Acceptable bias? Using corpus linguistics methods with critical discourse analysis. *Critical Discourse Studies*, *9*(3), 247–256.

Ball, S. J., Maguire, M., & Braun, A. (2012). *How schools do policy: Policy enactments in secondary schools*. Routledge.

Barnes, M. (2022). Framing teacher quality in the Australian media: The circulation of key political messages? *Educational Review*, *74*(7), 1305–1321.

Baroutsis, A. (2016). Media accounts of school performance: Reinforcing dominant practices of accountability. *Journal of Education Policy*, *31*(5), 567–582.

Baroutsis, A., & Lingard, B. (2017). Counting And comparing school performance: An Analysis of media coverage of PISA in Australia, 2000–2014. *Journal of Education Policy*, *32*(4), 432–449.

Baroutsis, A., & Lingard, B. (2023). *Exploring education policy through newspapers and social media: The politics of mediatisation*. Routledge.

Beames, J. R., Christensen, H., & Werner-Seidler, A. (2021). School teachers: the forgotten frontline workers of Covid-19. *Australasian Psychiatry*, *29*(4), 420–422.

Bednarek, M., & Caple, H. (2017). *The discourse of news values: How news organizations create newsworthiness*. Oxford University Press.

Berkovich, I., & Benoliel, P. (2019). Understanding OECD representations of teachers and teaching: A visual discourse analysis of covers in OECD documents. *Globalisation, Societies and Education*, *17*(3), 132–146.

Blackmore, J., & Thorpe, S. (2003). Media/ting change: The print media's role in mediating education policy in a period of radical reform in Victoria, Australia. *Journal of Education Policy*, *18*(6), 577–595.

Brezina, V., Weill-Tessier, P., & McEnery, T. (2021). *#LancsBox 6.0 [software package]*.

Cabalin, C. (2015). Mediatizing higher education policies: Discourses about quality education in the media. *Critical Studies in Education*, *56*(2), 224–240.

Cohen, J. L. (2010). Teachers in the news: A critical analysis of one US newspaper's discourse on education, 2006–2007. *Discourse: Studies in the Cultural Politics of Education, 31*(1), 105–119.
Commonwealth of Australia Education Ministers Meeting. (2022). *National teacher workforce action plan.* Department of Education.
Craig, C. J. (2017). International teacher attrition: Multiperspective views. *Teaching and Teacher Education, 23*(8), 859–862. https://doi.org/10.1080/13540602.2017.1360860
Creagh, S., Thompson, G., Mockler, N., Stacey, M., & Hogan, A. (2023). Workload, work intensification and time poverty for teachers and school leaders: A systematic research synthesis. *Educational Review*, 1–20. https://doi.org/10.1080/00131911.2023.2196607.
Department for Education UK. (2019). *Teacher recruitment and retention strategy.* DfE.
Department for Education UK. (2024). *How to become a teacher.* DfE.
Doan, S., Steiner, E. D., Pandey, R., & Woo, A. (2023). *teacher well-being and intentions to leave: Finding from the 2023 state of the American teacher survey.* RAND Corporation.
Easthope, C., & Easthope, G. (2000). Intensification, extension and complexity of teachers' workload. *British Journal of Sociology of Education, 21*(1), 43–58.
Edling, S., & Liljestrand, J. (2020, 2020/05/26). Let's talk about teacher education! Analysing the media debates in 2016-2017 on teacher education using Sweden as a case. *Asia-Pacific Journal of Teacher Education, 48*(3), 251–266. https://doi.org/10.1080/1359866X.2019.1631255
Fairclough, N. (1992). *Discourse and social change.* Polity Press.
Fairclough, N. (2000). *New labour, new language?* Routledge.
Gautreaux, M., & Delgado, S. (2016). Portrait of a teach for all (TFA) teacher: Media narratives of the universal TFA teacher in 12 countries. *Education Policy Analysis Archives/Archivos Analíticos De Políticas Educativas, 24*, 1–28.
Hansen, A. (2009). Researching 'teachers in The news': The portrayal of teachers in The british national and regional press. *Education 3–13, 37*(4), 335–347. https://doi.org/10.1080/03004270903099900
Hattam, R., Prosser, B., & Brady, K. (2009). Revolution or backlash? The mediatisation of education policy in Australia. *Critical Studies in Education, 50*(2), 159–172.
Henry, J. (2023, November 5). Newly-qualified teachers quit UK for schools abroad due to abject pay and conditions. *The Guardian (UK).*
Hopfenbeck, T. N., & Görgen, K. (2017). The politics of PISA: The media, policy and public responses in Norway and England. *European Journal of Education Research, Development and Policy, 52*(2), 192–205.
Karamperidou, D., Brossard, M., Peirolo, S., & Richardson, D. (2020). *Time to teach: Teacher attendance and time on task in Eastern and Southern Africa.* UNICEF Office of Research-Innocenti,
Kemmis, S., Wilkinson, J., Edwards-Groves, C., Hardy, I., Grootenboer, P., & Bristol, L. (2014). *Changing practices, changing education.* Springer.
Keogh, J., & Garrick, B. (2011). Creating catch 22: Zooming in and Zooming out on the discursive constructions of teachers in a news article. *International Journal of Qualitative Studies in Education, 24*(4), 419–434.
Kim, L. E., Owusu, K., & Asbury, K. (2024). The ups and downs in perceived societal appreciation of the teaching profession during COVID-19: A longitudinal trajectory analysis. *British Educational Research Journal, 50*(1), 93–111. https://doi.org/https://doi.org/10.1002/berj.3914
Kinman, G., Wray, S., & Strange, C. (2011). Emotional labour, burnout and job satisfaction in UK teachers: The role of workplace social support. *Educational Psychology, 31*(7), 843–856.

Knodel, P., Martens, K., & Niemann, D. (2013). PISA As an ideational roadmap for policy change: Exploring Germany and England in a comparative perspective. *Globalisation, Societies and Education, 11*(3), 421–441.

Ladd, J. M., & Lenz, G. S. (2009). Exploiting a rare communication shift to document the persuasive power of the news media. *American Journal of Political Science, 53*(2), 394–410. https://doi.org/10.1111/j.1540-5907.2009.00377.x

Lewis, S. (2017, 2017/05/04). Governing schooling through 'what works': The OECD's PISA for schools. *Journal of Education Policy, 32*(3), 281–302. https://doi.org/10.1080/02680939.2016.1252855

Lingard, B., & Rawolle, S. (2004). Mediatizing educational policy: The journalistic field, science policy, and cross-field effects. *Journal of Education Policy, 19*(3), 361–380.

Lingard, B., & Sellar, S. (2016). The changing organizational and global significance of the OECD's education work. In K. Mundy, A. Green, B. Lingard, & A. Verger (Eds.), *The handbook of global education policy* (pp. 357–373). Wiley.

Madigan, D. J., & Kim, L. E. (2021). Does teacher burnout affect students? A systematic review of its association with academic achievement and student-reported outcomes. *International Journal of Educational Research, 105*, 101714.

Mautner, G. (2009). Corpora and critical discourse analysis. In P. Baker (Ed.), *Contemporary corpus linguistics* (pp. 32–46). Bloomsbury.

McLeod, J. (1989). Debating English curriculum in the 1980s: Questions about ideology, discourses and commonsense. *Critical Studies in Education, 31*(1), 107–120.

Meyer, H.-D., & Benavot, A. (2013). PISA And the globalization of education governance: Some puzzles And problems. In H.-D. Meyer, & A. Benavot (Eds.), *PISA, power and policy: The emergency of global education governance* (pp. 9–26). Symposium Books Oxford.

Mills, M., & Keddie, A. (2010). Cultural reductionism and the media: Polarising discourses around schools, violence and masculinity in an age of terror. *Oxford Review of Education, 36*(4), 427–444.

Mockler, N. (2014). Simple solutions to complex problems: Moral panic and the fluid shift from 'equity' to 'quality' in education. *Review of Education, 2*(2), 115–143.

Mockler, N. (2022). *Constructing teacher identities: How the print media define and represent teachers and their work*. Bloomsbury Academic.

Mockler, N. (2023). *Constructing teacher identities: Print media representations of Australian teachers 1996 to 2020* Sarah Fielden Lecture, University of Manchester, March 30, 2023.

Nerlino, E. (2023). "From Heroes to Scapegoats": Teacher Perceptions of the Media and Public's Portrayal of Teachers during COVID-19. *The Educational Forum, 87*(4), 282–303.

Office for Standards in Education UK (2019). *Teacher well-being at work in schools and further education providers*. Ofsted.

Pettigrew, M., & MacLure, M. (1997). The press, public knowledge and the grant maintained schools policy. *British Journal of Educational Studies, 45*(4), 392–405.

Precel, N. (2023, March 11). 'Just up and quitting': Victorian schools short 1000 teachers. *The Age*.

Punakallio, E., & Dervin, F. (2015). The best and most respected teachers in the world? Counternarratives about the 'Finnish miracle of education' in the press. *Power and Education, 7*(3), 306–321.

Rawolle, S. (2010). Understanding the mediatisation of educational policy as practice. *Critical Studies in Education, 51*(1), 21–39.

Richards, K. A. R., Hemphill, M. A., & Templin, T. J. (2018). Personal and contextual factors related to teachers' experience with stress and burnout. *Teachers and Teaching, 24*(7), 768–787.

Richardson, J. E. (2007). *Analysing newspapers: An approach from critical discourse analysis*. Palgrave.

Rizvi, F., & Lingard, B. (2010). *Globalizing education policy*. Routledge.

Schleicher, A. (2011). Building a High-Quality Teaching Profession: Lessons from around the World. *OECD*. https://doi.org/http://dx.doi.org/10.1787/9789264113046-en

Shine, K. (2015). Are Australian teachers making the grade? A study of news coverage of NAPLAN testing. *Media International Australia, 154*(1), 25–33.

Shine, K. (2017). 'Everything is negative': Schoolsteachers' perceptions of news coverage of education. *Journalism, 21*(11), 1694–1709.

Singh, P., Thomas, S., & Harris, J. (2013). Recontextualising policy discourses: A Bernsteinian perspective on policy interpretation, translation, enactment. *Journal of Education Policy, 28*(4), 465–480.

Sørensen, T. B., Ydesen, C., & Robertson, S. L. (2021). Re-reading the OECD and education: The emergence of a global governing complex–an introduction. *Globalisation, Societies and Education, 19*(2), 99–107.

Spicksley, K., & Franklin, E. (2023). Who works on the 'frontline'? Comparing constructions of 'frontline' work before and during the COVID-19 pandemic. *Applied Corpus Linguistics, 3*(3), 100059. https://doi.org/10.1016/j.acorp.2023.100059

Stack, M. (2007). Representing school success and failure: Media coverage of international tests. *Policy Futures in Education, 5*(1), 100–110.

Takayama, K. (2008). The politics of International league tables: PISA In Japan's achievement crisis debate. *Comparative Education, 44*(4), 387–407.

Takayama, K. (2010). Politics of externalization in reflexive times: Reinventing Japanese education reform discourses through Finnish PISA success. *Comparative Education Review, 54*(1), 51–75.

Tamir, E., & Davidson, R. (2011). Staying above the fray: Framing and conflict in the coverage of education policy debates. *American Journal of Education, 117*(2), 233–265.

Thomas, S. (2003). 'The trouble with our Schools': A media construction of public discourses on Queensland schools. *Discourse: Studies in the Cultural Politics of Education, 24*(1), 19–33.

Ulmer, J. B. (2016). Re-framing teacher evaluation discourse in the media: An analysis and narrative-based proposal. *Discourse: Studies in the Cultural Politics of Education, 37*(1), 43–55.

UNESCO. (2015). *Education for All Global Monitoring Report: Policy Paper 19*. UNESCO.

UNESCO (2023). *The teachers we need for the education we want: The global imperative to reverse the teacher shortage*.

UNESCO Institute of Statistics (2022). *Covid-19 education response: Dashboards on the global monitoring of school closures caused by the COVID-19 pandemic*.

Viac, C., & Fraser, P. (2020). *Teachers' well-being: A framework for data collection and analysis*. OECD.

Vickers, M. (2015). Neglecting the evidence: Are we expecting too much from quality teaching? In H. Proctor, P. Brownlee, & P. Freebody (Eds.), *Controversies in education: Orthodoxy and heresy in policy and practice* (pp. 81–89). Springer.

Waldow, F. (2009). What PISA did and did not do: Germany After the 'PISA-shock. *European Educational Research Journal, 8*(3), 476–483.

Waldow, F., Takayama, K., & Sung, Y. (2014). Rethinking the pattern of external policy referencing: media discourses over the Asian Tigers' PISA success in Australia, Germany and South Korea. *Comparative Education, 50*(3), 302–321.

Wallace, M. (1993). Discourse of derision: The role of the mass media within the education policy process. *Journal of Education Policy, 8*(4), 321–337.

Warmington, P., & Murphy, R. (2004). Could do better? Media depictions of UK educational assessment results. *Journal of Education Policy, 19*(3), 285–299.

Watkins, K. (2000). *The Oxfam education report*. Oxfam.

Whitehead, A., Ryba, K., & O'Driscoll, M. (2000). Burnout among New Zealand primary school teachers. *New Zealand Journal of Psychology, 29*(2), 52–52.

Wilkins, C. (2015). Education reform in England: Quality and equity in the performative school. *International Journal of Inclusive Education, 19*(11), 1143–1160.

Yemini, M., & Gordon, N. (2017). Media representations of national and international standardized testing in the Israeli education system. *Discourse: Studies in the Cultural Politics of Education, 38*(2), 262–276.

Yorke, H. (2020, July 30). Public sector job drive key to PM's 'build back better' plan. *The Daily Telegraph*.

Part II
Labor Market Policies and Teachers' Careers
Shifting Toward Flexibility and Fragmentation

5 Teacher Shortages and Contract Teachers in the Global South

Amita Chudgar and Martial Dembélé

Introduction

At the time of writing this chapter, echoes of UNESCO's Director-General Audrey Azoulay's October 2022 remarks are still reverberating in the global education policy discourse. In the context of a global learning crisis and the urgent need to transform education, the Director-General's vision statement in 2022 noted that a fundamental change is needed in the considerations of the role and the treatment of teachers. Yet challenges of teacher shortage remain vast. For instance, the recent UNESCO Teacher Task Force report released during the 14th Policy Dialogue Forum, on February 26, 2024, projects that 44 million additional teachers are needed globally to reach the goal of attaining universal primary and secondary education by 2030 (UNESCO, 2023). The region with the largest deficit of teachers is still Sub-Saharan Africa (5.4 million teachers are needed at primary level, and 11.1 million teachers at secondary level), followed by Southern Asia (1.7 million and 5.3 million teachers at primary and secondary levels, respectively). For perspective, the size of the teacher labor force in the entire European Union is a little over 5 million (Eurostat, n.d.), and the size of the teacher labor force in the United States is just over 3 million (U.S. Bureau of Labor Statistics, n.d.). Collectively across the world, many countries dealing with multiple crises are also facing the daunting prospect of increasing their teacher labor force in magnitudes that far exceed the entire teaching labor force of affluent and relatively well-funded educational systems.

In this chapter, we focus on contract teacher policies as a response to teacher shortages and the resultant implications for the education system in low- and middle-income countries (LIMCs), given the magnitude and urgency associated with considerations of teacher shortage and contract-based hiring in these countries. It is important to distinguish between different types of teacher employment arrangements from the outset. Historically, civil service or regular government teachers, also referred to as civil/public service employees or civil/public servants (*fonctionnaires* in French), have been dominant. These are individuals hired by government authorities, with permanent employment status. The chapter's primary focus is government contract teachers hired by public authorities, whether on fixed or open-ended terms, who do not have civil/public

DOI: 10.4324/9781003441731-8

service status. The phenomenon emerged in the public sector in the 1990s and has not waned in most countries. Hired on such terms, contract teachers, as we will see, typically have poor employment conditions compared to their civil service colleagues or regular government teachers. Finally, while it is not central in our chapter, we also acknowledge and briefly discuss contract-based hiring of teachers in the private sector in many of these countries. Throughout the chapter, unless we specify otherwise, we use the term "contract teachers" to refer to contract teachers hired by government authorities. We specify clearly when we are discussing contract teachers working in private schools.

While we focus on LMICs, it is important to acknowledge that the concerns of teacher shortage and related mechanisms for alternative forms of teacher hiring have also been present in high-income countries, including the United States, France, several Canadian provinces, etc. In the United States for instance, teacher vacancy in the last few years has increased rapidly. According to a recent report, schools across this country collectively have about 55,000 vacant teacher positions.[1]

In the United States, scholars have noted concerns about shortages of mathematics and science teachers or teachers with special education training (Dee & Goldhaber, 2017). In recent years in this country, the challenge of teacher shortage has also been exacerbated by a large turnover in the teaching profession (e.g., Goldhaber & Theobald, 2023) and declining enrollment in teacher education programs (e.g., McMurdock, 2022). This has led to the emergence of what is often called "Grow Your Own" (GYO) programs which help create a local and diversified supply of teachers across the country (Edwards & Kraft, 2024). In their recent review of the literature, Edwards and Kraft found that such GYO programs are prevalent across 40 out of the 50 states of the United States. They also note that "[t]he single, near universal feature of GYO initiatives is that they aim to increase teacher supply by targeting individuals who work in, live in, or attend schools near a specific district. Outside of this, GYO programs vary widely in their purposes, participants, and program features" (Edwards & Kraft, 2024, p. 3). This US-focused literature review does not acknowledge the widely prevalent contract-based hiring in the Global South where several issues that are now being considered in the United States are extensively studied, especially nuances of teacher demand and supply in local communities and the implication of these practices for students, teachers, and school systems. In addition, in the US context, various other measures have also long existed to bring teachers into schools facing urgent needs, including alternate certification routes and residency programs.[2]

It is easy to see several parallels between the contract teacher phenomenon in the Global South and various aspects of the GYO and TFA programs in the United States. In other words, some of the concerns we explore in this chapter are common across the world with some context-specific variation. Yet, there are also important distinctions; to our knowledge, US teachers hired through these alternate routes do not face similar job precarity that contract teachers generally face in our study context. While we acknowledge concerns of teacher shortage in the Global North and varying responses to these concerns, many aligned with the general umbrella term of "contract-based hiring," for this chapter we focus on the Global South where there is a longer and more well-established literature on these questions and where in absolute terms (of both size and cost) these concerns are more acute.

The central goal of the chapter is to explain and explore the complex phenomenon of contract-based hiring in LMIC education systems, with a primary attention to this phenomenon in the government sector. In doing so the chapter embraces a system-level perspective by first discussing the various interrelated considerations regarding teacher shortages. We then unpack contract-based teacher hiring as a response to these shortages, and we note how these responses while similar can also present important context-specific variation. We devote the third and final section of the chapter to broader implications of teacher shortages and contract-based hiring as a policy solution. We draw on existing literature, including our own works and reports by various international organizations to observe how this decidedly inadequate response to an urgent challenge of teacher shortage has yielded mixed results. We conclude with thoughts on future research and next steps for the field.

Teacher Shortages, Three Complex and Interrelated Considerations

The challenge of growing the teacher labor force brings to fore three complex and interrelated considerations: teacher education and training, teacher remuneration, and teacher distribution. Addressing teacher shortage typically requires education systems to invest more heavily in pre-service teacher preparation. In many education systems pre-service teacher education is connected with the tertiary education system. This makes it a complex and costly investment to rapidly scale-up while maintaining quality. In recent years, for instance, scholars have observed the ways in which lack of adequate government funding and oversight in pre-service teacher education has resulted in proliferation of low-quality private teacher education providers in many countries in the Global South (e.g., CETE, 2023; Sirois et al., 2021a, b).

Once these future teachers are trained and join the teaching profession, their salary bills can create a significant pressure on current expenditure budgets in education. These extensive financial commitments associated with growing the teacher labor force can be made more acute by historical policies, often imposed by donors, such as the World Bank and the International Monterey Fund (IMF) since the 1990s which have required countries to systematically disinvest from their public service provision, including their teacher labor force as a part of financial restructuring (for a brief review, see Chudgar et al., 2014). A 1996 report by the International Labor Organisation (ILO) documents the impact of these financial restructuring efforts. The report explains that the key message to governments in several parts of Africa and Asia was "to reduce the teacher wage bill, particularly by keeping teachers' salaries low and replacing experienced, more highly paid teachers with unqualified ones" (ILO 1996, pp. 43–44).

The challenge of growing the teacher labor force is also complicated by the fact that teacher shortage can often be very specific, requiring either particular types of teacher preparation, or requiring also specific policies for allocating teachers to specific areas or students with specific needs. This causes challenges of teacher distribution, or the problem of finding teachers who are appropriately suited for specific needs of children. For instance, a push for universal primary enrollment since the 1990s has meant that many countries now have a far greater need for qualified teachers at secondary levels. These needs are often felt acutely in fields like science, mathematics, technology education, and in some instances also in languages. For instance, UNESCO's 2023 report on Global Teacher Shortage notes that out of 10 new global recruits 7 are required for secondary education. The same report also notes that globally 85% of secondary-level teachers have minimum required qualifications and just over 60% in Sub-Saharan Africa (UNESCO, 2023). Even though belated, the dedication to attend to children with special learning needs has created a welcome but challenging need for teachers who are trained to work with these children. The unprecedented global refugee crises, fueled by wars, persecution, and climate change have similarly created a need for teachers who are able to support children learning under these unprecedented circumstances.

Contract-based Hiring: A Response to Teacher Shortage and Related Considerations

Contract-based teacher hiring by governments, which is the primary focus of this chapter, has emerged as a relatively common response to the above issues related to teacher shortage. Briefly, contract-based hiring policies allow education systems to circumvent teacher preparation, pay lower salaries, and recruit teachers from non-traditional, local community routes to urgently and affordably fill teaching positions in public (government) schools. Since in most countries government teachers are part of the regular government service (often referred to as civil service), the contract-based hiring in public schools creates a two-tiered system of civil service (regular) teachers and contract teachers. Civil service teachers (usually) have a permanent employment status from the day they are hired. In opposition, contract teachers do not enjoy such a status, and their contracts can be fixed-term or open-ended. Contract teachers are found in both the public and private sectors. Contract-based hiring has historically been a common and widely prevalent practice in private schools. We acknowledge some nuances below, though that is not our primary focus.

That contract-based teacher hiring for public education has contributed significantly to widening access to primary education in resource-constrained contexts is a consensual fact. For instance, Bernard et al. (2004) showed that it allowed 270,000 additional children to attend school in Niger in 2002, representing almost 50% more children in schools than would have been possible otherwise. The gain in Mali was 230,000 in 2003. This was achieved through "a steady increase in the number of primary school teachers in [both] countries between 1997/1998 and 2002/2003. The teacher stock was more than doubled in Mali, recording an average annual increase of 18.3%, and it was nearly doubled in Niger, with an average annual increase of 12.1%. [...] This growth trend has continued after 2002/2003" (Dembélé & Mellouki, 2013, p. 41).

While hiring teachers on contract basis may appear to be a viable solution to the problem of teacher shortage, this policy creates several challenges of its own. As noted in the introduction, the Global South context is the primary focus of this chapter, but it is important to acknowledge that concerns of teacher shortage and related mechanisms for alternative forms of teacher hiring have also been present in the Global North.

Contract-Based Hiring: A Common but Complex Response to Teacher Shortage

The practice of contract-based teacher hiring is a worldwide phenomenon. It has a long history in many countries, regardless of income level (see Duthilleul, 2005). What is new is the massive recruitment of contract teachers in the public education sector in developing countries in the drive toward universal primary education following the 1990 World Conference on Education For All (EFA) in Jomtien. Initially conceived as a stopgap measure and a cost-effective way to increase the number of teachers in a context of increased social demand and imposed reduction of public expenditure on education, the policy has been institutionalized in most countries that have resorted to it, leading to the fast growth of contract teachers while the proportion of civil/public service (i.e., permanent) teachers declined drastically in just a few years in some of them (Dembélé & Mellouki, 2013).

Magnitude of Contract-Based Hiring: A Glimpse of Recent Statistics

UNESCO's International Teacher Task Force for Education 2030 (2020) report provides one of the most current and comprehensive treatments of the contract teacher phenomenon in the sub-Saharan Africa region. Drawing from 23 country case studies, this report makes several important observations about the contract teacher phenomenon.

For instance, the report notes that in Kenya 37% of all teachers at the primary level are hired on contract basis. In Zambia 15% of teachers are working on contract basis and in Sudan contract teacher proportions are at 9% and 17% at the primary and secondary levels, respectively. In places like the Gambia or Uganda, the number of contract teachers has declined but still remains noteworthy.

In Francophone countries, however, there has been a sizable growth in contractual recruitment since the mid-1990s. For instance, in Chad, the *maîtres communautaires* (community teachers) were 64% and 36% of the primary and secondary level teaching force. Cameroon has hired several cohorts of contract teachers since the policy was introduced in 2006. In Benin, the report notes "the quasi-disappearance of teachers with civil service status due to retirement and limited recruitment," with an increase in teachers hired on contract basis where they now account for 40% of the primary teaching force. As the report shows, in Burkina Faso also the proportion of contract teachers grew rapidly, from 0.6% in 2002/2003 to 81% in 2015. In Mali, the trends have somewhat reversed since 2010 with a decreasing reliance on contract teachers. In Guinea as well contract teachers represent 20% of the primary teaching force due to the transfer of contract position to civil service position more than a decade ago.

A recent report on contract teachers from India (CETE, 2023) discusses how the practice of hiring contract teachers evolved in the Indian state of Rajasthan as an effort to mobilize youth in remote communities where government teachers were unwilling to work. The authors document the various ways in which this low-cost, locally driven model continued to get formally enshrined in various state education systems often creating a parallel teaching track. According to them, in India "11% of government school teachers are contractually employed." (CETE, 2023, p. 5) The report goes on to state that in some specific states[3] and Union Territories between 24% and 69% of the government school teachers are contractual.

Contract-based Hiring: Common Practices and Context-Specific Variations

In general, scholars have observed that those hired on contract basis tend to be less well-paid compared to regular civil service teachers, receiving as little as 25–33% of civil service salary. Contract teachers often have similar levels of education as regular teachers, but have limited pre- or in-service teacher professional development, ranging from a few days to a few weeks. In some instances, however, the training has been longer notably in places like Burkina Faso and Guinea. These teachers are also often hired locally and are younger and less experienced (see Chudgar et al., 2014, for a systematic review of these trends).

While the contract teachers are clearly distinguished from regular or civil service teachers in the above manner, the distinctions also offer glimpses into the specific ways in which these teachers are hired, trained, or supported and into how they can vary tremendously from location to location. The UNESCO's International Teacher Task Force For Education 2030 report notes that there is "a fair amount of variation in what the term 'contract teacher' applies to within and across countries, and indeed who is considered to be a contract teacher due to context-specific hiring conditions" (UNESCO, 2020, p. 23). Depending on the country context, particularly in Anglophone African countries, contract teachers can be retired teachers working on open-ended contracts and drawing retirement benefits, or they could be volunteer parents and community helpers with limited to no teacher training. In Francophone African countries, as the report explains, there are various types of contract-based arrangements depending on the country. While government contract teachers are common, in various countries part-time teachers, volunteers, and community teachers are also identified as contract teachers.

What these distinctions within the term "contract teachers" highlight is that in general we may expect contract teachers to be less experienced, but this may not be true if they are retired teachers. We may expect them to be less-trained, but this too will depend on if the teacher is a student teacher, a retired teacher, an expatriate teacher, or truly a community member or volunteer with no teacher training. Their contract conditions make their jobs uncertain, but here again there appear to be variations in the length of contract, and if and how they may be converted to regular arrangements depending on the country. Finally, an important variation is the source of remuneration. Contract teachers paid by the local management, school, parents, or community may find different employment conditions and support compared to those who are on regular government payroll.

Contract Teachers in Private Schools: An Understudied Area

A category of contract-based hiring our chapter highlights, and which has hitherto been understudied in the literature, are teachers who work in the private sector. With a rapid growth in the private education sector in many countries in the Global South, private schools have become significant employers of teachers. For instance, Chudgar and Sakamoto (2021) note that in India private schools employ nearly 3 million teachers. While large-scale and systematic understanding of private school teachers' working conditions in India and elsewhere is limited, in general it is documented that these teachers also work on contract basis (or without a job guarantee). While the actual private school environment (in terms of infrastructure, or students) may be better than or comparable to public school environment, in terms of employment conditions such as salary, benefits, and job security, private school teachers fare poorly compared to public school teachers (e.g., CETE, 2023; Chudgar & Sakamoto, 2021; UNESCO, 2020).

Implications of Teacher Shortages and Contract-based Hiring

After discussing contract teachers as one widely exercised policy response to teacher shortage, we turn our attention to the broader implications of both teacher shortages, and practices such as contract-based hiring on teachers, students, and education systems. We divide this discussion into three parts.

Unequal Distribution of Trained and Qualified Teachers

A deeply problematic feature of teacher shortages and contract-based hiring is that it is more commonly experienced by communities and children who are otherwise already marginalized. These phenomena have important distributional implications that ultimately may impact educational opportunities available to children most in need of greater investment and support.

The most important inequality resulting from teacher shortages, and contract-based hiring, when resorted to, is that significant financial resources are allocated unevenly toward children with more privileges and those in greater need. This uneven allocation of resources happens through at least two related channels. As noted previously, the challenges of teacher shortage are more likely to affect children and communities which are rural, remote, and otherwise underserved. These are also the communities whose teachers are either allocated on contract basis (receiving lower salaries) or less experienced and less trained (on a lower salary schedule). Together these mechanisms result in unfavorable distribution of financial resources to such communities. For instance, in an extensive analysis of more than 20 education systems, Luschei and Chudgar (2016) documented that teachers teaching the more marginalized children (by socio-economic status, parental education, language) also tended to be less experienced and less qualified.

The unfavorable distribution is not just financial. A related feature of such teacher allocation is that teachers with more qualification and experience are unlikely to be teaching in the context where learners need maximum support. For instance, the challenges of finding teachers to teach indigenous languages in Mexico are well documented (e.g., Santibañez, 2016). While there is a policy in place to assign teachers who speak indigenous languages to teach children in schools that offer education in indigenous languages, often the teachers and students do not speak the same indigenous language. In the same manner, children who are refugees or affected by conflicts are often deeply underserved in education systems that receive them, as their teachers may not be able to communicate in their language, or may not be trained to deal with their complex, trauma affected background (e.g., Richardson, 2018). In Cambodia, the Khmer Rouge regime targeted qualified teachers; so, after the regime ended and schools re-opened in former areas of conflict, it was difficult to prepare/qualify a new batch of teachers quickly. This led to reliance on contract teachers (called *kru jat-tang* or appointed teachers, or *kru kij-sanaya* or contract teachers) (Duthilleul, 2005; Geeves & Bredenberg, 2005). So, while the teachers in this instance may have had language and cultural familiarity, they lacked the benefit of professional development. In general, because teacher shortages are more acute in remote, rural, and otherwise challenging locations, contract teachers and less trained and qualified teachers often find themselves working in schools with limited resources and infrastructure and schools with multi-grade classrooms. A 2010 case study from India for instance observed a contract teacher teaching in a classroom with children from preschool to grade 7 all in the same room (Raval et al., 2010). We turn next to exploring the implications of these practices for student learning and the teaching profession.

Implications for Student Learning: Mixed Evidence

A lot has been and continues to be said and written about the quality and effectiveness of contract teachers versus teachers with permanent/civil service status during the past two decades (see e.g., Atherton & Kingdon, 2010; Bernard et al., 2004; Bourdon et al., 2006, 2010; Chandra, 2015; Chudgar, 2015; Chudgar et al., 2014; Duflo et al., 2015; Lei et al., 2018; Michaelova & Wechtler, 2006; Muralidharan & Sundararaman, 2013). There is, however, no consensus in the literature.

In their synthesis of PASEC[4] data, Bernard et al. (2004) concluded that "there are no significant differences related to teacher status in terms of pedagogical effectiveness. When observed, the differences are moderate and are not systematically in favor of a particular category of teacher" (p. 14). On the contrary, in their survey-based study of the relative effectiveness and costs of contract and regular teachers in India, Atherton and Kingdon (2010) found that "contract teachers are substantially more effective than regular teachers in [the state of Uttar Pradesh] and weakly more effective than regular teachers in [the state of] Bihar" (p. 14), despite working in less favorable conditions, namely, more deprived communities, schools and children. They put forward two possible explanations for this: "One way through which contract teachers may have beneficial effects on child learning is by lowering pupil-teacher ratios and reducing or eliminating multi-grade teaching. [...] An additional possible explanation is that contract teachers, due to their short-term insecure contracts which can be terminated, face greater accountability pressures and thus exhibit more effort than regular teachers" (pp. 14 and 15). They argue further that "[i]t could be that contract teachers are of a different type than regular teachers; for example, lower salaries of contract teachers may imply that only persons intrinsically motivated towards teaching children take these low paid jobs, whereas regular teachers are individuals attracted more by the high salaries of regular teacher posts but have less intrinsic motivation for teaching" (p. 20). This latter explanation is not supported by Duflo et al. (2015). These researchers set up and studied an experimental program in Kenya "under which school committees at randomly selected [...] schools were funded to hire an additional teacher on an annual contract renewable conditional on performance, outside normal Ministry of Education civil-service channels, at one-quarter normal compensation levels. For students randomly assigned to stay with existing classes, test scores did not increase significantly, despite a reduction in class size from 82 to 44 on average. In contrast, scores increased for students assigned to be taught by locally-hired contract teachers" (p. 2).

Duflo et al. attributed these positive results in part to contract teachers being less absent and more hardworking than their civil service colleagues "because they believed this would help them obtain a civil-service position" (Duflo et al., 2015, p. 18). In other words, the contract teachers in this study were extrinsically motivated. Muralidharan and Sundararaman (2013) also provide experimental evidence from India showing that "the marginal product of contract teachers is positive, and [refuting] the conventional view that [contract] teachers will not help improve learning" (p. 15). Finally, a more recent study aimed at estimating the effects of contract teachers (versus civil service teachers) on student achievement in rural Western China found that "contract teachers have a negative effect on gains in student performance on standardised examinations in mathematics and Chinese relative to civil service teachers" (Lei et al., 2018, p. 302).

From the foregoing, and as suggested by Chudgar (2015) as well as Lei et al. (2018), it appears that the evidence from studies comparing the effectiveness of contract versus regular teachers is largely inconclusive, and this may be in part because context matters; and so do teacher characteristics and contract types. Chudgar (2015) for instance shows how the association between contract-based teaching and student learning is negative (Benin and Cameroon), positive, only with some specific controls (Mali and Chad), and consistently positive (Guinea) where the contract system is well organized and implemented with adequate teacher support.

A striking observation is that the studies that find positive effects of contract teachers on student learning are primarily experimental ones. But we know that taking experimental programs to scale is generally a challenging task, especially in education. We also know that randomized control trials are not always feasible in this sector; and even when they are, scale is limited to a particular context, making it hard to generalize the results. One thing is sure, the debate remains unsettled.

Implications for the Teaching Profession: Status, Composition, and Turnover/Attrition

Another aspect of the debate to which we now turn has to do with the effects of contract-based hiring on the composition, status, and attractiveness of the teaching profession, and on teacher attrition and retention. We do so in reference to the useful distinction that the Organization for Economic Co-operation and Development (OECD) drew between two basic models shaping teacher employment in the public sector in its oft-cited and still largely current *Teachers Matter* report: career-based and position-based. We summarize them in Table 5.1.

The situation in several countries has evolved since 2005 due to increasing teacher shortages. Nowadays, countries such as France are resorting to contract-based hiring (see for instance Bertron et al., 2021; Cour des comptes, 2018; Pons, 2021). In this country, between 2010–2011 and 2017–2018, the number of contract teachers increased by 24%, against 0.6% for permanent teachers. However, the above distinction remains valid. In fact, as the OECD argued, no country is a pure case of either model.

In low-income countries that were French colonies, public sector employment, including in education, was shaped by the career-based model until

Table 5.1 Basic models of teacher employment in the public sector.

	Career-based	Position-based
Features	• Initial entry at a young age, based on academic credentials and/or a civil service examination • Demanding entry criteria • Expectation of entire working life in the public service • Teacher deployment according to requirements; and assignments to teaching positions follow principles and procedures of centralized bureaucratic deployment rather than discretion of local school administrators • For promotion, use of a system of grades attached to individual rather than a specific position • Often relatively low starting salaries but clear pathway to higher ones • Usually relatively generous pension schemes • Public-sector employment often seen as superior to private-sector employment on criteria such as average salary, job security, and pension benefits • Generally no problems of teacher supply as usually more applicants than positions available.	• Focus on selecting (by external recruitment or internal promotion) the best-suited candidate for each position • Access opened to a wide range of ages, to entry from other careers • Movement from teaching to other jobs and later returns are not uncommon • Often attractive initial salaries but tendency to level off relatively early in the career • Career advancement tied to competing successfully for vacancies • Number of higher-level vacancies usually restricted • Decentralization of personnel selection and management to schools or local authorities
Concerns/ shortcomings	• Disconnect between initial teacher education (ITE) and school needs • Lack of emphasis on competencies needed for effective teaching in entry selection criteria • After tenure, no strong incentive to continue developing professionally • Limited school capacity and incentives to respond to diverse local needs due to strong emphasis on regulations • Lack of appeal to individuals uncertain to commit early to a lifetime teaching career or with experience in other careers	• Teacher recruitment problems, especially in areas like mathematics, science and information and communication technology, with attractive opportunities in other occupations • Market-like employment conditions but lack of capacity and flexibility to compete on private sector terms • Difficulty in retaining a core of experienced teachers beyond the 30–40-year-old age bracket • High staff turnover, especially in schools located in disadvantaged or unpopular areas • Greater disparities among schools in terms of teacher qualifications and experience due to less reliance on regulation than career-based systems in staff assignment to schools

(Continued)

Table 5.1 (Continued)

	Career-based	Position-based
Recommended policy responses	• Stronger connections between ITE, selection, and professional development • More flexible employment positions • Offering possibilities for external recruitment • More scope to local education authorities and school principals for personnel decisions • Management by objectives	• Greater emphasis on system-wide criteria for staff selection, performance evaluation, and building career pathways • Comparatively greater emphasis on the selection and training of principals and other school leaders given their critical role in personnel management • Provision of significantly more resources to schools in disadvantaged or unpopular areas for them to compete for quality teachers in a market-like system • Need for much more differentiation in salaries and working conditions in order to attrach the types of teachers in short supply
Examples of countries where model is dominant	France, Japan, Korea, and Spain	Canada, Sweden, Switzerland, and the United Kingdom

Source: OECD (2005, pp. 11–12).

the late 1980s or early 1990s. Since then, and under the structural adjustment programs imposed by the World Bank and the IMF, and in response to EFA objectives and the Millennium Development Goal 2 (Achieve Universal Primary Education by 2015), most of them implemented contract teacher policies as presented earlier in this chapter. However, the contractualization models, still in place in several of these countries, do not have all the features of the position-based model. Selecting the best-suited candidates is clearly not a focus; there is an age limit (usually 35 years) to be recruited into public service either as a civil servant or a State contractual; and, as we already indicated, the salaries of contract teachers are low compared to those of their civil servant colleagues. This resulted in the emergence of two-tiered teacher workforces progressively dominated by contract teachers. In countries such as Burkina Faso, Mali, Niger, and Senegal, there was a complete reversal of proportions in just a few years, with fewer and fewer teachers with civil service status. However, where contract teachers progressively formed a critical mass, they forced the government to create pathways to become civil servants (see Dembélé & Mellouki, 2013). Burkina Faso, a country that resisted massive contractualization until the early 2000s, went a step further. Indeed, after a decade and a half of implementation, the government made the decision to grant civil service status to all 16,000 state contract teachers as of January 1, 2016, thus putting an end to the policy.

One of the most visible effects of contract-based hiring is the segmentation of the teaching force engendered by the multiplicity of types of contract teachers in the same national or local context. In some cases, this has led to its recomposition, particularly in former French colonies in Sub-Saharan Africa (see Dembélé & Mellouki, 2013). As documented by Dembélé and Mellouki in four French-speaking West African countries, attrition, which is usually low in career-based systems in part due to job security, emerged as another visible effect of contractualization. Chandra's (2015) review of the implications of contract teaching in India suggests this may be the case in that country too.

In other words, staff turnover is a reality in the contract-based systems put in place in the Global South, just as it is a concern in position-based systems in the Global North. As already noted above, contract teachers are more often than not assigned to hard-to-staff, rural or remote schools. In addition, they have uncertain career prospects; which makes it difficult to develop a long-term professional project in teaching. The combination of these predicaments translates into precarity, precariousness, and "proletarization."

Drawing on Huberman (1993), Dembélé and Mellouki (2013) argued that "[h]igh turnover and difficulties in retaining highly experienced teachers must be of particular concern given the time it generally takes for an individual to complete the initial phases of teaching" (p. 40). In Huberman's model of a teacher's career, these phases span a period of survival and discovery (the first two or three years), followed by a period of stabilization and consolidation of a pedagogical repertoire (fourth to sixth years). A key event usually occurs during the stabilization and consolidation phase: the individual makes a definite or durable commitment to the profession. This phase is followed by a long period (years 7–25) of diversification, experimentation, and reassessment. It is during this long period that a teacher attains professional maturity. Indicators of maturity include (i) attempts to increase one's impact in the classroom; (ii) embarking on a series of personal experiments by diversifying one's instructional materials, methods of evaluation, modes of grouping students, or instructional sequences; (iii) a heightened awareness of instructional factors blocking one's impact in the classroom; (iv) confronting more boldly those aberrations of the system that reduce this impact but were previously unseen or taken as given; (v) pursuit of administrative responsibilities; and (vi) becoming involved in professional activities beyond one's classroom and school, e.g., district curriculum committees or collective action (Huberman, 1993). In a career that can span up to 40 years, it takes 5–10 years to reach this maturity. It is therefore critical to help and ensure that new teachers successfully pass through the initial two phases and this is the sort of support that contract teachers clearly seem to lack. This must be a concern and taken seriously, given the well-documented positive association between teaching experience and student achievement gains, and the fact that (younger) colleagues and more generally schools also benefit from returns to experience (Podolsky et al., 2019). Although Podolsky et al.'s review focuses on US research, it is plausible that their findings apply elsewhere. However, it would be worth conducting such research in low-income countries. Another argument in favor of supporting novice teachers or contract teachers with limited qualifications, and ensuring teacher retention in the Global South, is the evidence that teacher effect on student learning is greater in low-income countries compared to high-income countries (see for instance Bernard et al., 2004).

Conclusion

Contractualization policies and their implications for education systems have been and remain a controversial subject. This chapter provides a brief overview of contract teaching in LMICs and highlights some of the reasons why these policies have been so controversial.

In light of the global push for EFA, contract-based hiring has proven to be a solution for nations facing a sudden surge of new children in their education systems. But as we note in this chapter, these same global forces have also played a conflicting role in many of these countries when, under the guise of structural adjustment policies and financial restructuring, the teacher labor force in many education systems was systematically defunded. The phenomenon of contract teaching is thus a hyperlocal response to specific kinds of teacher shortage, but it is important to recognize the global forces at play, including, on the one hand, a drive to increase enrollment (and now increasingly student learning) in classrooms which requires more teachers and, on the other hand, increasing privatization and policies such as structural adjustment which have led to a steady erosion of civil service teacher labor force in many instances, and the ways in which these current and historical factors have shaped national policy responses.

Speaking to this context-specific nature of the contract teacher policies, the chapter also underscores cross-national variation in the extent and type of contract teacher reliance. In general, though, we note that contract teachers tend to be less well-paid and receive less pre- and in-service teacher education support compared to regular or government teachers. We posit that regardless of the number of contract teachers in any context, how they are recruited, their characteristics and employment conditions, including salary, can affect how the profession is perceived by the public and by teachers themselves. In turn, these perceptions are likely to affect the profession's attractiveness, teachers' motivation and professional satisfaction, and the system's and its schools' capacity to retain them. While we draw attention to the potential and growing role of the private sector in the contract-based hiring practice, it is noteworthy that at a system level this practice, or the related policy solutions, has been led by the state apparatus in most cases.

Many education systems are currently caught in a vicious cycle, with high attrition rates among both practicing and future teachers, depletion of collective expertise due to attrition, and difficulty to attract candidates into "traditional" teacher preparation programs. In these circumstances, and against the backdrop of historical teacher shortages, we understand that some elements of contract-based hiring are likely to remain part of most education systems across the world. At various times nationally, or locally, the government, or the community will find it necessary to rely on teachers who have received limited (initial) teacher education to fulfill emerging needs. Such teachers may be needed to address shortages or address the needs for specific types of teachers in specific circumstances (for instance, educating refugee children who do not speak the local language).

However, as we note in the chapter, the contract teaching "solution" is not a long-term fix. The "solution" of contract teaching raises several other challenges within the education system of unequal resource/teacher quality distribution, uneven quality of learning, and lack of attractiveness of the teaching profession. The segmentation of the teaching force, with more and more precarious members, has implications for the very fabric of the profession, especially, as has often been the case in many (developing) countries, if such members are recruited with lower credentials. This runs counter to the professionalization discourse that has been fashionable since the 1980s around the world.

Thus, while acknowledging the possibility that some form of reliance on contract-based teaching is likely to continue in various forms across the world, we note that reliance on contract teachers in this manner ultimately allows nations to circumvent the more complex problems of improving and extending their teacher education systems, and the challenge of covering higher salary bills for teachers. We argue that thinking about ways to carefully address these challenges of providing affordable and quality teacher education and sustainably building the teaching profession is necessary to address the long-term health of the teaching profession in any education system. Given that the fast-growing private sector in many countries also relies on practices similar to public or government contract-based hiring, attention to these lasting questions about the quality of teacher education, and the ability of nations to sustainably support their teacher labor force becomes more urgent.

Collectively these observations present researchers with a robust scholarly agenda. Within the specific focus on contract-based hiring by governments, many more system-level studies are needed to better understand the specific local circumstances that lead to the adoption of this policy and to understand what specific form this policy solution takes on the ground. Similarly, the research remains divided on the implications of these hiring practices on various educational outcomes (for students, teachers, and the system); more research from diverse educational contexts can add important nuances to our understanding. Beyond the specific issue of contract-based hiring by governments, the implications of these practices in the private sector, especially the so-called low-cost private education sector, are also important.

We began the chapter with a system-level understanding of the factors that have led to these forms of teacher hiring. Each of those factors, teacher education and training, teacher remuneration, and teacher distribution also deserve close scholarly attention. The research agenda in each of those sub-fields is vast, but briefly as they pertain to the issue of contract teaching, exploring effective, accessible, and affordable modes of teacher pre- and in-service education is crucial to ensure all teachers are well supported regardless of their contract status. The challenge of considering how government systems may sustain vast teacher salary bills while staffing their classroom similarly requires more research and policy discussions. That all sectors have both permanent and contract-based employees is a given. The issue that divides and needs to be addressed is what proportion of the latter is acceptable in the education sector in light of conceptualizations of teachers' careers, such as Huberman (1993) and demonstrated returns to experience (Podolsky et al., 2019)? This also raises the question about what sorts of support may be needed in a system that must rely on an effective corps of contract teachers. Finally, the questions about who teaches where and to whom are at the heart of why many low-resourced and otherwise marginalized communities have to resort to contract-based teaching. Understanding these dynamics can better illuminate the factors that shape local teacher shortages and the need for reliance on these hiring practices.

Notes

1 https://www.teachershortages.com/
2 Founded in 1989 and still operating, Teach For America (TFA) is a case in point. It has been both highly praised and strongly criticized (see for instance https://www.brookings.edu/articles/teach-for-america-is-shrinking-is-this-cause-for-celebration/).
3 India is a federal republic with 28 states and 8 union territories.
4 PASEC is a program designed to assess (through large scale evaluations of student achievement in grades 2 and 6) the education systems of the member countries of CONFEMEN, the international organization of Francophone Ministers of Education.

References

Atherton, P., & Kingdon, G. (2010). The relative effectiveness and costs of contract and regular teachers in India. Research Papers in Economics (RePEc) https://ideas.repec.org/p/csa/wpaper/2010-15.html

Bernard, J.-M., Tiyab, B. K., & Vianou, K. (2004). Profils enseignants et qualité de l'éducation primaire en Afrique subsaharienne francophone: Bilan et perspectives de dix années de recherche du PASEC. PASEC/CONFEMEN.

Bertron, C., Buisson-Fenet, H., Dumay, X., Pons, X., & Velu, A.-É (2021). Les enseignants contractuels de l'Éducation nationale: Vers l'institutionnalisation d'une gestion coûtumière de la pénurie? *Revue Française de Socio-Economie*, (27), 121–140. DOI: 10.3917/rfse.027.0121

Bourdon, J., Frölich, M., & Michaelowa, K. (2006). Broadening access to primary education: Contract teacher programs and their impact on education outcomes in Africa – An econometric evaluation for Niger. *Pro-Poor Growth: Issues, Policies, and Evidence, Schriften des Vereins für Socialpolitik*.

Bourdon, J., Frölich, M., & Michaelowa, K., (2010). Teacher shortages, teacher contracts and their effect on education in Africa. *Journal of the Royal Statistical Society Series A (General)*, 173, Part 1. http://halshs.archives-ouvertes.fr/halshs-00426678

CETE (2023). *The right teacher for every child. state of teachers teaching and teacher education for India Report 2023*. Tata Institute of Social Sciences, Mumbai. SoTTTER-2023_CETE-TISS.pdf

Chandra, M. (2015). The implications of contract teaching in India: A review. *Policy Futures in Education, 13*(2), 247–259. https://doi.org/10.1177/1478210314567288

Chudgar, A. (2015). Association between contract teachers and student learning in five francophone African countries. *Comparative Education Review, 59*(2), 261–288.

Chudgar, A., Chandra, M., & Razzaque, A. (2014). Alternative forms of teacher hiring in developing countries and its implications: A review of literature. *Teaching and Teacher Education, 37,* 150–61.

Chudgar, A., & Sakamoto, J. (2021). Similar work, different pay? Private school teacher working conditions in India. *International Journal of Educational Development, 86,* 102478.

Cour des comptes (2018). *Le recours croissant aux personnels contractuels dans l'Éducation nationale. Communication à la commission des finances du sénat.* https://www.vie-publique.fr/files/rapport/pdf/194000071.pdf

Dee, T. S., & Goldhaber, D. (2017). Understanding and addressing teacher shortages in the United States. *The Hamilton Project, 5,* 1–28.

Dembélé, M., & Mellouki, M. (2013). The drive towards UPE and the transformation of the teaching profession in French-speaking sub-saharan Africa. In J. Kirk, M. Dembélé and S. Baxter (Eds.) *More and betters teachers for quality education for all: Identity and motivation, systems and support* (chapter 3). Collaborative Works.

Duflo, E., Dupas, P., & Kremer, M. (2015). School governance, teacher incentives, and pupil–teacher ratios: Experimental evidence from Kenyan primary schools, *Journal of Public Economics, 123,* 92–110, https://doi.org/10.1016/j.jpubeco.2014.11.008

Duthilleul, Y. (2005). *Lessons learnt in the use of 'contract' teachers: Synthesis report.* International Institute for Education Planning, UNESCO.

Edwards, D. S., & Kraft, M. A. (2024). Grow your own: an umbrella term for very different localized teacher pipeline programs. (EdWorkingPaper: 24-895). Retrieved from Annenberg Institute at Brown University. https://doi.org/10.26300/0s8x-c050

Eurostat. (n.d.). *Teachers in the EU.* Products Eurostat News. https://ec.europa.eu/eurostat/web/products-eurostat-news/-/edn-20201005-1

Geeves, R., & Bredenberg, K. (2005). *Contract teachers in Cambodia.* IIEP-UNESCO.

Goldhaber, D., & Theobald, R. (2023). Teacher attrition and mobility in the pandemic. *Educational Evaluation and Policy Analysis, 45*(4), 682–687.

Huberman, M. (1993). *The lives of teachers* (translated by J. Neufeld). Teachers' College Press.

International Labour Office (1996). *Impact of structural adjustment on the employment and training of teachers.* ILO, Sectoral Activities Programme.

Lei, W., Li, M., Zhang, S., Sun, Y., Sylvia, S., Yang, E., & Rozelle, S. (2018). Contract teachers and student achievement in rural China: Evidence from class fixed effects. *Australian Journal of Agricultural and Resource Economics, 62*(2), 299–322. https://onlinelibrary.wiley.com/doi/epdf/10.1111/1467-8489.12250

Luschei, T. F., & Chudgar, A. (2016). *Teacher distribution in developing countries: Teachers of marginalized students in India, Mexico, and Tanzania.* Springer.

McMurdock, M. (2022, September 22). Traditional university teacher ed programs face enrollment declines, staff cuts. *The 74 Newsletter.* https://www.the74million.org/article/traditional-university-teacher-ed-programs-face-enrollment-declines-staff-cuts/

Michaelova, K., & Wechtler, A. (2006). The cost-effectiveness of inputs in primary education: Insights from the literature and recent student surveys for Sub-Saharan Africa. Working Document prepared for the Association for the Development of Education in Africa for its 2006 Biennial Meeting. ADEA.

Muralidharan, K., & Sundararaman, V. (2013). Contract teachers: Experimental evidence from India. Working Paper No. 19440. National Bureau of Economic Research. https://www.nber.org/papers/w19440

OECD. (2005). *Attracting, developing and retaining effective Teachers—Final report: Teachers matter.* Author. https://www.oecd-ilibrary.org/education/teachers-matter-attracting-developing-and-retaining-effective-teachers_9789264018044-en

Podolsky, A., Kini, T., & Darling-Hammond, L. (2019). Does teaching experience increase teacher effectiveness? A review of US research. *Journal of Professional Capital and Community*, 4(4), 286–308. https://doi.org/10.1108/JPCC-12-2018-0032

Pons, X. (2021). Le recours croissant aux enseignant.es contractuel.les : vers un effet papillon? *Mouvements*, 3(107), 63–73. https://www.cairn.info/revue-mouvements-2021-3-page-64.htm

Raval, H., McKenney, S., & Pieters, J. (2010). A conceptual model for supporting parateacher learning in an Indian non-governmental organization (NGO). *Studies in Continuing Education*, 32(3), 217e234.

Richardson, E. (2018). Teachers of refugees: A review of the literature. Education Development Trust.

Santibañez, L. (2016). The indigenous achievement gap in Mexico: The role of teacher policy under intercultural bilingual education. *International Journal of Educational Development*, 47, 63–75.

Sirois, G., Dembélé, M., Kyélem, M., Morales-Perlaza, A., & Johnson, M. C. (2021b). La privatisation de la formation initiale des enseignants du primaire en afrique de l'Ouest francophone: Le cas du bénin et du burkina faso. In D. C. Depover, J.-P. Jarousse, P. Y. Dieng, & C. Armand (Eds.), *Perspectives pour la formation des maîtres en francophonie: Où en est l'Initiative francophone de formation à distance des maîtres?* (pp. 364–399). Éditions Autrement.

Sirois, G., Morales-Perlaza, A., & Dembélé, M. (2021a). *Offre privée de formation initiale des enseignants: cartographie et études de cas du phénomène en Afrique subsaharienne, Amérique latine et Asie du Sud et de l'Ouest*. Background Paper for the 2021 Global Education Monitoring Report. https://unesdoc.unesco.org/ark:/48223/pf0000380061

U.S. Bureau of Labor Statistics. (n.d.). *Learning about employment and wages of elementary and secondary school employees*. https://www.bls.gov/opub/ted/2023/learning-about-employment-and-wages-in-elementary-and-secondary-schools.htm#:~:text=There%20were%20about%202.0%20million,U.S.%20schools%20in%20May%202022.

UNESCO. (2020). *A review of the use of contract teachers in Sub-Saharan Africa*. 89 pp.

UNESCO. (2023). *Global report on teachers: Addressing teacher shortages—Highlights*. 36 pp.

6 The Expanded Presence of Second-Career Teachers
Redefining the Teaching Profession and Career

Thibault Coppe

Setting the Stage: The Global Emergence of Second-Career Teachers

The topic of second-career teachers (SCTs) has gained significant attention among educational researchers and policymakers in recent years. This chapter delves into discussions surrounding the expanded presence of SCTs and the associated challenges. It examines the impact of this expansion on our understanding of the contours of the teaching profession and career. As an introduction, the following lines shed light on the pivotal role of teacher shortages, which the scholarship on SCTs has consistently reported as being at the core of their growing proportion in teacher workforces.

Over the past two decades, severe teacher shortages have emerged as a global issue. The phenomenon of teacher shortages is intricate, involving various intertwined factors. Some of these factors certainly remain unknown, while others are deeply rooted in societal and cultural contexts, such as the perceived social status of the teaching profession. These complexities make addressing this issue particularly challenging. What has become clear over the past 20 years is that teacher shortages are a pressing societal challenge that has proven exceptionally hard to resolve with core aspects of the problem varying depending on the context (e.g., problem of retention versus problem of recruitment; Ingersoll & Smith, 2003). Given the imperative to find solutions and the undeniable fact that inaction is not viable, educational systems have experienced a "state of crisis" regarding teacher shortages for the past two decades (Aragon, 2016). Notably, this crisis was foreseen as early as 40 years ago (Darling-Hammond, 1984).

Crises require prompt decisions during the course of the action, in this case to alleviate the weight of the shortages on the educational systems. A crisis is "a critical moment or turning point that calls for consideration and judgment" (Biesta, 2022). Such consideration and judgment require knowledge and expertise, leading to decisions that are ideally well-balanced and determined to be optimal (Rosenthal & Hart, 1991). In the case of the teacher shortage crisis, it could be argued that this necessary knowledge was and is still missing, or at least missing in a form that could help a decision-making process to address it. Consequently, decisions have been – and are still being – made

DOI: 10.4324/9781003441731-9

without proper reflection about their adequacy and potential unexpected consequences (Darling-Hammond, 1990). The well-known contribution from Ingersoll and Smith (2003), "The Wrong Solution to the Teacher Shortage" illustrated that quite well in criticizing the idea that increasing the intake of new teachers would solve the shortage, a belief that was an early and dominant response to teacher shortages globally.

One of these decisions that governments made almost worldwide was to open the doors of schools widely to people from professions other than teaching, namely, SCTs[1] (Baeten & Meeus, 2016; Coppe, 2022). In line with this, many governments have implemented or further developed policies to make the requirements for entry into the teaching profession more flexible (Bertron & Buisson-Fenet, 2022; Mathou et al., 2022), and we have witnessed the emergence of more and more alternative certification programs aimed at training SCTs. This decision was also characterized by a lack of reflection about its potential consequences for the teaching profession. Almost 40 years ago, Darling-Hammond (1988) had already coined the term "apparent schizophrenia" to describe the questionable logic of investing in SCT attraction and recruitment without thinking about the consequences it would have for the profession (see Section The "Schizophrenia" about Standards for Teachers for more details on this point). The situation now is that the proportion of SCTs is growing in educational systems worldwide. They represent a significant part of the teaching workforce nowadays (see Section A Glance at the Numbers for national figures). Data from the TALIS 2018 survey show that 35 out of the 48 participating countries had a teacher workforce with an average of 2 years of experience outside teaching.[2]

While the expanded presence of SCTs originated from the search for solutions to one of the major current challenges for educational systems, namely, teacher shortages, it has also introduced fundamental changes and new challenges in the teaching profession – some that were not foreseen in this context of looking for solutions to the shortage crisis. The main purpose of this chapter is to highlight and discuss these changes and challenges. In discussing the case of SCTs, it is important to note that this chapter does not adopt a stance similar to the one described in "the wrong solution to the teacher shortage" (Ingersoll & Smith, 2003), questioning neither the quality nor the relevance of SCTs. This remains a debate connected to alternative certification programs that are still not consensual in the literature (see e.g., Bowling & Ball, 2018; Boyd et al., 2007) with strong opponents (e.g., Watts, 1986) and defenders (e.g., Hawk & Schmidt, 1989), a debate that has been ongoing for more than 35 years. Instead, this chapter focuses on the importance of discussing the changes, challenges, and contradictions that need to be considered – and have not received enough consideration so far – now that these teachers represent, and will likely continue to represent, a significant part of teaching workforces. In doing so, this chapter is framed around four main topics of discussion. First, it offers an international perspective on the expanded presence of SCTs and discusses the difficulty of defining this specific population of teachers. Second, the chapter reflects upon two paradoxes associated with this expansion: on the one hand, the effort aiming at tackling teacher shortages by massively recruiting a population of teachers who suffer from a dramatically high attrition rate; on the other, the opening of schools' doors to "unqualified/quickly qualified" teachers while also strengthening the teacher quality, education, and professional development narrative. Third, this chapter describes how the growth in the proportion of SCTs and the associated challenges contribute to redefining and shaking up the foundations of the contours of the teaching profession. Fourth, the chapter provides reflections on addressing these paradoxes by drawing upon what we can learn from a comparative view of teacher-related policies and scholarship on SCTs.

I also want to inform the reader that while this chapter discusses SCTs from an international perspective, it is not intended to provide a precise view of different national contexts, but rather seeks to highlight trends and common challenges. Given the heterogeneities in what it means to be a teacher from one country to another (Dumay & Burn, 2023), these trends cannot be an exact reflection of each particular situation and may even diverge from the realities of very specific contexts.

A Glance at the Numbers: The Complex Landscape of Research on Second-Career Teachers

Researchers on SCTs agree that the exponential growth in their recruitment is a consequence of policies aiming at tackling the teacher shortage by purposefully attracting SCTs into the teaching profession (e.g., den Hertog et al., 2023; Ruitenburg & Tigchelaar, 2021). While they represented a rare minority of teachers 30 years ago (Grossman & Loeb, 2008), they now represent a significant part of the teacher workforce internationally. In the United States, approximately 25% of starting teachers in secondary schools were SCTs, according to figures from a few years ago (Paniagua & Sánchez-Martí, 2018). Grossman and Loeb (2008, p. 3) wrote that in the United States, "In 1985, only 275 teachers were prepared through alternative certification programs; in 1995, the number had jumped to 6,932, and in 2005, that number increased almost tenfold to 59,000." In the United Kingdom, the corresponding proportion was 27% (Paniagua & Sánchez-Martí, 2018). The proportion of starting SCT in secondary school rose to approximately 40% for French-speaking Belgium in 2021, with continued growth over the past 10 years (Coppe, 2022). In 2022, they represented about 25% of the current teacher population in Québec (Mukamurera et al., 2023), and their number doubled between 2013 and 2019 (Harnois & Sirois, 2022). From 2016 to 2023, the number of starting SCTs increased from 8.4% to 13.3% in Germany (Bresges et al., 2023). These figures are available for a few countries only, even though many others have also reported a growing population of SCTs, such as the Netherlands (Meijer, 2021), Italy (Bresges et al., 2023), Switzerland (Berger & D'Ascoli, 2012), Australia (Varadharajan, 2014), and the region of

Hong Kong (Trent & Gao, 2009). Looking at the 2018 Teaching and Learning International Survey results for what teacher training certificate respondents held, for all participating countries taken together, the proportion of teachers who reported not having followed a traditional teacher training program represented 13.3% of the total sample of teachers (OECD, 2018). This is further evidence of the significant proportion of SCTs in our educational systems. Although alternate route teachers are not solely SCTs, a significant portion of them are (Hammerness & Reininger, 2008).

The trends reported above are mainly approximations and are available only for a few countries. Indeed, we critically lack data identifying the proportion of SCTs in educational systems. Most national databases about teachers do not track whether they are first- or SCTs; so far, the international surveys have not done so either. Because of this lack of data, decisions on how to look at SCTs and define them in practice are highly heterogeneous in the literature. Some researchers have restricted their scope to "alternatively certified teachers" (e.g., Lucksnat et al., 2022), emphasizing the characteristic that these teachers often followed an alternative teacher training program. Others have used the age of entry in the teaching profession as a proxy to identify SCTs in a national database (Bresges et al., 2023), considering that if they start to teach at more than 30 years old, it is likely that they have had a previous professional life (Coppe, 2022). Some have defined SCTs as "non-legally qualified teachers," emphasizing that in some contexts, they often do not hold any teacher certificate (Harnois & Sirois, 2022). Different terminologies are also used, whatever is the chosen way to operationalize them, such as "career-changer teachers" (Cuddapah & Stanford, 2015), "career-switchers" (Boyd et al., 2011), or "non-traditional teachers" (Flores et al., 2004). All these studies using different terminologies build the current scholarship on SCTs. However, despite their intention to investigate SCT-related phenomena, depending on how they define their population of SCTs, they are referring to entirely different realities (e.g., alternatively certified teachers versus non-legally qualified teachers). This heterogeneity in the practical operationalization of the population of SCTs causes difficulties in building a coherent literature. Now that we have enough evidence that SCTs represent a significant part of the teaching workforce, I believe it has become urgent to adopt the same terminology and add information about the status of SCTs to national databases and international surveys in order to refine our understanding of their realities.

Most of our educational systems worldwide, and especially the many reporting teacher shortages, have more and more SCTs in their teaching workforce. Still, it is very difficult to know the exact proportion they represent and to develop precise knowledge about the consequences of this growth, as every research team uses its own way of trying to define the population of SCTs. However, some of the challenges that are consequences of this increase can be highlighted and are discussed in the following sections of this chapter.

Two Paradoxes around the Expanded Presence of Second-Career Teachers: Balancing Attraction, Retention, and Standards

Investing Massively in Second-Career Teachers' Recruitment without Investing in Their Retention

While SCTs represent, indeed, a new influx in the recruitment of teachers, recruiting them massively does not mean that the teacher shortages are solved. Research has shown that SCTs are more at risk of attrition than first-career teachers[3] (Redding & Smith, 2016). Some studies have presented results highlighting that they are twice as likely to leave the teaching profession during the first years as first-career teachers (Chambers Mack et al., 2019; Coppe, 2022), who already suffer from quite a high attrition rate (Dupriez et al., 2016).

Continually investing in their recruitment without investing in their retention is not a sustainable solution to the teacher shortages (Coppe, 2022). Scholarship on SCTs has highlighted several reasons that explain this high attrition rate, which we can categorize as macro-, meso-, and micro-level reasons.

At the macro-level, results from empirical research showed that beginning SCTs often suffer from a lack of employment security (e.g., Bertron et al., 2023; Coppe et al., 2023; Dufour et al., 2023). As discussed in the literature, in countries such as Belgium and France,[4] these measures have tended to create a dualization of the teacher labor market – meaning, structural differences between first and SCTs, leading to inequalities. In France, this dualization has been characterized as institutionalized and explicit (Bertron et al., 2021, 2023), with a clear separation between the employment status of traditional-entry teachers (known as "titular" teachers in France) and lateral-entry teachers. This dualization is also a reality in French-speaking Belgium, but its institutionalization is less clear, or at least not explicit (Coppe, 2022). For both these examples, being on the margins of traditional teacher status implies much less employment security than for traditional teachers (Bertron et al., 2023; Coppe et al., 2023). The same dualization trend with the same consequences in terms of employment security has begun to be visible in Quebec as well (Dufour et al., 2023; Harnois & Sirois, 2022). This situation implies a clear contradiction between the expectations of SCTs and the reality of their employment status. To attract more and more SCTs, governments advertise with recruitment campaigns highlighting teacher shortages and a form of job security for future teachers, as we lack teachers (Coppe, 2022). Research has also shown that when they enter the teaching profession, SCTs expect this relative employment security[5] (Berger & D'Ascoli, 2012; Coppe et al., 2021). But the reality is that in many systems, they are used to fill the gaps of the teacher shortages, without having the same rights in terms of job security as other teachers. Empirical large-scale research has shown that in the United States, this instrumental use of SCTs leads to them being more likely to work in hard-to-staff schools (Redding & Smith, 2016), which are known for their more difficult working conditions (e.g., salary and student population).

Employment insecurity and difficult working conditions put SCTs in a precarious situation and are factors that lead them to quit the profession soon after deciding to enter it (Coppe et al., 2021; Redding & Smith, 2016).

At the meso-level, research has shown that SCTs tend to experience a complex induction process in school (e.g., Coppe, März, & Raemdonck, 2022; Coppe et al., 2023; Haggard et al., 2006; Ruitenburg & Tigchelaar, 2021). As they often go through a fast certification track or no teacher training at all, their first step in the profession is truly a learning process (Coppe, Enthoven, et al., 2022; van Heijst et al., 2023). Recent literature has shown that in several national contexts, SCTs do not feel supported in this learning process (Brindley & Parker, 2010; Redding & Smith, 2016; Ruitenburg & Tigchelaar, 2021). Specifically, research has shown that while SCTs need support from colleagues to become familiarized with the teaching profession, they are often isolated and not seen as "real" teachers by their colleagues (Coppe et al., 2023; Varadharajan, 2014). Research has also shown that when they have the chance to enter into a supportive environment, school principals and mentors sometimes do not know how to support them adequately, as their needs differ from those of traditional-entry teachers (Ruitenburg & Tigchelaar, 2021). This lack of support adds to the well-known difficulty of beginning teachers' induction process (e.g., Colognesi et al., 2020) and is likely to contribute to their attrition, as evidenced by the empirical study from Redding and Smith (2016).

At the micro-level, literature investigating the alignment between SCTs' motivations and expectations and the reality of the teaching profession has shown that some of them experience a mismatch (Anthony & Ord, 2008; Coppe, März, & Raemdonck, 2022). Examples of this are thinking teaching was a collaborative profession but realizing it is very individualistic (Anthony & Ord, 2008; Coppe et al., 2023), or thinking teaching would be a stable and secure job because of the shortages but realizing that is not the case (Coppe et al., 2021). In addition, most SCTs in some educational systems start to teach while they are also starting an alternative teacher certification program; the heavy workload also represents a challenge that has been reported as difficult to overcome (Coppe, März, & Raemdonck., 2022).

The challenges reported above, albeit most certainly not consistently representative of the reality in every country, show that SCTs encounter other, often additional, challenges compared to first-career teachers. It is noteworthy to witness the number of initiatives aiming to attract them into the teaching profession versus the very little evidence of initiatives aiming to keep them in the profession (Coppe, 2022). Because "teacher shortages" are viewed as a crisis, policy measures to tackle teacher shortages are short-term measures that are implemented without proper reflection on their relevance and consequences. While there is (at the moment) no right answer to the question, "Is it efficient and relevant to attract SCTs into the teaching profession to tackle the teacher shortages," there is definitely an answer to the question, "Is it efficient and relevant to attract SCTs without putting as much effort into their retention as into their attraction." This answer is clearly no. Scholarship on SCTs has primarily focused on their motivations for joining the teaching profession, leaving aside reflections about how to support their retention (Ruitenburg & Tigchelaar, 2021) – an issue that future research ought to address.

The "Schizophrenia" about Standards for Teachers

The two mainstream discourses about teachers do not fit together well: the teacher quality discourse and the teacher shortages discourse. On the one hand, supra-national organizations, such as the OECD, seek insights about teacher quality, as one of the most important factors in the quality of educational systems (OECD, 2005; Paine & Zeichner, 2012). On the other hand, the global teacher shortage crisis is pushing governments to staff schools with teachers who do not follow the traditional qualification path (i.e., SCTs). Alternative certification programs are typically shorter than traditional certification programs, and the increased flexibility of the conditions for entry to the teaching profession often allows SCTs to start teaching without any teaching degree. The juxtaposition of the need for high-quality teachers – usually taken as a synonym of "highly qualified teachers"[6] (Darling-Hammond & Sykes, 2003) – and the need to make professional non-teachers become teachers as fast as possible paints a wicked portrait of our perception of "what is a teacher."

This is an apparent paradox that, in substance, tells the population of SCTs: we need you, but we do not want you. A recent event in Quebec illustrates that well, as it has had direct consequences for how SCTs are treated by their colleagues in schools. In 2023, a movement began that has been called, "Display your diploma (i.e., "affiche ton diplôme," Dion-Viens, 2023), which was born as a reaction against SCTs who do not have (yet) their teaching degree. This movement, launched by first-career teachers, aimed at showing parents and students that some teachers have the necessary training to be high-quality teachers but some do not, by displaying their diploma in their classroom. This initiative generated much debate in the Quebec press.

This raises a crucial but complex question. How can educational systems continue their quests for teacher quality while having to deal with teacher shortages, with the preferred solution being to recruit SCTs who are not trained or trained faster? Brewer referred to this complex question as "the grand paradox in teacher preparation and certification policy" (Brewer, 2003, p. 3).

This question becomes even more crucial when looking at where teacher shortages are more prevalent. Research has shown that teacher shortages are worst in schools located in disadvantaged areas with students from a lower socio-economic background (e.g., Cobbold, 2017). The teaching gaps that must be filled are wider in these schools, which means that the proportion of SCTs would be expected to be higher there (Carver-Thomas & Darling-Hammond, 2017). Large-scale empirical research conducted by Redding and Smith (2016) showed also this trend. However, it can be argued that these schools also need high-quality teachers, as the task of education is particularly challenging there (Jacob, 2007).

A Redefinition of the Contour of the Teaching Career and the Teaching Profession

I believe these two paradoxes contribute to modify the very roots of our view of the teaching career and profession. Historically, the teaching profession has been strictly regulated in most countries, with clear training pathways, clear standards, and clear contours of its workforce, even though some contexts did allow the existence of "regulated flexibility"[7] (Mathou et al., 2022). This regulation works in parallel with particular care for the quality and training of teachers, with different ways to ensure it between national or state contexts. The expanded presence of SCTs contributes to the creation of a double dualization of the teacher labor market: one that relates to whom we want as teachers and, in turn, with whom we staff the schools, and the other that relates to how we define what a teacher is and, in turn, how we perceive their professional status.

First, when it comes to "whom we want as teachers," I want to re-emphasize the peculiar reasoning behind the persistent recruitment of SCTs, but with very little focus on their retention, and what this reveals about the current view of the teaching workforce. While it is understandable that governments sought a new influx of individuals to augment the teaching workforce, it is noteworthy how quickly these individuals influx are disregarded once they are in the system. The prevailing discourse on the teaching profession expresses the hope of equipping schools with teachers prepared to address the challenges of educating youth and addressing societal disparities, by ensuring that they received the necessary training. However, many educational systems now permit teachers to enter the profession without ensuring they have obtained this training, and there is very little subsequent effort to ensure that these SCTs develop professionally and find their place in schools (Coppe, 2022). This leads to a significant number departing the profession prematurely and re-starts the cycle through the need to recruit new teachers. This logic suggests that the emphasis on and priority of staffing schools with highly qualified teachers holds only when the influx of teachers via traditional pathways is adequate. However, when this influx is insufficient, the priority switches to filling classrooms with personnel. This is not to say that these SCTs are not high-quality teachers; that is not the point I want to make here. But no institutional means provide a way to make sure they are indeed qualified to teach, and that tells us something about the priorities. In the face of the teacher shortage, is being a teacher about being a skilled professional dedicated to imparting high-quality education, or is it about filling a position to ensure that educational institutions continue to operate—a logic that has been elegantly described previously as "funneling warm bodies into classrooms" (Darling-Hammond & Podolsky, 2019, p. 8)?

This first point brings us to the second, to "how we define what is a teacher," which is referred in this chapter and elsewhere (Darling-Hammond, 1988) as schizophrenia about teacher qualification standards. It raises the question of the professional status of teachers. The coexistence of both the implicit narrative that being a teacher does not require long education and fast alternative certification program can adequately prepare teachers and the strong narrative about teacher qualification and professional development blurs the very meaning of our understanding of teachers as professionals. In an era characterized by a decline in the attractiveness of the profession, its public recognition (Udave et al., 2013), and the trust given to teachers (Goepel, 2012), alongside growing demands to strengthen the perception of teachers as professionals (Biesta, 2015), muddling this very notion does not serve the teaching profession as a whole.

An Unsolvable Problem?

This dual discourse in terms of both "whom we want in our school" and "what is a teacher" represents paradoxes in several countries, though these paradoxes are not inevitable. I am convinced that SCTs have a place in our educational systems without having to suffer from occupying a paradoxical position. At least two aspects seem promising avenues that could inspire educational systems.

While I referred mainly to educational contexts in which SCTs were on the margins of the profession, because I believe they represent the global picture, some national contexts have evolved historically to become a less complex environment for SCTs' integration in the teaching workforce. England is an example of this form of institutional evolution. That context has seen more of a diversification of the labor market than a dualization (Mathou et al., 2023; Menter et al., 2019). In England, SCTs are not on the margins of traditional teacher status but are incorporated within a system that allows for integration of different routes toward the teaching profession (Tatto, 2019). Helgetun (2022), using the example of France versus England, argued that this difference between dualization and diversification is due to a view of the teaching profession as a profession requiring strong initial education (i.e., France) and a view of teachers as "craftpersons" (i.e., England) who can be properly trained on-the-job and during the first years of the profession, without lowering the quality standards (see also Helgetun & Dumay, 2021). Explicitly recognizing that teachers could achieve the qualification standards by qualifying on the job gives room for creating the mechanisms and instruments that make it possible. It is then also possible to reflect upon the efficacy of these mechanisms and instruments and to improve them if required. Conversely, when SCTs are not integrated and are relegated in the margins of the teaching workforce, as in most contexts presented in this chapter, there is de facto a "hidden" population of teachers, which jeopardizes the potential implementation of instruments and mechanisms to support their professional growth that can eventually lead to their retention. Of course, in the case of England, such diversification comes with strong accountability mechanisms aimed at regulating the quality of the teaching workforce that raise other questions about the teaching profession, such as the extent to which these mechanisms impair the professional autonomy of teachers (Sugrue & Mertkan, 2017). Without taking the entire English system as an inspiration, I think its integration of alternative routes within the system rather than on its margins deserves attention from other contexts.

Another avenue that has barely been addressed by the literature, but for which we are starting to see some evidence, is the need to see SCTs for what they are, rather than what they are not. SCTs may not be trained in the same way as other teachers, but they bring with them transversal competencies, professional maturity, and real-world experience (Hogg et al., 2023). Recognizing SCTs for their added value is undoubtedly a way to demarginalize them, integrate them, and allow them to contribute, in their own way, to high-quality education (Ruitenburg & Tigchelaar, 2021). A body of literature has recently begun to explicitly highlight the added value of SCTs in schools (see den Hertog et al., 2023).

Fortunately, more and more researchers are taking an interest in the population of SCTs, and it is to be hoped that the coming years will see the flourishing of reflections on how to integrate these teachers into the system as a strength rather than a weakness. I believe this will necessitate examining local contexts, as well as conducting systematic comparative investigations across different contexts, to learn from what appears to be promising or not.

Notes

1 Second-career teachers are defined as professionals who decided to leave a prior occupation to become teachers as a second, third, etc., career. As a note in relation to Chapter 5 that discusses the case of contractual teachers, while some contractual teachers might be second-career teachers and vice versa, these statuses are not overlapping per se.
2 The five countries/regions reporting the highest average are the United States, Sweden, Argentina, Brazil, and New Zealand. The five reporting the lowest average are Shanghai, Korea, Japan, and Vietnam, all of which are Asian countries.
3 With, for example, attrition rates for second-career teachers being as high as 50% in French-speaking Belgium during the first five years (Coppe, 2022) and the estimated attrition probability being 40% for a cohort of lateral entry teachers from North Carolina during the first three years (Zang & Zeller, 2016).
4 In France, these measures relate to the recruitment of contractual teachers, which is presumably the status of most beginning second-career teachers.
5 Note that it is not the most prevalent motivation that led them to transition to the teaching profession (Coppe et al., 2021).
6 Since the Bologna Declaration, many countries have lengthened their teaching training programs in search of higher quality teaching (Bauer & Prenzel, 2012).
7 For instance, England introduced alternative routes to obtaining qualified teacher status quite early, with careful consideration of how to regulate quality at the conclusion of these routes (Whitty, 1993).

References

Anthony, G., & Ord, K. (2008). Change-of-career secondary teachers: Motivations, expectations and intentions. *Asia-Pacific Journal of Teacher Education, 36*(4), 359–376.

Aragon, S. (2016). *Teacher shortages: What we know.* Teacher Shortage Series. Education Commission of the States.

Baeten, M., & Meeus, W. (2016). Training second-career teachers: A different student profile, a different training approach? *Educational Process: International Journal, 5*(3), 173–201.

Bauer, J., & Prenzel, M. (2012). European teacher training reforms. *Science*, *336*(6089), 1642–1643.

Berger, J. L., & D'Ascoli, Y. (2012). Becoming a VET teacher as a second career: Investigating the determinants of career choice and their relation to perceptions about prior occupation. *Asia-Pacific Journal of Teacher Education*, *40*(3), 317–341.

Bertron, C., & Buisson-Fenet, H. (2022). Au guichet du rectorat. Le travail de recrutement des enseignant·es contractuel·les dans le second degré [at the rectorate counter. The recruitment process of contractual secondary school teachers], *Formation Emploi*, *159*, 10890, https://doi.org/10.4000/formationemploi.10890

Bertron, C., Buisson-Fenet, H., Dumay, X., Pons, X., & Velu, A. (2021). Les enseignants contractuels de l'Éducation nationale: Vers l'institutionnalisation d'une gestion coutumière de la pénurie [Contractual teachers of the national education: Towards the institutionalization of a daily management of the shortage]? *Revue Française De Socio-Économie*, *27*, 121–140, https://doi.org/10.3917/rfse.027.0121

Bertron, C., Vélu, A.-E., Buisson-Fenet, H., & Dumay, X. (2023). The dualisation of teacher labour markets, employment trajectories and the state in France. *Work, Employment and Society*. https://doi.org/10.1177/09500170221128681

Biesta, G. (2015). What is education for? On good education, teacher judgement, and educational professionalism. *European Journal of Education*, *50*(1), 75–87.

Biesta, G. (2022). Have we been paying attention? Educational anaesthetics in a time of crises. *Educational Philosophy and Theory*, *54*(3), 221–223. https://doi.org/10.1080/00131857.2020.1792612.

Bowling, A. M., & Ball, A. L. (2018). alternative certification: A solution or an alternative problem? *Journal of Agricultural Education*, *59*(2), 109–122.

Boyd, D., Goldhaber, D., Lankford, H., & Wyckoff, J. (2007). The effect of certification and preparation on teacher quality. *The Future of Children*, *17*(1), 45–68.

Boyd, D., Grossman, P., Ing, M., Lankford, H., Loeb, S., O'Brien, R., & Wyckoff, J. (2011). The effectiveness and retention of teachers with prior career experience. *Economics of Education Review*, *30*(6), 1229–1241. https://doi.org/10.1016/j.econedurev.2011.08.004

Bresges, A., Dawkins, D. J., Del Gobbo, G., & Kramp, D. (2023). Second-career teachers and lateral entry programmes: The state of the art in England, Germany, and Italy. In D. Frison, D. Dawkins, & A. Bresges (Eds.), *Teaching as a second career: Non-traditional pathways and professional development strategies for teachers*. Pensa Multimedia.

Brewer, T. (2003). The "grand paradox" in teacher preparation and certification policy. *Arts Education Policy Review*, *104*(6), 3–10. https://doi.org/10.1080/10632910309600974.

Brindley, R., & Parker, A. (2010). Transitioning to the classroom: Reflections of second-career teachers during the induction year. *Teachers and Teaching: Theory and Practice*, *16*(5), 577–594.

Carver-Thomas, D., & Darling-Hammond, L. (2017). *Teacher turnover: Why it matters and what we can do about it*. Learning Policy Institute.

Chambers Mack, J., Johnson, A., Jones-Rincon, A., Tsatenawa, V., & Howard, K. (2019). Why do teachers leave? A comprehensive occupational health study evaluating intent-to-quit in public school teachers. *Journal of Applied Biobehavioral Research*, *24*(1), 1–13. https://doi.org/10.1111/jabr.12160

Cobbold, T. (2017). *Resource gaps between advantaged and disadvantaged schools among the largest in the world*. Save Our Schools. https://saveourschools.com.au/equity-in-education/resource-gaps-between-advantaged-disadvantaged-schools-among-the-largest-in-the-world/

Colognesi, S., Van Nieuwenhoven, C., & Beausaert, S. (2020). Supporting newly-qualified teachers' professional development and perseverance in secondary education: On the role of informal learning. *European Journal of Teacher Education*, *43*(2), 258–276.

Coppe, T. (2022). *Untangling second career teachers' entry process in TVET schools: From the suitability of entry profiles to the benefits of social capital for a successful work socialization process*. Doctoral dissertation. UCLouvain.

Coppe, T., Enthoven, S., März, V., & Raemdonck, I. (2022). L'insertion professionnelle des enseignants de deuxième carrière: Un processus de professionnalisation par et au travail [Second-career teachers' induction: A professionalization process by and at work]. *McGill Journal of Education, 57*(1), 45–61.

Coppe, T., März, V., & Raemdonck, I. (2022). Rencontre entre l'enseignant de deuxième carrière et son établissement scolaire: Un mariage sans idylle [Encounter between second career teachers and the school, a marriage without romance]. *Revue Des Sciences De l'éducation De McGill*.

Coppe, T., März, V., Coertjens, L., & Raemdonck, I. (2021). Transitioning into TVET schools: An exploration of second career teachers' entry profiles. *Teaching and Teacher Education, 101*, 103317

Coppe, T., März, V., & Raemdonck, I. (2023). Second career teachers' work socialization process in TVET: A mixed-method social network perspective. *Teaching and Teacher Education, 121*, 103914.

Coppe, T., Sarazin, M., März, V., Dupriez, V., & Raemdonck, I. (2022). (Second career) teachers' work socialization as a networked process: New empirical and methodological insights. *Teaching and Teacher Education, 116*, 103766.

Cuddapah, J. L., & Stanford, B. H. (2015). Career-changers' ideal teacher images and grounded classroom perspectives. *Teaching and Teacher Education, 51*, 27–37.

Darling-Hammond, L. (1984). *Beyond the commission reports. The coming crisis in teaching*. The Rand Corporation.

Darling-Hammond, L. (1988). The futures of teaching. *Educational Leadership, 46*(3), 4–10.

Darling-Hammond, L. (1990). Teaching and knowledge: Policy issues posed by alternate certification for teachers. *Peabody Journal of Education, 67*(3), 123–154.

Darling-Hammond, L., & Podolsky, A. (2019). Breaking the cycle of teacher shortages: What kind of policies can make a difference? *Education Policy Analysis Archives, 27*, 34. http://dx.doi.org/10.14507/epaa.27.4633

Darling-Hammond, L., & Sykes, G. (2003). Wanted, a national teacher supply policy for education: The right way to meet the "highly qualified teacher" challenge. *Education Policy Analysis Archives, 11*, 33–33.

den Hertog, G., Louws, M., van Rijswijk, M., & van Tartwijk, J. (2023). Utilising previous professional expertise by second-career teachers: Analysing case studies using the lens of transfer and adaptive expertise. *Teaching and Teacher Education, 133*, 104290.

Dion-Viens, D. (2023, August 22). Embauche de profs non qualifiés: Des enseignants lancent le mouvement « affiche ton diplôme » [Hiring non-qualified teachers: Teachers initiate the movement "display your diploma"]. *Le Journal Du Québec*. Retrieved from https://www.journaldequebec.com/2023/08/22/des-profs-lancent-le-mouvement–affiche-ton-diplome

Dufour, F., Gareau, M., Dubé, F., Piché-Richard, A., & Labelle, K. (2023). Défis d'enseignants non légalement qualifiés: Développement professionnel et identitaire d'enseignants non légalement qualifiés au québec [Challenges of non-legally qualified teachers: Professional and identity development of non-qualified teachers in Quebec]. *Éducation Et Formation, 318*, 39–52.

Dumay, X., & Burn, K. (2023). Introduction: The status of the teaching profession. In X. Dumay, & K. Burn (Eds.), *The status of the teaching profession* (pp. 1–14). Routledge.

Dupriez, V., Delvaux, B., & Lothaire, S. (2016). Teacher shortage and attrition: Why do they leave? *British Educational Research Journal, 42*(1), 21–39.

Flores, B. B., Desjean-Perrotta, B., & Steinmetz, L. E. (2004). Teacher efficacy: A comparative study of university certified and alternatively certified teachers. *Action in Teacher Education*, 26(2), 37–46.

Goepel, J. (2012). Upholding public trust: An examination of teacher professionalism and the use of teachers' standards in England. *Teacher Development*, 16(4), 489–505.

Grossman, P., & Loeb, S. (2008). *Alternative routes to teaching: Mapping the new landscape of teacher education*. Harvard Education Press.

Haggard, C., Slostad, F., & Winterton, S. (2006). Transition to the school as workplace: Challenges of second career teachers. *Teaching Education*, 17(4), 317–327.

Hammerness, K., & Reininger, M. (2008). Who goes into early-entry programs? In P. Grossman & S. Loeb (Eds), *Alternative routes to teaching: Mapping the new landscape of teacher education* (Chapter 2). Harvard Education Press.

Harnois, V., & Sirois, G. (2022). Les enseignantes et enseignants non légalement qualifiés au québec: état des lieux et perspectives de recherche [Non-legally qualified teachers in Quebec: State of the art and research perspectives]. *Éducation Et Francophonie*, 50(2). https://doi.org/10.7202/1097038ar

Hawk, P. P., & Schmidt, M. W. (1989). Teacher preparation: A comparison of traditional and alternative programs. *Journal of Teacher Education*, 40(5), 53–58.

Helgetun, J. B. (2022). The importance of context: Teacher education policy in England and France compared. In I. Menter (Ed.), *The palgrave handbook of teacher education research* (pp. 1403–1430). Springer International Publishing.

Helgetun, J., & Dumay, X. (2021). From scholar to craftsperson? Constructing an accountable teacher education environment in England 1976–2019. *European Journal of Teacher Education*, 44(1), 80–95. https://doi.org/10.1080/02619768.2020.1832986.

Hogg, L., Elvira, Q., & Yates, A. (2023). What can teacher educators learn from career-change teachers' perceptions and experiences: A systematic literature review. *Teaching and Teacher Education*, 132, 104208.

Ingersoll, R. M., & Smith, T. M. (2003). The wrong solution to the teacher shortage. *Educational Leadership*, 60(8), 30–33.

Jacob, B. A. (2007). The challenges of staffing urban schools with effective teachers. *The Future of Children*, 17(1), 129–153.

Lucksnat, C., Richter, E., Schipolowski, S., Hoffmann, L., & Richter, D. (2022). How do traditionally and alternatively certified teachers differ? A comparison of their motives for teaching, their well-being, and their intention to stay in the profession. *Teaching and Teacher Education*, 117, 103784.

Mathou, C., Sarazin, M. A., & Dumay, X. (2022). Reshaping the teaching profession: Patterns of flexibilization, labor market dynamics, and career trajectories in England. In I. Menter (Ed.), *The palgrave handbook of teacher education research* (pp. 185–210). Springer International Publishing.

Mathou, C., Sarazin, M., & Dumay, X. (2023). Reshaped teachers' careers? New patterns and the fragmentation of the teaching profession in England. *British Journal of Sociology of Education*, 44(3), 397–417. https://doi.org/10.1080/01425692.2023.2167703.

Meijer, P. C. (2021). Quality under pressure in Dutch teacher education. In D. Mayer (Ed.), *Teacher education policy and research* (pp. 101–111). Springer.

Menter, I., Mutton, T., & Burn, K. (2019). Learning to teach in England: Reviewing policy and research trends. In M. Tatto, & I. Menter (Eds.), *Knowledge, policy and practice in teacher education: A cross-national study* (pp. 60–68). Bloomsbury Academic.

Mukamurera, J., Tardif, M., & Borges, C. (2023). Un regard sociohistorique sur Les pénuries de personnel enseignant au québec: Les facteurs en jeu [A socio-historical view on shortages of teachers in Quebec: Factors at play]. *Apprendre Et Enseigner aujourd'hui*, 12(2), 8–11. https://doi.org/10.7202/1101205ar

OECD. (2005), *Teachers matter: Attracting, developing and retaining effective teachers*. https://doi.org/10.1787/9789264018044-en
OECD. (2018). *TALIS 2018 database*. https://www.oecd.org/education/talis/talis-2018-data.htm
Paine, L., & Zeichner, K. (2012). The local and the global in reforming teaching and teacher education. *Comparative Education Review*, 56(4), 569–583.
Paniagua, A., & Sánchez-Martí, A. (2018). *Early career teachers: Pioneers triggering innovation or compliant professionals?* OECD. https://doi.org/10.1787/4a7043f9-en
Redding, C., & Smith, T. M. (2016). Easy in, easy out: Are alternatively certified teachers turning over at increased rates? *American Educational Research Journal*, 53(4), 1086–1125.
Rosenthal, U., & Hart, P. T. (1991). Experts and decision makers in crisis situations. *Knowledge*, 12(4), 350–372.
Ruitenburg, S. K., & Tigchelaar, A. E. (2021). Longing for recognition: A literature review of second-career teachers' induction experiences in secondary education. *Educational Research Review*, 33, 100389.
Sugrue, C., & Mertkan, S. (2017). Professional responsibility, accountability and performativity among teachers: The leavening influence of CPD? *Teachers and Teaching*, 23(2), 171–190.
Tatto, M. T. (2019). Professional knowledge and theories of teaching and learning. In M. Tatto, & I. Menter (Eds.), *Knowledge, policy and practice in teacher education: A cross-national study* (pp. 257–268). Bloomsbury Academic.
Trent, J., & Gao, X. (2009). At least i'm the type of teacher i want to be': Second-career English language teachers' identity formation in hong Kong secondary schools. *Asia-Pacific Journal of Teacher Education*, 37(3), 253–270. https://doi.org/10.1080/13598660903052449.
Udave, J., Carlo, A., & Valette, S. (2013). *Study on policy measures to improve the attractiveness of the teaching profession in Europe: final report. Volume 1*, Publications Office. https://data.europa.eu/doi/10.2766/40827
van Heijst, I., Volman, M., & Cornelissen, F. (2023). Coping strategies used by second-career student teachers. *British Journal of Educational Psychology*. https://doi.org/10.1111/bjep.12652.
Varadharajan, M. (2014). *Understanding the lived experiences of second career beginning teachers* (Doctoral dissertation, University of Technology Sydney).
Watts, D. (1986). Alternate routes to teacher certification: A dangerous trend. *Action in Teacher Education*, 8(2), 25–29.
Whitty, G. (1993). Education reform and teacher education in England in the 1990s. *Journal of Education for Teaching*, 19(4), 263–275. https://doi.org/10.1080/0260747930190422

7 The Teaching Profession in India: Growth, Diversification, and Feminization

Padma M. Sarangapani, Mythili Ramchand, and Jyoti Bawane

Introduction

Teacher supply and quality have acquired global significance both for their perceived value in contributing to school quality and hence economic competitiveness among countries and the fact that teachers' salary constitutes the largest public expenditure within the education sector (Cochran-Smith, 2021; OECD, 2019; Sayed et al., 2018). The focus on teachers has also been fuelled by research linking teacher quality to student achievement (Hanushek, 2002; McKinsey and Company 2007; Organization for Economic Co-operation and Development, 2005; World Bank, 2010). Identifying teacher qualification as a key indicator of teaching quality, the Sustainable Development Goal 4.c aims at "substantially increasing the supply of qualified teachers" by 2030 (Teacher Task Force, 2019). Even as "evidence-based" policy and research interest in teacher quality is growing, critics (Furlong et al., 2009, p. 3) have been questioning policy interventions that seek greater state control over teacher education and in defining quality of teachers and teaching, leading to an increasing proletarianization of the occupation of teaching in a neoliberal, globalized economy (Densmore, 1987). In the context of holding teachers accountable to standards, it is important to note that linear linkages between teacher quality and subject knowledge or technical skill are problematic (Humphrey et al., 2008; Luschei & Chugdar, 2016), and narrow accountability measures have debilitating effects on equity and inclusion (Batra, 2019; Connell, 2009; Darling-Hammond, 2021; Fullan, 2012).

Teacher availability and quality is a complex reflection of multiple factors including policy formulations, systemic structures, and resource allocation affecting recruitment, preparation, compensation and career advancement, continuing professional learning, and working conditions of teachers (Darling-Hammond, 2017; Goodwin et al., 2021; UNESCO, 2019). Despite the trend toward adopting transnational universalistic discourses on teacher quality and pushes for policy borrowing from countries of the global north by financial and aid agencies, the teaching profession is largely shaped by history, culture, politics, constitutional values, and economics of the nation-state (Cochran-Smith, 2005; Sayed & Sarangapani, 2021).

DOI: 10.4324/9781003441731-10

This chapter examines the teacher workforce in India, identifying the key features of who teachers are, and the characteristics of their employment, and locating the profession in the forces of culture, history, politics, and economics uniquely associated with teachers and the teaching profession in India, leading to a discussion on the shape of the future workforce and where the profession seems to be heading. In the first section, we provide an overview of teachers in India, drawing on recent analysis reported in our report *The Right Teacher for Every Child: State of Teachers Teaching and Teacher Education in India 2023* (CETE, 2023a), and identify some of the key emerging trends. In the second section, we present and discuss three interacting fields shaping the professional landscape: India's unique cultural-colonial legacy; State policy, its federal structure and financing; and the growth of the education market. These shape perceptions of status, aspirations to become a teacher, and opportunities and conditions of employment. In the third and final section, we argue that these interacting fields have given rise to a complex dynamic of contradictory pulls and pushes, skewing supply and demand. Current policy initiatives that focus on perception of status and choose to skirt the economics of employment will only exacerbate a downward trend in teacher status and employment terms and eventually have a negative impact on quality of teacher supply.

Teachers in India: A Diverse, Differentiated Workforce

The teaching workforce in India at 9.5 million (excluding the early childhood education sector) is among the largest in the world. The workforce is characterized by considerable diversity: by level of school (primary generalist teachers and subject specialist teachers for middle, secondary and senior secondary school), type of school management, and location of the schools in which teachers work. This huge and diverse workforce is expected to grow with increased enrolment in secondary and senior secondary schooling, pre-school being integrated into the school structure and the addition of teachers for art, music and physical education and special needs – all hitherto neglected and under-staffed. It is also estimated that approximately 10–15% will need to be replaced every 5 years on account of retirement (CETE, 2023a).

The analysis presented in this section provides an overview of teachers in India. Demographic details including caste, gender, and age of teachers along with the nature of their employment contract and wages are comparatively examined to bring out features linked to regional differences (interstate/rural-urban), and the sector of employment (government or private sector). The analysis is based on data from the Government of India database, Unified District Information System for Education Plus (UDISE+) for 2020–21 (CETE, 2023b), the Periodic Labour Force Survey 2020–21 (PLFS) (CETE, 2023c) and primary data gathered as a part of the State of Teachers, Teaching and Teacher Education Report 23 (SOTTTER 23) survey (CETE, 2023d, 2023e).

Schools in India are managed and financed by state and non-state entities. In the federal structure of India, school education is a state subject, and states and union territories not only run schools and employ teachers, but they also regulate privately managed schools which are financed through student fees. About 49% of teachers in India are under the employment of respective state governments and union territories (28 states and 8 union territories, respectively). The eight most populous states account for close to 50% of the workforce. Teacher salaries account for about 90% of the education budget in most states. About 10% of the teachers working in State government schools are contractually employed. State governments also provide grants in aid to some privately managed schools – mostly to cover teacher salaries. About 8% of the teacher workforce work in such schools. State governments also regulate several aspects of privately managed schools, which are financed through student fees, drawing primarily from norms and standards prescribed in the Right to Education Act (Government of India, 2009). Approximately 37% of teachers are employed in privately managed schools. This is a sector which is growing in the last two decades at about 1–3% annually. Effectively this leads to teachers having different types of employment contracts and status and wages. State-employed teachers employed through recruitment processes against cadres created and approved by respective finance departments are full-fledged civil servants and identify themselves as having "regular" employment – they are state employees – they enjoy tenure and pay fixed as per state pay commissions. Teachers working in private sector schools are contractual and their employment may be terminated at any point. Salary terms are negotiated and vary widely in the private sector.

The Central government does not employ teachers (the Ministry of Education, Government of India does fund a small number of schools run by autonomous bodies), and its role is primarily limited to setting policy, norms, and standards, regulating schools and teacher qualifications and teacher education. From the 1980s onwards, after education was shifted from the state to concurrent list, the Center has extended its influence on States and on the sector, through large-scale funded schemes and missions addressing infrastructure, access, employing teachers teaching quality (in-service teacher education) extending to data gathering and management and most recently the use of central technology platforms and technology-mediated programs.

Interstate and Rural–Urban Differences

States in India are mostly organized on linguistic lines – most states having one unique dominant regional language, except for several states in North India where the dominant language is Hindi (the so-called "Hindi Belt"). The overall rural population is 66%, and agriculture employs the majority of the working age-population (35%). Only one-tenth of the working-age population have regular wage employment of which about 50% is in the public sector/government (Sarangapani & Pappu, 2021, pp. 9–10).

There are interstate differences in development with states in the North and Northeast, having larger rural population and lagging behind the more urbanized South in most economic and social indicators. 85% of government school teachers and 52% of private school teachers work in rural areas. Interstate differences in overall teacher deployment indicate varying conditions of difficult-to-staff regions (rurality or geographies), overall governance and fiscal well-being affecting timely recruitment, and policy toward grants in aid and privatization. Three of the very large states in the Hindi belt have high PTRs (between 40:1 and 57:1, in Uttar Pradesh, Jharkhand and Bihar). 90% of all single-teacher schools are in rural areas. A high proportion of single-teacher schools (20–30%) is seen in Himalayan states and in the Northeast. Several states especially in the North East have a very high proportion of teachers working in government schools on contract (between 37% and 69%). Mostly this is on account of fiscal problems and unresolved legal cases leading to courts staying recruitments for more than a decade (Sarangapani, 2023). In total, 90% of government contract teachers are in rural schools.

In most other states this scheme is being discontinued. The proportion of private school teachers varies widely between states. In eight states, the proportion in the private sector is more than 50% of the total teacher workforce (Karnataka, Tamil Nadu, Telangana, Punjab, Uttar Pradesh, Uttarakhand, Haryana, and Madhya Pradesh). The workforce in grant-in-aid schools is significant in only three states indicative of continued political influence of the community (Maharashtra) and the Church (Kerala and Goa) (CETE 2023b, p30).

Age

The median age of the workforce is 38 years. The workforce is skewed with the government teacher workforce being older with a median age of 42 and a younger workforce in private school teachers with a median age of 35. This could be because recruitment is irregular and entry into government service is delayed; it could also be because government recruitment itself has decreased over time. A very large proportion of teachers in the 20–24 age bracket and the 25–29 age bracket are in the private school sector. It is likely that most teachers find their first employment in the private sector.

Social Category

Indian society is hierarchically stratified on caste lines which has led to structural inequalities. The State provides affirmative action to its citizens from scheduled castes and tribal (SC and ST) groups – among the most backward and historically suffering discrimination including untouchability, and socially and educationally backward classes called "other backward castes (BC/OBC)". This includes reservation of seats up to 50% in state-funded educational institutions (school and higher education) and government employment. "General" category includes castes higher in the social hierarchy and also more advanced educationally and economically.

Differences are seen in the caste composition of the teacher workforce in comparison with the overall population and between government and private school sectors. In the government sector, the proportion of SC and ST is

15.4% and 10%, respectively, and it reflects their proportion in the population; this is likely on account of affirmative action in employment. In comparison, the private sector has a higher proportion of general category teachers (51%) and a much lower proportion of SC category (9%) and ST category (3.5%).

Gender

Across India, 51% of schoolteachers are women. However, comparisons between states, between levels of school and rural-urban and government-private show both over-representation and under-representation of women. Some Southern and more urbanized states have a very high proportion, over 75% women teacher workforce (Delhi, Goa, Kerala, Puducherry, Punjab, and Tamil Nadu). Others, mostly from the North India Hindi belt, have a very low proportion, with less than 40% women teachers (Bihar, Jharkhand, Rajasthan). Overall, the proportion of women in government schools is 44% (55% in contractual government). Government recruitment which is otherwise gender neutral has in the past followed policies favoring employment of women in a bid to ensure at least one woman teacher in every school. In private schools the proportion of women is 63% (73% in urban private schools). In initial teacher education, women comprised 73% of the sample of secondary school teacher preparation (BEd) and 63% of the sample for primary school teacher preparation (DElEd) in the primary survey of pre-service teacher education colleges across India (SOTTER 23 survey data; CETE, 2023e).

Sixty-two percent of secondary school teachers and 73% of primary school teachers in the age group of 20–24 are women, while in the age group 45 years and upwards, the balance is tilted toward men. Feminization of the government workforce seems to be taking place over the last decade. Feminization of the private school teacher workforce seems to have begun some 20–30 years ago (PLFS data; CETE, 2023c).

Gender intersects with caste. A larger proportion of general category teachers tend to be women (58% vs 42% men), OBC is gender balanced (49% women, 51% men), while SC and ST categories have a much higher proportion of men (42–43% women vs 57–58% men). This suggests greater access to higher education among women from socially advanced communities and far lower access for women from tribal communities.

Qualifications

The National Council of Teacher Education is the statutory body mandating and regulating minimum teacher qualifications for different levels of school. The minimum qualifications to be a primary school teacher (grades I to V) are having a senior secondary school certificate and either the two-year Diploma in Elementary Education (DElEd) or four-year Bachelor in Elementary Education (BElEd). For subject teaching at the middle and secondary level, the requirement is an undergraduate degree in the relevant subject and the BEd (earlier one year and two years since 2014), or a four-year integrated BSc/BABEd. Senior secondary school teachers are required to have a postgraduate degree in the relevant subject in addition to the BEd (or equivalent).

Overall 83% of school teachers are graduates and 90% of them have some form of professional qualification. The private school sector is the primary employer of teachers without any professional qualification: 16% of teachers in this sector do not have a professional qualification and 61% of those without professional qualification are in this sector. States with a higher proportion of teachers without professional qualifications include the North Eastern (between 15 and 38%) and the Himalayan States, as well as Uttar Pradesh and Bihar (15%). Interstate migration to balance the problems of qualified teacher supply is not feasible or has not found favor politically.

In August 2023, the Supreme Court of India ruled that the BEd will not be considered the appropriate qualification for teaching at the primary level (with the appropriate qualification now being Diploma in Elementary Education ie DElEd or equivalent). Only 46% of government school teachers and 22% of primary school teachers in the private sector had the appropriate qualification (ie DElEd). Seventy-nine percent of teachers at the secondary school level had the appropriate qualification (Bachelor in Education, i.e., BEd). Private schools appear to favor the BEd degree over the DElEd qualification. This could also be attributed to the fact that employers from schools with English as a medium of instruction may perceive that BEd degree holders are more proficient in English. Whereas government schools, social, tribal, and labor department schools typically adopt the regional language as the medium of teaching, they follow the government regulations for recruitment and hence are individuals with a DElEd qualification (CETE 2023b).

Recruitment and Employment

State recruitment is an intensely political matter, with all state governments adopting norms and criteria to favor in-state over out-of-state aspirants. Announcement of large-scale teacher recruitment around the time of state elections is common (see CETE, 2023a, p. 1). Starkly different employment terms are found between the government and private school sector, and within the government between "regular" and "contractual" (CETE 2023c).

Fifty percent of teachers in private schools report working without any written contract (equally for men and women) while for those with written contracts for three years or more, the proportion is 30% men to 21% women. Private school teachers receive salaries far lower than that of government school teachers: in the case of primary and secondary school teachers, private school teachers receive only 35–36% of the respective government school teachers' salary. The bulk of private school teachers who are working without any written contract are also the worst paid, receiving about 50–60% of the salary of private school teachers with contracts for three years or more or about 25% the average salary of a government school teacher. Women primary school teachers in the private sector earn about 61–67% of the salary of men. Between 55% and 63% of government school teachers receive a range of benefits including gratuity, provident fund, maternity leave, and health cover. Between 52% and 57% of teachers in private schools are not eligible for any benefits.

The SOTTER 23 survey found that 45% of private school teachers and 34% of contractual teachers in government schools reported receiving monthly pay of Rs 10,000/- to Rs 20,000, which is less than half the pay of a regular government school teacher (CETE 2023c). 75% of contractual government teachers also said that they did not receive any vacation pay (CETE, 2023a).

Overview

In sum, the following features of Indian teacher workforce stand out:

1 The Indian teacher workforce continues to grow and there continues to be a significant teacher requirement in the system. Teaching is a significant form of white collared waged/salaried employment in urban and rural India and has a significant participation of women.
2 The private school sector is growing; for every 10 teachers in government schools, there are 7.6 teachers in private employment. Most teachers find their first job with the private sector and the wait time for those who succeed in securing government employment is between 5 and 7 years. Private school teachers are in the majority of the workforce in several states.
3 The extent of contractualization in the government sector is about 10%; however, it is very high in States in the Northeast and the Hindi belt. Contractualization has also become invisible in a few states which have effectively stopped recruiting to the notified teacher cadre. Although employed on contract at far lower salaries, by extending contracts until retirement, and providing some benefits, these teachers are being classified as "regular" in government data.
4 Private schools employ more teachers without any professional qualifications and prefer to employ BEd teachers to DElEd ones. Private schools employ more women and younger teachers.
5 Teaching in government schools continues to be an attractive employment option for rural men and for men from the Hindi-speaking North Indian belt. Elsewhere the profession is becoming feminized. Primary school teaching is increasingly feminized, as younger teachers tend to be women.
6 Government school teachers tend to represent the population demography by social category; in contrast, private school teachers have a much higher proportion of teachers (mostly women) from upper castes and far fewer teachers from scheduled tribes.
7 Teachers in private schools have far lower salaries compared to government school teachers, often work without any written contract, and do not enjoy any benefits. Women in private primary schools receive far less compensation

compared to men. The average salary of a private school teacher is at best a second income and cannot support a family.

8 There are very significant differences between states and between rural and urban areas with regards to the proportion of private school teachers; extent of feminization of the workforce; extent of contractual teachers in government schools, single-teacher schools, and availability of qualified teachers in the workforce. However, the workforce is practically localized within states, and there is little or no movement from regions of oversupply to regions of teacher demand. Government recruitment favors local, in-state aspirants and although private schools are so-called English medium, their employment terms and compensation, as well as localized modes of recruitment, do not make migration feasible or attractive. Teachers are mostly not mobile.

Shaping the Landscape of the Teaching Profession: Culture and History, the State and the Market

We profiled teachers in the previous section and identified some of the key current features of the Indian teacher workforce. The overall growth in teaching employment opportunities is taking place in a context of stagnating or shrinking government recruitment and growth in private school employment producing contradictory pulls shaping aspiration to become a teacher. Women teachers dominate the urban private sector and males dominate the rural government sector. Moreover, an overall feminization of teaching is taking place, visible in a larger proportion of women entering into ITE programs and more women among younger teachers. In this section, we contextualize these trends in the unique and distinctive culture, history, politics, and economy of the region. We begin with a discussion of the continued contradictory influences of Indian culture and history on the status of the profession. We follow this with a discussion of State policy and the growing influence of the market. Working together as "fields" (Bernstein, 2000; Webb et al., 2002) these influences shape the professional identity and social status of teachers, aspiration to become a teacher, and the resultant characteristics of the workforce and direction of the profession.

Under the theme of culture and history, we discuss the cultural-colonial legacy: Indigenous/traditional/patriarchal and colonial educational ideals and institutions shaping the profession. In the theme of the State and market, we provide a brief review of state policy and guiding ideals of the profession and reform in the sector, the impact of fiscal stress in states, the growing influence of neo-liberalism and new public management, and the related growth of the education market.

Cultural-Social-Colonial Legacies: Between Respectability and Low Status and Pay

South Asian teachers and the profession of teaching bear twin, oppositional legacies from culture and colonization. On the one hand, the institution of "guru" – a civilizational inheritance widespread in the region's religious, folk, and secular epistemic traditions – places teachers next to god and one's parents. On the other hand, colonial education policies, which are the foundation of the modern education system, relegated teachers to the position of subservient civil servants at the bottom of the administrative hierarchy (Sayed & Sarangapani, 2021, p. 1205).

Kumar (2014) has persuasively argued that Indian school teachers inherited the cultural mantle of "guru." Along with this, several tropes such as enjoying respect in the community, having extensive moral and epistemic authority over students, and pedagogical practices such as discipline and memorization, which are traceable to this formidable legacy, became a part of their professional identity. The ideas of a teacher being a member of a higher social class, and a respected member of society and of teaching being a noble profession draw from this cultural ideal and continue to be widespread in society, generally contributing to the view that teaching is a respectable occupation suitable for educated persons (see Kale, 1970; Sarangapani, 2003, 2021; Sharma & Sarangapani, 2018). This inheritance comes with problematic casteist and gender-biased dimensions, which are aspects of structural inequalities that are integral parts of Indian society. Nevertheless, as cultural ideals, they have recently found renewed political favor and are frequently invoked in recent policy which seeks to draw from "Indian traditions and knowledge systems" (see for example, the recent National Education Policy, 2020).

Patriarchal social values endemic in Indian society which earlier were a barrier to girls' access to and participation in education are now nudging educated women into teaching. The perception is widespread that teaching is a respectable job for women. It enables them to work in "safe" spaces with minimal contact with strangers/unknown men and to work with children, to which it is believed women have a natural proclivity. It is regarded as a positive feature that women are able to work and earn, with convenient working hours and vacations, thus enabling them to fully meet all demands of the family. Women teachers cite how their decision to choose teaching was shaped from early childhood by family or through encouragement of their in-laws or husband (Latha, 2020). Conveniences of teaching in schools in one's neighborhood, flexibility in teaching hours, and in taking leave are cited by women teachers as reasons to prefer private school jobs even if the pay is poor (Sarangapani, 2018). Even if government jobs pay far better, they mostly involve working with children from poor and marginalized communities, they carry inconveniences of posting in far away, rural, places involving travel time, as well as the possibility of being transferred. The entry of more educated women into the workforce has provided private schools with a steady supply of teachers willing to work for less pay.

While these cultural, social, and civilizational legacies have largely ensured a modicum of respectability continues for the profession, the colonial legacy on the other hand has left the profession battling a "deficit view" (Sayed & Sarangapani, 2021). The prevalent institution of "guru" notwithstanding, the education system that was developed in the course of colonization over 200 years placed teachers at the bottom of the educational hierarchy. They were reduced to servile, poorly paid employees of the state under the control of supervisors. Teachers, like other colonial subjects, were regarded as having low competence and poor morals. Their practice was completely circumscribed and controlled, being required to teach from prescribed textbooks and for centrally conducted examinations – giving rise to what Kumar (2014) has characterized as "the textbook culture." The deficit view of the State-employed teacher – of being incompetent and immoral – continued in post-independence India, merging into more recent perceptions that they are also overpaid and unaccountable, and requiring New Public Management principles to tightly administer teachers and their work (Sarangapani et al., 2018). We discuss these developments in the next section.

The State and the Market: Changing Terms of Employment

The period between the 1980s and 2020 has been especially significant in terms of defining the size, form, and expectations of the teaching profession. Initial focus on mass enrolment has given rise to an expanded state system where all children from the ages of 6 to 14 attend school compulsorily. The Right to Education was enacted in 2009. The Act provides a vision of quality, laying down expectations from teachers and from the State vis a vis teacher availability (Pupil Teacher Ratio (PTR) norms), teacher quality (qualification), and teaching quality (pedagogy). Alongside the development of the mass government education system, the private school sector has also grown, providing low-cost English medium education. The period has seen tensions and shifts in policy pertaining to teacher employment terms in the government and in the private sectors.

While the themes of the professional status of teachers and quality of teaching have been recurrent themes in Indian policy, policy analyses and responses in the form of initiatives schemes and programs have differed over the years.

The professional status of teachers, quality of teachers, and teacher education have been recurring concerns with substantive recommendations made in the last two national education policies (Government of India (GoI), 1986, 2020). Two national commissions were set up to specifically look into reforms of teachers and their education (GoI, 1985, 2012). The National Council for Teacher Education was set up as a statutory body to regulate teacher education by an Act of parliament in 1993.

The low professional status of teachers in India has been of concern to policymakers for a considerable period of time. "The destiny of India is now being shaped in her classrooms" (GoI, 1966, p. 1), the opening statement of the first national education commission in independent India, caught the imagination of academicians, bureaucrats, and the general public alike. The commission was concerned about the status of teachers and had devoted an entire chapter to it, giving suggestions for increasing remuneration, improving service and work conditions, and providing retirement benefits, recommending "high quality recruits, best quality preparation and satisfactory working conditions" (p. 46). Noting wryly that "appeals to motives such as love for children...idealism and desire for social service" are not tenable, the policy pointed out that it is necessary to make "an intensive and continuous effort to raise the economic, social and professional status of teachers in order to attract young men and women of ability to the profession, and to retain them in it as dedicated, enthusiastic and contented workers" (p. 46).

Almost two decades later, the national commission on teachers devoted considerable attention to the status of teachers was the focus of the terms of reference given to the commission. Noting that teachers' status is "a complex sociological concept and can mean different things in different cultural contexts" (GoI, 1985, p. 44), it speculated that the tendency to underpay teachers possibly stems from a misconception around the idea of "guru." The 1986 national education policy and the subsequent program of action also recommended increased pay and improved working conditions (GoI, 1986, 1992).

Suggestions for improved pay, fixing a pay scale and extending benefits such as medical insurance and pension scheme have been institutionalized to varying degrees for teachers in state-run schools. However, salary structures and service conditions of teachers within and between states are very uneven with increasing stratification among government schools (CETE, 2023e; Sarangapani et al., 2018). The 1986 National Policy on Education (GoI, 1986) initiated steps to expand and standardize initial teacher preparation as a part of its efforts to achieve universalization of elementary education, with the introduction of District Institutes of Education and Training (DIET). However, it also legitimized non-formal education and the participation of underqualified local youth as teachers.

The 1990s expansion of the school system saw a huge expansion in the teaching workforce but primarily led to state governments employing underqualified teachers, contractually and at salaries lower than that of state teacher cadres. Initially argued as necessary to enhance local community linkage to schools, this soon developed into a full-fledged system of contractually employed underpaid teachers, adopted in many states with fiscal deficits (Govinda & Josephine, 2005; Ramachandran et al., 2016). Shifting from the initial argument favoring such schemes claiming that contract teachers enabled community participation, later arguments cited neo-liberal principles of higher accountability and lower absence resulting in better learning outcomes (CETE, 2023b). Recent studies point to lowered levels of motivation of such teachers, after a few years of working in unequal conditions (Chandra, 2015; Chudgar et al., 2014; UNESCO, 2021).

We find that broadly there are two diverging strands in policy. One emerges from commission reports and National curriculum guidelines, headed by academicians and based on "liberal and humanistic" principles. This discourse seeks autonomy for teachers nurtured through professional development and strong professional identity, and envisions state support to empower them so that they can help their students flourish as individuals in a democratic society. The second strand is based on neo-liberal perspectives in administration and governance, and linked to globalized market forces. This is seen from the 1986 policy onwards (Nambissan, 2016; Velaskar, 2010) and also in the recent National Policy on Education. The discourse of inefficient teachers in the public schooling system has been used to build a case to curtail public expenditure on teacher salaries (Batra, 2012; Sarangapani et al., 2018) and adopt principles of New Public Management in teacher governance.

The last two decades have seen the growing influence of the market, with the growth of private schools, providing English medium education at relatively low fees (Nambissan, 2016.). Private schools, i.e., schools funded primarily through student fees, have always been a part of the Indian school scape – a part of the colonial legacy (Jain, 2018). They have traditionally offered English medium education and served elites and upper-middle-class groups, in opposition to the mass education system, which until recently has favored mother tongue/regional language as the medium of instruction. As per data from the UDISE 2021–22, private schools now account for 22.55% of all schools, serving about 33.3% of students and employing 37% of teachers (CETE 2023a, p. 3). The sector has been growing at about 1–3% annually. Generally offering English as the medium of instruction, they are associated with higher status. In comparison, state government schools are perceived as being of lower quality, generally offering education in the regional languages/mother tongue, and disproportionately attended by children from lower socioeconomic groups, lower castes, and girls (Mukhopadhyay & Sarangapani, 2018; Nambissan, 2016).

Social stratification is reproduced across schools with reference to their clientele (Sarangapani, 2018). The presence and growth of the private sector of schools, which optimizes costs in order to be profitable, is a significant development in the Indian education system. Among the key costs that these schools seek to optimize and minimize are the salaries of teachers. Although state schools offer better job security and high pay, they cater to lower-status clientele. Recruitment, while irregular, is increasingly norm-based and follows government policies of affirmative action.

Reflecting stratification in school clientele, a stratification in the teaching workforce is also becoming evident. Private schools have a disproportionately larger representation from higher social classes/castes (mostly women) and very limited representation from scheduled tribes. Operating with minimal state oversight and given the limits on the state's ability to regulate this sector as per the norms of the Right to Education Act, private schools also tend to employ locally educated women, who may be under-qualified and without professional degrees, through a range of informal undocumented arrangements, and involving very low salaries and no benefits. The lack of certainty of securing a government job, the wait time to secure a government job along with poor pay in private schools work as disincentives, encouraging men to look for other employment opportunities, while keeping their options for employment in the government sector open. The market therefore favors feminization, lowering of working conditions of teachers, and lowering teacher status from the point of view of reasonable pay and working conditions. The high likelihood that one's teaching career will start in a poorly paying private school job, and the overall uncertainty that attends government employment also works against rigorous and time-consuming professional preparation programs in the eyes of teacher aspirants, leading them to seek out shortcuts to acquire the relevant certification with minimum investment.

State policy and the growth of the market of private schools have led to expansion of employment opportunities in the teaching profession which along with the colonial legacy have influenced the perception of teaching as having low status and relatively undesirable. At the same time, the cultural social legacy of the region influences perception that teaching is respectable, has status, and is desirable as a form of white collar employment. We find rural men and high-caste women in the profession. Government school teaching continues to be a respectable job option for men, especially when they are from rural areas and have fewer alternatives. School teaching is also a respectable option for women in general and high-caste women in particular, even when it does not pay well. At the same time, it also places teachers in a very vulnerable position vis-a-vis administrators.

Trends and Future Directions of Teacher Workforce in India

This chapter has examined the teacher workforce in India, identifying the key features of who teachers are, the characteristics of their employment, and locating the profession in the complex interplay of forces of culture, history, politics, and economics. This gives an indication of the contours of the future workforce and where the profession seems to be heading.

The trends in the profession indicate continued aspirations for teaching among the rural youth and urban women with the latter seeking to supplement income of the family and the former hoping for a white-collared, secure job in the government sector. The Indian teacher workforce continues to grow, and there is a significant demand for teachers in the system, especially in the growing private sector. Increasing feminization of the teaching workforce in this sector at lower salaries combined with the ad-hoc or contractual nature of appointment in government schools has been reshaping the teaching workforce. There are very significant regional differences between rural and urban areas with regard to the proportion of private school teachers, extent of feminisation of the workforce, extent of contractual teachers in government schools, single-teacher schools, and availability of qualified teachers in the workforce. The teacher workforce is also localized within states, and teachers are mostly not mobile.

Culturally, teachers in India have had to contend with the two opposing notions of teaching as a traditionally valued occupation with the colonial legacy of the teacher as a deficit, low-level state bureaucrat. The neoliberal state and a capitalist market interact with this unique cultural-colonial legacy in shaping the profession. The federal structure and education being a state subject has meant the central government taking on a more directive role and providing shared financial support through centrally sponsored schemes. The de facto policy of most state governments favors limiting the teacher salary budget through means such as avoiding direct recruitment, delaying appointments, hiring teachers on contracts, or through various other ad hoc means. Concomitant growth of the education market with minimal regulation has allowed the private school sector in India to benefit from the current availability of educated women willing to work under disagreeable and exploitative conditions. While increased participation of women in the teaching workforce is beneficial, this growth, taking place mostly in the private low fee paying school sector, has lowered the professional status of teachers, lowered working conditions and lowered salaries. In this scenario, policy drives and initiatives that focus on quality improvement through rigorous teacher education remain rhetorical and cannot support the development of a cadre of teaching workforce with strong professional identity.

In lieu of ensuring that the salary and working conditions of teachers are attractive to aspirants and comparable in both the government and private sectors, the state has resorted to external assessment and accountability measures including appointment based on teacher eligibility tests and professional growth based on meeting the national professional standards for teachers. The National Education Policy 2020 expects that increasing the length of professional preparation of teachers to four years and motivating elite institutions to offer teacher preparation programs will lead to enhancing the profession's status and making it more aspirational. However, this is unlikely to have any significant impact unless government employment is regularized, enhanced, and expanded, and the trend of private schools growth is reversed.

Persistence of cultural norms of respecting a teacher and the colonial legacy of teacher as a low-level bureaucrat overlays neoliberal policy measures of accountability and efficiency, resulting in a growth of tensions related to the teaching profession workforce. Further research is needed to explicate these forces and to make sense of their complex interplay in shaping the profession and understand future directions. We do not have adequate data on the large workforce employed in the private sector, their career trajectories, and working conditions. Robust data sets on teachers' academic specialization and the subjects they teach and the diversity of teacher workforce correlated with the demography of the students they teach are required. Longitudinal studies on teachers' growth trajectories and trends in fiscal spending on teachers would help provide more nuanced indicators of status of teachers.

Acknowledgement

We thank our Research Associates Kamlesh, Goyal, Aishwarya Rathish, Anitha Bellappa and Arpitha Jayaram who are co-authors of The Right Teacher for Every Child: State of Teachers, Teaching, and Teacher Education Report for India 2023, on which the analysis presented in this chapter is based.

References

Batra, P. (2012). Positioning teachers in the emerging education landscape. In *India infrastructure report* (IDFC Foundation ed., pp. 257–269). Routledge.

Batra, P. (2019). Comparative education in South Asia: Contribution, contestation, and possibilities. In C. C. Wolhuter & A. W. Wiseman (Eds.), *Comparative and international education: Survey of an infinite field* (Vol. 36, pp. 183–211). Emerald Publishing Limited.

Bernstein, B. (2000). *Pedagogy, symbolic control, and identity: Theory, research, critique* (Rev ed.). Rowman & Littlefield.

CETE (2023a). The Right Teacher for Every Child. State of Teachers Teaching and Teacher Education Report for India 2023. Tata Institute of Social Sciences.

CETE (2023b). Teachers in India in 2021-22: The picture from UDISE+. Background paper 1: State of Teachers, Teaching and Teaching Education Report 2023. Tata Institute of Social Sciences.

CETE (2023c). Teachers in India: A snapshot from the Periodic Labour Force Survey. Background paper 2: State of Teachers, Teaching and Teaching Education Report 2023.

CETE (2023d). Public and Private Sector Contract Teachers in India: An analytical research paper. Background Paper 3, State of Teachers, Teaching and Teaching Education Report 2023.

CETE (2023e). Status of teachers in the workforce in eight states: A report based on SOTTTER 23 Survey. Background paper 5: State of Teachers, Teaching Education Report 2023.

Chandra, M. (2015). The implications of contract teaching in India: A review. *Policy Futures in Education*, 13(2), 247–259. https://doi.org/10.1177/1478210314567288

Chudgar, A., Chandra, M., & Razzaque, A. (2014). Alternative forms of teacher hiring in developing countries and its implications: A review of literature, *Teaching and Teacher Education*, 37, 150–161, https://doi.org/10.1016/j.tate.2013.10.009

Cochran-Smith, M. (2005). Studying teacher education: What we know and need to know. *Journal of Teacher Education*, 56(4), 301–306. https://doi.org/10.1177/0022487105280011

Cochran-Smith, M. (2021). Exploring teacher quality: International perspectives. *European Journal of Teacher Education*, 44(3), 415–428. https://doi.org/10.1080/02619768.2021.1915276

Connell, R. (2009). Good teachers on dangerous ground: Towards a new view of teacher quality and professionalism. *Critical Studies in Education*, 50(3), 213–229. https://doi.org/10.1080/17508480902998421

Darling-Hammond, L. (2017). Teacher education around the world: What can we learn from international practice? *European Journal of Teacher Education*, 40(3), 291–309. https://doi.org/10.1080/02619768.2017.1315399.

Darling-Hammond, L. (2021). Defining teaching quality around the world. *European Journal of Teacher Education*, 44(3), 295–308. https://doi.org/10.1080/02619768.2021.1919080

Densmore, K. (1987). Professionalism, proletarianization and teachers' work. In T. Popkewitz (Ed.). *Critical studies in teacher education* (pp. 130–160). Routledge. https://doi.org/10.4324/9780429450150

Fullan, M. (2012). *Change forces: Probing the depths of educational reform*. Routledge.

Furlong, J., Cochran-Smith, M., & Brennan, M. (Eds.). (2009). *Policy and politics in teacher education: International perspectives*. Routledge.

Goodwin, A. L., Lee, C. C., & Pratt, S. (2021). The poetic humanity of teacher education: Holistic mentoring for beginning teachers. *Professional Development in Education*, 1–18. Published Online: September 02, 2021. https://doi.org/10.1080/19415257.2021.1973067

Government of India (GoI) (1966). *Education and National Development: Report of the Commission (1964-66)*. Government of India. New Delhi.
Government of India (GoI) (1968). *National Policy on Education, 1968*. New Delhi: Ministry of Education, Government of India.
Government of India (GoI) (1985). *The Teacher and Society: Report of the National Commission on Teachers-I (1983–85)*. Government of India. New Delhi: Ministry of Human Resource Development.
Government of India (GoI) (1986). *National Policy on Education 1986*. Government of India. New Delhi: Ministry of Education.
Government of India (GoI) (1993). *Learning without Burden: Report of the National Advisory Committee appointed by the Ministry of Human Resource Development*. Government of India, Ministry of Human Resource Development. New Delhi: Department of Education.
Government of India (GoI) (2009). *Right of Children to Free and Compulsory Education Act 2009*. Ministry of Law and Justice.
Government of India (GoI) (2020). *National Education Policy 2020*. Ministry of Human Resource Development.
Govinda, R., & Josephine, Y. (2005). Para teachers in India: A review. *Contemporary Education Dialogue*, 2(2), 193–224. https://doi.org/10.1177/097318490500200204.
Hanushek, E. A. (2002). Teacher quality. In L. T. Izumi, & W. M. Evers (Eds.), *Teacher quality* (pp. 1–12). Hoover Press.
Humphrey, D. C., Wechsler, M. E., & Hough, H. J. (2008). Characteristics of effective alternative teacher certification programs. *Teachers College Record*, 110(1), 1–63.
Jain, M. (2018) Public, private and education: A historical overview. In M. Jain, A. Mehendale, R. Mukhopadhyay, P.M. Sarangapani, and C. Winch (Eds) *School education in India.: Market, state and quality*. Taylor and Francis Group.
Kale, P. (1970). The guru and The professional: The dilemma of The secondary school teacher in Poona, India. *Comparative Education Review*, 14(3), 371–376.
Kumar, K. (2014). *Politics of education in colonial India*. Taylor & Francis Ltd.
Latha, K. (2020). *Beginning Teachers in India: An exploratory study*. Unpublished doctoral dissertation submitted to Tata Institute of Social Sciences.
Luschei, T., & Chugdar, A. (2016). *Teacher distribution in developing countries; Teachers of marginalized students in India, Mexico, and Tanzania*. Springer Nature.
McKinsey & Company. (2007). *How the world's best performing school systems come out on top*. http://mckinseyonsociety.com/downloads/reports/Education/Worlds_School_Systems_Final.pdf
Mukhopadhyay, R., & Sarangapani, P. M. (2018). Introduction: Education in India between the state and market – Concepts framing the new discourse: Quality, efficiency, accountability. In M. Jain, A. Mehendale, R. Mukhopadhyay, P.M. Sarangapani, and C. Winch (Eds) *School education in India.: Market, state and quality*. Taylor and Francis Group.
Nambissan, G. B. (2016). *Poverty, Markets and Elementary Education in India*, Working Papers id:10966, eSocialSciences. https://ideas.repec.org/p/ess/wpaper/id10966.html
National Education Policy. (2020). Policy document released by Government of India, https://www.education.gov.in/sites/upload_files/mhrd/files/NEP_Final_English_0.pdf.
OECD. (2019). *Education at glance 2019*. https://doi.org/10.1787/f8d7880d-en
OECD (2005), *OECD Annual Report 2005*, OECD Publishing, Paris. https://doi.org/10.1787/annrep-2005-en
Ramachandran, V., Béteille, T., Linden, T., Dey, S., Goyal, S., & Chatterjee, P. G. (2016). *Teachers in the Indian education system: How we manage the teacher workforce in India* (NUEPA research report publication series no. NRRPS/001/2016). NUEPA.
Sarangapani, P. M. (2003). *Constructing school knowledge: An ethnography of learning in an Indian village*. Sage Publications.

Sarangapani, P.M. (2018) In Hyderabad's education market. In M. Jain, A. Mehendale, R. Mukhopadhyay, P.M. Sarangapani, and C. Winch (Eds) *School education in India.: Market, state and quality*. Taylor and Francis Group.

Sarangapani, P. (2021). A cultural view of teachers, pedagogy, and teacher education. In P. M. Sarangapani, & R. Pappu (Eds.), *Handbook of education systems in South Asia. Global education systems* (pp. 1247–1270). Springer Nature.

Sarangapani, P., Mukhopadhyay, R., Parul, & Jain, M. (2018). Recovering the practice and profession of teaching: Market, state and quality. In M. Jain, A. Mehendale, R. Mukhopadhyay, P.M. Sarangapani, and C. Winch (Eds) *School education in India.: Market, state and quality*. Taylor and Francis Group.

Sarangapani, P.M. and Pappu, R. 9(2021) Education systems in South Asia. In P.M. Sarangapani and R. Pappu (Eds) *Handbook of education systems in South Asia*. Springer Nature.

Sayed, Y., Carrim, N., Badroodien, A., McDonald, Z., & Singh, M. (Eds.). (2018). *Learning to teach in post-apartheid South Africa: Student teachers' encounters with initial teacher education*. African Sun Media.

Sayed, Y., & Sarangapani, P. M. (2021). Understanding teachers and teaching in South asia. In P. M. Sarangapani, & R. Pappu (Eds.), *Handbook of education systems in South Asia. Global education systems* (pp. 1199–1218). Springer Nature.

Sharma, N., & Sarangapani, M. P. 2018. Teaching because it matters: Beliefs and practices of government school teachers. In M. Jain, A. Mehendale, R. Mukhopadhyay, P.M. Sarangapani, and C. Winch (Eds) *School education in India.: Market, state and quality*. Taylor and Francis Group.

Teacher Task Force. (2019). Learning for All: Teachers as Agents for Inclusion. https://teachertaskforce.org/blog/learning-all-teachers-agents-inclusion

UNESCO (2019). Teacher Policy Development Guide. https://teachertaskforce.org/knowledge-hub/teacher-policy-development-guide

UNESCO (2021). Teachers' working conditions in state and non-state schools. Paper commissioned for the 2021/2 Global Education Monitoring Report, Non-state actors in education. https://unesdoc.unesco.org/ark:/48223/pf0000380078/PDF/380078eng.pdf.multi

Velaskar, P. (2010). Quality and equality in Indian education: Some critical policy concerns. *Contemporary Education Dialogue*, 7(1), 58–93. https://doi.org/10.1177/0973184913411200

Webb, J., Schirato, T., & Danaher, G. (2002). *Understanding bourdieu*. Allen and Unwin.

World Bank. (2010). *Does linking teacher pay to student performance improve results (English). From evidence to policy*. World Bank Group. http://documents.worldbank.org/curated/en/346571468043459067/Does-linking-teacher-pay-to-student-performance-improve-results

8 The Future of Teacher Education and Teacher Professionalism in the Face of Global Policy Trends

Maria Teresa Tatto

Introduction

Since the introduction of universal schooling worldwide in the mid-1800s, teachers' recruitment, retention, and preparation have been a concern. The expansion of schools first meant that systems were pressed to bring individuals into classrooms with at least minimum levels of knowledge than that of the pupils they were expected to teach. Teachers were seen as apprentices and expected to follow a prescribed curriculum; therefore, much effort was invested in textbooks and materials to support these teachers and in developing rules of conduct for teachers. Quality concerns began to appear after increased access to public education was considered sufficient as part of the education systems' commitment to universal education. In other words, education providers began to realize that it was not enough to have all children attend school but that the time spent in school needed to result in the acquisition of worthwhile knowledge and skills. Universal education was seen as a human right and a means to develop future citizens (Cummings, 1999; Tatto, 2007).

While sociological and cultural values were attributed to universal education, a primary concern in dominant global economies was determining whether education resulted in individuals' learning and a rise in productivity and income (see Psacharopoulos & Patrinos, 2018, but also Klees et al., 2012). Quality became redefined as the relationship between school characteristics (textbooks, writing materials, teacher quality, more efficient school management) and pupil achievement (Fuller, 1985). The search for the school factors that boost achievement highlighted the need to ensure quality in teaching, including classroom organization, thus leading to concerns about the education of teachers as worth exploration and investment.

Evolution of Formal Teacher Education

There have been different conceptions concerning teachers' best preparation, with three dominant approaches: school-based, Normal Schools, and Higher Education Institutions (HEI); however, this trajectory has yet to be exclusive,

DOI: 10.4324/9781003441731-11

linear, or universal (Tatto & Menter, 2019, p. 259). According to school-based approaches, teaching is a craft that may be acquired through long practice periods in educational settings and by observing others teach. The other two approaches see teaching as a complex undertaking at the same level as other professions, assuming that teachers must acquire specialized knowledge to be competent. Western models of teacher education began with the Normal School, which emerged in France more than 300 years ago from a practical knowledge conception of the ideal teacher – an individual who must follow moral standards (norms) originally conceived by the church and state. This approach emphasizing pedagogical knowledge initially helped prepare primary school teachers and has been highly influential worldwide. Furlong and Whitty (2017) argue that the influence of the Normal School on the preparation of primary teachers initially separated them from the preparation that secondary and upper secondary teachers received, as these were seen as needing specialized education in their academic discipline. In many settings, such separation continues to exist. Between the late-1800s and the mid-1900s, beginning with England, France, and the United States and eventually extending to the rest of Europe and Latin America, the education of teachers became the purview of higher education (Tatto & Menter, 2019). Education in universities became oriented toward providing future teachers with theory, specialized disciplines of knowledge, the liberal pursuit of questions, intellectual curiosity supported by academic freedom and autonomy, deep-level understandings of current circumstances and prospective long-term change, all the hallmarks of liberal education traditions (Furlong & Whitty, 2017, p. 32).

Educating teachers in universities profoundly affected their status and careers, bringing them closer to professionals in education (Tatto, 2021b). Such a critical reform eventually spread worldwide, albeit with some exceptions, and continues today. However, as time passed, it encountered challenges from policy-makers and school teachers who preferred practical traditions, arguing a disconnect between what school demands entail and what academia can provide.

The English and US Cases: As Examples of Convergence and Divergence in Progress

The preparation of teachers, including the approaches discussed above, had been, until recently, a responsibility of the (welfare) state, as had public schools. However, recent reforms have challenged these traditions in these two countries – we use them as examples because they represent policy convergence and divergence (Windzio & Martens, 2022), markedly affecting university-based teacher education systems, teacher recruitment, employment, and careers.

Beginning in the 1980s, the governments of Margaret Thatcher and Ronald Reagan introduced market approaches to education, initiating a pivotal shift in the relationship between the state and education, increasing privatization and competition. Policies resulting from these changes diminished the importance of teacher education in universities and encouraged the creation of the so-called alternative-routes to teacher certification. The economic crisis of 2008 and then the Great Recession accelerated these trends and opened the way to the "enterprise narrative" and the "shadow state," defined as a parastate apparatus comprising voluntary sector organizations administered outside traditional democratic politics (Ellis et al., 2024, pp. 14–15). These shifts emerged from a knowledge tradition exemplified by Gibbons et al. (1994), where "knowledge is generated in the process of providing solutions to problems which have been identified on the ground in the context of application" (Furlong & Whitty, 2017, p. 36). In these contexts, this conception of knowledge has devolved the state's education responsibilities to corporate entities and schools.

England presents the most extreme case where state-supported multi-academy trusts manage finances, staffing, buildings, and even the curriculum. Furlong and Whitty (2017, p. 37) report that these alternative school systems are almost entirely responsible for teacher professional development and, more recently, for initial teacher training through "school-led teacher education." England has taken this model to the point that, as of 2020, 35% of primary and 77% of secondary schools are academies (operated by multi-academy trusts with state funding). Such a revamping of the English school system substantially affects teacher preparation in a fragmented system that follows the professional model of teacher education while also, paradoxically, an apprenticeship model, as stated in the new standards for teacher education and early career teaching (DfE, 2024).

The trajectory of the teaching career in England depends on the many different routes to becoming a teacher, which has affected teacher recruitment and retention. According to Corbert (2024, p. 1), "In eight of the past nine years, too few people have entered the teaching profession in the UK. In 2023–24, only half of the targeted secondary trainee teacher places have been filled...[t]he government needs over 13,000 more secondary teachers to meet the 2023-24 teacher recruitment target."

In contrast, the United States has also embraced the entrepreneurial spirit with a growing shadow state; however, the country's democratic tradition and decentralized system of governance moderate these forces. In contrast with England, in the United States, most schools are governed and supported by the state, with 7% of the total number of schools being charter schools.[1]

Nevertheless, as in England, the trajectory of teacher careers is variable. After the COVID pandemic, there were fewer educators in the American public school systems, with 18% of public schools having one teaching vacancy and 26% having multiple teaching vacancies (U.S. IES-NCES, 2022). At the same time, university-based teacher education programs have seen a reduction in aspiring teachers, with alternative-route programs seeing increasing enrolment.

The conservative political discourse against teacher education programs has intensified in both countries. In England, for instance, Fazackerley (2022) of The Guardian reports that the government is pushing teacher training out of universities with the justification that "education departments are "hotbeds of leftwing intellectualism" and full of "Marxists." In the United States, according to Pace et al. (2022) of the Brookings Institution, attacks on "Critical Race Theory" have driven bans on teaching about systemic racism, sexism, and other politically charged topics, affecting, to some degree, the curriculum of teacher education institutions.

While these reforms and political movements have spread quickly across England and the United States, not all countries have followed, as Sahlberg (2015) reminds us.

The English and the US cases illustrate one model among many in the evolution of teacher-related policy in the current globalization dynamic. The following section explores each of these aspects.

Teachers' Professional Status and Careers

Since formal schooling was established, improving teachers' status and careers has been a priority for educators. Renewed attention to these issues underlines UNESCO's Sustainable Development Goal 4, which seeks to ensure inclusive and equitable quality education for all by 2030 by, among other strategies, "increasing the supply of qualified teachers [.] including teacher training" (UNESCO, 2024, p. 327). A key argument concerning teachers' status and careers has evolved around whether teachers can be considered professionals, challenging the general view that has traditionally regarded them as semi-professionals (Hodson & Sullivan, 2007). As in many fields seen as "semi-professions," efforts at professionalization are in progress. Hence, in this chapter, to discuss teachers' status and careers, it is essential to attempt a definition of the characteristics of a profession based on Gardner and Shulman's (2005) work. When applied to teaching, such characterization outlines an ambitious agenda for the profession.

As in other professions (Tatto, 2021b), teachers constantly negotiate a *dual ethical responsibility and engage in decision-making under technical and ethical uncertainty*. This is manifested by, for instance, the state's requirements to comply with accountability requirements and curriculum standards and what pupils' learning needs demand, which can have opposing aims. A much-needed aspect of teacher education is to help teachers learn how to deal with these ethical responsibilities. Determining *the knowledge base for the teaching profession*, however, while it is an essential characteristic of a profession, is a complex undertaking as conceptions of knowledge requirements for qualified teachers are highly contested; thus, a concern is how to create coherence around professional knowledge for teachers that will also allow them to engage effectively with knowledge for teaching as well as their ethical and technical responsibilities. Professionalism in teaching also entails the need to *learn from and, in practice,* develop more coherence between the norms of the state, the academy, and the professional practice community. Indeed, being part of a professional learning community requires knowledge production and diffusion to learn from experiences and continue building a solid profession. *Oversight and monitoring quality in professional education and practice* is the hallmark of any profession. It is much needed to elevate teaching status; it requires creating the capacity for self-studies to learn how to improve programs and demonstrate internal and external accountability. Elevating the status of teaching as a profession has profound repercussions not only in their careers but also in the field's capacity to recruit and retain highly qualified individuals.

While much research on teachers has been and continues to be descriptive (i.e., examining their characteristics, attributes, effectiveness, and "professional" development, among others), few studies explore what it would take for the field to equip teachers as professionals according to the conditions described above (Cohen, 1967). For instance, an in-depth examination of the teaching profession using a conceptual review of the research literature and Germany, Poland, and the United States as case studies found deficiencies in all of these areas, the most concerning being the oversight and monitoring from inside the profession or, in other words, who should regulate the profession, with consequences for all other professional areas (Tatto, 2021b).

The attractiveness and status of teaching as a profession depend on the meso and micro-level regulatory policies (Tatto et al., 2012). For instance, research results from the Teacher Education and Development Study in Mathematics (TEDS-M) Study[2] found that systems that promoted policies that preserved or raised the quality of their teaching workforce, offered a stipend for prospective teachers, or introduced a competitive admissions process resulted in great demand for teaching positions in Canada, Chinese Taipei, and Singapore but less so in nations where the status of the teaching profession is lower including Germany, Poland, the Russian Federation, Spain, Switzerland, and the United States (Tatto et al., 2012, pp. 42–43). Current conditions show little improvement, with a growing teacher shortage worldwide (UNESCO, 2024). Teachers are also dropping out of the profession and leaving schools in more significant numbers. Much of this phenomenon results from accountability pressures that value competition more than learning (Kraft et al., 2018).

Accountability reforms seem to affect teachers' typical career paths, with forces outside the profession gradually assuming more control, determining the needed knowledge for teaching, and creating standards that often contradict teachers' professional responsibilities (Santoro, 2017). The resulting policies have deterred potential teachers from entering the profession or led to early career exits across the United States (Kraft et al., 2018). The lack of teachers has created a real crisis in some education systems to the point that individuals with minimal or no teacher preparation are being recruited to teach. In addition, these policies are transforming what it means to be a professional teacher. This situation has been exacerbated by the COVID crisis, the rapid growth of digitization, and the incursion of AI into education (Dorn et al., 2021).

Teachers' Recruitment and Selection

Despite policies attempting to regulate and increase the recruitment of future teachers, UNESCO (2023, p. 3) recently estimated that by 2030, the global teacher shortage will be 44 million, including primary and secondary teachers, with the direst need in Southern Asia and Sub-Saharan Africa. It is increasingly challenging to attract secondary teachers as countries work hard to expand education opportunities beyond primary education.

Low salaries, poor working conditions, and lack of recognition of professional qualifications have resulted in high attrition rates among primary teachers (from 4.62% globally in 2015 to 9.06% in 2022), with alarming rates for males (9.2% in 2021 compared to the rate of 4.2% in 2015).

UNESCO (2023, p. 3) concludes:

> The teacher shortage is a global phenomenon affecting developing and developed countries. In Europe and Northern America, retirement and a lack of interest in entering the profession pose challenges in recruiting 4.8 million teachers to secure quality primary and secondary education.

The degree to which governments can control teacher recruitment varies according to the policies adopted. For instance, government authority over teacher supply, governance, and recruiting exists in strongly regulated nations, such as Malaysia and Singapore; both nations allocate seats proportionally to the number of teachers required by the educational system. Countries with lax regulations for entry into initial teacher education (ITE) have few restrictions on prospective teachers. In contrast, countries with localized control structures may allow institutions to set enrollment caps or promote alternative providers. Some countries have mixed control policies. For instance, Germany and Switzerland have open-entry policies that rely on strict secondary school graduation requirements (Tatto et al., 2012, pp. 41–42).

Teacher Recruitment

Recruiting qualified teachers, especially to teach in far-to-reach schools or disadvantaged areas, has been challenging (Guarino et al., 2006; Ingersoll et al., 2019). Education systems have developed schemes that are expected to recruit future teachers and retain those teachers once qualified in difficult-to-staff schools. For instance, China's Special Post Program, funded by central finances, has expanded recruitment to 950,000 college graduates for rural compulsory education. The program ensures that teachers' salaries are not lower than those of local civil servants (Zhen, 2023).

Paradoxically, policies that have been developed to increase the quality of the teaching workforce have, in some cases, complicated recruitment. Recently, systems have developed national accreditation standards and procedures to ensure high-quality classroom-ready teachers. In Australia and England, for instance, these standards include a pre-determined desirable level of knowledge, skills, and attributes for teachers at different stages of their careers, including behavior management, parental engagement strategies, and curriculum understanding. The Australian Institute for Teaching and School Leadership limits entry into ITE programs to high academic performers. This has exacerbated recruitment issues as many candidates do not qualify as high academic performers, with close to 40% of classes being taught by out-of-field teachers. In England, teachers are expected to fulfill all the Teachers' Standards for Qualified Teacher Status; the lack of qualified teachers, however, prompted the introduction of school-centered initial teacher training (SCITT) in 1986, which highlighted the tension between HEIs and governments over the leadership of teacher education. School-led partnerships account for 52% of all ITE provisions in England (Shea, 2019).

Several other factors complicate how recruitment to teaching occurs and who is being recruited. At the macro level, policy concerning teachers does not support successful recruitment. Confronted by low salaries and difficult working conditions – teachers, especially secondary teachers, find better-remunerated jobs elsewhere. The devaluation of professional knowledge for teaching in recent years with reforms that emphasize content knowledge and deemphasize pedagogical content knowledge and pedagogy, plus the "entrepreneurial spirit" and the growth of the "shadow state," has given rise to alternative ways of becoming a teacher. The global expansion of "Teach for All" (TFA) is a salient example of an enterprise that has created a deceptively "easy" solution to a complex problem. Introducing these market models into education has diminished the importance of HEI's role in teacher education. For instance, as of this writing, in the United States, of the 3.8 million public school teachers working in the school year 2015–16, approximately 676,000 (18%) had entered teaching through an alternative route to certification program (U.S. DOE-NCES, 2022). This number is only expected to increase.

Teacher Selection

In the past, teachers were typically selected at two stages: first, as they applied to enter teacher education programs in HEI, and second, once they obtained qualified teacher status (QTS) when seeking employment (although this is also variable as in some systems, once selected for ITE institutions, graduates are assigned to schools who promptly hire them). The return to the apprenticeship model of teachers' knowledge acquisition has resulted in a direct entry into school teaching, whether with scant training or no training at all – thus, in theory, strict selection of these individuals would seem of paramount importance.

According to Stronge and Hindman (2006), policymakers in the United States have seen careful and methodic teacher selection as a precursor to teaching quality. Recruiters are typically expected to select individuals according to specific attributes, including verbal ability, content knowledge proficiency, education course work (including a strong dose of content and pedagogical content knowledge), teacher certification, and teaching experience. In contrast, alternate route recruitment is wide-ranging.

Globally, education requirements to enter teacher education programs have varied from possessing a secondary level education certificate and no requirement to demonstrate an acceptable domain of the knowledge of school subjects or pedagogy to more robust requirements concerning a deep understanding of pedagogy and the subjects teachers will be expected to teach, including tertiary-level studies in their subject (Tatto et al., 2012, pp. 44–46). Studies have shown that depending on the fidelity of implementation, those teachers who were required to demonstrate high levels of the subject at the recruitment stage demonstrated deeper levels of content and pedagogy content knowledge and a growth mindset when expressing their views on the nature of teaching and learning school subjects (i.e., mathematics) at graduation (Tatto et al., 2018). Current research argues that for the selection of prospective teachers and teachers for teaching posts, methods must focus on aspects that show high and significant correlations with measures of teacher effectiveness, such as learning opportunities, teaching competence, teaching behaviors, and student and teacher outcomes, plus academic and non-academic attributes and background factors to answer the question "Is it likely that this applicant will be (or develop into) an effective teacher?" (Klassen & Kim, 2019, p. 34).

Initial Teacher Education

Teachers' initial preparation has been considered a societal concern for many years across diverse countries, significantly when expanding education systems required hiring many unqualified teachers between 1950 and 1970, in what some scholars have called the world educational revolution (Meyer et al., 1977). More recently, while contested, significant progress in the conceptions of teachers' knowledge and expertise has been marked by the recognition that teachers need to possess deep knowledge of their subjects as well as knowledge to teach that subject to an increasingly diverse population to ensure that their pupils are not only mastering the content but also learning how to flourish as human beings. Cross-national research has backed up these knowledge conceptions, showing the value of well-designed teacher education programs with *internal* solid accountability in universities as measured by the performance of their graduates in knowledge and pedagogy assessments (Mayer et al., 2017; Tatto et al., 2012, 2018).

However, we are reminded that many teachers worldwide need help accessing the required preparation for teaching (UNESCO, 2023). At the same time, alternative-routes into teaching have emerged worldwide, with many allowing individuals with no pedagogical preparation or teaching experience to enter the classroom. This is the case for TFA,[3] a global network of 61 countries, and an example of the "entrepreneurial spirit," which emerged in 2007 as a worldwide disruption to teacher education in HEI despite the lack of robust evaluation reports of its effectiveness, as the organization rarely releases data for independent research (for exceptions, see Glegg, 2024; Penner, 2014).

While reforms generally claim to improve educational quality, the tension between the so-called traditional approaches to teacher education based on HEI and the alternative-routes to teaching fashioned under market models has created confusion and fragmentation as to what counts as a qualified teacher, reduced the principles that have marked teaching as a profession, and threatened the university project of teacher education (Furlong, 2013).

However, the concept of quality is contested and multifaceted (Bradford et al., 2021). While there has been a growing rise in accountability schemes, the new accountability (Tatto, 2007) represented a shift from measuring inputs (e.g., programs' number of credits hours or program length) to holding programs accountable for content, outputs, and outcomes. Thus, there is not only more accountability but also a different type of accountability primarily dictated from outside the profession. Under market models, conceptions of teacher education quality include the performance of initial teacher preparation programs as measured by future teachers' expected knowledge, skills, and dispositions, early career teachers' practice, and even their pupils' learning. Such a conception of quality is more prominent in wealthier countries such as England and the United States, where it has been defined as the "value-added" of teacher preparation and demonstrated by periodic teacher evaluations and achievement tests administered to pupils as part of external accountability interventions. This value-added method to evaluate the effectiveness of teacher education has been questioned by the education community and measurement experts (American Educational Research Association, 2015; Sass et al., 2014). The assumption that compliance with standards and external accountability measures can enhance education quality has gained global traction without solid empirical backup (Mayer, 2020; Mayer et al., 2017), to the dismay of scholars asserting that professional self-regulation yields more positive results (Harris, 2011; Plecki et al., 2012; Sahlberg & Walker, 2021). Paradoxically, these policies have deterred potential teachers from entering the profession, diminished the professional status of teachers, or led to early career exits (Jerrim & Sims, 2022).

Modalities of Initial Teacher Education

ITE in HEI typically has two modalities: concurrent or consecutive. It prepares teachers as generalists or specialists, with future primary teachers predominantly prepared as generalists and secondary teachers as specialists in the subjects they will teach. Entry into teacher education also varies, with some systems requiring a deep knowledge of the subjects the teacher will teach for admittance into the program. Other systems follow a more open approach, including the school-direct approach. Programs in higher education include courses on the curricular content of the subjects teachers will teach, content pedagogy, pedagogy, and a practicum period. HEI and schools work in partnerships as they introduce future teachers to the profession, and this phase can be highly variable, lasting only a few months to an entire year and occurring in one or more schools (see Tatto et al., 2012, 2018). Alternative routes to teaching vary in their approaches. Some rely strongly on schools to prepare teachers, while others offer a combination of direct placement into schools with additional preparation provided by alternative-route organizations or HEI.

Despite this variability, the professional field's substantial evidence on university-based teacher education's effectiveness has supported the global spread of this approach (Mayer et al., 2017; Tatto et al., 2012). While research on the efficacy of alternative-routes to teacher education has been limited, these continue to proliferate rapidly. Still, there is debate within and across education systems about how best to prepare teachers while increasing the supply of qualified teachers. Different cultural and knowledge traditions represent contested views of what a professional teacher must be able to know and do.

Teacher Employment

The selection of qualified teachers as employees is probably one of the most important decisions a school can make – especially in systems where teachers are offered, after probation, a permanent job and expected to work until retirement. Policies that regulate entry into the profession vary. For instance, the TEDS-M Study revealed that graduation automatically leads to official entry to the teaching profession in some countries, such as Botswana, Chile, Georgia, Malaysia, Norway, Poland, the Russian Federation, Singapore, Spain (private school teachers), Switzerland, and Thailand. In Canada (Ontario), Oman, Philippines, and Spain (for public school teachers), in addition to graduation, entry into the profession depends on passing further tests set by external agencies (e.g., licensure tests of professional knowledge). In countries such as Chinese Taipei, Germany, and the United States, entering the profession or gaining employment depends on passing further tests of professional knowledge and performance assessments (Tatto et al., 2012, p. 49). These policies do not apply to alternative-route pathways, which typically have decision-making autonomy.

Each system has explicit regional or national requirements for hiring teachers. While systems that have introduced alternative-routes may or may not need qualified teacher status for hiring, most school systems generally require a formal qualification, often from a HEI, demonstrating the knowledge of the subjects they will teach, preparation in pedagogy, and some field experience. Some systems have a combination of employment-based pathways and more traditional pathways, like the United States, New Zealand (Hoben, 2021), and England (Shea, 2019), while others, such as Finland, have firmly rejected involvement with TFA, requiring a master's degree in a HEI for permanent teaching positions (Moilanen & Räihä, 2021).

Discussion

In our previous work based on the study of reforms in ten countries (Tatto & Plank, 2007, p. 274), we mapped teacher-oriented policy as traditional (e.g., the point where the reform initiates), aspirational (e.g., reform intended ambitions), and reform as implemented (e.g., current implementation status). Our analysis distinguished formal vs. organic systems of control as regulating the degree to which teachers were considered bureaucrats vs. professionals. These systems of control and conceptions of the professional status of teachers conditioned teacher preparation, whether in HEI or alternative-routes (e.g., technical with teachers receiving "scripted knowledge" vs. professional with teachers receiving discretionary knowledge). Technical orientations consider teaching procedural and independent of context, while professional orientations consider teaching as requiring critical reflection and being highly contextual. At the time of our study, we could not find evidence of convergence in teacher education policy. However, we did find a tendency for states to treat teachers as bureaucrats exerting a higher degree of control over teaching. We also found a "general movement toward closer supervision of teachers' careers and teaching practice accompanied by far more heterogeneous set of reforms targeting the preparation of teachers, the knowledge they require and the manner they are expected to teach" (Tatto & Plank, 2007, pp. 274–275). A finding that shines light on the paradoxes of reforms is that not all reforms were able to achieve change due to strong cultural norms related to traditional ways of thinking about teachers and their preparation and, in many cases, due to frank resistance emerging from teachers and their unions or the community.

A more recent study in twelve countries found that the traditions of control over teachers' work and careers persist even more (Tatto & Menter, 2019). The notion of teachers as professionals has been weakened by the entrance of market models in education in some systems. Still, in most countries, the two models discussed above co-exist (the teacher as a bureaucrat and the teacher as a professional). In our study, however, we found the emergence of two additional co-existing teaching models not as much inspired by preparing the ideal teacher for the ideal citizen but instead by what Ellis et al. (2024, pp. 14–15) call the entrepreneurial spirit.

Start-ups such as Teach for America – discussed above – have extended globally and are an example of one such approach. Under this approach (and possibly other alternative-routes to teaching), a teacher is conceived as a worker in a gig economy, with the idea that the ability to teach can be summoned possibly as an innate ability and that some knowledge of the subject is sufficient to teach.

A fourth approach has emerged recently in England and the United States, where the forms of control do not come from the state (i.e., teachers as bureaucrats) but rather from enterprises that can be considered as the "shadow state" (Ellis et al., 2024, pp. 83–84 and 108–109) effectively transforming teachers into "bureaucrats working for the shadow state." Such enterprises have state support and have managed to control the education market, the curriculum, and even conceptions of teachers' knowledge, status, and careers. This approach conceives prospective teachers as apprentices expected to learn from their school supervisors and mentors. Such a model considers teaching scripted, dominated mainly by standards, and disregards the importance of discretionary knowledge contrary to that provided by Normal or Higher Education preparation (Hordern & Tatto, 2018). While not universally spread, such a model is attractive to politicians, especially in an era of teacher shortages when traditional recruitment and retention strategies have not been as effective. Direct entry into teaching solves recruitment, selection, and employment issues, even if it may not improve these individuals' professional status or their students' learning.

While there is still some convergence on the notion of teachers as professionals and as technicians, the market model, together with the entrepreneurial spirit and the shadow state they create, powerfully influence teachers' status, preparation, and careers. There is resistance from educators in those countries that have implemented policies that threaten the status of teachers as professionals or as possessors of solely technical knowledge (Hordern & Brooks, 2023). Given the state's role and how deeply these policies have transformed education, however, we may see more experimentation in this direction.

Implications and Areas for Further Exploration

Research is needed on the traditional and divergent approaches to preparing teachers. Despite more convergence regarding the preparation teachers must receive, emerging approaches diverge significantly, as shown throughout this chapter. There is general agreement that teachers must have a firm foundation on the disciplines they will teach, but there is variation in what counts as pedagogical preparation. While apprenticeship and alternate route models seem to take practice immersion as the source of learning, a practicum is recognized as an essential aspect of ITE, highlighting the critical role of partnerships between HEI and schools (Menter, 2019). It is essential to understand, for instance, whether and how these partnerships work and what factors account for success or failure; more work is also needed to investigate the disjointed nature of ITE with induction and professional development. The divergent approaches seem to emphasize the role of schools as the sole formative force for future teachers, disregarding academic traditions as those supported by HEI (Normal Schools and University-based teacher education). Research into these later approaches is urgently needed to document their evolution and impact.

Teachers' complex work has intensified as they are asked to document their compliance with regulations and standards. Teachers are unhappy with their salaries, and recruitment is challenging in many countries, especially for those needed in rural areas (UNESCO, 2022). While the general agreement in the field is that performativity, accountability, and the rise of standards negatively impact teachers' status and careers, these aspects deserve more rigorous study.

Given the widespread proliferation of market models in education systems in several globally influential contexts (e.g., Australia, England, New Zealand, and the United States), the weakening of the profession and the state's authority to encourage these forces, it is possible to anticipate a future where teacher education and teaching professional status is reduced and where forces external to the profession continue to dominate. We see systems that have used accountability to curtail teachers' professional status by restricting autonomy, imposing a narrow curriculum, and demanding teacher evaluations based on the results of pupil achievement measurements (Ellis et al., 2024; Furlong, 2013; Hordern & Brooks, 2023; Jerrim & Sims, 2022; Kraft et al., 2018; Mayer, 2020). This is concerning because it fragments the teaching profession and education overall and because there is no empirical evidence that these policies will improve education access and quality.

There is a different foreseeable future as other models exist, such as those that we see in Finland, where more democratic policy mechanisms and an active profession moderate and contextualize policy, thus managing to maintain the integrity of teaching as a profession. Creating a more vital profession would require operating around a strong and sustainable vision of teacher professionalism paired with a vision of the purposes of education (Tatto, 2021a, 2021b).

Let us hope for a promising future where the professionalization of the teaching force predominates in interdisciplinary environments. This is essential to fulfilling the purposes of education: to educate flourishing human beings for a democratic, knowledgeable, and sustaining future. This future will require hard work and close collaboration among the members of the profession of education and associated disciplines.

Notes

1 Academies and free schools are state-funded, non-fee-paying schools in England, independent of local authorities. Free schools are funded by the government but are not run by the local authority, having considerable autonomy (Gov.UK, n.d.). As of 2021–22 in the United States, there are 99, 239 schools of which 75% are

funded by the state, 3% are magnet schools focusing on STEM subjects and 8% are charter schools (publicly funded but privately ran regulated by their own contracts rather than education laws). Twenty-five percent are private fee-charging schools (U.S. DOE-NCES, 2023).
2 TEDS-M is the only large-scale comparative study of teacher education to date that collected nationally representative data from teacher education programs in higher education institutions (HEI) in 17 countries including future teachers, teacher educators and the teacher education curriculum (see Tatto et al., 2012).
3 See the Chapter on TFA in Section 3 of this volume.

References

American Education Research Association (2015). AERA statement on the use of value-added models (VAM) for the evaluation of educators and educator preparation programs. *Educational Researcher, 44*(8), 448–452.

Bradford, K., Pendergast, D., & Grootenboer, R. (2021). What is meant by 'teacher quality' in research and policy: A systematic, quantitative literature review. *Education Thinking, 1*(1), 57–76.

Cohen, E. G. (1967). Chapter VI: Status of teachers. *Review of Educational Research, 37*(3), 280–295. https://doi.org/10.3102/00346543037003280

Corbert, S. (2024, February 16). Teacher apprenticeships may encourage more people into the profession – but greater change is needed to get them to stay. *The Conversation.* https://theconversation.com/teacher-apprenticeships-may-encourage-more-people-into-the-profession-but-greater-change-is-needed-to-get-them-to-stay-216218

Cummings, W. K. (1999). The Institutions of education: Compare, compare, compare! *Comparative Education Review, 43*(4), 413–437.

DfE (2024). *Initial teacher training and early career framework.* Department for Education. London. https://www.gov.uk/government/publications/initial-teacher-training-and-early-career-framework

Dorn, E., Hancock, B., & Sarakatsannis, J. (2021, July). *COVID-19 and education: The lingering effects of unfinished learning.* McKinsey & Co. https://www.mckinsey.com/industries/education/our-insights/covid-19-and-education-the-lingering-effects-of-unfinished-learning#/

Ellis, V., Gatti, L., & Mansell, W. (Eds.) (2024). *The new political economy of teacher education: The Enterprise narrative and the shadow state.* Policy Press.

Fazackerley, A. (2022, May). Government 'pushing England's universities out of teacher training' over leftwing politics. *The Guardian.* https://www.theguardian.com/education/2022/may/28/government-pushing-universities-out-of-teacher-training-over-leftwing-politics-say-leaders

Fuller, B.(1985). *Raising school quality in developing countries: What investments boost learning?* World Bank. https://documents1.worldbank.org/curated/en/161041468741003695/pdf/multi-page.pdf

Furlong, J. (2013). *Education - an anatomy of the discipline. Rescuing the university project?* Routledge.

Furlong, J., & Whitty, G. (2017). Knowledge traditions in the study of education. In G. Whitty, & J. Furlong (Eds.), *Knowledge and the study of education* (pp. 1–57). Symposium Books.

Gardner, H. E., & Shulman, L. S. (2005). The professions in America today: Crucial but fragile. *Daedalus, 134*(3), 13–18. doi: 10.1162/0011526054622132.

Gibbons, M., Limoges, C., & Nowotny, H. (1994). *The new production of knowledge.* SAGE.

Glegg, A. K. P. (2024). *Heroism, complexity and core tensions: An appreciative exploration of schools as teacher learning environments within the teach first training programme*. University College London: https://escholarship.org/content/qt6cj5h6h5/qt6cj5h6h5.pdf

Gov.UK (n.d). *Schools and education*. The Crown. https://www.gov.uk/types-of-school/free-schools.

Guarino, C. M., Santibañez, L., & Daley, G. A. (2006). Teacher recruitment and retention: A review of the recent empirical literature. *Review of Educational Research*, 76(2), 173–208. https://doi.org/10.3102/00346543076002173

Harris, D. N. (2011). *Value-added measures in education: What every educator needs to know*. Harvard Education Press.

Hoben, N. (2021). Initial teacher education in New Zealand. *Bloomsbury education and childhood studies*. Bloomsbury. http://dx.doi.org/10.5040/9781350993709.0004

Hodson, R., & Sullivan, T. A. (2007). *The Social Organization of Work*. Cengage Learning. ISBN 9780495003717.

Hordern, J., & Brooks, C. (2023). The core content framework and the 'new science' of educational research. *Oxford Review of Education*, 49(6), 800–818. https://doi.org/10.1080/03054985.2023.2182768

Hordern, J., & Tatto, M. T. (2018). Conceptions of teaching and educational knowledge requirements. *Oxford Review of Education*, 44(6), 686–701. https://doi.org/10.1080/03054985.2018.1438254

Ingersoll, R., May, H., & Collins, G. (2019). Recruitment, employment, retention, and the minority teacher shortage. *EPAA*, 27, 37, http://dx.doi.org/10.14507/epaa.27.3714

Jerrim, J., & Sims, S. (2022). School accountability and teacher stress: International evidence from the OECD-TALIS study. *Educational Assessment, Evaluation and Accountability*, 34, 5–32, https://doi.org/10.1007/s11092-021-09360-0

Klassen, R. M., & Kim, L. E. (2019). Selecting teachers and prospective teachers: A meta-analysis. *Educational Research Review*, 26, 32–51.

Klees, S., Samoff, J., & Stromquist, N. P. (2012). *The World Bank and education critiques and alternatives*. Sense.

Kraft, M. A., Brunner, E. J., Dougherty, S. M., & Schwegman, D. (2018). Teacher accountability reforms and the supply of new teachers. https://scholar.harvard.edu/files/mkraft/files/kraft_et_al._2018_teacher_accountability_reforms.pdf

Mayer, D. et al. (2017). Studying the effectiveness of teacher education. In: *Studying the effectiveness of teacher education* (pp. 13–26). Springer. https://doi.org/10.1007/978-981-10-3929-4_2

Mayer, D. (2020). The connections and disconnections between teacher education policy and research: Reframing evidence. *Oxford University Research Archives*. Retrieved from Oxford University Research Archives.

Menter, I. (2019). The interaction of global and national influences. In M.T. Tatto and I. Menter (Eds.). *Knowledge, policy and practice in learning to teach: A cross-national study* (268–279). Bloomsbury. https://doi.org/10.5040/9781350068711.0025

Meyer, J. W., Ramirez, F. O., Rubinson, R., & Boli-Bennett, J. (1977). The world educational revolution, 1950–1970. *Sociology of Education*, 50(4), 242–258. https://doi.org/10.2307/2112498

Moilanen, P., & Räihä, P. (2021). Initial teacher education in Finland. *Bloomsbury education and childhood studies*. Bloomsbury. http://dx.doi.org/10.5040/9781350996533.011

Pace, J. L., Soto-Shed, E., & Washington, E. Y. (2022, January 31). Teaching controversial issues when democracy is under attack. Brookings. https://www.brookings.edu/articles/teaching-controversial-issues-when-democracy-is-under-attack/

Penner, E. K. (2014). *Teaching for all? Variation in the effects of Teach for America*. [Dissertation]. UC Irvine.

Plecki, M., Elfers, A., & Nakamura, Y. (2012). Using evidence for teacher education program improvement and accountability: An illustrative case of the role of value-added measures. *Journal of Teacher Education, 63*, 318–334. http://dx.doi.org/10.1177/0022487112447110

Psacharopoulos, G., & Patrinos, H. A. (2018). *Returns to investment in education: A decennial review of the global literature* (Policy Research Working Paper 8402). World Bank. https://documents1.worldbank.org/curated/en/442521523465644318/pdf/WPS8402.pdf

Sahlberg, P. (2015). *Finnish Lessons 2.0: What can the world learn from educational change in Finland?* Teachers College Press.

Sahlberg, P., & Walker, T. (2021). *In teachers we trust: The Finnish way to world-class schools.* W. W. Norton & Company.

Santoro, D. A. (2017). Teachers' expressions of craft conscience: Upholding the integrity of a profession. *Teachers and Teaching: Theory and Practice, 23*(6), 750–761.

Sass, T., Semykina, A., & Harris, D. (2014). Value-added models and the measurement of teacher productivity. *Economics of Education Review, 38*, 9–23.

Shea, J. (2019). Initial teacher education in England. *Bloomsbury education and childhood studies.* Bloomsbury. http://dx.doi.org/10.5040/9781350996274.0009

Stronge, J. H., & Hindman, J. L. (2006). *The teacher quality index: A protocol for teacher selection.* ASDC.

Tatto, M. T. (2007). *Reforming teaching globally.* Symposium Books. (Reprinted in 2009 Information Age Publishers). DOI: https://doi.org/10.15730/books.11

Tatto, M. T. (2021a). Developing teachers' research capacity: The essential role of teacher education. *Teaching Education, 32*(1), 27–46. https://doi.org/10.1080/10476210.2020.1860000

Tatto, M. T. (2021b). Professionalism in teaching and teacher education. *European Journal of Teacher Education, 44*(1), 20–44. https://doi.org/10.1080/02619768.2020.1849130

Tatto, M. T., & Menter, I. (2019). Understanding teacher education policy and practice cross-nationally. In M.T. Tatto, & I. Menter (Eds.). *Knowledge, policy and practice in learning to teach: A cross-national study* (pp. 3–8). Bloomsbury. https://doi.org/10.5040/9781350068711

Tatto, M. T., & Plank, D. N. (2007). The dynamics of global teaching reform. In M. T. Tatto (Ed.), *Reforming teaching globally* (pp. 267–277). Oxford Studies in Comparative Education. Symposium.

Tatto, M. T., Rodriguez, M., Smith, W., Reckase, M., & Bankov, K. (Eds.) (2018). *Exploring the mathematics education of teachers using TEDS-m data.* Netherlands: Springer. https://doi.org/10.1007/978-3-319-92144-0

Tatto, M. T., Schwille, J., Senk, S. L., Ingvarson, L., Rowley, G., Peck, R., Bankov, K., Rodriguez, M., & Reckase, M. (2012). *Policy, practice, and readiness to teach primary and secondary mathematics in 17 countries. Findings from the IEA teacher education and development study in mathematics (TEDS-m).* IEA.

Teach for All (TFA). (n.d.). https://teachforall.org/

U.S. DOE-NCES (2022). *Characteristics of public school teachers who completed alternative-route to certification programs.* U.S. Department of Education, Institute of Education Sciences. https://nces.ed.gov/programs/coe/indicator/tlc

U.S. DOE-NCES (2023). *Number of educational institutions, by level and control of institution: 2010–11 through 2020–21.* U.S. Department of Education, Institute of Education Sciences https://nces.ed.gov/programs/digest/d22/tables/dt22_216.10.asp;216.30.asp; 205.50.asp

U.S. IES-NCES (2022, December 6). Forty-four percent of public schools operating without a full teaching staff in october, New NCES Data Show. https://nces.ed.gov/whatsnew/press_releases/12_6_2022.asp.

UNESCO (2022). *Promising policy options: Teacher deployment, teacher retention for equity and inclusion.* UNESCO-IIEP. https://policytoolbox.iiep.unesco.org/policy-option/teacher-deployment-teacher-retention/#promising-policy-options

UNESCO (2023). *The teachers we need, the teachers we want. International task force on teachers for education.* https://unesdoc.unesco.org/ark:/48223/pf0000387001.

UNESCO, (2024). *Global report on teachers: Addressing teacher shortages and transforming the profession.* https://unesdoc.unesco.org/ark:/48223/pf0000388832

Windzio, M., & Martens, K. (2022). The global development, diffusion, and transformation of education systems: Transnational isomorphism and 'Cultural spheres.' In Martens, K., &Windzio, M. (Eds.) *Global pathways to education. Global dynamics of social policy* (1–35). Palgrave Macmillan. https://doi.org/10.1007/978-3-030-78885-8_1

Zhen, J. (2023). Initial teacher education in China. *Bloomsbury education and childhood studies.* Bloomsbury.

Part III

New Configurations of Teachers' Work and Learning

9 Platformed Professionalities

What Digital Platforms Do to Teacher Professionality[1]

Mathias Decuypere and Steven Lewis

Introduction

Faced with the increasing platformization of schooling and society (Decuypere et al., 2021), this chapter seeks to understand new forms of teacher professionals and teacher learning as made possible by *digital platforms*. While research to date has often focused on the ability of platforms to link people and places together via data infrastructures (for instance, see Decuypere, 2021; Lewis & Hartong, 2022; Lewis & Lingard, 2023), critical attention is increasingly being paid to platforms in terms of how they have the potential to fundamentally change what it means to *be* a teacher; how they shape notions of "effective" teaching professionals, such as undertaking professional learning; and, finally, how these reconfigure the teaching profession (for instance, see Bradbury, 2019; Lewis & Holloway, 2019; Williamson et al., 2020).

Building on this existing work, in particular our own previous work (Lewis & Decuypere, 2023), our purpose here is, based on an interface analysis of one platform to explore what digital platforms (can) do to *teacher professionality*. With many definitions and conceptions of teacher professionalism prevailing (Demirkasımoğlu, 2010), in this chapter we understand teacher professionalism as the combination of professional knowledge, discretion and responsibility that enables a teacher to be a professional and undertake professional practice. We advance the argument that digital platforms reshape teacher professionality by investing in digital organizational forms and, relatedly, investing in specific ways of thinking about, and acting upon, desired ways of organizing education in general, and the professional development of teachers in particular (Decuypere et al., 2021; Thévenot, 1984). More specifically, through an inquiry into the European Commission's (EC) teacher professional learning platform, the *European School Education Platform (ESEP)*, this chapter analyzes one such example of a dedicated digital organizational form: the *project*. By "form," we mean ways of organizing social practices in dedicated ways that make those practices "dividable, intelligible, knowledgeable and actionable" (Decuypere et al., 2021, p. 7; see equally Thévenot, 1984). By contrast, "project" refers specifically to a temporary, activity-focused enterprise with clear aims that is usually established to achieve certain known objectives or outcomes (see Büttner & Leopold, 2016, p. 43).

DOI: 10.4324/9781003441731-13

ESEP was officially launched in 2022 and is the merger of two previously existing platforms: (i) the *School Education Gateway* (SEG) platform on the one hand, and (ii) the *eTwinning* (eT) platform on the other hand. As of October 1, 2023, ESEP has over 175,000 registered users (European Commission, 2023b). Before the merger into ESEP, the SEG platform was primarily concerned with informing teachers and schools about EU policies providing online resources (including teaching material), as well as providing overviews of how to acquire Erasmus+ funding. By contrast, the eT platform has always been more community oriented and has aimed to establish communities of teachers that can work together with other European and non-European teachers across the boundaries of the nation-state (see Decuypere & Lewis, 2023).[2] An interesting commonality between the SEG and the eT platform is that both are centrally making use of *projects* as an organizational form that at once promotes specific forms of teacher professionality. In that regard, our purpose with this chapter is to explore the various means by which the ESEP platform promotes a particular version of teacher professionality that is thoroughly *projectified* (i.e., based on the project form) and *platformed* (i.e., occurring in the digital space of the platform).

Drawing on recent scientific work on "projectification," or the ability of the project form to shape work practices (Berglund et al., 2020; Fred, 2020; Godenhjelm et al., 2015; Jensen et al., 2016), we investigate how ESEP contributes to the remaking of teacher professionality. Although projectification and its impacts have admittedly been explored at the level of student learning (e.g., Miller et al., 2021) and education more generally (see Vanden Broeck, 2020b), to our knowledge, it has arguably *not* yet been considered systematically at the level of the teacher and teacher professionality. Indeed, we argue that a projectified teacher professionality is now increasingly constituted as a perpetual *project-in-itself*, with this mechanism uniquely enacted by and through platform dynamics.

Analytical and Methodological Approach

The Project Form

In recent decades, the *project form* has emerged as a central organizational trope (see Kalff, 2017). Correspondingly, *projectification* entails the proliferation of this "temporary, future-oriented, purposeful, time-limited organisational form" (Jensen et al., 2016, pp. 25–26). The significance of projectification as a shift toward "non-permanent structures" extends beyond mere administrative or logical changes, in which actors are encouraged to adopt "practices, assumptions, values, beliefs and rules associated with projects" (Fred, 2020, p. 352). Rather, projects are now an omnipresent feature of contemporary life (including education), shaping both what we do and how we do it, as well as informing the more fundamental ontological concerns of who teachers and students are deemed to be within the "project society" (Jensen et al., 2016).

Projects, then, are not mere technical tools for the organization of activities but have instead become instruments that challenge and reshape educational practices and ideals (Ylijoki, 2016).

We can see in this the emergence of the project as a *generalized* organizational solution to all manner of institutional problems, but also, interestingly, the development of *specific* projects as solutions to specific problems. Such an orientation introduces a significant solution-focused and temporally limited logic to projects, whereby projects are brought into existence for only so long as they are required to solve a given problem. Furthermore, the project form is increasingly used as a means of governing the educational sector (Vanden Broeck, 2020b). This is perhaps best typified by the EC's broader Erasmus+ program, which supports education, training, youth, and sport activity in Europe via the funding of *projects*, but which, notably, financially supports educational activities *only if* they are presented as projects (Vanden Broeck, 2020b, p. 664). More broadly, it has been suggested that projects now arguably comprise the *modus operandi* of the EC, insofar as it provides the means of implementing a large proportion of its policy agendas (Godenhjelm et al., 2015). This can be witnessed in both the SEG and the eT platforms, as both platforms within the ESEP heavily draw on the project as an organizational form (see Figure 9.1).

Developing this constitutive nature of the project form, projects can be said to exist within a series of "self-established casualties, moving from a problem (cause) to its solution (effect)" (Vanden Broeck, 2020b, p. 669). Moreover, projects are amorphous in terms of their specific form and potential: they are

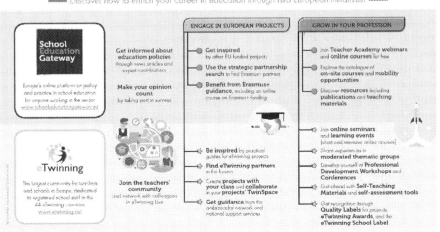

Figure 9.1 The SEG and eT are two platforms that heavily draw on the project form, and that are now mutually integrated into the ESEP.

Source: European Commission (2019).

at once indistinct phenomena that nevertheless have a very particular way of organizing, constituting so-called "formless forms" that continuously come into and then fade from existence (Vanden Broeck, 2020a, p. 845). While it is impossible to predict the exact shape a project will take in pursuit of a solution, it is possible to determine the shaping conditions or parameters within which the project will emerge and be practiced. For instance, at least in professional contexts, a project must work along specific rules and within rigid structures; and yet, at the same time, it offers the freedom for any given project to flexibly unfold within the parameters of these rules (Berglund et al., 2020; Godenhjelm et al., 2015). Herein lies the ultimate paradox of professional projects, insofar as they are meant to enable versatility to respond to changing environments and contingencies, and yet they provide an exceptionally prescriptive and standardized approach to perceiving and approaching problems *as projects*.

Beyond the constitution of projects through problems, and the associated rendering of problems in such a way as to be amendable to intervention through projects, projects equally have distinct spatiotemporal qualities that are intrinsically linked to project activity. Jensen et al. (2016, p. 22) argue in this respect that projects possess four distinct characteristics: *i)* what is done (*activity*); *ii)* where it is done (*space*); *iii)* when it is done (*time*); and *iv)* with whom it is done (*relations*). Three of these project characteristics (space, time, relations) are considered thoroughly subordinate to *activity*, which itself has the power to "decide and format space, time and relations" (Jensen et al., 2016, p. 26). In many respects, the priority granted to activity necessarily emerges in response to the needs and contingencies of projects. For instance, some activity or outcome (a "milestone" or "deliverable") needs to get done within a certain limited number of activities that can be done in the confines of virtual timespaces, such as digital platforms.

Finally, the embedding of time-space within the project itself constitutes, in turn, a series of emergent project times and project spaces, or what we describe as *project timespace:* the experience of timespace by those *within* the project (see Thrift & May, 2001). We offer the concept of "project timespace" to emphasize how the clear temporal boundaries of projects mean time will be experienced differently by those within a project than by those outside of it.

The Projectified Self

With the project so prevalent and "indispensable" for coordinating work and society, it is perhaps unsurprising that the project form and logics also exert an affective (and ontological) influence, thereby helping to constitute what Kalff (2017) terms the *projectified self*. Kalff contends that, within the professional realm, the project assumes the role of a biography or life plan for individuals who are shaped by the "subjectivising antinomy of predictability and flexibility" (Kalff, 2017, p. 10), in which ongoing transformation and objective deadlines are inescapably embedded within oneself. The projectified self thus helps reify both the project form and, at the same time, the professional identity of the project worker (see also Lindgren & Packendorff, 2007). Central to this projectified ontology is the need to *be active* as the undergirding premise of professional identity: "if you are not active, you become invisible or, at best, just *boring*" (Jensen et al., 2016, p. 27; emphasis added).

While each individual accomplishment is itself important for the projectified self, what ultimately matters most is the cohering narrative of successive activities and successes, and especially the ability to "project" (i.e., communicate) this tangible value to others. The project form thus also shapes how individuals see themselves, both objectively and in relation to others, in project terms, with self-worth now predicated upon one's ability to produce and then *project* oneself as a "self-controlling, self-improving, self-commercialising, life-compartmentalising, and deadline-driven human being" (Berglund et al., 2020, p. 367). We see the multiple interpretations of the verb "to project" as especially telling here, meaning not only to *broadcast* but also, importantly, to show oneself *as a project*. In short, it captures the shaping of reality, whereby projectified individuals seek to be understood (by themselves and others) through the lens of the project form.

Over and beyond our interest in how the project form aims to constitute projectified individual teachers, we situate our work in conversation with a now extensive literature that has sought to document and problematize how teacher professionalism has been actively reconstituted in response to certain discursive and material constellations (for instance, see Brass & Holloway, 2021; Hardy & Melville, 2019; Moore & Clarke, 2016; Sachs, 2016). These constellations are diverse and vary, but they often include such aspects as the discursive framing of teacher expertise, the technical infrastructures made available to schooling systems and actors (e.g., software, hardware), and the policies that shape factors such as initial teacher education and professional development. As Holloway (2021, p. 412) notes, "constructs like 'teacher quality' and 'professionalism' are always being (re)made as products of available discourses at a particular time and place." To this discursive focus, we would also add digital technologies and practices, as well as the platform interface itself.

Methodology

In methodological terms, this chapter adopts what Decuypere et al. (2021, p. 2) describe as a critical platform gaze: "an analytical stance that approaches platforms not as neutral 'digital tools', but ... as connective artefacts constitutive of, as well as constituted by, active socio-technical assemblages." Putting this gaze to practice, we conducted initial exploratory interviews with a select amount of informants that were involved in rolling out the transition from eT to ESEP in various European countries, Internet searches to provide an initial overview of ESEP and collected all publicly available information on the ESEP website (https://school-education.ec.europa.eu/en), as well as information that can only be found whilst logging-in to the ESEP, including webpages and embedded multimedia content such as videos, infographics, and press releases.

In this way, we were able to work across most of the platform elements to methodically collect materials for subsequent analysis. Finally, we conducted multiple read-throughs to collect analytic memos (i.e., written reflective notes that were shared amongst the authors and that reflect and record "how the process of inquiry is taking shape; and the emergent patterns, categories and subcategories, themes, and concepts in your data" – Saldaña, 2016) regarding instances where ESEP was used to *i)* shape teacher professionality (e.g., by mobilizing new concerns and priorities amongst participating users), and *ii)* orient participating teachers favorably toward project-based learning, both for themselves and for their students. These segments were then extracted and subjected to subsequent rounds of analysis, using our theoretical framework to analytically track the ways that ESEP contributes to the promotion of particular schooling discourses, practices and teacher subjectivity within teacher professional learning. As an important note, we should add that, for the purposes of this chapter, we have focused on those aspects of ESEP that are emblematic of governing teacher discourses (and identities) through the promotion and infrastructural provision of project logics.

Platforms, Projects, and Educational Forms

Embedding the Project: Staging Teachers

In this section, we discuss the various ways and means in which ESEP embeds projects, including the different ways in which teachers are given the possibility to be trained (e.g., via webinars) to be able to work within a projectified platform environment. In that respect, it is important to argue that, first, ESEP states very clearly the eT platform is designed not merely to foster interaction between teachers, but that it is equally a space where teachers *can develop professionally*. To do so, ESEP focuses on the facilitation of project work and, at the same time, embeds this project work in a broad program of professional development initiatives. As one of the eT-related courses, *Setting up your eTwinning project* (a course that helps teachers understanding the projectified logics of eT) makes clear, the objectives of teaching activities undertaken on eT are very much in line with the project-related thinking we outlined above, and should more particularly be *specific, measurable, achievable, relevant*, and *time bound* (see Figure 9.2). Next to such courses, ESEP equally provides professional development initiatives (including webinars, events, conferences, and teaching materials developed in cooperation with the EU Academy, another EC-backed digital platform) that are related to learning to act and operate in projectified platform environments. Moreover, ESEP very clearly frames eTwinning as a (sub)platform that can be involved in the training of future teachers. For instance, it is stated that eTwinning "can help in the development of new generations of teachers" and, as such, "that introducing eTwinning into the education of student teachers is very valuable to them and their institutions" (European Commission, 2023a, np).

EDUCATIONAL OBJECTIVES

SPECIFIC
Clear and simple.

MEASURABLE
Quantifiable objectives.

ACHIEVABLE
Realistic and attainable objectives.

RELEVANT
Actual, pertinent in the context of school and students.

TIME BOUND
Clear time frame, reasonable deadlines.

PEDAGOGICAL APPROACHES AND TEACHING PROPOSALS

VARIETY OF PEDAGOGIC METHODS
That encourage active, autonomous learning.

STUDENT CENTRED
Students are actors in the process of learning and creating products.

INNOVATION & CREATIVITY
New and creative use or combining of pedagogical methods and techniques.

Figure 9.2 Objectives and pedagogical approaches characteristic of eTwinning projects.
Source: EU Academy (2023a).

What becomes clear from this variety of learning opportunities, which are all retrievable from the "professional development" subsection of the ESEP (a subsection previously belonging to the SEG), is not only that many of them are focusing on the adequate adoption of eT. Equally, professional development and training itself very strongly revolve around *the figure of the expert*; that is, someone who is standing *outside* the actual project work that teachers perform, but who is ultimately in charge of activities that foster teacher professional development (ESEP often designates such experts as "speakers"). These experts include representatives from the various country-centered National Support Organizations (NSOs), which are frequently housed within the respective Ministries of Education for ESEP-participating countries; as such, these non-teachers are positioned as "education experts," even if they are, strictly speaking, not educators *per se*. These expert-led activities are offered to provide teachers with knowledge they themselves cannot obtain (or cannot obtain as quickly) through merely interacting with one another on the eT platform. This implies that *expert expertise* is a form of expertise surrounding, but distinct from, *teacher professional expertise*. The latter is a form of expertise that teachers *can* (and are at once promised and "responsibilized" to) gain through working on the project, whereas the former is a form of expertise that teachers can draw on, but which is clearly distinguished from their own expertise. As such, through staging teachers as *professionals* who can perform (in) the project form, the platform at once positions those teachers as *non-experts*: experts are framed as those persons who contribute to teachers' professionalism *from outside* the project form.

As argued elsewhere, providing tutorials, webinars, sample projects, etc. is not a neutral endeavor. Instead, such practices should be conceived as a way of *governing the possible* (i.e., how teachers will use those in their concrete practice) through staging these many initiatives as actual potentials. That is, they act and operate as potential initiatives that one can draw from, and that, in doing so, circumscribe and delimit what is seen as exemplary teacher professionalism, and what is *not* (Decuypere & Simons, 2020; see equally Holloway & Lewis, 2022; Simons, 2015). Indeed, the extent to which ESEP governs what it means to teach and be a teacher through projects is captured in the considerable affective responses to the transition from eTwinning to ESEP. While tangential to our main argument here, it is worth noting that our interview participants shared many negative reactions to the forced migration to ESEP, reflecting both the joy of doing projects on eTwinning and, equally, the "horror" associated with the transition toward (the first version of the) ESEP. We mention this here to emphasize the extent to which the project form and logics exert a considerable affective (and onto-epistemological) influence on its participants, (re)shaping not only what teachers think of their practice but also, importantly, what they think of themselves.

Commencing the Project: Steering Teachers

Despite its overall interest in, and promotion of, the project form, the ESEP platform is not just interested in *any* project, and neither is it aiming to make just *any* project possible. ESEP clearly positions educational projects as projects that are to be done in, by, and through collaborating, and it makes explicit that the lion's share of activities done on the platform (after logging in) are to be *collaborative* in nature. In doing so, the platform makes it very clear that not anything goes; for a project to start and for teachers to embark on a project, collaboration is key. In other words, educational projects are only to be considered as valuable projects – and, in a strong sense, are only considered to be projects *as such* – when they generate collaboration. Moreover, in addition to the collaborative nature of projects, eTwinning equally offers the possibility for teachers to discuss didactic and pedagogical matters in dedicated groups (e.g., "Integrating migrants and refugees at school"; "Creativity with eTwinning"). Arguably, this is a way of demarcating, or steering, teacher activity in a very specific manner, whereby favored forms of teacher professionality and practice are necessarily and significantly collaborative, rather than individualized. As the broader ESEP platform makes clear when one consults the "apply" page, "eTwinning promotes school collaboration in Europe through the use of information and communication technologies by providing support, tools and services for schools" (European Commission, 2020, np). Such an emphasis on collaboration in many respects mirrors and endorses significant research and policy trends over the last few decades that have sought to encourage teacher professionalism *through* collaboration (for instance, see Hargreaves, 2019; Muckenthaler et al., 2020; Nguyen & Ng, 2020).

At the same time, however, we would note that this collaborative focus does not entirely preclude the individual, insofar as participating teachers are encouraged to engage with ESEP (and collaborative eTwinning projects) for the purpose of their own self-improvement, as the following section on the same page of the platform equally illustrates: "Thanks to all individual tools, each member of the community can build interesting and useful partnerships with teachers throughout Europe in an easy, convenient and quick manner" (ibid.). Thus, the collaborative and the individual decidedly clearly come together on ESEP: it is collaboration through individualism, and (at the same time) collaboration to the benefit of the individual. In addition, another aspect of teacher professionalism worth mentioning here is the fact that users need an approved institutional affiliation to successfully create project themselves: teachers need to "apply" to become institutionally affiliated to the school they are working in, and it is only when the national support organization (NSO) of the country in question has approved this request, that a teacher can start joining projects. This, equally, is a measure to ascertain that only "real" teachers can submit projects, and it is therefore a tool to curate (the quality of) the projects that will eventually be submitted.

Doing the Project: Responsibilizing Teachers

A third operation performed by the ESEP platform is stringently outlining what actually doing a project entails, which clearly reflects how projects operate as formless forms. As Figure 9.3 showcases, even though no claim is being made regarding what the *content* of a project should look like (in that sense, projects are a formless form), project *activities* are nonetheless to be performed in a precise step-by-step manner, logically succeeding one another and applicable regardless of the specific project being undertaken. In this sense, projects very much have a designated form. This concatenation and "logical" ordering of steps *responsibilizes* teachers strongly: if they aim to act professionally, they *should* adhere to project logics, which commences with making a strong project introduction (including title and findable keywords), and eventually ends with "expected results" that will be the outcome of the project.

Figuring Idealized Forms of Teacher Professionality: Awarding and Labeling Teachers

Thus far, this chapter has made clear how *educational* projects (i.e., projects that are both educational in content *and* serve to "educate" the participating

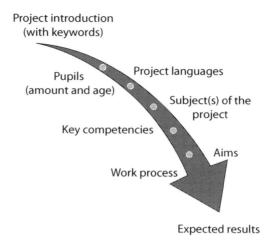

Figure 9.3 Steps for a successful project. Adapted from EU Academy, 2023b.

teachers) are being platformed; that is, the specific ways in which projects take shape through being hosted on ESEP. We have tried to show how each of these ways has distinct implications for teachers and teacher professionality. As argued above, *eTwinners* on ESEP are enticed to extensively prepare for a project (via self-teaching professional development materials), to complete a current project, or to develop a subsequent project by seeking out additional like-minded teachers. One might describe this as the *project lifecycle* on the platform. Projects thus serve as the key orienting mechanism within ESEP in terms of both user activity and platform structure, with both characteristics recursively shaping one another, whereby teacher users develop projects on the eTwinning platform, and the platform content prepares teachers for undertaking project work.

We would argue that particularly the eTwinning section of the ESEP *figures* an idealized form of teacher professionality (Suchman, 2012), in which being a good teacher presumes first being a good project worker who is constantly in a state of readiness and receptiveness for embarking on and starting projects. This imbrication of teacher and project is perhaps most prominent in the manner that ESEP recognizes teacher performance through projects. On the "recognition" page of ESEP, one can clearly discern the coming together of awards and labels that were previously developed under the auspices of the original SEG and eTwinning platform. As far as eTwinning is concerned, ESEP grants *eTwinning National Quality Labels*, *eTwinning European Quality Labels*, and *eTwinning School Labels*. The former two labels are nationally awarded to the participating teachers of international projects, and the premise upon which this performance is recognized is explicit *via the project*, indicating that a certain project has reached a certain *national* (in the case of the National Quality Label) or *European* (in the case of the European Quality Label) standard. Thus, even when participating teachers are being rewarded for their project performance, it is the *project* itself, arguably, that is the actual recipient, and acknowledging the project provides a key means of teaching teachers about exemplary performance. Put differently, it is as much the *project-as-teacher*, as it is the *teacher-as-project*, that is being awarded, which clearly emphasizes the project form and, specifically, the educational nature of the project within the platform. The exception to this is the *eTwinning School Label*, which is awarded to whole schools. Again, one of the prime "drivers" behind this label is projects, as eligibility for this label requires schools to first have at least three active eTwinning teachers (European Commission, 2023c).

Next to labels, ESEP equally grants awards. The *eTwinning European Prize* is an award that can only be granted to those projects that have already received a national and a European Quality Label. Next to a trophy and a certificate, winners of this award are granted free entry to the yearly eTwinning conference, where they have the opportunity to run a workshop based on their project (European Commission, 2023d). A second type of award is the *European Award for Initial Teacher Education*, which is based on the intention of eTwinning to expand awareness of eTwinning amongst prospective and early career teachers. Significantly, the platform encourages mandated teacher education curricula to develop *projectified* logics and practices amongst trainee teachers, and this by minimally including two activities:

> [I]ncluding an 'Introduction to eTwinning' module in the initial teacher education curriculum, [and] creating small collaborative eTwinning projects for teacher educators and/or student teachers (at local, national, and international level), or small eTwinning projects with pupils when student teachers are on placements in schools.
> (European Commission, 2023a, np)

Despite the suggestion here that eTwinning provides trainee teacher with opportunities to acquire new projectified knowledge and skills, the active promotion and equating of *project-focused* skills and logics with (teaching) *professional* skills is particularly telling in eTwinning, constructing ideas of teaching professionalism that exceed more conventional domains of teacher professional knowledge (e.g., curriculum, pedagogy). Embedding the project form within initial teacher training and having dedicated awards for those teacher training institutes that maximally embed the project logics of eTwinning reflects, arguably, how eTwinning is squarely situated within the broader discursive terrain of the project society (Jensen et al., 2016). Here, projects are not mere technical tools but instead work to challenge and reshape educational practices and ideals (see Ylijoki, 2016).

Finally, we would note an interesting tension between the discrete nature of individual eTwinning projects and self-teaching materials on ESEP and, at the same time, the continuous nature of teacher development as an ongoing project. When Jensen et al. (2016, p. 25) describe the "freedom of the project," we can observe in this the apparent flexibility for eTwinners to pick and choose their own projects and teacher collaborators, as well as customize their online profiles and learning modules. However, this freedom is ultimately curtailed, insofar as the completion of each project or self-teaching material can only ever be a stepping-stone to the *next project*. Given the central importance for the "successful" project worker (and, thus, eTwinner) to be active, all past and present activity on the platform is necessarily superseded by demands for yet further future activity toward the ultimately unrealizable teacher-as-project, where teachers are deemed possible of improvement but never perfection (see also Holloway & Lewis, 2022; Lewis & Holloway, 2019).

Given how the platform is promoted, there is no grand arc or goal toward which all teachers or eTwinners move; rather, it is about each individual teacher getting better, project by project, but entirely heterogeneously, thereby establishing what Vanden Broeck (2020b, p. 671) has called an *unsynchronized simultaneity*. Ultimately then, we would argue that even though some sort of universalized experience of the project is promoted within ESEP, this homogeneity exists only at a distance. Up close, it is highly specific and fragmented, as each ESEP user makes their own decisions and takes their own paths to achieve their own goals, again and again (see also Decuypere & Simons, 2020). This means that eTwinners are figured to create their own project timespaces independent of chronological timespace, which builds on but transcends the individual projects in which they participate, and ultimately bounds their own experiences of teacher-as-project within the ESEP platform.

Conclusion: Projectified Teacher Professionality Running Out of Space and Time

In this chapter, we have sought to demonstrate how educational projects occupy a central place on the ESEP platform, as well as how project and platform logics are now increasingly shaping contemporary teacher professionality and learning. Rather than merely seeing the platform as a passive or neutral vehicle for hosting projects, we would instead suggest that ESEP provides an exemplary environment for repositioning project thinking as a central, and even *necessary*, aspect of teacher professionality. Moreover, the ongoing development of teacher professionality via projects (i.e., teacher-as-project) is also accompanied, at the same time, by the educative work of projects themselves on the platform (i.e., project-as-teacher). In this respect, we see the emergence of a simultaneously platformized and projectified form of teacher professionality (and other professionalities more broadly). In the beginning of this chapter, we advanced our understanding of teacher professionalism as situated within the combination of knowledge, discretion, and responsibility. What this chapter has shown, is that – and how – platforms reconfigure each of these dimensions. First, ESEP and eT both advance and require new sorts of knowledge and new ways of knowledge promotion (e.g., with regard to the project lifecycle). In terms of discretion, it was rendered clear that platforms install new dependencies (e.g., being dependent on the project form) as much as they advance new forms of teacher autonomy (e.g., being completely autonomous with regards to which projects are being made). Lastly, in terms of responsibility, the chapter showed how platforms responsibilize teachers to adhere to the project form, and thus both at once open up (e.g., working internationally with other teachers) and curtail (e.g., only being able to do so via projects) teachers' space of action. We should be clear here that we are not critiquing the content or methods of ESEP, or the staff who helped produce them. Indeed, there is seemingly a broad consensus amongst the NSO and CSS staff with whom we have spoken that the ESEP content, digital community, and project learning benefits teacher professional development and classroom practice. Nevertheless, this does not preclude that such a singular focus on the teacher-as-project and the project-as-teacher is actively reshaping the possibilities for how teachers negotiate what it means to be a teaching *professional* (i.e., ontological) and for what it means to think and act *professionally* (i.e., epistemological). While concerns for the changing nature of teacher professionalism are by no means an entirely recent development (for instance, see Holloway, 2021; Sachs, 2016), we would nonetheless argue that idealized forms of teacher professionality – emphasizing the teacher-as-project/project-as-teacher and the importance of connecting with like-minded teachers – are being actively constituted via the ESEP platform. In this sense, future research on digital education platforms and teacher professionality should explicitly adopt a mutual concern for both platform and project logics, as well as their respective effects on one another (Hartong & Decuypere, 2023). Moreover, this chapter has limited itself to discussing the projectified logics that are present on ESEP. As such, we did not focus on how teachers themselves use the platform and how they experience such projectified understandings of teacher professionality, which are important avenues for further research.

In addition, this chapter contributes to our understanding of how projectified logics are increasingly at work in the fields of teacher education, development, and learning. Whereas a plethora of literature has emerged around "project based learning" in the classroom, and how to use project-based learning in order to enhance the learning of students (see, for instance, Blumenfeld et al., 1991; Kaldi et al., 2011; Miller et al., 2021), this chapter disentangles how the project form is increasingly deployed as a governance technique to stimulate and instill specific forms of learning in teachers as well. Moreover, the usage of badges and awards is emblematic of new forms of learning, where teacher professionality is not (only) evidenced through the following of workshops or official trainings, but equally through the recognizing – and credentialing – of (project) work conducted on a platform that can subsequently be shared (e.g., on social media) with other teachers and/or schools (see equally Berry et al., 2016; Lewis, 2022). We can see in this an ongoing evolution regarding processes of projectification and the teacher in both their sense of self and, importantly, their teaching *practice*. For instance, ESEP exemplifies not only the role of platforms and projects in teacher professional learning but also in their didactics and pedagogy; that is, teachers learn and know themselves through projects, *and* they increasingly come to teach their students (as well as other teachers) through projects. This suggests that platformisation and projectification provide prolific avenues for further research beyond theorizing different modes of governing teacher knowledge, learning and practice, and incorporating the role that projects are now playing in didactics and pedagogy. However, it should be noted that the platform we have analyzed is a distinctively European one (even though users worldwide theoretically have access to it). In a context of increasing platformization around the globe, including the Global South (see Cobo & Rivas, 2023), it seems particularly interesting to further explore if, how, and to what extent, projectification is a worldwide tendency impacting teacher professionalism.

In closing, we would like to reiterate here the explicit connection between new forms of projectified teacher professionality and digital platforms, like ESEP. Such platforms now typify how individuals seeking the idealized form of teacher professionality are forever starting individual projects anew and yet, at the same time, are never quite finishing anything. The ultimate life-long project – that is, the self-as-project – instead stretches indeterminably and unattainably before them. Indeed, the personal project timespace of each eTwinner reflects a projectified teacher professionality that requires there always be *another project* and another opportunity for yet further improvement. As such, meaningful progress toward attaining the idealized teacher professionality becomes impossible: for every step forward taken by the teacher, the horizon recedes further in the form of yet un-attempted and incomplete projects. While this may not differ from a conventional understanding of profession(al)s and the premise that they are permanently seeking to improve, what we see with ESEP is this logic taken fully to a different (and previously unseen) projectified and platformed conclusion. Teacher professionality is thus being governed in ESEP through new platformed and projectified temporalities. Given that being part of a project is the *sine qua non*e of the contemporary teaching professional, such teachers may well find themselves "out of space" and "out of time": caught in the never-ending task of completing an infinite series of projects within an infinite series of project timespaces.

Funding

This work was supported by the Australian Research Council [grant number DE190101141] and the KU Leuven Research Council [grant number C14/18/041].

Notes

1 This chapter is a profound reworking and update of: Lewis, S., & Decuypere, M. (2023). 'Out of time': Constructing teacher professionality as a perpetual project on the eTwinning digital platform. *Tertium Comparationis*, 29(1), 22–47. https://doi.org/10.31244/tc.2023.01.02

2 First launched in 2005 and funded by the EC's *Erasmus+* program, the original eTwinning platform (2005–2022) has become a flagship education initiative for the EC, reportedly connecting more than 215,000 European schools and more than 945,000 European teachers together via its online professional learning community before the merger into ESEP (eTwinning, 2021).

References

Berglund, K., Lindgren, M., & Packendorff, J. (2020). The worthy human being as prosuming subject: 'Projectified selves' in emancipatory project studies. *Project Management Journal*, 51(4), 367–377.

Berry, B., Airhart, K. M., & Byrd, P. A. (2016). Microcredentials: Teacher learning transformed. *Phi Delta Kappan*, 98(3), 34–40.

Blumenfeld, P. C., Soloway, E., Marx, R. W., Krajcik, J. S., Guzdial, M., & Palincsar, A. (1991). Motivating project-based learning: Sustaining the doing, supporting the learning. *Educational Psychologist*, 26(3–4), 369–398.

Bradbury, A. (2019). Datafied at four: The role of data in the 'schoolification' of early childhood education in England. *Learning, Media and Technology*, 44(1), 7–21.

Brass, J., & Holloway, J. (2021). Re-professionalising teaching: The new professionalism in the United States. *Critical Studies in Education*, 62(4), 519–536.

Büttner, S., & Leopold, L. (2016). A 'new spirit' of public policy? The project world of EU funding. *European Journal of Cultural and Political Sociology*, 3(1), 41–71.

Cobo, C., & Rivas, A.(Eds.). (2023). *The new education policy landscape: From education systems to platforms*. Routledge.

Decuypere, M. (2021). The topologies of data practices: A methodological introduction. *Journal of New Approaches in Educational Research*, 9(2), 67–84.

Decuypere, M., Grimaldi, E., & Landri, P. (2021). Introduction: Critical studies of digital education platforms. *Critical Studies in Education*, 62(1), 1–16.

Decuypere, M., & Lewis, S. (2023). Topological genealogy: A methodology to research transnational digital governance in/through/as change. *Journal of Education Policy*, 38(1), 23–45.

Decuypere, M., & Simons, M. (2020). Pasts and futures that keep the possible alive: Reflections on time, space, education and governing. *Educational Philosophy and Theory*, 52(6), 640–652.

Demirkasımoğlu, N. (2010). Defining "Teacher professionalism" from different perspectives. *Procedia-Social and Behavioral Sciences*, 9, 2047–2051.

eTwinning. (2021). *Homepage*. Retrieved 10/10/2021 from https://www.etwinning.net/en/pub/index.htm.

EU Academy. (2023a). *Setting up your eTwinning project*. Retrieved October 10, 2023, from https://academy.europa.eu/courses/setting-up-your-etwinning-project/view/?fromPath=dashboard.

EU Academy. (2023b). *eTwinning projects and Twinspace*. Retrieved October 10, 2023 from https://academy.europa.eu/enrol/index.php?id=1615.

European Commission. (2019). *Your journey through education in Europe!* Retrieved October 10, 2023, from https://www.schooleducationgateway.eu/downloads/SEG-eTwinning%20Infosheet_June-2019_EN.pdf.

European Commission. (2020). *eTwinning: the community for schools in Europe*. Retrieved October 10, 2023, from https://www.schooleducationgateway.eu/en/pub/resources/tutorials/etwinning–the-largest-commun.htm#:~:text=eTwinning%20 promotes%20school%20collaboration%20in,online%20professional%20development%20 for%20educators.

European Commission. (2023a). *eTwinning for future teachers*. Retrieved October 10, 2023, from https://school-education.ec.europa.eu/en/about/etwinning-future-teachers.

European Commission. (2023b). *European school education platform: People*. Retrieved October 10, 2023, from https://school-education.ec.europa.eu/en/networking/people.

European Commission. (2023c). *eTwinning school label*. Retrieved October 10, 2023, from https://school-education.ec.europa.eu/en/recognition/etwinning-school-label.

European Commission. (2023d). *More information about the eTwinning European prizes*. Retrieved October 10, 2023, from https://school-education.ec.europa.eu/en/more-information-about-etwinning-european-prizes.

Fred, M. (2020). Local government projectification in practice: A multiple institutional logic perspective. *Local Government Studies*, 46(3), 351–370.

Godenhjelm, S., Lundin, R. A., & Sjöblom, S. (2015). Projectification in the public sector: The case of the European union. *International Journal of Managing Projects in Business*, 8(2), 324–348.

Hardy, I., & Melville, W. (2019). Professional learning as policy enactment: The primacy of professionalism. *Education Policy Analysis Archives*, 27(90), 1–27.

Hargreaves, A. (2019). Teacher collaboration: 30 years of research on its nature, forms, limitations and effects. *Teachers and Teaching*, 25(5), 603–621.

Hartong, S., & Decuypere, M. (2023). Platformed professional(itie)s and the ongoing digital transformation of education. *Tertium Comparationis*, 29(1), 1–21.

Holloway, J. (2021). Teachers and teaching: (Re)thinking professionalism, subjectivity and critical inquiry. *Critical Studies in Education*, 62(4), 411–421.

Holloway, J., & Lewis, S. (2022). Governing teachers through datafication: Physical-virtual hybridity and language interoperability in teacher accountability. *Big Data & Society*, 9(2), 1–14.

Jensen, A., Thuesen, C., & Geraldi, J. (2016). The projectification of everything: Projects as a human condition. *Project Management Journal*, 47(3), 21–34.

Kaldi, S., Filippatou, D., & Govaris, C. (2011). Project-based learning in primary schools: Effects on pupils' learning and attitudes. *Education*, 39(1), 35–47.

Kalff, Y. (2017). The knowledge worker and the projectified self: Domesticating and disciplining creativity. *work organisation. Labour & Globalisation*, 11(1), 10–27.

Lewis, S. (2022). An apple for teacher (education)? Reconstituting teacher professional learning and expertise via the apple teacher digital platform. *International Journal of Educational Research*, 115, 1–14.

Lewis, S., & Decuypere, M. (2023). 'Out of time': Constructing teacher professionality as a perpetual project on the eTwinning digital platform. *Tertium Comparationis*, 29(1), 22–47.

Lewis, S., & Hartong, S. (2022). New shadow professionals and infrastructures around the datafied school: Topological thinking as an analytical device. *European Educational Research Journal*, 21(6), 946–960.

Lewis, S., & Holloway, J. (2019). Datafying the teaching 'profession': Remaking the professional teacher in the image of data. *Cambridge Journal of Education*, 49(1), 35–51.

Lewis, S., & Lingard, B. (2023). Platforms, profits and PISA for schools: New actors, by-passes and topological spaces in global educational governance. *Comparative Education*, 59(1), 99–117.

Lindgren, M., & Packendorff, J. (2007). Performing arts and the art of performing: On co-construction of project work and professional identities in theatres. *International Journal of Project Management*, 25(4), 354–364.

Miller, E. C., Severance, S., & Krajcik, J. (2021). Motivating teaching, sustaining change in practice: Design principles for teacher learning in project-based learning contexts. *Journal of Science Teacher Education, 32*(7), 757–779.

Moore, A., & Clarke, M. (2016). 'Cruel optimism': Teacher attachment to professionalism in an era of performativity. *Journal of Education Policy, 31*(5), 666–677.

Muckenthaler, M., Tillmann, T., Weiß, S., & Kiel, E. (2020). Teacher collaboration as a core objective of school development. *School Effectiveness and School Improvement, 31*(3), 486–504.

Nguyen, D., & Ng, D. (2020). Teacher collaboration for change: Sharing, improving, and spreading. *Professional Development in Education, 46*(4), 638–651.

Sachs, J. (2016). Teacher professionalism: Why are we still talking about it? *Teachers and Teaching, 22*(4), 413–425.

Saldaña, J. (2016). *The coding manual for qualitative researchers* (3rd ed.). Sage.

Simons, M. (2015). Governing education without reform: The power of the example. *Discourse: Studies in the Cultural Politics of Education, 36*(5), 712–731.

Suchman, L. (2012). Configuration. In C. Lury, & N. Wakeford (Eds.), *Inventive methods: The happening of the social* (pp. 48–60). Routledge.

Thévenot, L. (1984). Rules and implements: Investment in forms. *Social Science Information, 23*(1), 1–45.

Thrift, N., & May, J. (2001). *Timespace: Geographies of temporality*. Routledge.

Vanden Broeck, P. (2020a). Beyond school: Transnational differentiation and the shifting form of education in world society. *Journal of Education Policy, 35*(6), 836–855.

Vanden Broeck, P. (2020b). The problem of the present: On simultaneity, synchronisation and transnational education projects. *Educational Philosophy and Theory, 52*(6), 664–675.

Williamson, B., Bayne, S., & Shay, S. (2020). The datafication of teaching in higher education: Critical issues and perspectives. *Teaching in Higher Education, 25*(4), 351–365.

Ylijoki, O.-H. (2016). Projectification and conflicting temporalities in academic knowledge production. *Theory of Science, 38*(1), 7–26.

10 Working from Professional and Political Scripts

Teach for All and the Globalization of a (Domestic) Teacher Education Model

Matthew A. M. Thomas and Elisabeth E. Lefebvre

Introduction

How do teachers learn to become teachers? Who chooses to teach? And what impact does their work have on the communities they serve? These and related questions remain central to the teaching profession but deserve special consideration in an increasingly globalized world (Paine et al., 2016). While virtually all countries have mechanisms in place for recruiting, training, placing, supporting, and monitoring (or surveilling) the work that teachers do, new forms of global attention, comparison, and governance have called these mechanisms into question. As Paine and Zeichner (2012) argue:

> where previous waves of education reforms, in the United States and internationally, have directed energies to questions of access to education, systems, and curriculum, the past decade has shown a marked shift as national and international policy makers turn their gaze toward teachers and teaching.
>
> (p. 569)

The expansion of global testing regimes such as NAEP, TIMSS, and PISA has only made these efforts seemingly more urgent (e.g., Sorensen et al., 2021). Part catalyst for, part response to a growing number of critiques surrounding teachers and teaching, several organizations have emerged as proposed alternatives to traditional models of training, licensure, placement, and support. They tend to rely on a number of adaptable scripts that position them as different and purportedly better at addressing the perceived deficient status quo within the teaching profession, and education in general.

Teach For All (TFAll) represents a significant example of such organizations in terms of both its international scope and impact on global conversations about teaching. Indeed, since its inception, TFAll has positioned itself as a disruptor. It does not recruit or train its teachers in the usual ways, nor generally work with existing teachers. Instead, it proposes a new, heterarchical approach to teaching and teacher education policy that it sees as replicable or

DOI: 10.4324/9781003441731-14

adaptable across multiple country contexts (Olmedo et al., 2013), regardless of their unique histories or contemporary sociopolitical contexts. TFAll has grown from its initial programs (Teach For America and Teach First UK) to now include affiliates across six continents, all of which voice a shared mission: "... a world where all children have the education, support, and opportunity to shape a better future" (TFAll, 2024a).

To articulate this alternative, shareable approach to teacher learning and teaching, TFAll has relied on a number of professional and political scripts. In this chapter, we explore and highlight several examples of these scripts in action, describing the type of teacher/leader TFAll seeks to recruit, how they expect recruits to act, and the systems they are meant to change. Building on Matsui's (2015) previous work focused on Teach For America corps members, we use the term "scripts" intentionally to point toward TFAll's corporate emphasis on the replicability of its approach (i.e., its "scripted" solution to deeply rooted challenges across diverse contexts) and instrumentalist teacher training methods (i.e., follow these "learning scripts" to ensure the hoped-for outcome). Our use of the term "scripts" also points to an inherent adaptability; though scripted, TFAll's manifestations may involve notable variations. In the following sections, we first briefly outline the history of TFAll, before describing the five generic but adaptive scripts used by TFAll and its affiliates. We conclude with a discussion of what these scripts suggest for research, teacher learning, and practice, as well as for the future of the teaching profession *writ large*.

Becoming a Global Trend

Teach For America (TFA) was conceptualized by Wendy Kopp in 1989 as part of her undergraduate honors' thesis at Princeton. She was drawn to issues related to workforce development, and particularly how to unite the business and education communities by recruiting and placing ambitious, young teachers who could help reduce teacher shortages, ideally while simultaneously improving the quality of education and human capital in the United States (Kopp, 1989, 2001). Her thesis outlined plans for a new form of teacher corps, drawing inspiration from other similar programs in the United States (Blumenreich & Rogers, 2021; Kopp, 1989). With a significant amount of social capital and gumption (see Thomas & Baxendale, 2022), she subsequently raised enough economic capital to launch the program the following year with approximately 400 eager recruits.

Despite some rough patches as the organization found its footing (Rauschenberger, 2021), TFA rapidly expanded both the number of teachers it recruited and placed, as well as the geographic regions where it worked. It eventually became one of the single largest providers of new teachers in the United States, capitalizing on the increasing percentage of teachers entering through alternative routes rather than four-year college-recommending programs (Grossman & Loeb, 2008; Lefebvre & Thomas, 2019). TFA's successful expansion laid the groundwork for the global spread of TFA through its soon-to-be umbrella organization, TFAll, launched in 2007 at the Clinton Global Initiative with the expressed purpose of supporting the development of TFA-like programs in other national contexts (Thomas et al., 2021). TFAll programs now exist in 60+ countries worldwide, with continued plans for expansion (see Lefebvre et al., 2022).

To accomplish such scaling, TFAll has explicitly and implicitly utilized a number of professional and political "scripts" to shape its work. These scripts help structure the programs in similar yet adaptable ways, supporting both organizational discourses and individual and social practices. As noted above, we build on the notion of scripts as employed by Matsui (2015), who drew on key phrases used commonly within TFAll – and particularly TFA – to highlight underpinning ideologies and practices framing the advancement of these organizations. Her discussion examined both an overall, generic "TFA Script" as well as more specific discourses, such as "nothing elusive," "closing the achievement gap," "work hard, get smart," and "more" (p. 21). While there is some overlap in the five scripts we present below – perhaps most notably in terms of "working relentlessly" – our central and overarching argument moves beyond Matsui's in at least two ways. First, we posit these scripts are no longer limited simply to TFA (the central focus of her work), but serve as an adaptable ideological framework guiding the spread of TFAll as well as similar programs around the world. Second, we see them as flexible narratives that allow for embodied improvisation, reinterpretation, and even revision. Viewed in this way, scripts are value-laden frameworks that guide action and justify a particular approach to educational reform but may not be applied uniformly across contexts.

Scripting (Global) Teacher Learning and Work

Broadly speaking, there are two mutually reinforcing sets of scripts employed by TFAll. The first set includes "professional" scripts, which focus on the characteristics and behaviors expected of recruits, and arguably by extension, their students. Enacting these scripts, TFAll proposes to enlist a new and better cadre of educational professionals, in some cases displacing those who might have otherwise been hired. In subsequently demonstrating their success, largely through measurable forms of academic achievement, TFAll further aims to justify its comparatively technicist approach. The second set of scripts is more "political" in orientation, seeking to disrupt existing educational systems themselves. The entry-point for these scripts is that extant national educational systems are broken, in need of fixing, and that TFAll offers a global – though not necessarily uniform – solution to issues of inequity. With these scripts, TFAll both argues for its necessity and justifies its particular brand of intervention, seeking to ensure its longevity and embeddedness in professional and political systems alike.

Professional Scripts: The Best Teachers, Learning Quickly and Working Relentlessly

Script 1: The Best and Brightest

From its roots in TFA and Teach First UK, TFAll programs have largely operated under the premise of recruiting a nations' "best and brightest" (Blumenreich & Rogers, 2016; Elliott, 2018), or as Nimer and Makkouk (2021) noted about Teach For Lebanon, the "cream of the cream of the cream" (p. 106). In the United States, for instance, TFA's acceptance rate – often reported as approximately 10–15% (Maier, 2012) – has been used to bolster this claim, though TFA's exclusivity and corps size has waned in recent years (Lefebvre & Thomas, 2024). Across the TFAll network, the "best and brightest" motto and ethos galvanizes the interests of highly ambitious and driven individuals who are drawn to TFAll programs. For example, the websites of TFAll and its affiliate programs are replete with references to their remarkable, high-achieving *recruits* who go on to become remarkable, high-achieving *alumni* (in India: Blumenreich & Gupta, 2015; in the United States, United Kingdom, China, and Norway: Ellis et al., 2016; and in Ghana, Nigeria, Uganda, and TFAll: Lefebvre et al., 2022).

As TFAll frames its mission, affiliate organizations "recruit their nations' diverse, promising leaders to commit to at least two years to teach in marginalized communities" (TFAll, 2023). Teach For Kenya (2023) and other affiliates draw on similar language in their mission statements: "We recruit Kenya's most promising university graduates and high-performing young professionals to serve as full-time teachers in low-income schools for two years." Afterward, alumni "continue to work with other educators, allies, and communities to improve the quality of education for students and effect the systemic changes needed to enable all children to thrive" (TFAll, 2023). In this way, as Elliott (2018) argues in her analysis of Teach First UK, TFAll teachers are "constructed – and construct themselves – as elites who are other and better than teachers, doing heroic, philanthropic, life-changing work" (p. 272). This is perhaps one of the reasons they are typically branded as Corps Members (United States), Associates (Australia), or Fellows (Nigeria, Uganda, etc.) – to further distinguish them from "just" "regular" teachers (see Crawford-Garrett & Thomas, 2018).

Elliot's (2021) work comparing teachers recruited by Teach First UK and Teach South Africa highlights how this particular script manifests itself through their framing of teacher learning and identity. In looking across two national organizations, Elliott shows how various TFAll affiliates adapt their "unifying principles" to apply to their specific contexts, while maintaining remarkably similar language. She references as one example a Teach South Africa podcast in which its recruits are referred to as "the heroes of 2015…who volunteer not just their time but their lives" (p. 89). Similar discourses and practices are adopted by Teach First and Teach South Africa teachers themselves, who rely on philanthropic language to describe their work. Across both organizations, Elliott (2021) found that graduates recruited into the programs, as well as the programs themselves, described the teachers as "elite, special, and 'other'" (p. 87).

This script that TFAll teachers are set apart from – or even a step above – other (likely traditionally trained) teachers has important implications for teacher learning and work. First, it reinforces existing discourses in some contexts that blame traditionally trained teachers for educational woes (see Goldstein, 2015). Second, the script maintains exclusivity not by improving the esteem of all teachers, but in setting apart its teachers (fellows/corps members) as different and special, thereby making an otherwise potentially "unattractive" career worthy of pursuit (see Labaree, 2010). Third, and more importantly for TFAll teachers themselves, a related assumption is often made: because of their brightness and uniqueness, these "remarkable individuals" can become teachers in considerably condensed timeframes.

Script 2: Learning Quickly

TFAll programs generally follow a similar operational model, predicated on the exceptionality of their recruits. Specifically, most TFAll programs prepare their teachers through a short "Summer Institute" program consisting of 5–8 weeks of study and practice. The condensed nature of these training programs has led to TFAll's branding as a so-called "fast-track" model. Although fast-track models are not necessarily unique to TFAll, the organization is certainly one of the earliest and most prominent examples (Blumenreich & Rogers, 2021; Thomas & Baxendale, 2022).

In the United States, for instance, TFA's five-week Summer Institute program has been comprised of sessions focused on foundational educational concepts, the "learning cycle,"[1] instructional "best practices," curriculum and lesson planning, and real-life teaching with students completing summer school programs. The pace and intensity of Summer Institute programs speak to vital issues of andragogy – how adults learn, process, and make use of new information. Moreover, the practical teaching component wherein new recruits teach summer school students is extremely short in comparison with more traditional teacher education programs – estimated to be as little as 18 hours throughout the five weeks (Brewer, 2013). It also may not necessarily align with the actual content area or level in which the TFA teacher will eventually teach, a stark departure from other models of teacher education. Thomas (2018) notes: "As a hypothetical but germane example, an accounting major who co-teaches sixth-grade math during a 5-week Summer Institute does not have requisite background knowledge of approaches and processes to begin a placement in Grades 7 to 12 special education" (p. 451).

With such a condensed period and potential mismatch of age- or content-level expertise, it is not surprising that many TFA teachers find Summer Institute immensely stressful (see Brewer & deMarrais, 2015; Matsui, 2015). Stoneburner (2018) studied the experiences of TFA teachers during their time in this condensed pre-service teacher learning program, writing that "for the majority of participants who have limited or no previous teaching experience, there is a lot to learn in a short amount of time" (p. 67). Indeed, one of his key recommendations for teacher learning practice (in the TFA program) was to "decrease workload and increase meaning making" (p. 72), further noting that "a review of the daily Summer Institute schedule shows that there is very little, if any, opportunity for participants to make meaning of what they are learning" (p. 73).

Interestingly, Smith (2023) notes that one of TFA's responses to criticism about its shortened model has been to offer corps members admitted as juniors (i.e., third-year university students) additional opportunities to prepare by engaging in early, optional training focused on understanding inequality and classroom management. In other words, TFA's response to criticism has been to increase the time spent on training – moving the program slightly closer to the much longer training model followed by more traditional teacher education programs. Perhaps this is also why some newer affiliates, like Teach For Uganda (2023), require longer periods of training, though at three months, it is still fairly short. Despite these shifts and differences across contexts, there remains little public research about TFAll's fast-track model for pre-service teacher learning across its network. In sum, we are only starting to address a wide range of questions about the teacher learning that occurs (or doesn't) before TFAll teachers enter the classroom, even as the model has been transferred around the world based on its presumed effectiveness.

Professional Script 3: Working Relentlessly

A third professional script is that TFAll teachers must work relentlessly in pursuit of educational excellence and equity. At face value, this is admirable; there is much to accomplish in reforming educational systems, processes, and vitally, learning outcomes. How this script is operationalized may be problematic, however, particularly when pursuing an unattainable and discursive "more" leads to serious personal issues.

Matsui (2015), for example, chronicled how the corps members she interviewed experienced negative effects to their social and emotional health because of TFA, including increased alcohol consumption, significant changes to their weight and/or physical health, strains to relationships, and most commonly, fatigue. Veltri (2010) and Crawford-Garrett (2013) noted similar stresses in their analyses, and in our own work we found TFA teachers internalized the notion of "relentless pursuit" as they sought to outwork larger systemic challenges (Thomas & Lefebvre, 2018). Notions of meritocracy were also commonplace among TFAll teachers in New Zealand and the United States (Crawford-Garrett et al., 2021), creating a competitive environment in which recruits both felt individually responsible for tackling the problems they saw and compelled to do so more successfully than the next recruit. Collectively, these patterns contributed to the notion that bright, dedicated, and well-meaning TFAll teachers should help students overcome any barrier they faced.

This third script is also related to TFA teachers' "internal locus of control," a phrase popularized by *Teaching as Leadership* (Farr, 2010), a key organizational text.[2] Within TFA, the intensity of being a novice teacher working in an underserved school is compounded by significant organizational pressures to single-handedly overcome systemic issues. Brewer (2014) highlights how the onus to (re)position students for success despite both school-based and external sociocultural and socioeconomic influences, encourages disenfranchisement and in some cases burnout. The script that many TFAll teachers learn is that they cannot "blame" any external factors for their students' lack of "significant gains" (initially defined by the organization as 1.5–2 years of growth, albeit with less-clear mechanisms for measurement), but should instead focus on what is within their "internal locus of control." In Southern's (2021) study, a Teach First Cymru (Wales) teacher "explained to his peers that 'self-leadership' was the way to overcome any challenge; a term which derives from the Teach First Values, and which implies a singular, potentially aloof, approach to teaching" (p. 187). Thus, if a student is failing, it must be due to shortcomings on the part of the teacher (Kretchmar, 2014). Coupled with the fourth script described below, this causes some TFAll teachers to presume they care more about student success than non-TFA teachers.

Political Scripts: Fixing Systems, Everywhere

Script 4: Traditional Systems Are Broken

Operating in tandem with the professional scripts explored above, the generic political script that traditional educational systems are broken and likely to remain so without outside intervention, underpins TFAll programming. In this framing of the "problem," the disruption and innovation delivered by TFAll is a panacea to improve student learning and outcomes (e.g., Ellis et al., 2024; Lefebvre et al., 2022). These taken-for-granted assumptions about "failing schools" occur across multiple levels: traditionally trained teachers are ineffective, public/government schools are inadequate, and teacher education institutions are unwilling or unable to meet the needs of communities and classrooms. Importantly, non-TFAll teachers serve as crucial evidence for this script. To return to an example from Farr's (2010) work, referenced above, *Teaching as Leadership* includes an extended vignette describing Ms. Lora, a TFA teacher who worked ardently to improve educational outcomes in her school, including rejecting the low expectations and work ethic of her traditionally trained teaching colleagues.

While it is certainly true that not all teachers are equally good at or committed to their work, this "broken systems" script permeates through TFAll organizations, such that recruits are habituated to see themselves as protagonists within an antagonistic system, a phenomenon unfortunately sometimes reinforced by tensions with non-TFA teachers (see Anderson et al., 2022; Thomas, 2018). The role played by TFAll mentors also reinforces this conflict. In many TFAll programs, there are designated supervisors or instructional coaches who observe and offer feedback to the TFAll teachers on a regular basis. For instance, Teach For Uganda (2023) – which describes its fellows as "transform[ing] their classrooms by setting high expectations for their students" (presumably in contrast to the educational experiences students might have otherwise) – provides fellows with dedicated leadership coaches as well as in-service trainings and online resources. On the one hand, this is a wonderful strategy and seeks to address many of the challenges faced by novice teachers in their first and second years of teaching. We know from research that early career teachers need significant support and instructional coaching, and this is one of the benefits that TFAll programs provide. Some recruits may even opt to join TFAll because they are eager to receive this type of tailored feedback (see Lefebvre & Thomas, 2024). On the other hand, the trainers, mentors, and instructional coaches provided by TFAll generally work outside the traditional/standard educational system (in part as a means to ensure fidelity to the model) – and themselves often have only a few years of teaching experience. Teach For Lebanon, for instance, initially held a four-week training at a local university; however, the agreement broke down because the university coordinators wanted to include additional discussions of mechanisms and theories for cultivating robust systemic change. Eventually, "TFL implemented the training themselves in one of the partner schools, bringing in two teaching mentors from Teach For America, one trainer from Teach For All" (Nimer & Makkouk, 2021, p. 109). In this way, TFAll's model sometimes displaces rather than works within traditional structures; instead of connecting novice TFA teachers to experienced mentor teachers outside various TFAll programs, they provide their own supervisors, who themselves often have only slightly more experience than the teachers they mentor (see Anderson et al., 2022).

Public/government schools and systems are also a part of the "broken" script and TFAll programs frequently work closely with charter schools in the United States (Lefebvre & Thomas, 2017), KIPP-inspired schools in Taiwan (Thomas & Xu, 2022), and other related alternatives such as the ARK chain of academies in the United Kingdom (Ellis et al., 2024). Subramanian (2018, 2020) further highlighted in her research efforts to reshape the Indian system of primary education, noting that Teach For India has played a significant role in "facilitating a number of managerialistic NGOs" that emphasize "'technologies of reform' such as performance measures, contracts, targets, monitoring and evaluation" (p. 44). Similar efforts have been evidenced in Bangladesh (Adhikary et al., 2021). In these and other contexts, teachers involved in TFAll programs are prepared to teach, often in mechanistic ways, while also being taught that high-level reform and systems change are necessary. This reflects the enduring script within TFAll organizations that traditional public systems are broken and seemingly replaceable, albeit in a more privatized, corporatized, and philanthropized form.

The institutions that traditionally prepare teachers form the last part of this script. Teacher education programs and institutions have been a common target of TFAll organizations, though paradoxically many programs have also used them as a means to establish legitimacy when launching new national programs. In the United States, for instance, many TFA teachers are required to take graduate-level coursework in education while teaching full time in their classrooms. This is often a very challenging experience, particularly because they are what we have termed "synchronous-service teachers", operating in the liminal space between pre-service and in-service teachers (see Thomas & Lefebvre, 2020). As a result, when they enter the classroom as students, TFA teachers seem to want more challenging work while also being unable or disinterested in putting forth the effort. Other research has highlighted similar issues wherein the expectations of university-based teacher educators do not necessarily match those of TFAll teachers or national affiliate programs (e.g., in Australia: Moss et al., 2021; in the United States: McNew-Birren et al., 2018). Here engagement with theory in traditional teacher education programs is proffered as evidence of its brokenness; it is often perceived as preventing further opportunities to "do" or "practice" teaching.

Unfortunately, these scripts related to broken systems are not just learned by TFAll teachers, but by the general public as well. Several studies have highlighted how media portrayals of TFAll programs commence from the assumption that public, traditional systems are broken; therefore, innovation and disruption are essential to save students, schools, and societies. Gautreaux and Delgado (2016) analyzed 32 newspaper articles from across 12 countries where TFAll programs operate, and Chan et al. (2023) analyzed 122 newspaper articles about Teach For Australia; both studies highlighted the distinct media framing of TFAll programs as poised to solve unsolvable problems and TFAll teachers as uniquely equipped to address educational equity. Gautreaux and Delgado (2016), in particular, highlighted the consistent framing of TFAll teachers as better than others due to their possession of "exceptional traits and attributes" (p. 17). This attention:

> diverts the public's attention away from asking questions such as: Why do teachers have to manage with limited resources in the first place? It steers attention away from conversations about adequate and equitable state funding of public schooling and puts the focus and responsibility on the individual teacher.
>
> (p. 17)

Although national education systems are not equally or irrevocably broken, these tropes help lay the foundation for the global proliferation of such programs.

Script 5: The Solutions Are Shareable

The fifth and final script is that the solutions for solving the world's most endemic educational challenges are easily shareable. Indeed, "solutions are shareable" was an explicit TFAll motto in previous years (see Elliott, 2021). In many ways, this script is consistent with broader discourses within education and international development, which for decades have sought to improve educational systems around the world by transferring effective approaches to teaching, learning, and schooling across contexts. By design, TFAll advances this script through the continued "scaling" of fast-track programs and the recruitment of similar teachers/leaders across contexts (Thomas et al., 2021a). An indication of scaling efforts, for example, includes the purchase of website domain names for all countries around the world, such that www.teachfortuvalu.com, www.teachfortuvalu.org, etc., all redirect back to TFAll (see Lefebvre et al., 2022).

This script is perhaps most clearly operationalized by TFAll's annual Global Conference, through which it might "accelerate" its impact (Lefebvre et al., 2022). In October 2023, for example, approximately 600 TFAll "CEOs, staff members, teachers, alumni, students, and board members from more than 60 countries, as well as policymakers, civil society practitioners, supporters, and allies from the African continent and beyond" gathered in Kenya to share insights across the network (TFAll, 2023). The network also hosts regular webinars meant to foster information sharing and hires staff whose purpose is to facilitate these information flows across its heterarchical, networked form of governance (see Olmedo et al., 2013). In affiliating themselves with the TFAll network, programs commit to a "common purpose and approach" through the "exchange of ideas and solutions across borders and adapt them to local needs" (TFAll, 2023).

Scholars within comparative education have highlighted the fact that these (and related) events are where power brokers interact, policies and resources flow, and new constructions of educational systems are made (e.g., Adhikary & Lingard, 2018). At the same time, hierarchical relationships are sometimes (re)made through the process of policy borrowing (Lefebvre et al., 2022). For example, Friedrich et al. (2015) highlighted how new forms of discourse and datafication are used at events like the TFAll Global Conference to address lingering concerns about the particularities of certain contexts while reinforcing the "shared problems, shared solutions" approach (see Ahmann, 2015; Ellis et al., 2024). In this way, the development of new versions of the same program can be initiated from above, while legitimated by the illusion of bottom-up, grassroots organizing (Friedrich, 2014). One small example of this can be seen through the conflicting origin stories of various TFAll programs, such as in Lebanon (Nimer & Makkouk, 2021) and China (Lam, 2020), where initiatives were made to appear "local" despite their support from corporate and/or international organizations, including TFAll. It is through this final script – which in turn rests on the four other scripts – that TFAll substantiates its practices.

Concluding Thoughts on TFAll's Purposes, Processes, and Impact

Through the scaling of the TFAll program over the past 25 years, a new model for teacher learning and teachers' work has emerged, framed by several key professional and political scripts. First, the "best and brightest" recent college graduates are recruited, providing an alternative to a presumably problematic status quo "teacher." Second, these recruits are expected to learn quickly through a fast-track model, absorbing as much as four years of study and field experience in a few weeks, then apply their nascent teaching knowledge and experience in the classroom. Third, they must embody these scripts relentlessly, viewing anything less than success as a personal failure. Fourth, they operate within (presumedly) broken educational systems and are tasked with making a significant and structural difference. Fifth, and finally, TFAll suggests its work has been "proven" and can be replicated across contexts through its shareable solutions and extensive alumni network.

Taken collectively, these scripts represent an important reconfiguring of teachers' learning and work. As one important example, traditional mechanisms for teacher learning and teaching are cast by these scripts as both inadequate and seemingly endlessly condenseable into smaller forms, thereby warranting disruptive, fast-track solutions. There is no need to build a robust system for teacher training to ensure better student outcomes when you can shrink it down and have teachers learn while they are already teaching. Thus, the first and second scripts beg critical questions about the time needed to prepare teachers for effective, career-long practice, though TFAll's theory of change is less concerned with preparing career teachers than positioning change makers. This is also particularly concerning within an environment in which teaching career patterns, and the profession more broadly, have become increasingly fragmented (Mathou et al., 2023).

TFAll's approach also embodies broader moves toward the responsibilization of teachers – both requiring much more of individuals and schools, while expecting them to accomplish this with less. In emphasizing the efforts of individual teachers to ensure that "all children have the education, support, and opportunity" (TFAll, 2024a), TFAll seems to suggest that existing teachers are themselves a primary cause of educational challenges and therefore changing teacher recruitment and training is a key goal of their reforms. Yet simultaneously, this undermining of the credibility of traditional training mechanisms and their respective teachers raises concerns about the costs of these scripts to the broader profession. We see these framings of social change – with the individual at the foundation – as embodying a seemingly equity-focused form of progressive neoliberalism (see Lefebvre et al., 2022) that is deeply problematic and a barrier to advancing more systemic and enduring equity and societal change.

These scripts also call into question what warrants the replicability of particular models for educational intervention and reform. To be clear, there are important variations in how TFAll has operated within particular educational systems: such as its varied types of partnerships with universities and governments (e.g., Nesje, 2021, 2024; Thomas & Lefebvre, 2020); the length and style of the initial training and other alumni leadership programs, including TFA's Leadership for Educational Equity (e.g., Trujillo et al., 2017); the forms of mentoring and support provided to recruits whilst teaching (Moss et al., 2021); the levels taught, including at kindergartens, middle schools, and polytechnics in Austria (Symeonidis & Eloff, 2023), primary schools in Bangladesh (Adhikary et al., 2021), and (mostly) secondary schools in Australia (Rowe et al., 2023); the subjects taught (science, English, mathematics); and more (see Thomas et al., 2021, for additional variances). Despite these differences, however, there remains remarkable consistency in TFAll's programmatic approaches: such as recruiting the best and brightest, requiring a two-year teaching commitment, training recruits through a condensed model, prioritizing leadership and policy change after teaching, connecting alumni and developing cross-network knowledge sharing, adopting consistent affiliate branding, and more (e.g., Ellis et al., 2024; Lefebvre et al., 2022; Thomas & Xu, 2023).

Indeed, rather than work within existing educational structures to identify challenges and propose tailored reforms, TFAll follows the same sort of disruptive script or "pattern": input highly motivated individuals for (at least) a short time, train them to follow a particular set of mechanistic approaches to classroom instruction and management, then facilitate their leadership post-program wherein they may be poised to make a broader systemic difference. Yet as research from various TFAll affiliates demonstrates and we highlight above, educational intervention is often considerably more complicated. Reform is also more complicated. Teacher training is more complicated. And of course, teaching itself is much more complicated. In sum, and given TFAll's efforts to date to alter existing educational landscapes, we invite critical conversations about the contemporary impacts and residual effects of TFAll on the teaching profession and the work, lives, and learning of all teachers.

Notes

1 This is a four-step process wherein corps members observe, practice, teach, and then reflect and receive feedback on their teaching, before engaging with the cycle again (see Rappaport et al., 2019).
2 Likely in response to some of the criticisms levied at TFA and TFAll, this framework is now described as Teaching as Collective Leadership. See TFAll (2024b).

References

Adhikary, R. W., & Lingard, B. (2018). A critical policy analysis of 'Teach for Bangladesh': A travelling policy touches down. *Comparative Education, 54*(2), 181–202.

Adhikary, R. W., Lingard, B., & Hardy, I. (2021). *Global-national networks in education policy: Primary education, social enterprises and Teach for Bangladesh*. Bloomsbury.

Ahmann, C. (2015). Teach for All: Storytelling 'shared solutions' and scaling global reform. *Education Policy Analysis Archives, 23*(45), 1—27.

Anderson, A., Thomas, M. A. M., & Brewser, T. J. (2022). Teach for America's influence on non-TFA teachers in TFA-hiring schools. *Education Policy Analysis Archives, 30*(98), 1–26.

Blumenreich, M., & Gupta, A. (2015). The globaliszation of Teach for America: An analysis of the institutional discourses of teach for America and teach for India within local contexts. *Teaching and Teacher Education, 48*, 87–96.

Blumenreich, M., & Rogers, B. L. (2016). TFA and the magical thinking of the best and the brightest. *Education Policy Analysis Archives, 24*(13), 1–35.

Blumenreich, M., & Rogers, B. (2021). *Schooling teachers: Teach for America and the future of teacher education*. Teachers College Press.

Brewer, T. J. (2013). From the trenches: A Teach for America corps member's perspective. *Critical Education, 4*(12), 1–17.

Brewer, T. J. (2014). Accelerated burnout: How teach for America's academic impact model and theoretical culture of accountability can foster disillusionment among its corps members. *Educational Studies, 50*(3), 246–263.

Brewer, T. J., & deMarrais, K. (Eds.). (2015). *Teach for America counter-narratives: Alumni speak up and speak out*. Peter Lang.

Chan, S. S. W., Thomas, M. A., & Mockler, N. (2023). Amplifying organisational discourses to the public: Media narratives of Teach for Australia, 2008–2020. *British Educational Research Journal, 49*(2), 231–247.

Crawford-Garrett, K. (2013). *Teach for America and the struggle for urban school reform: Searching for agency in an era of standardization*. Peter Lang.

Crawford-Garrett, K., Oldham, S., & Thomas, M. A. M. (2021). Maintaining meritocratic mythologies: Teach for America and ako mātātupu: Teach First New Zealand. *Comparative Education, 57*(3), 360–376.

Crawford-Garrett, K., & Thomas, M. (2018). Teacher education and the global impact of Teach for All. *Oxford Research Encyclopedia of Education*. https://oxfordre.com/education/view/10.1093/acrefore/9780190264093.001.0001/acrefore-9780190264093-e-417

Elliott, J. (2018). Teach First organisational discourse: What are teach first teachers really being trained for? *Power and Education, 10*(3), 264–274.

Elliott, J. (2021). The Teach for All 'brand': Exploring TFA's successful transferability through case studies of teach South Africa and teach first. In M. A. M. Thomas, E. R. Rauschenberger, & K. Crawford-Garrett (Eds.), *Examining Teach for All: International perspectives on a growing global network* (pp. 79–95). Routledge.

Ellis, V., Gatti, L., & Mansell, W. (2024). *The new political economy of teacher education*. Policy Press.

Ellis, V., Maguire, M., Trippestad, T. A., Liu, Y., Yang, X., & Zeichner, K. (2016). Teaching other people's children, elsewhere, for a while: The rhetoric of a travelling educational reform. *Journal of Education Policy, 31*(1), 60–80.

Farr, S. (2010). *Teaching as leadership: The highly effective teacher's guide to closing the achievement gap*. John Wiley & Sons.

Friedrich, D. S. (2014). Global microlending in education reform: Enseñá por Argentina and the neoliberalization of the grassroots. *Comparative Education Review, 58*(2), 296–321.

Friedrich, D., Walter, M., & Colmenares, E. E. (2015). Making all children count: Teach for All and the universalizing appeal of data. *Education Policy Analysis Archives, 23*(48), 1–21.

Gautreaux, M., & Delgado, S. (2016). Portrait of a Teach for All (TFA) teacher: Media narratives of the universal TFA teacher in 12 countries. *Education Policy Analysis Archives, 24*(110), 1–28.

Goldstein, D. (2015). *The teacher wars: A history of America's most embattled profession*. Anchor.

Grossman, P., & Loeb, S. (2008). *Alternative routes to teaching – Mapping the new landscape of teacher education*. Harvard Education Press.

Kopp, W. (1989). *An argument and plan for the creation of the teacher corps*. (Unpublished Master's Thesis). Princeton University.

Kopp, W. (2001). *One day, all children…The unlikely triumph of Teach for America and what I learned along the way*. Public Affairs.

Kretchmar, K., Sondel, B., & Gerrare, J. J. (2014). Mapping the terrain: Teach For America, charter school reform, and corporate sponsorship. *Journal of Education Policy*, 29(6), 742–759.

Labaree, D. (2010). Teach For America and teacher ed: Heads they win, tails we lose. *Journal of Teacher Education*, 61(1–2), 48–55.

Lam, S. (2020). *From Teach for America to Teach for China: Global teacher education reform and equity in education*. Routledge.

Lefebvre, E. E., Crawford-Garrett, K., & Thomas, M. A. M. (2022). The progressive neoliberalism of Teach for America. In A. Sharma, M. Schmeichel, & B. Wurzburg (Eds.), *Progressive neoliberalism in education* (pp. 135–150). Routledge.

Lefebvre, E. E., Pradhan, S., & Thomas, M. A. M. (2022). The discursive utility of the global, local, and national: Teach for All in Africa. *Comparative Education Review*, 66(4), 620–642.

Lefebvre, E. E., & Thomas, M. A. M. (2017). 'Shit shows' or 'like-minded schools': Charter schools and the neoliberal logic of Teach for America. *Journal of Education Policy*, 32(3), 357–371.

Lefebvre, E. E., & Thomas, M. A. M. (2019). Alternative routes to teaching. In M. A. Peters (Ed.), *Encyclopedia of teacher education*. Springer Nature.

Lefebvre, E. E., & Thomas, M. A. M. (2024). "I knew i had to leave": A bourdieusian analysis of why Teach for America teachers quit early. *Teaching and Teacher Education*. https://doi.org/10.1016/j.tate.2024.104520

Maier, A. (2012). Doing good and doing well: Credentialism and Teach for America. *Journal of Teacher Education*, 63(1), 10–22.

Mathou, C., Sarazin, M., & Dumay, X. (2023). Reshaped teachers' careers? New patterns and the fragmentation of the teaching profession in England. *British Journal of Sociology of Education*, 44(3), 397–417.

Matsui, S. (2015). *Learning from counternarratives in Teach for America – Moving from idealism towards hope*. Peter Lang.

McNew-Birren, J., Hildebrand, T., & Belknap, G. (2018). Strange bedfellows in science teacher preparation: Conflicting perspectives on social justice presented in a Teach for America–university partnership. *Cultural Studies of Science Education*, 13(2), 1–26.

Moss, J., Mccandless, T., Walker-Gibbs, B., Dixon, M., Hitch, D., Johnstone, K., & Loughlin, J. (2021). Teacher educators and the pedagogical and curriculum complexity of Teach for All in Australia. In M. A. M. Thomas, E. R. Rauschenberger, & K. Crawford-Garrett (Eds.), *Examining Teach for All: International perspectives on a growing global network* (pp. 157–178). Routledge.

Nesje, K. (2021). The origin and adaptation of Teach First Norway. In M. A. M. Thomas, E. R. Rauschenberger, & K. Crawford-Garrett (Eds.), *Examining Teach for All: International perspectives on a growing global network* (pp. 63–78). Routledge.

Nimer, M., & Makkouk, N. (2021). Bringing a global model to the Lebanese education context: Adaptation or adoption? In M. A. M. Thomas, E. R. Rauschenberger, & K. Crawford-Garrett (Eds.), *Examining Teach for All: International perspectives on a growing global network* (pp. 96–114). Routledge.

Olmedo, A., Bailey, P. L., & Ball, S. J. (2013). To infinity and beyond…: Heterarchical governance, the Teach for All network in Europe and the making of profits and minds. *European Educational Research Journal*, 12(4), 492–512.

Paine, L., Blömeke, S., & Aydarova, O. (2016). Teachers and teaching in the context of globalization. In C. Bell, & D. Gitomer (Eds.), *Handbook of research on teaching* (pp. 717–786). American Educational Research Association.

Paine, L., & Zeichner, K. (2012). The local and the global in reforming teaching and teacher education. *Comparative Education Review*, 56(4), 569–583.

Rappaport, S., Somers, M., & Granito, K. (2019). A redesigned training program for new teachers: Findings from a study of Teach For America's Summer Institutes. *MDRC*. https://files.eric.ed.gov/fulltext/ED594050.pdf

Rauschenberger, E. (2021). From Teach for America to teach first. In M. A. M. Thomas, E. R. Rauschenberger, & K. Crawford-Garret (Eds.), *Examining Teach for All: International perspectives on a growing global network* (pp. 13–35). Routledge.

Rowe, E., Langman, S., & Lubienski, C. (2023). Privatising public schools via product pipelines: Teach for Australia, policy networks and profit. *Journal of Education Policy*, 1–26.

Smith, S. (2023, June 21). Teach For America. *Oxford Research Encyclopedia of Education*. https://oxfordre.com/education/view/10.1093/acrefore/9780190264093.001.0001/acrefore-9780190264093-e-1879.

Sorensen, T. B., Ydesen, C., & Robertson, S. L. (2021). Re-reading the OECD and education: The emergence of a global governing complex – An introduction. *Globalisation, Societies and Education*, 19(2), 99–107.

Southern, A. (2021). Teach First Cymru: Whose mission? Teach first and the Welsh government's 'national mission' for education. In M. A. M. Thomas, E. R. Rauschenberger, & K. Crawford-Garrett (Eds.), *Examining Teach For All: International perspectives on a growing global network* (pp. 179–199). Routledge.

Stoneburner, J. D. (2018). *Understanding teacher stress and wellbeing at Teach For America's Summer Institute* [Unpublished doctoral Dissertation]. UCLA.

Subramanian, V. (2020). Parallel partnerships: Teach for India and new institutional regimes in municipal schools in new Delhi. *International Studies in Sociology of Education*, 29(4), 409–428.

Subramanian, V. K. (2018). From government to governance: Teach for India and new networks of reform in school education. *Contemporary Education Dialogue*, 15(1), 21–50.

Symeonidis, V., & Eloff, I. (2023). Addressing teacher shortages to achieve inclusive and equitable education for all: Policies for the supply of and demand for qualified teachers in Austria and South Africa. In S. Hummel, et al. (Eds.), *Shaping tomorrow today: SDGs from multiple perspectives* (pp. 161–184). Springer VS.

Teach For All. (2023, July 6). Looking ahead to the 2023 Teach For All Global Conference. https://teachforall.org/news/looking-ahead-2023-teach-all-global-conference

Teach For All. (2024a). Our Purpose. https://teachforall.org/our-purpose

Teach For All. (2024b). Teaching as Collective Leadership. https://teachforall.org/our-learning-insights/teaching-collective-leadership

Teach For Kenya. (2023). What we do. https://teachforkenya.org/what-we-do/

Teach For Uganda. (2023). Life in the fellowship. https://teachforuganda.org/life-as-a-fellow

Thomas, M. A. M. (2018). 'Policy embodiment': Alternative certification and Teach for America teachers in traditional public schools. *Teaching and Teacher Education*, 70, 186–195.

Thomas, M. A. M., & Baxendale, H. (2022). Wendy Kopp. In Geier, B. A. (Ed.), *Palgrave's handbook of educational thinkers* (pp. 1–16). Palgrave MacMillan. https://doi.org/10.1007/978-3-030-81037-5_208-1#DOI

Thomas, M. A. M., Crawford-Garrett, K., & Rauschenberger, E. (2021). A growing global network: The development of international research on Teach for All. In M. A. M. Thomas, E. R. Rauschenberg, & K. Crawford-Garrett (Eds.), *Examining Teach for All: International perspectives on a growing global network* (pp. 36–59). Routledge.

Thomas, M. A. M., & Lefebvre, E. E. (2018). The dangers of relentless pursuit: teaching, personal health, and the symbolic/real violence of Teach for America. *Discourse: Studies in the Cultural Politics of Education, 39*(6), 856–867.

Thomas, M. A. M., & Lefebvre, E. E. (2020). Teaching synchronous-service teachers: Traditional teacher education at a crossroads. *Teachers College Record, 122*(7), 1–34.

Thomas, M. A. M., Rauschenberger, E. R., & Crawford-Garrett, K. (Eds.). (2021). *Examining Teach for All: International perspectives on a growing global network*. Routledge.

Thomas, M. A. M., & Xu, R.-H. (2023). The emergence and policy (mis)alignment of Teach for Taiwan. *Journal of Education Policy, 38*(4), 686–709.

Trujillo, T., Scott, J., & Rivera, M. (2017). Follow the yellow brick road: Teach for America and the making of educational leaders. *American Journal of Education, 123*(3), 353–391.

Veltri, B. T. (2010). *Learning on other people's kids: Becoming a Teach for America teacher*. IAP.

11 Teacher Leadership and Professional Status in World Culture[i]

Gerald K. LeTendre

Introduction

Over the last two decades, teacher effectiveness and teacher quality have become the focus of intense international attention by the OECD, World Bank, and UNESCO, which have promoted policies to "improve" teacher quality (OECD, 2005; UNESCO, 2014). More recently, international organizations have tended to focus specifically on how teachers can play a more active role in leading reforms, Andreas Schleicher, Director for Education and Skills, and Special Advisor on Education Policy to the Secretary-General at the OECD, wrote: e.g., "effective school autonomy depends on effective leaders, including system leaders, principals, teacher leaders, senior teachers and head teachers, as well as strong support system" (Schleicher, 2012, p. 14).

However, the causal logic of these policies (Stone, 1989) and their implications for the teaching profession have not been well analyzed. Many nations have not adopted the US system of educating and certifying school administrators on a separate path from teachers. We have not examined the global consequences of diffusing a school leadership reform model that encodes logical assumptions about teachers and their work that are derived from a single, highly specific national context. We know that teachers take on different leadership roles around the world (Webber & Okoko, 2021). To address this gap, I analyze the development of the concept of teacher leadership diffusing in globalized reforms and trace it to US research, where contemporary versions of the concept have been forged. Examples from Japan illustrate how older cultural logics (*shidō* 指導) can influence globally diffusing logics resulting in reconfiguration of the understanding of teachers' roles in the school and community, and hence the concept of "leadership" itself.

"Cultural logics" refers to the inter-related sets of taken-for-granted assumptions that inform our understandings of "teacher" or "school" within a dynamic world culture (Anderson-Levitt, 2003; LeTendre, 2023). In their analysis of

---

i I would like to acknowledge the detailed and insightful feedback provided by Xavier Dumay on the drafts of this manuscripts.

DOI: 10.4324/9781003441731-15

neoliberalism, Lerch et al. (2022) use a similar term – "cultural order" – to identify key beliefs about the human person, individual agency, and school that are globally diffused. These globalized cultural logics may affect different aspects of teaching. As Voisin and Dumay (2020) show, nations display different "professional models for regulating the teaching profession" which allocate differential professional autonomy within schools to teachers. This allocation of autonomy, or agency to teachers is broadly consistent with global cultural logics that emphasize the rights of all individuals to determine their own life course.

Inconsistencies or even contradictions can occur when policies or reforms which originated in one national context are transferred to another. Steiner-Khamsi argued that in international policy borrowing, reforms become disconnected from their original cultural contexts (e.g., deterritorialization, see Steiner-Khamsi, 2014). This is true of the global diffusion of teacher-focused policies. In Nordic and East Asian nations, Woo and LeTendre (2022) discussed how nations also reformulated policies from the transnational levels of discourse (e.g., reterritorialization), but with changes that allow the policies to better fit within the national political environment (e.g., see Akiba, 2017 on "sensemaking" in the dynamic interplay of global and national environments). In particular, the concept of "leadership" has been disconnected from its historical meaning and is widely used in international policy discourse to create policies for teacher learning and work norms. The vagueness of the construct makes it useful to transnational policymakers. Some would call this a "floating" or "empty" signifier, teacher leadership can be defined to fit with the agendas of the reform at hand. However, applying such a diffuse or amorphous construct may have a deleterious effect on national cultures in countries where leadership in schools has been cultural constructed along very different lines from that in the United States.

The Development of Teacher Leadership as a Construct in North America

The idea that a teacher is a "leader" – either in the classroom or the community – can be found in many cultures across a long span of time, but "teacher leadership" as a field of academic study is relatively new and originates primarily in the United States (Wenner & Campbell, 2017). There is no commonly accepted definition of teacher leadership at the transnational level (LeTendre, 2022). Indeed, reviews of teacher leadership show there is a lack of consensus on how teacher leadership is conceptualized within the US context (Nguyen et al., 2018; York-Barr & Duke, 2004). Woo et al. (2022) have identified that teacher leadership typically involves engagement in collective action that has broader organizational effects.

In the United States, however, the image of "teacher leaders" is typically associated with leadership outside of the classroom even while teachers maintain their classroom responsibilities (Wenner & Campbell, 2017). Teacher leadership in US policy debates is promoted by various organizations (Institute For Teacher Leadership, 2018) without any common understanding of what precisely the competencies or qualifications are for "leadership". The concept caught the imagination of policymakers. Smylie (1995, p. 1) has demonstrated that at the end of the 1980s nearly every US state had adopted some kind of legislation around teacher leadership. He noted that few studies of teacher leadership used formal theory or empirical investigations. York-Barr and Duke (2004) reached a similar conclusion ten years later, and in 2017, Wenner and Campbell (2017) argued that there was little agreement among researchers about how to define the core construct of teacher leadership.

Part of the problem in defining teacher leadership is that little research has been conducted on how teachers shaped the institutionalization of mass schooling that was so critical to the development of the modern nation-state (LeTendre, 2023). Teachers are missing from early work on the development of mass schooling and the nation-state, their relationship to the state was also ignored, and the status or actorhood (Meyer & Jepperson, 2000) of teachers was not fully articulated. As national systems of education developed, particularly in the late 1800s and early 1900s, the institutional logic of mass schooling in many states was founded on the idea of enculturation of future citizens. Yet the role of teachers in preparing those citizens varied significantly across nations. Unlike in nations that exhibit a professional model of teacher development (Voisin & Dumay, 2020), teachers in the United States failed to achieve professional control over a specific body of knowledge and to control setting the standards for professional entry (Ikoma, 2017). Most sociologists do not consider US teachers to be a profession, and instead use the term "mass profession" or "semi-profession" (Etzioni, 1969). Like police officers and nurses, teachers as a profession have little control over the creation of their own professional knowledge or certification standards. Ikoma (2017) has argued that teachers in the United States have largely been unable to gain sufficient autonomy and control over their work to the degree that other professions have.

Going back to Smylie's point (Smylie & Denny, 1990), in the two-tiered system of professional administration (principals as school leadership and superintendents as district leaders) teachers are relegated to worker status. Hence, there is a need to create a role for teachers as leaders. This makes sense (e.g., has an inherent logic to it) because in the system, teachers were considered workers, never leaders. The late 1970s in the United States saw reforms that promoted ideas like "Master Teacher" that provided a formal professional career ladder to improve the status of teaching. However, these reforms rarely expanded teacher authority and autonomy within the school.

The organizational context of mass schooling in the United States created a need or a "logic" for the promotion of leadership that requires specific intervention and the development of standards. But, due to the highly decentralized nature of the US education system, this process is fragmentary and typically results in incoherent policies (Cohen & Mehta, 2017).

For example, states create these licenses, certifications, or endorsements as a way to allow teachers to advance toward a higher professional standard. Multiple licenses or certifications that teachers can earn by completing series of requirements above and beyond entry-level requirements are supposed to create a more elaborated professional system. These advanced licenses are often connected to subject and grade specialty – and occasionally to teacher leadership.

This is where we can already begin to see the term "teacher leadership" functioning as a "floating signifier." With 50 States that largely set their own educational policy, we find a diverse and often contradictory set of state policy for teacher standards has emerged. The impetus for initiating these standards is often solving short-term problems, e.g., teacher shortages. Many states in the United States have experienced significant teacher shortages and have tried to develop career ladders that will make teaching a more desirable profession (Adams et al., 2009). Consequently "teacher leadership" has become an attractive mechanism for policymakers, despite a long-term failure to adequately define and enact policies that align with either current standards or empirical studies. This has resulted in a hodgepodge of policy adoption where states may enact policies that lower the requirements for teacher entry, while simultaneously creating special certification for teacher leadership, e.g., Arkansas and New Mexico.[1]

Loose terminology and policy inconsistencies across states create real issues with policy coherence. As Cohen and Mehta (2017) have shown, in the United States, policy coherence is foundational to the successful implementation of educational reforms and many policies fail simply due to a lack of consistency. Beyond this, a lack of coherent vision for the teaching profession on the national level (Akiba & LeTendre, 2009) further hinders the development of a strong professional status for teachers as well as the development of clear leadership standards. This lack of a coherent vision for teaching not only problematic for teacher education (see Hammerness et al., 2020) on the role of vision in effective teacher education programs), it is further detrimental in that it sets up a situation where new entrants to teaching are essentially workers with little training who need to be monitored for accountability. Training for leadership or other specialized positions is typically provided by master's programs at universities, but the selection and support of teachers typically relies on individual initiative or district policies around financial support for professional development.

None of the states in the United States appear to have enacted a coherent policy for teacher recruitment, induction, retention, and long-term professional development. The National Center on Teacher Quality (https://www.nctq.org/) has documented this lack of policy coherence (see Fuhrman, 1993) for many years. The fractionated policy environment within the United States makes it extremely difficult for a clear vision of a "teacher leader" to emerge. Despite the work of organizations like the National Board for Professional Teaching Standards (https://www.nbpts.org/) that argue board-certified teachers have strong leadership skills (Behrstock-Sherratt et al., undated), few teachers (less than 3% in most states) even obtain this certification.[2] In such an environment, "teacher leadership" has no common shared meaning for teachers, much less a common vision for what leadership means that is shared by teachers, students, and parents alike. This situation stands in stark contrast to other national systems where different cultural logics supported a clear vision of leadership, and where there are clear differentiated roles for teachers that include integrated systems for professional development and advancement.

International Reforms and the Global Cultural Dynamic

Teacher leadership (or middle school leadership in Europe) is now routinely used in transnational policy and educational reforms. Globalization – the increased exchange of peoples, goods, services, and information – has resulted in an elaborated and global cultural dynamic that some have styled "world culture" (Lechner & Boli, 2008). Overtime there has been considerable cross-national convergence of educational policies and practices while important national differences remain (Baker & LeTendre, 2005), particularly in how school leadership is organized. Within this global cultural dynamic, powerful organizations like UNESCO, the World Bank or the OECD typically promote both reforms and policies they consider supportive of better learning or training for teachers (see OECD, 2005). Critically, the attention of these groups has shifted significantly from a concern with the quality of national curriculum in the 1980s and 1990s to a concern with teachers and teacher quality (Akiba & LeTendre, 2017).

A clear specific example of this is UNESCO's Teacher Policy Development Guide (International Taskforce for Teachers 2030, 2019).[3] This book was developed to specifically guide nations in formulating policies about their national teaching forces (for a critique of UNESCO's policies, see Cerqua et al., 2014). Leadership, typically denoted by the term "school leadership" occurs frequently as a topic and is linked to effective reform of schools, better conditions for teachers, and improved student performance. An example of what "leadership" means (p. 55) suggests that training for school leaders "… will likely include management and instructional leadership focusing on managing teachers, including monitoring teachers' assiduity, time keeping, professionalism and performance."

The document incorporates empirical research and elaborates a strong rationale for why leadership matters, but this rationale is based on a specific definition of leadership. It is a package or "packet of meaning," and following Berger et al. (1974) "packets of meaning" are transmitted or diffused in a globalized world by the spread of institutions, like the modern system of mass schooling. I take the position that teacher leadership is a cultural product – a "packet of meaning" that is diffusing globally but has a definite origin in a specific national context, within the cultural logics of that nation. These national logics may not align completely with the global cultural logics or "cultural order" that Lerch et al. (2022) have formulated. There is a dynamic tension between national logics that inform national sense-making activities around policies and global cultural logics that informs many of the reforms promoted by international organizations.

The power of the global cultural dynamic may also wax and wane (Bromley et al., 2021), but certain actors (e.g., the OECD) have more access to visibility and influence in this world culture. Numerous theorists have argued that international organizations play a key role in transmitting educational reforms globally (Chabbott, 2002) or setting standards that drive similar reforms (Meyer & Benavot, 2013), although some evidence suggests that such activity may be declining (Bromley et al., 2021). We must therefore consider the timeframe during which the concept of leadership as a construct played a central role in in many globally diffusing educational reforms. Although "teacher leadership" and "middle level leadership" are relatively new terms for INGOs, "distributed leadership" has long been incorporated into global policy dialogs. The last few decades, both the accountability and the decentralization movements, assume that there will be a more active and informed leadership in schools. These movements also encode ideas about human capital functions of schools (and school leaders) that may clash with local understandings (see Aydarova, 2015). To clearly understand the ramifications of the diffusion of teacher leadership requires some understanding of the historical roots of the concept.

Leadership and Professional Status in Japan

Japan's educational system relies heavily on teachers for non-instructional labor (e.g., for guidance, see LeTendre, 1994a; Sato, 1996; for administrative work, see LeTendre et al., 2001). While aspects of this labor may be onerous to teachers, it also provides opportunities for increased professional activity. Similarly, as Akiba and Liang (2016) and Akiba and Wilkinson, 2016) have argued, Japanese teachers are expected to engage in long-term professional development around teaching, moving from novices who present their first demonstration lesson to seniors who play a guiding role in school and district "lesson study." Formal positions reflect this change in responsibilities and status.

Differentiation and specialization are often associated with stronger professional status (e.g., medical specializations, see Abbott, 1988). While teaching, in general, is clearly marked by clear specialization (e.g., elementary education, special education, etc.), this specialization is the result of initial training not, long-term professional development. The absence of career ladders that allow further advancement and training may hinder the recruitment of talented people to the profession. Thus, career stages and long-term changes in work duties (and status) are critical aspects of professionalization that have often been ignored in the literature on teachers.

In a review of teacher and principal quality, the Center on International Benchmarking notes that both the salary and leadership incentives are commonly used in Japan:

> Japanese teachers are able to move up within schools over the course of their careers, with the most straightforward path being teacher, head teacher and then principal. Within each of these steps, there are multiple salary grades based on performance and experience. There are 36 steps within the teacher level, 20 within the head teacher level and 15 within the principal level. Some teachers may never be promoted to head teacher, but they are able to see their salary climb from about US$29,000 to more than US$60,000 over a lifetime.
>
> Japan's system of personnel relocations also plays a part in developing school leaders. Rather than being transferred to new schools, high-performing teachers in middle to late-career stages are sometimes transferred to administrative offices, including local boards of education, and expected to contribute to the prefecture's educational planning with their practical experience. After several years in such an assignment, they are transferred back to leadership positions within schools.[4]

Finally, these formal roles encode an expectation of ongoing development. While the formal requirements for entry are not specified beyond a teaching license, there are strong cultural expectations for teacher professional identity that are tied to experience and a status hierarchy among teachers. These informal expectations play a large role in shaping how teachers exercise leadership in Japanese schools, but they also set up powerful sources of conflict.

Japanese teacher's salary structure suggests that there is a long-term expectation of career building and development. As Akiba et al. (2012) have shown, new teachers in Japan do not do well in international comparisons of average salaries. However, Japan ranks fifth overall for senior teacher salaries. They further show, that while new teacher salary is not associated with higher national achievement, average salaries for 15-year veterans are associated with higher achievement. They argue that this indicates an association between a strong career ladder of professional development and increased effectiveness in teaching.

While there are some regional differences in the kinds of duties and expectations, we see a clear pattern of long-term opportunities for career advancement for teachers in Japan. The Ministry of Education has officially recognized this, and notes roles such as "Head of Curriculum" or "Grade Chair."[5] There is some variation in how these duties are assigned and what specific tasks are associated with specific roles.

Hirata (2012, p. 184) noted that many schools created a "teacher council" that "... includes all teachers in the school and facilitates their cooperation. Teacher councils had significant influence on decision-making, which was sometimes beyond the principal's authority, based on the principles of democracy in education and the self-governance of teachers." He argues that these councils were most powerful in the immediate post-war period. Although such councils were granted legal status under a law passed in 2000 (The School Education Act Implementation Regulation of 2000), he argues that this law also strengthened the power of principals, making such councils merely advisory. This reinforcing of existing hierarchies within school administration, thus runs counter to the idea that teachers with formal roles have a greater professional responsibility in the school.

MEXT (The Japanese Ministry of Education, Culture, Sports, Science and Technology) offers specific guidelines. For example, the head of guidance (教務主任) is expected to: "Under supervision of the principal, coordinate communication and guidance and advice on matters concerning educational planning and other matters concerning teaching (such as planning and implementation of educational plans, comprehensive adjustment of the school timetable, handling of textbooks and teaching materials)."[6] As shown in Figure 11.1, these formal positions involve mixtures of guidance and administrative and pedagogical expertise. Some terms may differ depending on the prefecture, but these roles are typically recognized at all three levels (elementary, middle, and high school) of Japanese schooling.[7] This formal structure is important to teacher professional status in several respects.

Term	Approximate Period	Skills Knowledge
若い先生/教師 new teacher/young teacher	1-3 years	Basic classroom management; subject specific instruction
担任先生 homeroom teacher	1-15 years	Student counseling (生徒指導); classroom life; dealing with parents
クラブ担当 club advisor	1-15 years	Student activity; club finances
学年主任・学年長 grade chair	10+	Developmental goals of grade, social activities, learning goals of grade
教科担当 subject chair	10+	Subject specific expertise; mentoring techniques; research on subject-specific instruction
生徒指導主任 head of guidance	15+	School-wide safety, health and social issues
進路指導主任 head of academic guidance	15+	Academic issues, test preparation, future school placement
教務主任 head of curriculum	15+	School-wide curricular and testing issues
教頭・副校長 head teacher/vice principal	20+	Integrated management of entire range of school functions outside of budget

Figure 11.1 Cultural roles of Japanese teachers.

The first aspect of these roles that is important for the professional status is that they are open to all teachers with a basic teaching license. As opposed to countries like the United States, where specialized or advanced degrees would likely be required for such a position, all of these (with the exception of the health chair) simply require a basic teaching license. Of course, this does not mean that novice teachers would immediately qualify for such positions (see the next section on the importance of seniority). However, it augments the professional status of teachers, *per se*. Rather than a set of distinct professional educator/administrator roles (e.g., Principal, Curriculum Development Specialist, Counselor) as in the United States and many other nations, these important professional roles are all staffed by teachers.

Second, the roles encode the authority of teachers in core administration and governance of the school. Again, in many nations, teachers struggle to have influence in basic school decisions (Brezicha et al., 2015; Brezicha et al., 2019). Across the globe, teachers typically feel that they have little role in making important decisions within the school (Ingersoll et al., 2017). The formal work roles in Japan clearly provide teachers with far more direct influence on school matters than teachers in most other nations possess. This means that many of the issues caused by having a separate administrative track (Brezicha et al., 2015) are not present in Japan.

The terms used to designate differentiated roles for teachers are largely recognizable to the average Japanese individual. In the earliest stages, these roles are not formally recognized by the MEXT but are still considered essential stages in a teachers' career path. Indeed, both "homeroom teacher" [担任先生] and "club advisor" [クラブ担当] are typically roles that bring teachers into close contact with students and parents and are thus most visible to individuals outside the school system. The more formal roles like 指導部長 (head of guidance) might not have a clear image among the general populace but would be recognized as [えらい] – a position of importance.

While these roles are still at play in the Japanese system, many scholars have focused on the long-term decline in the power of the Japanese Teachers Union (see Okano & Tsuchiya, 1999) as well as the fact that Japanese teachers are legally "public servants" who do not have a "professional" consciousness (Sato et al., 1993). More recently, Gordon (2005) has argued that the social status of teachers is eroding, affecting the long-term ability of teachers to carry out these various roles. Multiple waves of reform have weakened the professional status of teachers (Roesgaard, 1998), by inserting state requirements around core activities. This includes erosion of organic mentor relationships (Lassila et al., 2017) and the imposition of government standards on professional development activities like lesson study (Akita & Sakamoto, 2015).

For example, the introduction of specific certification for counselors in the Japanese system created an inconsistency in the vision of what *shidō* means. Traditionally, Japanese homeroom teachers provided extensive socio-emotional counseling to children as part of their duties in "student guidance" (生徒指導 see Fukuzawa & LeTendre, 2001; LeTendre, 1995). Yagi (2008, p. 142) noted:

"In a society that perceives teachers to be all things to all students and regards teachers as 'almighty,' ... teachers, in fulfilling guidance and counseling role, made home visits ... During home visits, they might provide consultation and advice to students and their parents." Overtime, schools have increasingly relied on certified counselors to provide such counseling (Ito, 2014; Seto et al., 2005). The notion that "almighty" teachers could engage in counseling youth was challenged by MEXT which used policies to require schools to create a new staff position (school counselor) that took over important teacher functions.

While many teachers welcomed the introduction of school counselors, the creation of this specialized role undeniably reduced the scope of autonomy teachers could enact. In terms of school leadership, teachers were no longer the sole decision-makers on mental and emotional health issues within schools. Ministry policy also restricted teacher authority in other areas, for example, school placement guidance (LeTendre, 1994b) again diminishing teacher autonomy. As Yokota (2020) has shown, the focus on instructional leadership promoted by both OECD and UNESCO has not resonated well within Japan. "Instructional leadership failed to gain momentum as it did not correspond to the daily realities of schooling…" (p. 202).

As Yokota (2020) noted, Japanese policies on school leadership were heavily influenced by theories of transactional, instructional, transformation, and distributed leadership which originated in western contexts. Through the analysis of laws and educational policy documents, he clearly shows the influence of western theories in how these four dimensions of leadership were instantiated within documents and law. However, while it is clear that although policies and laws incorporate these concepts, how they are actualized by principals remains unclear and Yokota argues that there has been much alteration and adaptation. Citing cases from Malaysia and Turkey, he argues that the policies are modified when practiced in schools.

Ambiguity as Advantage: Teacher Leadership as a "Floating" or "Empty" Signifier

Globally, the diffusion of leadership has caused real problems for systems that are organized around different cultural and organizational logics. School leadership in the United States has often been narrowly defined in terms of school administration. Also downplayed in the United States is the role that teachers play in the socio-emotional development of children (at least once beyond the earliest elementary school years; see LeTendre, 2017). Thus, the term "homeroom teacher" [担任先生] causes much confusion when comparing the US and Japanese education. Homeroom teachers in the United States may do little more than take attendance during a brief (10–15 minutes) homeroom period. As I have previously written, the role of the homeroom teacher in Japan includes a broad range of activities and possibilities for leadership enactment (LeTendre, 2000).

Homeroom teachers became so critical to the selection process into high school, one of the critical steps in achieving higher social status in Japan, that

Japan needed to pass a law prohibiting public school teachers from using mock test scores to predict student placement on the high school exam (LeTendre, 1994b). Despite this ban, many teachers continue to guide students on what high schools to attend (Okano, 1993, 1995). This kind of *shidō* [指導] or "guidance" work is enormously consequential in the lives of students, and is relegated to senior leadership positions in schools, yet it is virtually absent in the global reform literature on how teacher leaders influence student life trajectories. This creates a dissonance or tension between the cultural logics of leadership promoted by International non-governmental organizations (INGOs) and the local or national logics most teachers in Japan are familiar with.

Dissonance between local and globally diffusing cultural logics (see LeTendre, 2023 for a discussion of dissonance and cultural logics) of "teacher leadership" mean that the vagueness of the term makes it an ideal candidate as a floating signifier. This vagueness means that policy can simultaneously appear to be in line with models emanating from major international organizations and from local sources. This ambiguous use of "leadership," "teacher leadership," "school leadership," or even "middle leadership" (Harris et al., 2019) appears increasingly in cross-national policy promotion. Detached from the original cultural and organizational contexts in which it evolved (see Steiner-Khamsi, 2014), teacher leadership appears to be increasingly used within a global cultural dynamic.

Beginning in the early 2000s, we see a shift in transnational policy focus away from an emphasis on reforming national curriculum to reforming national teaching workforces (Sorensen & Dumay, 2021). The joint ILO/UNESCO on the status of teachers adopted in 1967 makes no reference to leadership whatsoever, and it is not until 2005 that major transnational organizations begin to systematically promote the idea of teachers as critical to national educational success. Within the OECD's Teachers Matter (2005) leadership is mentioned 52 times. While UNESCO and Education International have been slower to adopt an emphasis on leadership, there is evidence that both are increasingly focusing on this construct.

For example, UNESCO (2019, p. 45) notes: "A teacher policy should provide for a recruitment of school leaders underpinned by the principles of efficiency, equity and transparency. Although it is possible in some contexts to combine school leadership with classroom teaching, all school leaders should be formally appointed to and remunerated for their leadership responsibilities." This recommendation for policy appears to allow for the multiple roles that the logic of *shidō* would require in Japanese schools, but at the same time the document enjoins nations to adopt policies around "Effective school governance and leadership, including managing and supporting teachers" (ibid., p. 29). The ambiguity in the term "teacher leadership" allows for multiple interpretations.

A study of student teachers and teacher leadership in Kosovo (Aliu & Kaçaniku, 2023, p. 37), "… reveals that there is no consensus on the definition of teacher leadership." A study of teacher leadership in the Philippines (Santos, 2023, p. 4299) suggests that "that giving encouragement is more than enough to promote leadership in their school...". Some might argue that this is simply a case of "decoupling" (Spillane et al., 2011). This term has been used by world society and world culture theorists to account for national variation in patterns of national school systems. Steiner-Khamsi (2012) argues that WC studies are overly reliant on loose coupling as a mechanism to explain local and national variation. As I argued (Letendre, 2021, p. 759), "Rather than simply defer to 'decoupling' as a theoretical explanation common to all rationalized bureaucratic systems, ... scholars should seek to identify disconnects, failures of diffusion, and why certain cases are promoted as exemplars of educational change. ... Understanding what aspects of teachers' work, education, or professional development become the focus of national reform movements would add a political dimension to WC theory that could link with theories of political mobilization of global reforms (Takayama 2010) and other theories of why national policy makers adopt globalized reforms (Verger 2014)."

Verger et al. (2012, p. 22) note that a floating signifier is a way "... for local actors to settle national and sub-national education agendas and advance their pre-established preferences in the educational field." In this case, there is a deliberative or strategic aspect to the use of the term "floating signifier." But, from a "sensemaking" perspective national educational policy formation (Akiba, 2017), words that have multiple meanings or nuances are often useful policy tools. (Burgos, 2003, p. 55) uses the terms "empty" and "floating" signifier and argues that "... the ambiguous character of a signifier is politically productive...". Thus, the rhetorical value of "teacher leadership" in the policy world lies in its ambiguity.

Akiba and LeTendre (2017, p. 3) have argued that "...both teacher quality and teacher policy are created within each nation as a result of collective sensemaking, negotiation, and contestation among policy actors at global, national, and local levels." This indicates that at all levels (local, national, or global) individuals engage in a process wherein they view "...a new idea through the lens of their preexisting beliefs and knowledge" but then reinterpret and adapt the idea based on interaction with others. In the United States, teacher leadership has been adapted to meet state needs for recruiting teachers in times of shortage, as well as in attempts to develop a more professionalized workforce. The fact that there is little empirical work that defines teacher leadership as a construct, makes the term useful in crafting policies.

Looking to the future, we are likely to see increased use of leadership and "teacher leadership" (or "middle leadership") as a construct in future policy documents. UNESCO has just recently commissioned a Global Education Monitoring (GEM) report on leadership.[8] This report will encode values like "Leadership is at the heart of quality education."[9] How well this, and future reports, are able to contextualize definitions of leadership, and account for alternative cultural logics that may apply in different national contexts, remains to be seen. Alternative formulations may also be proposed, for example, the Jakobs Foundation's "2030 Strategy"[10] tends to focus on "teacher agency" rather than "teacher leadership."

Conclusion

Whatever the term, a focus on leadership is consistent with the expanding and evolving global culture of educational policy and reform. This "world culture" is saturated with rationalized myths about the individual, state, and mass schooling that create self-sustaining cultural logics or "ideologies." Lerch et al. (2022) have argued, that "neo-liberalism" as part of a world cultural ideology re-envisions society as consisting not of structures but of individual human persons who are attributed immense agency, entitlement, and rationality" (p. 97). As global organizations have shifted more attention to the impact of teaching on national educational academic achievement, this logic encourages a broader consideration of the agency of teachers.

Yet few scholars have tried to analyze the widely different roles that teachers play in different national school systems. Much of the original theorizing on the development of world culture ignored teachers or assumed that a teacher's work, or the scope of professional duties, is invariant (see LeTendre, 2023). This is clearly not the case. As Tobin et al. (1989) showed, as early as preschool, teacher work roles and their relationship with the families and communities show clear and significant differences cross-nationally.

As the global discourse on leadership evolves, it will be important to continue to assert understandings of leadership that can account for concepts like *shidō* in terms of how teachers see themselves in their varied national cultures and their local communities. Within neoliberal ideology itself, there are inherent tensions between the need for accountability and the recognition of teacher agency, particularly over what teachers need to know. Production of knowledge for teachers in the United States is dominated by academic researchers, this predominance of academic over professional knowledge is not found in all nations. In particular, we are likely to see considerable strains between teacher organizations and academic researchers over what constitutes valid knowledge in teacher education and what role teachers should play in guiding the production of knowledge (see discussions in Tatto & Menter, 2019).

A further tension may be foreshadowed by the passage of laws in the U.S. regulating what teachers, and faculty at colleges of education, can teach about social inequalities. The core tenets of teacher leadership developed in the United States emphasize teachers taking leadership roles in the community and in policy development. This positions teachers (as leaders) to advocate for social justice for communities, and to take an active role in the political process. This expanded role for teachers as social justice leaders is consistent with the global cultural logics that emphasize the inherent rights of individuals, but clashes with the political aims of groups that seek to re-instate the control of religious communities and the hetero-normative family over education. An expanded vision of teachers as leaders of social change poses severe challenges to autocratic, authoritarian, and nationalistic parties and regimes. Where such parties and regimes dominate, we are likely to see increased state activity to limit teacher leadership.

Notes

1. See data from the Educational Commission of the States: https://www.ecs.org/50-state-comparison-school-leader-certification-and-preparation-programs-archive-2/
2. chrome-extension://efaidnbmnnnibpcajpcglclefindmkaj/https://www.nbpts.org/wp-content/uploads/2022/01/2021_StateRankings_All_NBCTs_Percent-of-Teaching-Population.pdf
3. (https://unesdoc.unesco.org/ark:/48223/pf0000370966)
4. http://ncee.org/what-we-do/center-on-international-education-benchmarking/top-performing-countries/japan-overview/japan-teacher-and-principal-quality/ Accessed June 24, 2019
5. http://www.mext.go.jp/b_menu/shingi/chukyo/chukyo3/031/siryo/06111414/001/003.htm#contentsStart
6. http://www.mext.go.jp/b_menu/shingi/chukyo/chukyo3/031/siryo/06111414/001/003.htm
7. Student guidance, academic guidance and subject chair are not recognized by MEXT for elementary schools.
8. https://www.unesco.org/gem-report/en/leadership
9. https://www.ipned.org/news-and-views/mp-consultation-education
10. https://jacobsfoundation.org/strategy-2030/

References

Abbott, A. (1988). *The system of professions: An essay on the division of expert labor*. University of Chicago Press.

Adams, S., Heywood, J., & Rothstein, R. (2009). *Teachers, performance pay, and accountability: What education should learn from other sectors* (Vol. 1). Economic Policy Institute.

Akiba, M. (2017). Editor's introduction: Understanding cross-national differences in globalilzed teacher reforms. *Educational Researcher*, 46(4), 153–168.

Akiba, M., Chiu, Y.-L., Shimizu, K., & Liang, G. (2012). Teacher salary and national achievement: A cross-national analysis of 30 countries. *International Journal of Educational Research*, 53, 171–181.

Akiba, M., & LeTendre, G. (2017). Teacher quality and the fate of nations. In M. Akiba, & G. LeTendre (Eds.), *The Routledge international handbook of teacher quality and policy* (pp. 572–585). Routledge.

Akiba, M. & G. LeTendre (2009). *Improving teacher quality: The U.S. teaching force in global context*. Teachers College Press.

Akiba, M., & Liang, G. (2016). Effects of teacher professional learning activities on student achievement growth. *Journal of Educational Research*, 21(1), 1–12.

Akiba, M. & B. Wilkinson (2016). Adopting an international innovation for teacher professional development: State and district approaches to lesson study in Florida. *Journal of Teacher Education*, 67(1), 74–93.

Akita, K., & Sakamoto, A. (2015). Lesson study and teachers' professional development in Japan. In K. Wood, & S. Sithamparam (Eds.), *Realising learning: Teachers' professional development through lesson and learning study* (pp. 25–40). Routledge.

Aliu, J., & Kaçaniku, F. (2023). An exploration of teacher leadership: Are future teachers ready to lead? *Center for Educational Policy Studies Journal*, 13(4), 37–62.

Anderson-Levitt, K. (Ed.) (2003). *Local meanings, global schooling: Anthropology and world culture theory*. Palgrave Macmillan.

Aydarova, O. (2015). Global discourses and local responses: A dialogic perspective on educational reforms in the Russian Federation. *European Educational Research Journal*, 47, 331–345.

Baker, D., & LeTendre, G. (2005). *National differences, global similarities: World culture and the future of schooling*. Stanford University Press.
Behrstock-Sherratt, E., Brookins, P., & Payne, G.. (undated). *Teacher leadership in uncertain times*.
Berger, P., Berger, B., & Kellner, H. (1974). *The homeless mind*. Random House.
Brezicha, K., Bergmark, U., & Mitra, D. (2015). One size does not fit all: Differentiating leadership to support teachers in school reform. *Educational Administration Quarterly*, 51(1), 96–132.
Brezicha, K., Ikoma, S., Park, H., & LeTendre, G. (2019). The ownership perception gap: Exploring teacher job satisfaction and its relationship to teachers' and principals' perception of decision-making opportunities. *International Journal of Leadership in Education*, 23(4), 428–456. doi:https://doi.org/10.1080/13603124.2018.1562098
Bromley, P., Overbey, L., Furuta, J., & Kijima, R. (2021). Education reform in the twenty-first century: Declining emphases in international organisation reports, 1998–2018. *Globalisation, Societies and Education*, 19(1), 23–40.
Burgos, R. B. (2003). Partnership as a floating and empty signifier within educational policies: The Mexican case. In *Educational partnerships and the state: The paradoxes of governing schools, children, and families* (pp. 55–79): Springer.
Cerqua, A., Gauthier, C., & Dembélé, M. (2014). Education policy, teacher education, and pedagogy: A case study of UNESCO. *Annual Review of Comparative and International Education 2014*, 25, 235–266.
Chabbott, C. (2002). *Constructing education for development: International organizations and education for all*. RoutledgeFarmer.
Cohen, D. K., & Mehta, J. (2017). Why reform sometimes succeeds: Understanding the conditions that produce reforms that last. *Amerian Educational Research Journal*, 54(4), 644–690.
Etzioni, A. (Ed.) (1969). *The semi-professions and their organization: Teachers, nurses, social workers*. Free Press.
Fuhrman, S. (1993). The politics of coherence. In S. Fuhrman (Ed.), *Designing coherent education policy* (pp. 1–34). Jossey-Bass.
Fukuzawa, R., & LeTendre, G. (2001). *Intense years: How Japanese adolescents balance school, family and friends*. RoutledgeFalmer.
Gordon, J. (2005). The crumbling pedestal: Changing images of Japanese teachers. *Journal of Teacher Education*, 56(5), 459–470.
Hammerness, K., Klette, K., Jenset, I. S., & Canrinuq, E. (2020). Opportunities to study, practice, and rehearse teaching in teacher preparation: An international perspective. *Teachers College Record*, 122, 1–46.
Harris, A., Jones, M., Ismail, N., & Nguyen, D. (2019). Middle leaders and middle leadership in schools: Exploring the knowledge base (2003–2017). *School Leadership & Management*, 39(3–4), 255–277.
Hirata, J. (2012). Standardization, deregulation, and school administration reform in Japan. In L. Volante (Ed.), *School leadership in the context of standards-based reform* (pp. 173–195). Springer.
Ikoma, S. (2017). Individual excellence vs. collaborative culture: Sociology of professions and professionalization of teaching in the U.S. In M. Akiba, & G. LeTendre (Eds.), *International handbook of teacher quality and policy* (pp. 38–52). Routledge.
Ingersoll, R., Sirinides, P., & Dougherty, P. (2017). *School leadership, teachers' roles in school decisionmaking, and student achievement*. Retrieved from University of Pennsylvania.
Institute for Teacher Leadership. (2018). *The teacher leadership competencies*. Institute for Teacher Leadership
International Taskforce for Teachers 2030 (2019). *Teacher policy development guide*. UNESCO.

Ito, A. (2014). School counselor roles and challenges in Japan. *Journal of Asia Pacific Counseling*, 4(2), 113.
Lassila, E., Uitto, M., & Estola, E. (2017). You're damned if you do and damned if you don't: The tension-filled relationships between Japanese beginning and senior teachers. *Pedagogy, Culture & Society.* https://doi.org/10.1080/14681366.2017.1412341.
Lechner, F. J., & Boli, J. (2008). *World culture: Origins and consequences.* John Wiley & Sons.
Lerch, J. C., Bromley, P., & Meyer, J. W. (2022). Global neoliberalism as a cultural order and its expansive educational effects. *International Journal of Sociology*, 52(2), 97–127.
Letendre, G. (2021). Teachers in neoinstitutional and world culture theory. *Comparative Education Review*, 65(4), 750–769.
LeTendre, G. (2000). *Learning to be adolescent: Growing up in U.S. and Japanese middle schools.* Yale University Press.
LeTendre, G. (1994a). Distribution tables and private tests: The failure of middle school reform in Japan. *International Journal of Educational Reform*, 3(2), 126–136.
LeTendre, G. (1994b). Guiding them on: Teaching, hierarchy, and social organization in Japanese middle schools. *Journal of Japanese Studies*, 20(1), 37–59.
LeTendre, G. (1995). Disruption and reconnection: Counseling young adolescents in Japanese schools. *Educational Policy*, 9(2), 169–184.
LeTendre, G. (2017). Socio-emotional learning and teacher quality. In M. Akiba, & G. LeTendre (Eds.), *International handbook of teacher quality and policy* (pp. 25–37). Routedge.
LeTendre, G. (2022). Teacher leadership in cross-national perspective. In *The Palgrave handbook of teacher education research* (pp. 1–22). Springer.
LeTendre, G. (2023). Globalization, cultural logics, and the teaching profession. Mattei, P. et al. (Eds.) *The Oxford handbook of education and globalization*, Oxford, UK: Oxford Publishing. 170–190.
LeTendre, G., Baker, D., Akiba, M., Goesling, B., & Wiseman, A. (2001). Teacher's work: Institutional isomorphism And cultural variation in the U.S., Germany And Japan. *Educational Researcher*, 30(6), 3–16.
Meyer, H.-D., & Benavot, A. (2013). *PISA, Power, and policy.* Symposium Books.
Meyer, J., & Jepperson, R. (2000). The "actors" of modern society: The cultural construction of social agency. *Sociological Theory*, 18(1), 100–120.
Nguyen, D., Harris, A., & Ng, D. (2018). A review of the empirical research on teacher leadership (2003–2017). *Journal of Educational Administration*, 58(1), 69–80.
OECD. (2005). *Teachers matter.*
Okano, K. (1993). *School to work transition in Japan.* Multilingual Matters Ltd.
Okano, K. (1995). Rational decision making and school-based job referrals for high school students in Japan. *Sociology of Education*, 68(1), 31–47.
Okano, K., & Tsuchiya, M. (1999). *Education in contemporary Japan: Inequality and diversity.* Cambridge University Press.
Roesgaard, M. (1998). *Moving mountains.* Aarhus University Press.
Santos, F. S. (2023). Understanding the role of organizational confidence on the culture of teacher leadership in public schools in the Philippines. *International Journal of Multidisciplinary: Applied Business and Education Research*, 4(12), 4294–4301.
Sato, M., et al. (1993). Practical thinking styles of teachers: A comparative study of expert and novice thought processes and its implications for rethinking teacher education in Japan. *Peabody Journal of Education*, 68(4), 100–110.
Sato, N. (1996). Honoring the individual. In T. Rohlen, & G. LeTendre (Eds.), *Teaching and learning in Japan* (pp. 119–153). Cambridge University Press.
Schleicher, A. (2012). Preparing teachers and developing school leaders for the 21st century: Lessons from around the world. OECD.

Seto, A., Inoue, T., & Forth, N. (2005). An overview of school counseling certifications in Japan. *Macro Counseling Studies, 4*, 29–34.

Smylie, M. (1995). New perspectives on teacher leadership. *The Elementary School Journal, 96*, 1–7.

Smylie, M., & Denny, J. (1990). Teacher leadership: Tensions and ambiguities in organizational perspective. *Educational Administration Quarterly, 26*(3), 235–259.

Sorensen, T. B. & X. Dumay (2021). The teaching professions and globalization: A scoping review of the anglophone research literature. *Comparative Education Review*, i(4), 725–749.

Spillane, J. P., et al. (2011). Organizational routines as coupling mechanisms: Policy, school administration, and the technical core. *American Educational Research Journal, 48*(3), 586–619.

Steiner-Khamsi, G. (2012). The global/local nexus in comparative policy studies: Analysing the triple bonus system in Mongolia over time. *Comparative Education, 48*(4), 455–471.

Steiner-Khamsi, G. (2014). Cross-national policy borrowing: Understanding reception and translation. *Asia Pacific Journal of Education, 34*(2), 153–167.

Stone, D. (1989). Causal stories and the formation of policy agendas. *Political Science Quarterly, 104*(2), 281–300.

Tatto, M., & Menter, I. (Eds.). (2019). *Knowledge, policy and practice in teacher education.* Bloomsbury Academic.

Tobin, J., Wu, D. Y., & Davidson, D. H. (1989). *Preschools in three cultures: Japan, China And the United States.* Yale University Press.

UNESCO. (2014). *Teaching and learning: Achieving quality for all.* Retrieved from Paris.

UNESCO (2019). *Teacher policy development guide.* UNESCO.

Verger, A., Novelli, M., & Altinyelken, H. K. (Eds.). (2012). *Global education policy and international development.* Bloomsbury Press.

Voisin, A. & Dumay, X. (2020). How do educational systems regulate the teaching profession and teachers' work? A typological approach to institutional foundations and models of regulation. *Teaching and Teacher Education, 96*, 1–16.

Walker, J. L. (1973). Comment: Problems in research on the diffusion of policy innovations. *The American Political Science Review, 67*(4), 1186–1191.

Webber, C. and J. Okoko (2021). Exploring teacher leadership across cultures: Introduction to teacher leadership. themed special issue. *Research in Educational Administration & Leadership, 6*(1), 1–5.

Wenner, J., & Campbell, T. (2017). The theoretical and empirical basis of teacher leadership: A review of the literature. *Review of Educational Research, 87*(1), 134–171.

Woo, H., & LeTendre, G. (2022). *Teacher leadership in Nordic and East Asian nations.* Paper presented at the San Diego, CA: American Educational Research Association.

Woo, H., LeTendre, G., Byun, S.-y, & Schussler, D. (2022). Teacher leadership – Collective actions, decision-making and well-being. *International Journal of Teacher Leadership, 11*(1).

Yagi, D. T. (2008). Current developments in school counseling in Japan. *Asian Journal of Counselling, 15*(2), 141–155.

Yokota, H. (2020). Mapping four leadership styles in Japan: How has the role of the principal been shaped by policies? *Journal of Educational Administration, 58*(2), 187–207.

York-Barr, J., & Duke, K. (2004). What do we know about teacher leadership? Findings from two decades of scholarship. *Review of Educational Research, 74*(3), 255–361.

12 The Socio-Politics of Teachers' Learning
Global Insights

Ian Hardy

Introduction

Teachers' work and learning is a heavily contested space. Stacey et al. (2022) highlight how teachers have become a focus of scrutiny and surveillance within a broader global knowledge economy that seeks to "capture" the nature of teaching practice and its effects. This is an environment in which teachers' work and learning are increasingly orchestrated and in which various kinds of accountability processes are implemented in an effort to manage and monitor teaching practices and educational outcomes, and in which such outcomes are often residualised to a relatively narrow range of typically quantitative measures/markers of achievement. Such measures include a range of global indicators that governments seek to corroborate against national indicators/measures and which, in turn, influence local educational practices.

This chapter builds from these initial insights into the global nature of the socio-political contexts of teachers' work and learning by elaborating key influences, particularly neoliberalism and managerialism, as well as more profession-oriented foci. The chapter reveals how these influences are not separate, "distinct" entities, but are simultaneously, often intricately, intertwined and co-exist in the various settings where they are enacted. These competing foci are expressed in multiple ways in different contexts.

The chapter begins by outlining the nature of more neoliberal and managerial influences as part of a broader globalized education policy space. It also delineates an alternative, "profession-oriented" conception of teachers' learning. The neoliberal and managerial section draws upon both policy and political theorizing literature, as well as academic literature in education, while the "profession-oriented" conception of teachers' learning section draws on more academic literature in the field of teachers' learning; the academic/'scientific' literature is used to assess the presence and the development of different conceptions and practices of teachers' learning and professional development (PD). The intertwined nature of these competing neoliberal, managerial, and more "profession-oriented" influences are then analyzed in relation to how teachers' work and learning are currently expressed in different educational systems in selected national settings, from both global "Northern" and "Southern" contexts;

this includes how such influences impact teachers' work and have sought to reframe teachers' learning. Literature was selected from within the past decade (with some key earlier studies included), and on the basis of whether they were either syntheses of literature on teachers' learning or academic sources that provided key/indicative insights into the nature of teachers' learning, including in specific education systems. Where relevant, some key policy/'grey' literature is also referred to vis-à-vis policy/political arguments. Overall, the orientation of the chapter is toward the need for more profession-oriented approaches to teachers' learning, and a general ethos that contests more reductive conceptions of neoliberal and managerial logics. The chapter concludes with a summative discussion of the contestation between these influences.

Neoliberalism and Managerialism within a Globalized Education Political Space

While neoliberalism is a heavily contested concept (Rowe et al., 2019), it is also a useful analytical resource for critiquing current policy and political developments within education. Welch (2021) highlights how neoliberalism has come to be associated with an increasingly economistic discourse which diminishes more traditional edu-bureaucratic processes of educational organizations, and residualizes social concerns. While neoliberalism is expressed in support and advocacy for competitive markets in educational provision, neoliberalism is perhaps more obviously evident in the application of privatization principles via state policies to public institutions, including education.

Emphasizing the ever-changing and active nature of neoliberalism – or what he describes as neoliberal*ization* – Peck (2010) refers to how neoliberal processes involve "an open-ended and contradictory process of politically assisted market rule" (p. xii). As he goes on to argue, this is an active process, rather than a "bloodless, semi-automatic process." This sheds light upon how neoliberalization is very much a "*constructed* project" (xii; emphasis original). Under such conditions, education is construed as a competitive undertaking that enables nation-states to compete more broadly.

Relatedly, and in conjunction with more neoliberal conditions, education reform can also be understood as characterized by increased attention to managing and monitoring the complexity of teachers' work and learning. These more "managerial" processes contribute to the deprofessionalization of educators, leading to an increasingly technicist approach toward, and understanding of, teachers' work and learning (de Saxe et al., 2020). As teachers' work becomes more technicized, they experience considerable loss of control over their work processes (Ball, 2016), often expressed via more standardized enumeration of educational processes (Ball, 2015). Under these more managerial conditions, various kinds of test are ascribed salience and cogency and used to evaluate the extent to which educational practices are considered "successful." Such assessment processes are also associated with more standardized curriculum and pedagogies, and these make it difficult to cultivate more substantive and productive educational approaches. These more substantive educational approaches constitute more "authentic accountabilities" that challenge neoliberal practices. "Authentic accountabilities" pertain to deeply interrogative governance practices, characterized by close inquiry into teachers' conditions and practices in more context-responsive, student-learning, and engagement-centered, situated ways – ways that challenge more performative approaches to accountability (Hardy, 2021).

Teacher Learning Under Current Policy Conditions: A Global Policy Agenda

These neoliberal and managerial processes have been taken up extensively within nation-states, indeed "globally." While contested, and politicized (Walter, 2021), globalization processes can be understood to have had intricate and imbricated effects upon education (Lingard, 2021). Globalization is a multifaceted concept, the effects of which pertain to economic, political, social, and cultural processes and practices. It can be understood to undertake both performative and analytical work – typically, to both assail particular kinds of practices as reductive and problematic in their limited (typically economic and managerial) scope, and as an analytical resource to articulate the extent to which particular kinds of practices and processes exert influence within different localities and sites.

The broader policy conditions in which teachers' learning has been undertaken have been influenced by what Sahlberg (2021) refers to as the "Global Education Reform Movement" (GERM). This phenomenon is characterized by: (1) increased competition between schools and school systems; (2) standardization of curriculum, pedagogy, and assessment; (3) emphasis on literacy, numeracy, and science, and reduction in the arts and social sciences; (4) focus on (often external) test-based accountability processes to hold both students and teachers accountable for their work and learning; and (5) emphasis on school choice as a vehicle to increase the options to parents. Such processes reflect broader "thickening" of global governance of teachers' work, including through specific technologies employed by institutions seeking to influence teachers' work across contexts, including the OECD and World Bank (Robertson, 2016).

The way in which teachers' learning is measured and monitored against specific markers of attainment, particularly various kinds of standards, reflects a more fragmented approach to learning. These standards indicate the atomization of educators' work and the tendency toward abstraction. Connell (2013) refers to the "technicization of professional knowledge" (p. 99) to capture how teachers' work and learning are influenced by large scale tests of student performance and correlational studies to identify "effects" and practices deemed necessary to enhance student learning. The teacher effectiveness literature, with its abstracted accounts of "best practice," also reveals how more business-oriented language permeates educational policy and practice (Connell, 2013). Such is the discursive power of notions of "best practice" that it becomes very difficult to challenge the broader principles upon which such abstractions are built, and to proffer more profession-oriented "authentic" accountabilities that are likely to have greater resonance in specific locations (Hardy, 2021). Abstracted modes of "best practice" are not in keeping with the sorts of teacher learning considered more beneficial, and which are "differentiated; contextualized; connected to teachers' problems of practice, curiosities and prior knowledge; collegial and collaborative; and encouraging of risk taking and experimentation" (Mockler, 2022, p. 170).

Of course, neoliberal policy conditions are far from uniform. "Actually existing neoliberalism" is a variegated and differentiated set of practices (Peck et al., 2018). Even ideas around neoliberalism are themselves contested, with neoliberalism understood as a keyword within education policy discourses which does considerable performative work but which may be used descriptively, analytically, and/or pejoratively (Rowe et al., 2019). Boylan and Adams (2023) neatly encapsulate how neoliberal principles of marketization and increased teacher and school autonomy sit alongside greater state control of primary mathematics teacher PD in England, for example. A multiplicity of logics is described as being at play, including greater prescription over the content of teachers' learning. Consequently, there are contradictory logics evident with more managerial practices and processes advocated alongside varied neoliberal influences and foci.

An Alternative: Cultivating More "profession-oriented" Teacher Learning

Under these conditions, it is difficult to cultivate the kinds of teacher learning initiatives that have been found to be beneficial for enhancing teachers' practice. This is in a context in which there is inconclusive evidence about the effects of strong accountability on student learning/achievement (Taylor, 2022). While more neoliberal and managerial pressures have exerted influence, encouraging more economistic and quantitatively oriented measures of teachers' learning, more substantive, "profession-oriented," and "authentic," forms of teacher learning have also been identified and cultivated. Such approaches foster more agentic standpoints on the part of teachers, enabling greater autonomy. This is significant, as enhancing teachers' autonomy, alongside more collaborative school cultures/collective teacher learning, is associated with collective teacher innovation (Nguyen et al., 2021). These more "profession-oriented," authentic' approaches also recognize and value the pedagogical content knowledge base that characterizes teaching, including the judicious use of resources to prepare classes, the representation of key ideas, selection of specific teaching strategies and differentiating subsequent experiences to cater for individual student needs (La Velle, 2023). This work is also supported internationally by the influence of academic researchers as well as more local teachers' professional networks and associations which foreground and support more agentic position-taking within contexts.

Drawing upon a review of what they describe as "35 methodologically rigorous studies that have demonstrated a positive link between teacher professional development, teaching practices, and student outcomes," Darling-Hammond et al. (2017, p. v) identify seven features of more substantive PD. Such development is construed as: (1) content focused, including in relation to discipline-specific curriculum and pedagogical development; (2) involving active learning, drawing upon interactive activities and artifacts to foster deeply contextualized professional learning; (3) fostering collaboration, including in their work contexts, so as to develop communities leading to change at grade, department and school and district levels; (4) drawing upon curriculum and pedagogical models as examples of "best practice"; (5) providing coaching and expertise about content and practice-based learning to address teachers' individual needs; (6) providing opportunities for reflection and ongoing feedback to cultivate greater expertise; and (7) requiring a sustained period of time to implement changes and embed them successfully in practice. More collaborative and job-embedded approaches to learning are construed as helping to build teachers' confidence and capabilities, leading to enhanced student learning/achievement.

Similarly, in their analysis of 156 articles focused on teacher PD in key journals, Sancar et al. (2021) put forward what they describe as a "comprehensive conceptual framework to define PD" (p. 8). These authors identify such learning as requiring attention to the nature of classroom practices. At the same time, various reforms and policies, school context, formal and informal supportive activities, and curriculum all need to be taken into account. Teacher learning is also understood as a continual process, requiring ongoing assessment of the effectiveness of initiatives, the need for a diversity of research processes to account for individual, institutional, and broader government needs, a longer-term approach to researching the effects of PD initiatives, collaboration between institutions and organizations as well as with teachers, context-oriented adjustments, and provision of long-term support to embed change. In relation to enhancing practice-embedded teacher learning, Gibbons et al. (2021) highlight the need to promote particular kinds of practices amongst facilitators of teachers' learning and how these practices can foster collaborative learning, greater experimentation on the part of teachers and provide emotional spaces for this work. These practices include: (1) promoting learning through collaboration; (2) advocating for experimentation and analysis of teaching practice; and (3) creating an emotional space in which participants feel supported to take risks. Collectively, such practices and processes can be understood as synonymous with more profession-oriented construals of teachers' learning which are grounded in teachers' everyday practices, and serve to challenge more standardized approaches to school reform (Hardy, 2021).

Teachers' Learning in Practice: International Insights

The literature in the remaining sections of the chapter comprise primarily academic/'scientific' literature to assess the presence and development of different conceptions and practices of teachers' learning and PD in varied national and systemic settings. However, it also includes more policy-oriented/'grey' literature, given the influence of key policy-focused bodies (such as the OECD). To understand the scope of how these competing influences and foci play out more broadly, the chapter draws upon literature into the nature of teachers' learning in education systems from across both "Northern" and "Southern" contexts. This includes research about global processes associated with neoliberalism and managerialism that seek to influence teachers' work and learning, albeit differently, in different settings.

However, these are not the only influences at play; at the same time, competing more profession-oriented foci also exert influence. These contested processes are not simply "theoretical" constructs but are manifest in practice in complex, multifarious ways. The chapter explores how these competing influences play out simultaneously, with more robust conceptions of teachers' learning in tension with more reductive and reactionary approaches oriented toward shorter term, managerial and economic foci.

There is evidence of how teachers' work and learning are advocated at a global scale, and how these broader processes seek to inform PD practices across different educational systems/jurisdictions. In this section, differences between profession-oriented and neoliberal-managerial conceptions, and how these play out in varied educational systems in Northern and Southern contexts, are elaborated.

Learnings from the Global North

In relation to more "Northern" settings, the work of the OECD provides useful insights into more dominant approaches to teachers' work and learning. The *Teachers' Professional Learning Study* was designed to foster teachers' PD by learning from productive and problematic practices in participating countries (OECD, 2023a). It focused on both initial and continuing professional learning (CPL). Importantly, the desire to "provide policy makers with rapid feedback," as well as to "improve the evidence base" (OECD, 2023a) portended an approach to teachers' learning that seems more remote from contextual concerns expressed in much of the teacher learning literature more broadly.

However, and simultaneously reflecting more contextually grounded, competing profession-oriented influences, this initiative also resulted in a number of "background reports" about particular national contexts, such as *Teachers' Professional Learning: Country Background Report of the Flemish Community of Belgium for the OECD TPL Study* (Flanders Department of Education & Training, 2021). The Flemish report provided insights into a range of features of CPL in this context, including content and process of CPL, teachers' motivations, accessibility, quality assurance processes, leadership relevant to CPL, and "challenges" to strengthen CPL. An equivalent report for Wales, entitled *Teachers' Professional Learning Study: Diagnostic Report for Wales*, provided more discursive insights into the systemic features that characterize the Welsh context, how professional learning is embedded in schools, and in teaching practice (Roy et al., 2021).

Similar sorts of tensions between the specificity of the local and the possibility of learning from across national systems are also evident in the OECD's efforts to foster enhanced teacher professionalism and capacity. This is evident in its recent focus on global engagement, sustainability and digital skills as part of its International Summit on the Teaching Profession series, in which it advocates PD seen as "best practice" from specific national settings (e.g., Singapore), at the same time as it seeks to recognize the need for increased professional discretion within schools and schooling systems (OECD, 2023b).

Similarly, in educational systems in the US context, for example, teachers' learning is variously described in relation to a range of competing approaches and foci. Reflecting the influence of randomized control evaluation studies, there is considerable emphasis upon what is described as the relative paucity of "rigorous" experimental studies (pre-test, post-test; control group), and relatively little attention to PD in these studies. This results in criticisms of analyses of the effects of PD interventions, and claims about the relative lack of attention to PD more broadly within such evaluation studies. In this vein, Fryer's (2017) analysis of the impact of 196 education interventions included just 9 PD studies. Similarly, other more specific PD studies in the United States have revealed a low number of studies with pre-test, post-test, and control group characteristics (e.g., Yoon et al., 2007). Furthermore, Fryer's (2017) overview evaluated studies on the basis of student outcomes on student test scores, reflecting the influence of such scores as the most credible markers of the evaluation of educational interventions – including those associated with teachers' professional learning. This is the case even as there are a multitude of studies critiquing the deleterious effects of high-stakes teacher evaluation as a vehicle for teacher learning (e.g., Warren & Ward's (2019) analyses of teacher evaluation in Tennessee, and Holloway's (2021) analysis of professional learning and evaluation in Arizona and Texas).

However, and reflecting how both neoliberal and profession-oriented logics are interwoven, these are not the only influences at play in the United States. This is also a environment characterized by contestation about the nature and value of initial teacher education, even as teachers prepared through teacher education programs feel significantly more prepared to teach than colleagues undertaking short courses or without teacher education preparation at all (Darling-Hammond et al., 2002). Reflecting a more agentic standpoint on the part of teachers, Sprott (2019) revealed how experienced teachers from a southern county in Texas valued: opportunities for collaborative reflection and how these collaborative reflections could be enabled by engaging with students as PD collaborators; traveling to different contexts (other teachers' classrooms, other schools – nationally and internationally); being challenged by scholars as critical friends; maintaining long-standing professional relations with colleague/s, and; drawing upon experiences from careers outside of education. At the same time, however, these teachers also recognized obstacles to such collaboration, particularly structural obstacles, such as unnecessary meetings, and bureaucratic duties.

Analyses of teachers' learning in different parts of Europe also reflect the effects of the intertwined nature of neoliberal and profession-oriented logics. More neoliberally oriented "fast policy" (Peck, 2010) logics are evident in Scandinavian contexts in which teachers and their learning have typically been afforded more recognition and value than in other (Anglo-American) contexts (Hardy et al., 2020). There has also been a push toward increasing the control over teachers' work, favoring more bureaucratic and market-oriented logics (Lindström, 2020). However, at the same time, there is also evidence of how Swedish teachers' professional learning is grounded in more research-based competencies and capacities, including more action research initiatives that are context-relevant, integrated, collaborative, and foster engagement between teachers, principals, and researchers. Such advocacy reflects a strong tradition of more democratic, action research-oriented approaches in Nordic countries more broadly (Salo & Rönnerman, 2023).

The focus upon various kinds of competencies – including digital competencies – also reflects how broader managerial processes seek to try to capture and compartmentalize knowledge in European country contexts, even as these are simultaneously contested. On the one hand, while digital competencies have attracted much attention, systematic reviews of literature in Europe, for example, reveal a relative lack of attention to teachers' learning around digitalization processes (Fernández-Batanero et al., 2022). This research indicated current PD/"training" approaches were insufficient, resulting in inadequate student learning. However, at the same time, there is also evidence of the use of digital tools as a vehicle for more sustainable learning and development and, indeed, democratization of learning across a range of European countries (Ovcharuk et al., 2020). This reflects not only the agency of teachers involved but also the influence of broad policy support for such interventions, including the European Council's *Reference Framework of Competences for Democratic Culture*, and the European Commission's *Digital Competence Framework for Educators*. Issues associated with teachers, the teaching profession and teachers' learning can also be read as a case of Europeanization, with the development of learning and labor market mobilities for teachers across Europe, and the development of various EU Teacher Academies (Sorensen & Dumay, 2024).

Learnings from the Global South

In more "Southern" settings, the intertwining of both more profession-oriented influences alongside more managerial and neoliberal logics is also evident. Reflecting more managerial logics, Popova et al. (2021) propose a set of indicators – the "In-service Teacher Training Survey Instrument" – to enable the standardization of reporting of teacher professional development programs. The application of this instrument to what are described as "33 rigorously evaluated PD programs" (p. 107) revealed that programs that make explicit links to career/salary advancement, focus on specific subject areas, include classroom practice as part of professional learning, and that include face-to-face in-service activities in the initial stages of the initiatives, led to higher student learning improvement.

However, when this model was applied to 139 large-scale government-supported PD programs across 14 middle and low-income countries, it was found that there were fewer incentives for teachers to be involved, fewer opportunities to practice and develop classroom skills, and fewer follow-up activities with teachers once they went back to their classrooms. Consequently, such initiatives flag the difficulties of enactment of broad-based, standardized markers of "effective" PD in actual school settings.

Nevertheless, and reflecting the simultaneous influence of more profession-oriented influences alongside more managerial logics, a systematic review of 170 studies on the use of technology in 40 low- and middle-income countries also revealed what it described as "promising, locally contextualized forms of technology-mediated TPD" [teacher PD], including social messaging, virtual coaching, blended learning, and engagement with subject-specific software/applications and video-stimulated reflection (Hennessy et al., 2022, p. 1). This was the case even as the sustainability, and cost-effectiveness of these initiatives, along with what were described as "tangible impacts on classroom practice and student outcomes," were described as "thin" (p. 1).

In education systems in South America, teacher performance and learning are often linked with student learning as measured against national assessment programs. In Chile, for example, teacher portfolios (including videotapes of teachers' classroom practice) are used for evaluation purposes, even as the outcomes of such analyses reveal mixed effects on student learning (Taut et al., 2019). Acuña (2023) refers to "bonsai pedagogies" to capture the nature and effects of neoliberal principles more broadly upon schooling in the Chilean context. In contrast to more autonomous approaches (Nguyen et al., 2021), such pedagogies controlled teachers' time, managed their practices, including through standardized tests against which students and teachers were evaluated, and limited creativity. However, these more managerial evaluative practices are challenged by approaches such as "pedagogical mentoring" in Chilean schools, involving long-term sustainable mentoring of teachers by colleagues and ongoing reflection on practice (Sutton et al., 2022). This initiative was also enabled by collaboration between academics from the United States and Chilean universities working together to support the development of school-based mentors as part of this work. The latter reflects the kinds of more international/"global" associations that can characterize support for substantive forms of teacher learning.

Similarly, and drawing upon an Argentinian example, Banegas and Glatigny (2021) refer to the "ateneo" approach which transformed teaching practice by focusing upon context-relevant and practical issues, which led to better lesson contextualization, lesson sequencing and transitions, and use of classroom time and resources. As in the Chilean example, through the agency of teacher educators and teachers working together to enhance the teaching of English as a foreign language, much more agentic position-taking was possible. Similarly, dialogic learning has proven useful for building schools as sustainable professional learning communities in South America, including in contexts as diverse as Mexico, Brazil, Colombia, and Peru (Garcia-Carrion et al., 2017). This is the case even as these countries have all simultaneously experienced either a strong or substantial governance turn characterized by increased accountability, control over schooling processes and prescribed curricula (Rivas & Sanchez, 2022). Nevertheless, recognition of the knowledges and "cultural intelligence" within the communities these teachers served led to much more productive relations with students.

Education systems in many African countries, as with other Southern settings, are dependent upon aid for much of their educational provision. Education in Sub-Saharan Africa in particular is challenging, with this region having the highest rates of education exclusion in the world (UNESCO, 2020). There is inadequate time spent teaching, high rates of student and teacher absenteeism, and insufficient teachers, who are poorly prepared and resourced (Bold et al., 2017). Provision of PD under such circumstances is deeply challenging.

In spite of such circumstances, in a review of multiple studies of education provision in Africa as a whole, Evans and Acosta (2021) show how a variety of structured teaching interventions (including lesson plans and training provision for teachers) have been found to have promising effects. Also, in contrast with some of the more reductive "globally" oriented influences upon teachers' learning, there is also evidence of how teacher learning in different African contexts reflects the needs of particular communities and the specificity of teachers' work and student learning. In Kenya, Bett and Makewa (2020) reveal how Facebook is a potentially useful vehicle for teachers' learning, particularly where resources are inadequate and where PD is poorly planned. In South Africa, Moodley (2019) showed how online social media (*WhatsApp*) could foster a professional learning community but that this was also dependent upon participants being open to different views and perspectives and awareness of their educational context.

Discussion and Conclusion: The Socio-Politics of Teachers' Learning

Within education systems in varied settings, teachers' learning is a complex entity, characterized by intertwined, competing, and contested positions. There is considerable evidence of the continued influence of neoliberal approaches to education, with their emphasis upon increased competition between schools and school systems, and policy settings that frame comparative learning as a vehicle for enhanced competitiveness, often measured against standardized test results (as a proxy for future economic competitiveness). The "Global Education Reform Movement" (Sahlberg, 2021), with its continued emphasis upon standardization of curriculum, teaching, and testing practices, is of this ilk. The OECD's focus upon broader international assessment regimes ensures that more neoliberal technologies in the form of standardized enumerated conceptions of education (Ball, 2015) exert influence, even as these are contested (Rowe et al., 2019). However, at the same time, these policy and political spaces are not homogenous but also reflect the influence of more profession-oriented learning approaches. Consequently, within the OECD itself, through its ongoing development of various national and regional reports about teacher learning practices, there is also evidence of support for more context-relevant learning that addresses the needs of particular communities and their schools, *in situ*. While there has been a "thickening" of the global governance of teachers' work more broadly (Robertson, 2016), there is also evidence of efforts to flag a plurality of more context-relevant practices. Given that such learning is often intimately interspersed with more neoliberal and managerial logics, and while reflective of the influence of more profession-oriented approaches to teachers' learning, the literature also reveals the need for greater attention to and emphasis on the latter.

Within and across individual education systems, competing profession-oriented, managerial, and neoliberal approaches to teachers' learning are simultaneously evident. The United States provides examples of long-term, heated and strongly contested positions about teachers' learning. Reflecting more managerial and neoliberal influences, standardized assessment practices have exerted considerable influence, reflecting the power of such measures to impact all aspects of teachers' work and learning. However, at the same time, there is also evidence of much more agentic position-taking on the part of educators who value being able to collaborate with others. These collaborations can be wide-ranging, involving students, other teachers, scholars, and external career experiences.

In European countries more broadly, and in the area of digital learning for example, there is evidence of both the ineffectiveness of more traditional "training" approaches to PD, as well as broader policy support for building digital competence, including in more democratic ways. Policy support for digital competence development also reflects how broader policy conditions can enable more professional learning. In Scandinavian settings, such as Sweden, at the same time more neoliberal and managerial logics have exerted influence, a broader tradition of teacher-generated action research responsive to teachers' immediate classroom and schooling settings (Salo & Rönnerman, 2023) is also apparent. Again, competing influences are simultaneously at play.

Similarly, education in South American settings reflects the interplay of competing neoliberal, managerial and more profession-oriented logics. South America has long been influenced by a neoliberal reform agenda stimulated by upheaval in the 1960s and 1970s and introduced into education policies in the 1980s under the guise of various "adjustments" (Puiggrós, 2019). This is also a form of neoliberalism specific to these Southern contexts in which it is expressed, rather than a "universal trend" of reform that somehow characterizes the global North (Windle, 2019). It is also a form of neoliberalism which while open to contest is also resilient and adaptable (Rodríguez, 2021).

Neoliberalism is multifaceted in expression; it is able to shift and shape, depending on circumstances (Peck, 2010). However, these different manifestations of neoliberal teacher learning have not gone unchallenged in South America. The Chilean case reflects how even in a country that is heavily influenced by neoliberal logics (standardized testing; performance-based pay), more collaborative mentoring approaches also coexist. Such responses provide the opportunity for more responsive and agentic position-taking on the part of teachers working with one another, and teacher educators, to enhance their practice. Reflecting the valuing of teachers' professional knowledge (La Velle, 2023), and collective teacher learning (Nguyen et al., 2021), the dialogic learning that attends such collaboration is also explicitly valued and recognized. This is similarly evident in countries such as Colombia, Mexico, Peru, and Brazil (Garcia-Carrion et al., 2017), even as these contexts have all been influenced by a governance turn that instantiated more neoliberal logics. The various kinds of "cultural intelligence" that attend more successful communities of teacher learners also reflect the need to ensure that such learning is always culturally and contextually relevant. Such approaches also entail a level of risk as teachers share their experiences; fostering such risk-taking is crucial to substantive reform (Gibbons, 2021).

The African context also reveals competing, intertwined influences, which are further complicated by paucity of resource provision. Rigid and instrumental (and, ultimately, ineffective) approaches to PD provision reflect more managerial approaches within a heavily constrained fiscal environment in many African countries. Nevertheless, more grounded, structured teaching interventions (including lesson planning and training provision for teachers) in African settings provide promising insights into alternative approaches and foci (Evans & Acosta, 2021). This is within a broader African context in which some countries, such as South Africa, experience better material circumstances and in which technology can enable professional learning amongst teachers, even as this is challenging and dependent upon teachers remaining open to new learning (Moodley, 2019). Such approaches also reflect teacher professional autonomy, leading to greater innovation, itself enhanced by more collective teacher learning (Nguyen et al., 2021).

Advocacy for more progressive profession-oriented possibilities and accountabilities needs to be made cautiously, and in the knowledge that such approaches and foci to teachers' learning are intricately intertwined with, and exist alongside, both neoliberal and managerial pressures that mitigate against their effectiveness and contribute to more standardized schooling processes (Hardy, 2021). Reflecting the plurality of approaches to teachers' professional learning evident within the literature more generally (Darling-Hammond et al., 2017; Sancar et al., 2021), research from education systems in both Northern and Southern settings reveals how professional learning is simultaneously influenced by more neoliberal and managerial pressures, even as it seeks to be locally/contextually relevant.

Given the propensity for policy borrowing and policy transfer (Steiner-Khamsi, 2021), particularly via various supra-national bodies such as the OECD, there is a need to be cautious about more decontextualized teacher learning approaches, and how specific countries and contexts might "learn" from such initiatives. However, valuable learning is possible – when it takes context into account, draws upon teachers' knowledge and capacities to utilize relevant resources, ideas, teaching strategies and to differentiate learning (La Velle, 2023), and when teachers' professional autonomy and agency are promoted (Nguyen et al., 2021). Such a position contrasts with more reductive conceptions of neoliberal and managerial logics. Just as neoliberal approaches and foci were never taken for granted during their long ascendency (Peck, 2010), so too is it possible and necessary to consider how to actively encourage more profession-oriented, autonomous approaches that foreground the intrinsically context-sensitive nature of teacher learning. This is necessary to helping reimagine teachers' learning in more substantive, progressively "authentic" ways.

References

Acuña, F. (2023). Governing teachers' subjectivity in neoliberal times: The fabrication of The bonsai teacher. *Journal of Education Policy*. https://doi.org/10.1080/02680939.2023.2196954.

Ball, S. J. (2015). Education, governance and the tyranny of numbers. *Journal of Education Policy*, 30(3), 299–301.

Ball, S. J. (2016). Subjectivity as a site of struggle: Refusing neoliberalism? *British Journal of Sociology of Education*, 37(8), 1129–1146.

Banegas, D., & Glatigny, R. (2021). The Ateneo as an effective model of continuing professional development: Findings from southern Argentina. *Pedagogies*, 16(4), 363–377.

Bett, H., & Makewa, L. (2020). Can Facebook groups enhance continuing professional development of teachers? *Asia-Pacific Journal of Teacher Education*, 48(2), 132–146.

Bold, T., Filmer, D., Martin, G., Molina, E., Stacy, B., Rockmore, C., Svensson, J., & Wane, W. (2017). Enrollment without learning: Teacher effort, knowledge, and skill in primary schools in Africa. *Journal of Economic Perspectives*, 31(4), 185–204.

Boylan, M., & Adams, G. (2023). Market mirages and the state's role in professional learning: The case of English mathematics education. *Journal of Education Policy*. https://doi.org/10.1080/02680939.2023.2195854.

Connell, R. (2013). The neoliberal cascade and education: An essay on the market agenda and its consequences. *Critical Studies in Education*, 54(2), 99–112.

Darling-Hammond, L. et al. (2002). Variation in teacher preparation. *Journal of Teacher Education*, 53(4), 286–302.

Darling-Hammond, L. et al. (2017). *Effective teacher professional development*. Learning Policy Institute.

de Saxe, J. G., Bucknovitz, S., & Mahoney-Mosedale, F. (2020). The deprofessionalization of educators: An intersectional analysis of neoliberalism and education "Reform." *Education and Urban Society*, 52(1), 51–69.

Evans, D., & Acosta, A. (2021). Education in Africa: What are we learning? *Journal of African Economies*, 30(1), 13–54.

Fernández-Batanero, J. M., Montenegro-Rueda, M., Fernández-Cerero, J., & García-Martínez, I. (2022). Digital competences for teacher professional development: Systematic review. *European Journal of Teacher Education*, 45(4), 513–531.

Flanders Department of Education & Training. (2021). *Teachers' professional learning: Country background report of the Flemish community of Belgium for the OECD TPL study*. Flanders DET.

Fryer, R. Jr (2017). The production of human capital in developed countries: Evidence from 196 randomized field experiments. *Handbook of Economic Field Experiments, 2,* 95–322.

Garcia-Carrion, R., Gomez, A., Molina, S., & Ionescu, V. (2017). Teacher education in schools as learning communities: Transforming high-poverty schools through dialogic learning. *Australian Journal of Teacher Education, 42*(4). https://doi.org/10.14221/ajte.2017v42n4.4

Gibbons, L. (2021). Conceptualizing the work of facilitating practice-embedded teacher learning. *Teaching and Teacher Education, 101.* https://doi.org/10.1016/j.tate.2021.103304

Hardy, I. (2021). *School reform in an era of standardization: Authentic accountabilities*. Routledge.

Hardy, I., Heikkinen, H., & Olin, A. (2020). Conceptualising and contesting 'fast policy' in teacher learning: A comparative analysis of Sweden, Finland and Australia. *Teacher Development, 24*(4), 466–682.

Hennessy, S., D'Angelo, S., McIntyre, N., Koomar, S., Kreimeia, A., Cao, L., Brugha, M., & Zubairi, A. (2022). Technology use for teacher professional development in low- and middle-income countries: A systematic review. *Computers and Education Open, 3.* https://doi.org/10.1016/j.caeo.2022.100080

Holloway, J. (2021). *Metrics, standards and alignment in teacher policy*. Springer.

La Velle, L. (2023). Development of teachers' knowledge: The breadth, depth and detail. *Journal of Education for Teaching, 49*(4), 545–550.

Lindström, M. (2020). Swedish School reforms and teacher professionalism. *Professions & Professionalism, 10*(3). https://doi.org/10.7577/pp.3878

Lingard, B. (2021). Globalisation and education: Theorising and researching changing imbrications in education policy. In B. Lingard (Ed.), *Globalization and education* (pp. 2–27). Routledge.

Mockler, N. (2022). Teacher professional learning under audit: Reconfiguring practice in an age of standards. *Professional Development in Education, 48*(1), 166–180.

Moodley, M. (2019). WhatsApp: Creating a virtual teacher community for supporting and monitoring after a professional development programme. *South African Journal of Education, 39*(2). https://doi.org/10.15700/saje.v39n2a1323

Nguyen, D., Pietsch, M., & Gümüs, S. (2021). Collective teacher innovativeness in 48 countries: Effects of teacher autonomy, collaborative culture and professional learning. *Teaching and Teacher Education, 106*(2). https://doi.org/10.1016/j.tate.2021.103463

OECD. (2023a). *Teachers' professional learning study*. OECD. https://www.oecd.org/education/teachers-professional-learning-study/

OECD. (2023b) *Teaching for the future: Global engagement, sustainability and digital skills*. International Summit on the Teaching Profession. https://doi.org/10.1787/d6b3d234-en

Ovcharuk, O., Ivaniuk, I., Soroko, N., Gritsenchuk, O., & Kravchyna, O. (2020). The use of digital learning tools in the teachers' professional activities to ensure sustainable development and democratization of education in European countries. *E3Sweb of Conferences, 166.* https://doi.org/10.1051/e3sconf/202016610019

Peck, J. (2010). *Constructions of neoliberal reason*. Oxford.

Peck, J., Brenner, N., & Theodore, N. (2018). Actually existing neoliberalism. In D. Cahill, M. Cooper, M. Konings, & D. Primrose (Eds.), *Sage handbook of neoliberalism* (pp. 3–15). Sage.

Popova, A., Evans, D., Breeding, M., & Arancibia, V. (2021). Teacher professional development around the world: The gap between evidence and practice. *The World Bank Research Observer, 37*(1), 107–136.

Puiggrós, A. (2019). *Neoliberalism and education in the Americas*. Routledge.

Rivas, A., & Sanchez, B. (2022). Race to the classroom: The governance turn in latin American education. The emerging era of accountability, control and prescribed curriculum. *Compare, 52*(2), 260–268.

Robertson, S. (2016). The global governance of teachers' work. In K. Mundy, A. Green, B. Lingard, & A. Verger (Eds.), *The handbook of global education policy* (pp. 275–290). Wiley.

Rodríguez, J. (2021). The politics of neoliberalism in latin america: Dynamics of resilience and contestation. *Sociology Compass, 15*(3). https://doi.org/10.1111/soc4.12854

Rowe, E., Lubienski, C., Skourdoumbis, A., Gerrard, J., & Hursh, D. (2019). Templates, typologies and typifications: Neoliberalism as keyword. *Discourse: Studies in the Cultural Politics of Education, 40*(2), 150–161.

Roy, S., Cordingley, P., Nusche, D., & Timperley, H. (2021). *Teachers' professional learning study: Diagnostic report for Wales*. OECD Policy Perspectives.

Sahlberg, P. (2021). *Finnish Lessons 3.0: What can the world learn from educational change in Finland?* Teachers College Press.

Salo, P., & Rönnerman, K. (2023). Educational action research for being. *Nordic Studies in Education, 43*(1), 78–93.

Sancar, R. et al., (2021). A new framework for teachers' professional development. *Teaching and Teacher Education, 101*. https://doi.org/10.1016/j.tate.2021.103305

Sorensen, T. B., & Dumay, X. (2024). The European Union's governance of teachers and the evolution of a bridging issue field since the mid-2000s. *European Educational Research Journal, 23*(2), 237–260.

Sprott, R. (2019). Factors that foster and deter advanced teachers' professional development. *Teaching and Teacher Development, 77*, 321–331.

Stacey, M., Gavin, M., Gerrard, J., Hogan, A., & Holloway, J. (2022). Teachers and educational policy: Markets, populism, and im/possibilities for resistance. *Education Policy Analysis Archives, 30*(93). https://doi.org/10.14507/epaa.30.7407

Steiner-Khamsi, G. (2021). Policy borrowing and lending in comparative and international education: A key area of research. In J. Jules, R. Shields, & M. Thomas (Eds.), *The bloomsbury handbook of theory in comparative and international education* (pp. 327–344). Bloomsbury.

Sutton, S., Cuellar, C., Gonzalez, M., & Espinosa, M. (2022). Pedagogical mentoring in Chilean schools: An innovative approach to teachers' professional learning. *International Journal of Mentoring and Coaching in Education, 11*(1), 69–88.

Taut, S., Valencia, E., Palacios, D., Santelices, M., Jiménez, D., & Manzi, J. (2019). Teacher performance and student learning: Linking evidence from two national assessment programmes. *Assessment in Education: Principles, Policy & Practice, 23*(1), 53–74.

Taylor, E. (2022). Teacher evaluation and training. In E. Hanushek, S. Machin, & L. Woessmann (Eds.), *Handbook of the economics of education* (pp. 61–141). North Holland.

UNESCO, 2020. *Education in Africa*. https://uis.unesco.org/en/topic/education-africa

Walter, S. (2021). The backlash against globalization. *Annual Review of Political Science, 24*, 421–442.

Warren, A., & Ward, N. (2019). 'It didn't make me a better teacher': Inservice teacher constructions of dilemmas in high-stakes teacher evaluation. *School Effectiveness and School Improvement, 30*(4), 531–548.

Welch, A. (2021). Neoliberalism in comparative and international education: Theory, practice, paradox. In D. Jules, R. Shields, & M. Thomas (Eds.), *The Bloomsbury handbook of theory in comparative and international education* (pp. 201–216). Bloomsbury Academic.

Windle, J. (2019). Neoliberalism, imperialism and conservatism: Tangled logics of educational inequality in the global South. *Discourse: Studies in the Cultural Politics of Education, 40*(2), 191–202.

Yoon, K. S., Duncan, T., Lee, S., Scarloss, B., & Shapley, K. (2007). *Reviewing the evidence on how teacher professional development affects student achievement (Issues & answers report no. 033)*. Institute of Education Sciences, National Center for Education Evaluation and Regional Assistance, U.S. Department of Education; and Regional Educational Laboratory Southeast at Florida State University. http://files.eric.ed.gov/fulltext/ED498548.pdf

Index

academies 162, 203
accountability 4–7, 10, 11, 15, 16, 25–31, 43, 44, 57, 90, 153, 156, 163, 164, 168, 172, 224
aid agencies 2, 143
Akiba, M. 217, 218, 223
American public school systems 162
Archer, M. 57, 63, 68
assessment 10, 11, 13, 25, 26, 31–33, 35–37, 39–41, 43, 47, 48, 56, 59–62, 69, 89, 91, 123, 168, 169, 230, 231, 233, 237–239
Australian Research Council 192

Bascia, N. 9–11, 74
Bawane, J. 143
Bentham, J. 67, 69, 70
Bereday, G. F. 1, 3
Big Five Personality Model 64, 69
Bill and Melinda Gates Foundation 2, 27
Bologna Declaration 138
Brewer, T. 135, 202
bureaucratic accountability 6
Burkina Faso 116, 122

Canales, C. N. 9–11, 56
career ladder 214–215, 217–218
Chandra, M. 119, 123
Chudgar, A. 13, 111, 117–120
Clinton Global Initiative 198
collocation analysis 96, 98–99
commercial actors 10
contract-based hiring 111–125
Coppe, T. 129
COVID-19 pandemic 12, 33, 43, 89, 96–97, 100–103
Crawford-Garrett, K. 199, 201
cultural logics 212–213

Darling-Hammond, L. 4, 130, 233
Davies, W. 59, 65, 67
Decuypere, M. 15–17, 179
Dembélé, M. 13, 111, 123
democratic deficit 77, 81, 83
distributed leadership 217, 221
District Institutes of Education and Training (DIET) 153
diversification 12–14, 123
Dumay, X. 1, 7, 16, 30, 32, 213

economic recession 162
Education International (EI) 8, 10, 74
education policy 29, 33, 43, 88
educational system 1, 6, 7, 13, 26, 28, 44, 135–136, 205–206, 234
educationalization 10
Elliott, J. 199, 200
England 137, 162–163, 168
English medium 150
eTwinning (eT) 180–189
European School Education Platform (ESEP) 15, 179–180
evaluation 8, 11, 25–27, 29, 31–39, 43, 44, 123, 166, 168, 172, 203, 235, 237

Ferrer-Esteban, G. 8, 9, 11, 25
financial crisis 58, 62
Finland 61, 170, 172
Fontdevila, C. 25
Ford Foundation 2
France 120, 137

Germany 67, 131, 164, 165, 169
Gibbons, L. 162, 233

246 Index

Global Education Monitoring (GEM) report 223
global governance 2–6, 8–11, 14, 74, 83, 231, 239
Global North 13, 92, 113, 115
Global South 13, 92, 93, 112, 115, 124, 192
globalization: defined 1, 2; historical forms of 5; teacher policy 3; teaching profession 1, 6
governance 25–44, 74–85; defined 2; pluralization 2; public interest 10
Great Recession 162
Gruijters, R. 69, 70

Hardy, I. 229
Hausman test 44–45
higher education institutions (HEI) 12, 160
Hindi language 145
Huberman, M. 123, 126
human capital theory 10

Indian teacher workforce 144–156
individualism 187
initial teacher education (ITE) 4–6, 125; accountability 168; confusion and fragmentation 168; cross-national research 167; modalities of 169; teachers' knowledge and expertise 167
inspectors/external personnel observations 38
institutional agents 7
inter-governmental (IGOs) 2
International Labor Organisation (ILO) 113
international organizations (IOs) 14, 16, 25, 76, 82, 83, 113, 205, 217, 222
International Summits on the Teaching Profession 8, 76, 83, 84, 235
intra-organizational relations 9

Japan 16, 90, 217–221; Japanese teachers 219; Japanese Teachers Union 220
Jensen, A. 182, 189

Khmer Rouge regime 118
Kumar, K. 151, 152

labor markets 3, 4, 11, 12, 14, 17, 30, 136, 137
labor relations 6, 17
leadership and professional status 16, 81, 83, 166, 202, 234
learning gaps 29
Lefebvre, E. E. 15–17, 196
Lerch, J. C. 213, 217, 224
LeTendre, G. K. 16, 212, 213, 223
Lewis, S. 15, 16, 17, 179
low- and middle-income countries (LIMCs) 13, 111
Luschei, T. 4, 118

market models, in education systems 166, 168, 170–172
market regime 30, 35, 36
Matsui, S. 197, 198, 201
McKinsey & Company 2, 25, 143
mediatization 88, 94, 101, 102
merit pay 25
middle level leadership 217
Millennium Development Goal 2 122
Mockler, N. 88
monitoring methods 37–40

neoliberalism 57, 68, 224
New Zealand 170

Organisation for Economic Co-operation and Development (OECD) 2, 3, 8, 56–57, 74, 76, 120
organizational professionalism 15–17

Paine, L. 1, 196
Pearson 2
performance data 40
performance-based accountability 26, 43
personality psychology 57, 64, 68
platformization 179–190
policy and media: in Australia and England 94–97; COVID-19 pandemic 89; of education 89–91; teacher "shortages" in 97–101; teacher supply, global issue 92–93; transnational and national policy 89
political orientation 29, 39, 40, 42, 43
private corporations 2
privatization 82, 124, 146, 161, 230
professional accountability 7
professional associations 7, 18
professional skills regime 30

Program for International Student
    Assessment (PISA) 10, 31, 32, 56,
    58–61, 63, 65, 68, 70, 83, 84, 89,
    90, 196
project-focused skills 189
public education 114, 115, 160
publicness 3, 10

qualitative monitoring methods 39
quality assurance 29

Ramchand, M. 143
Rawolle, S. 88, 102
research community 18
resilience 17, 65–67, 70
Robertson, S. L. 9, 10, 56, 84

salary 14, 78, 101, 113, 114, 116–119,
    124–126, 133, 143, 145, 148–150,
    153–156, 165, 166, 218, 236
Sarangapani, P. M. 143, 151
Schleicher, A. 56, 212
School Education Gateway (SEG)
    platform 180
school leadership reform model 212
scientific management 77
second-career teachers (SCTs)
    129–138
self-care 17
self-leadership 202
"social justice" organizations 75
social movements 18, 75
social transformations 57, 68
social-democratic governments 29
sociology 17, 70, 153
Sorensen, T. B. 1, 76, 83, 84
specialization 217
Spicksley, K. 88
standardized tests 26, 43, 90,
    237, 238
Steiner-Khamsi, G. 213, 223

Tatto, M.T. 160
Teach First 199
Teach First Cymru (Wales) 202
Teach For All (TFAll) 15; adaptive scripts
    197; "best and brightest" motto
    and ethos 199–200; educational
    professionals 198; learning quickly
    200–201; professional and political
    scripts 197; purposes, processes, and
    impact 206–207; relentless pursuit,
notion of 201; shared mission 197;
    traditional systems 202–204
Teach For America (TFA) 171; Clinton
    Global Initiative 198; workforce
    development 197
Teach For Uganda 201, 203
Teach South Africa 199
teacher appraisal: accountability
    agenda 26, 27; data sources and
    methodological approach 31–32;
    external assessments 25; global
    debate 26–28; institutional fit
    and feasibility 28; international
    organizations (IOs) 25; partisan
    politics 39–42; performance-based
    incentives 25; policy adoption and
    adaptation 26; policy convergence
    and divergence 26; qualitative
    monitoring methods 39; teacher
    regulatory regimes and 33, 35–39;
    teacher-appraisal schemes 26;
    teachers' professional identities 25;
    use of performance data for 35;
    value-added models (VAMs) 26
teacher career 4–6, 16–17, 29, 78, 155,
    162, 170, 203; Huberman's model
    123; job security 123; labor market
    policies and 11–14; models in public
    sector 121–122; professional status
    163–165; second-career teachers
    129–138
teacher effectiveness 25, 43, 167, 231
teacher employment 111, 120–122, 152,
    169–170
teacher leadership 217; ambiguity
    221–223; in North America 213–216;
    transnational policy and educational
    reforms 216
teacher organizations 74–77, 81;
    strategic goals 76
teacher peer reviews 35
teacher policy 4–8, 95; governance,
    flexible employment, and learning
    4–8
teacher professional expertise 186
teacher regulatory regimes 8, 31
teacher shortages 1, 12; contract teachers
    112; and contract-based hiring
    111, 113–124; "Grow Your Own"
    (GYO) programs 112; LMICs 112;
    permanent employment status 111;
    policy and media 97–101; teacher

labor force 114; UNESCO's 2023 report 114; in United States 112
teacher/teachers well-being 17
teacher-evaluation methods: teacher regulatory regimes and teacher appraisal 33–39
teachers' governance and development: professional identities and societal valuation 25; teacher appraisal *see* teacher appraisal; teacher-effectiveness agenda 25
teachers' lifelong learning 5
teachers' organizational involvement: challenges 83–84; international organizations 82; TALIS concerns 83
teachers' practice: partisan politics and methods 54–55; teacher regulatory regimes and methods 52–54
teachers' unions 76; challenges 77–82; involvement in local governance 76; "labor" issues 78–79; teacher diversity 79–82
teachers' work: and careers 170; and contemporary policy-making 84; heterogeneity of 84; and learning 14–17; partisan politics and performance data 54
Teaching and Learning International Survey (TALIS) 60, 76, 83, 84, 95
teaching profession 74–85, 129–138, 143–156
teaching workforce 12, 136, 137, 144, 153–156, 222

Thomas, M. A. M. 15–17, 196, 200, 201
training regime 30

UN High-Level Panel on the Teaching Profession 8
UN Human Rights and Right to Education 152
United Kingdom 27, 33, 61, 90, 131, 199, 203
United Nations Educational, Scientific and Cultural Organization (UNESCO) 3, 8, 13, 114, 115, 163, 216; Teacher Policy Development Guide 216; Teacher Task Force 111
United States 112, 161–164, 166–172, 197, 199–201, 203, 204, 213–215, 220, 221, 223

value-added models (VAMs) 26
Verger, A. 25, 223
virtualized learning devices 15
Voisin, A. 7, 8, 16, 30, 32, 45, 213

well-being: student well-being 57, 63, 65; teacher well-being 8, 10, 17, 27, 56, 60, 68, 84
Wilkinson, R. 61, 217
World Bank 3, 14, 27, 76, 84, 113, 122, 212
World Conference on Education For All (EFA) 1990 115

Zeichner, K. 7, 196

Printed in the United States
by Baker & Taylor Publisher Services